ABSOLUTE POWER

ABSOLUTE
POWER

HOW THE POPE
BECAME THE MOST
INFLUENTIAL MAN
IN THE WORLD

PAUL COLLINS

PUBLICAFFAIRS
NEW YORK

PublicAffairs
Hachette Book Group
1290 Avenue of the Americas, New York, NY 10104
www.publicaffairsbooks.com
@Public_Affairs

Printed in the United States of America

First Edition: March 2018

Published by PublicAffairs, an imprint of Perseus Books, LLC, a subsidiary of Hachette Book Group, Inc. The PublicAffairs name and logo is a trademark of the Hachette Book Group.

The Hachette Speakers Bureau provides a wide range of authors for speaking events. To find out more, go to www.hachettespeakersbureau.com or call (866) 376-6591.

The publisher is not responsible for websites (or their content) that are not owned by the publisher.

Print book interior design by Trish Wilkinson

Library of Congress Control Number: 2018932568

ISBNs: 978-1-61039-860-2 (hardcover), 978-1-5417-6200-8 (ebook)

LSC-C

10 9 8 7 6 5 4 3 2 1

For two inspiring mentors:
Rev. John F. McMahon, MSC, and Professor Oliver MacDonagh

CONTENTS

ABBREVIATIONS

AAS	*Acta Apostolicae Sedis* (official Vatican bulletin)
AL	*Amoris laetitia* (apostolic exhortation of Pope Francis)
APSA	*Amministrazione del Patrimonio della Sede Apostolica* (Administration of the Patrimony of the Holy See)
CDF	Congregation for the Doctrine of the Faith (Vatican)
CDW	Congregation for Divine Worship (Vatican)
CELAM	Latin American and Caribbean Bishops Conference
COSEA	Reference Commission on the Organization of the Economic-Administrative Structure of the Holy See (Vatican)
DJ	*Dominus Jesus* (declaration of the Congregation for the Doctrine of the Faith)
FC	*Familiaris consortio* (apostolic exhortation of John Paul II)
GS	*Gaudium et spes* (Vatican II document on the church in the modern world)
HV	*Humanae vitae* (1968 encyclical of Paul VI on contraception)
ICEL	International Commission on English in the Liturgy
IOR	*Istituto per le Opere di Religione* (Vatican Bank)
ITC	International Theological Commission

JOC	*Jeunesse Ouvrière Chrétienne* (Young Christian Workers)
LG	*Lumen gentium* (Vatican II document on the church)
LS	*Laudato si'* (encyclical of Pope Francis on the environment)
NRM	new religious movement
OD	Opus Dei
PA	*Pastor aeternus* (Vatican I document on primacy and infallibility of the pope)
PPI	*Partito Populare Italiano* (Italian Popular Party)
RN	*Rerum novarum* (encyclical of Leo XIII)
SB	Polish Secret Police
SSPX	Society of Saint Pius X
Vatican I	First Vatican Council (1869–1870)
Vatican II	Second Vatican Council (1962–1965)
VS	*Veritatis splendour* (encyclical of John Paul II)
YCW	Young Christian Workers (see JOC)
WYD	World Youth Day

ACKNOWLEDGMENTS

BOOKS ARE NEVER solo efforts, even though it looks that way, with the author working alone at a computer. But at least in nonfiction, you are dependent on the other people who have worked in the field, and the only way to acknowledge them is through the Notes and the Bibliography. So special thanks to all those scholars and thinkers whose work I have read and who inspired me. I have already written on this topic previously in my books *Papal Power* (1997) and *Upon This Rock* (2000). It is the election of Pope Francis that has brought me back to the topic.

I especially want to thank Professor Zbigniew Kaźmierczak of the University of Bialystok for helping me understand John Paul II's concept of the priesthood and its influence on the Polish pope. His books are referenced in the Bibliography.

Clive Priddle edited *Absolute Power* and made many valuable suggestions; it's a much better book because of him. I am also in the debt of managing editor Michelle Welsh-Horst and copy editor Annette Wenda for all the care that they have taken to improve the manuscript. Special thanks also to my agent, Daniel Conaway, and to Taylor Templeton of Writers House in New York for all your work on behalf of the book.

Many friends provided both intellectual stimulation and social support during the task of writing, especially Frank Purcell from Catholics Speak Out and Peter Johnston and Peter Wilkinson from Catholics for Renewal. Attendance at the Gender, Gospel, and Global Justice Conference in Philadelphia in 2015 stimulated many ideas, especially in conversation with Kristina Keneally and Tony

Flannery. Friends like Moira and Tom Hayes and Mary and Justin Stanwix have made sure real human contact has been maintained during the writing.

As always, my special thanks to my wife, Marilyn Hatton, who, having already journeyed with me in my excursion into tenth-century Europe in *The Birth of the West* (2013), has now accompanied me on this trip through papal history. She critically read the whole text and made many helpful suggestions. Thanks for all your love and support.

Paul Collins
Canberra, July 2017

A PERSONAL INTRODUCTION

I FIRST BECAME intrigued with the way the papacy uses power back in the mid-1990s when I was preparing two books, one on the history of the papacy and another on the way authority has been understood in the church. One of these books, *Papal Power: A Proposal for Change in Catholicism's Third Millennium* (1997), was "delated" (reported) to the Congregation for the Doctrine of the Faith, the former Holy Office of the Roman Inquisition, the Vatican department that guards orthodox doctrine.[1] This led to an "investigation" of *Papal Power* by the CDF that dragged on for more than three years that led in the end to my resigning from the active priestly ministry. Interestingly, the CDF was no longer interested in the book once I rejoined the Catholic laity, and I heard nothing more of the investigation. As a result, I now apply the legal dictum *qui tacet consentit*, literally "who keeps silence consents" or "silence denotes consent," and assume that the book is perfectly orthodox.

The subtitle of the book, *A Proposal for Change in Catholicism's Third Millennium*, explained my real intention in writing the book: I wanted to suggest ways in which Catholicism might continue to realize in church life something of the renewal proposed by the Second Vatican Council (1962–1965). You need to remember that the mid-1990s was a difficult period for progressive Catholics, as the Vatican II vision of a renewed church was being slowly whittled away. John Paul II had been pope since 1978, and it was abundantly clear that he, supported by traditionalist Catholics, was aiming at a kind of "restoration" that had little to do with Vatican II and, as we shall see later in this book, a lot to do with his own idio-syncratic vision of Catholicism.

Papal Power was admittedly critically blunt about the Roman Curia, the bureaucracy that supports—and sometimes controls—the pope. I described it as an "incubus" that smothers creativity in the church and said that the CDF employed incompetent theologians, was "irreformable," and had "no place in the contemporary church and should be abolished." Clearly, this was not going to win friends and influence people in Rome, but I was not really talking to those people. The book was addressed to English speakers, and as an Australian I tend to call a spade a spade. The book was a piece of popular theology written to suggest ideas to keep the renewal movement going. I was convinced that the time had come for clarity and directness because of the serious nature of the crisis that Catholics in the Western world were experiencing as people abandoned the church in droves. Clearly, Catholicism was not addressing their needs.

It is twenty years now since the publication of *Papal Power*, and, except for the election of Pope Francis, little has changed in Catholicism. For instance, the Pew Research Center found that the Catholic population of the United States dropped by 3.1 million between 2007 and 2015, with 13 percent of all Americans calling themselves "former Catholics." It is Latino immigration that helps keep US Catholic numbers stable.[2] The situation is the same in Australia, where the recent 2016 national census shows that between 2011 and 2016, the Catholic proportion of the population has dropped from 25.3 percent to 22.6 percent, a drop of 2.7 percent. While Catholics are still the largest religious group in the country, again it is immigration that has to a considerable extent maintained the Australian Catholic population.

There are many reasons people abandon Catholicism, but they are often scandalized by the imagined wealth of the papacy and the way in which power is used in the church. So I decided it was time to look again at the question of authority in Catholicism, specifically papal power and how it distorts the message of the Gospel. Christ is the litmus test for any institution that claims to be Christian because, as the Letter to the Philippians says, Christ "emptied himself taking the form of a slave . . . and became obedient to the point of death—even death on a cross" (2:7–8). The term *emptied himself* is a translation of the Greek word κενόω, the verb meaning "to empty." The text is trying to say that Christ absolutely abandoned all the power and authority that accompanied his intimacy and equality with God and assumed not just the weakness of the human condition, but the utter powerlessness of a slave who, in the Roman world, had no legal rights and no ability to use the system; slaves were utterly powerless. The powerlessness of Jesus was reinforced by his death on the cross. Here he is stripped of everything, even of hope. The Gospel of Mark says that as he died, he "shrieked out" (this is what the Greek word really means), "My God, my God why have you abandoned me?" (15:34). Thus, he dies as a common criminal on a cross, bereft of everything.

It is hard to reconcile this with the popes who from the early twelfth century until 1978 were crowned with a tiara of three crowns and addressed as "the father of princes and kings, [and] ruler of the world." This ridiculous nonsense has, thankfully, now been swept away, but the fact that it was in use for almost eight centuries tells you that the papacy has forgotten Christ on the cross and become besotted with power. What I want to show in this book is that the modern papacy has risen from a near-death experience in 1799 at the end of the French Revolution to become more centralized and more powerful than even before in its entire history. Nowadays the papacy is one of the most influential institutions in the world and uses both "soft" and "hard" power with skill and ability.

That forces you to ask the question: What would Christ, the man who emptied himself to die on the cross and the final norm of everything Christian, really think?

PART I

EXTINCTION?

1

A DEATH IN VALENCE

AT DAYBREAK ON August 29, 1799, an eighty-one-year-old Italian, known to the French authorities as *Citoyen Giovanni Angelo Braschi*, died in the citadel of the city of Valence in southeastern France. His body lay unburied until late January 1800, when it was laid in unconsecrated ground in a local cemetery. Citizen Braschi was, in fact, Pope Pius VI (1775–1799), the man the French also called "the former so-called pope." As the news of his death spread, the *philosophes*, the public intellectuals of Europe, rejoiced because they were sure the papacy was at last extinct. "The death of Pius VI has . . . placed a seal on the glory of philosophy in modern times," boasted the *Courrier Universel* on September 8, 1799. The church and the papacy would be swept away with the rest of the detritus of the *ancien régime* by the progressive *bourgeoisie* of the French Revolution. When he died Pius VI had been the longest-serving pope in church history—twenty-four years. Even the most optimistic Catholic in 1799 must have felt that the papacy was finished.

The death of Pius VI as a prisoner was a fitting end to a century of ineffectual papal nonentities. No longer influential in European politics, the popes had retired to the Papal States, that odd principality straddling central and northeastern Italy, where they played the role of "enlightened" monarchs and covered up their weakness by pretending to be neutral in international affairs. Their influence in the wider church was also diminished. It reached its lowest ebb when the vacillating, weak, and depressed Clement XIV (1769–1774) capitulated to the European powers in August 1773 and suppressed the Jesuits, the order that had been the mainstay of the papacy for two centuries. The papacy had been in a slow decline since the late seventeenth century, and its ecclesiastical power had been weakened by theological theories that emphasized the dominance of the local ruler in the local church. The church in most of Catholic Europe was largely controlled by eighteenth-century enlightened despots like Emperor Joseph II who didn't hesitate to use the church for their own ends. This is generically called "caesaro-papism," when kings and rulers appoint bishops and restrict church government to the sacristy.

The eighteenth century was an age of strong, absolutist regimes in France, Prussia, Russia, and the Hapsburg Empire. Monarchical absolutism embraced the theory of the divine right of kings, which was characterized by the notion that not only was the king the source of law, but he also controlled the administrative machinery of the state and its judicial functions. The monarch also controlled the local church. There were three Catholic caesaro-papist theological theories that handed the church over to the control of the state: Gallicanism, Febronianism, and Josephism. Gallicanism, the most theologically sophisticated of these theories, was also the most ancient, with roots in the thirteenth century. It claimed for the French monarch authority to control the French church by appointing all bishops and restricting all papal interventions in France. While it theoretically accepted papal authority, it claimed that the pope was always limited by the absolute supremacy of a general council of the church. It accepted papal authority in matters of faith, while holding that papal teaching was binding only when the faithful accepted it. Febronianism and Josephism were really just variations on Gallicanism.

The eighteenth century was the age of the Enlightenment, which itself was characterized by a deep distrust of religious authority and tradition. The key characteristics of the Enlightenment were the development of science, empirical experimentation, skepticism, the emergence of theories of natural religion like those of Jean-Jacques Rousseau, John Locke's democratic theory of the people as the source of authority in society, Voltaire's attacks on superstition and organized religion (particularly Catholicism), and Denis Diderot's *Encyclopédie*. This was a cultural milieu that was deeply distrustful of the authority of the church. Thinkers tried to find a "natural" basis for ethics rather than a morality based on dogmatic principles. The Enlightenment is especially important for its political and social theory. English thinker John Locke (1632–1704) held that the monarch rules not by a God-given divine right, but on the condition that the people consent to the authority of the ruler, and he or she governs in the interests of the people. If power is abused, the people have the right to resist. Locke argued that the people enter into a contract with the government. He supported religious freedom, toleration, limited government, and separation of powers. This idea was picked up by Montesquieu in his vast outline of political science in *L'ésprit des lois* (*The spirit of laws*).

How did the church respond to the ferment of ideas that was the Enlightenment? Not very creatively, truth be told, but this must be seen against the fact that the rural population remained untouched by the influence of the *philosophes*, whose inroads were predominantly among the urban middle class, some of the nobility, and a minority of clergy. The vast majority of the rural population remained loyal to Catholicism. Pious religious literature still topped the best-seller lists. However, no significant theologian emerged from within Catholicism in this period to tackle the new culture creatively. The church had had an easy run for 150 years as part of the establishment, and it had become lazy and self-satisfied.

The final papal conclave of the eighteenth century elected Giovanni Angelo Braschi, who took the style Pius VI. Handsome, lordly, worldly, and strong, he was very vain. He faced a culture bristling with Enlightenment skepticism, atheism, and caesaro-papist theories of state control over the church. The Papal States were desperately poor and deeply in debt, one of the most backward regions of Europe. Trade and economic reform were constantly stymied by the corrupt and chaotic clerical administration. Most of the population of perhaps 3 million worked the land and were largely uneducated.

But what really mattered in the Europe of the last decades of the eighteenth century was what began in France between May and July 1789.

———

AT THE BEGINNING of 1789, France was on the edge of bankruptcy. King Louis XVI had run out of options, so he convened the Estates General, a kind of parliament representing the three major divisions of society, nobles, clergy, and commons—in English *estates* refers to classes or orders in society—for May 5, 1789. It had not met for 175 years. The financial crisis was symptomatic of a deeper malaise. From around 1770 economic growth stagnated, and crop failures in 1788 compounded restlessness, especially among the peasantry. The bourgeoisie resented their exclusion from positions of power, and many were influenced by Enlightenment ideas and the example of the American Revolution. They questioned the divine-right monarchy and noble privileges. The church was resented because it was perceived to be very wealthy. There was growing anticlericalism that focused on church tithes and the fact that religious orders and dioceses owned 6 percent of the land surface of France. These complaints featured regularly in the *cahiers de doléances* (complaint books) submitted to the Estates General.

When the Estates General met at Versailles, Louis XVI and his ministers hoped that the assembly would persuade the nobles and clergy to accept reforms and new taxes. Of the 296 clergy elected, 208 were *curés*, or parish priests, who usually came from the lower orders; only 47 were bishops. With almost 300 clergy out of a total representation of 1,200 (including 300 nobles and 600 commoners), the Estates General was far from anticlerical. The different estates met separately, but a group of *curés* "went over" to the commoners. Seizing the initiative, they declared themselves a "Constituent National Assembly." The assembly decided to break with the nobles and the more traditional clergy, and they retreated to a royal tennis court and took the Oath of the Tennis Court (June 20, 1789), swearing to maintain their unity and independence as an assembly until a constitution was approved. By late June there was pressure on the assembly to disperse, and, as a warning, Swiss and German mercenaries were deployed in Paris. Fearing a royal counterattack and the danger posed by the proletarian mob, on July 14, 1789, a group of Paris tradesmen and businessmen formed a national guard to defend themselves and seized guns from the royal armory. Seeking gunpowder, they stormed the Bastille fortress, killing the guards and freeing seven prisoners. Riots began in the provinces, and manor houses were burned. Some of the aristocracy began to flee France entirely.

At Versailles the National Assembly had now taken over the Estates General. On one emotional night (August 4–5, 1789), feudalism and the tithe were abolished, and the last remnants of serfdom and class privilege were swept away, again with the support of many lower clergy. Then, on August 26, the assembly issued the Declaration of the Rights of Man and of the Citizen. The declaration balances universal principles with a concern for the interests of the bourgeoisie. Property was "sacred," but there was no mention of the poor. On October 6 the palace of Versailles was stormed, and, under pressure, an unwilling king ratified the abolition of feudalism.

But France was still hopelessly in debt. It was an opportunist bishop who suggested the best source of revenue: the church. Charles Maurice de Talleyrand, bishop of Autun, proposed that the resources of the church be placed "at the disposal of the nation" and that, in return, the nation provide for the upkeep of the church and the clergy. Adrien Dansette describes Talleyrand as "the most irreligious, corrupt and cynical of all the prelates of the old *régime*"; he was also the great survivor of the Revolution.[1]

To seize ecclesiastical revenue, the assembly proceeded to nationalize the church and radically redraw the relationship between church and state. Between October 1789 and February 1790, the religious orders were abolished and their property confiscated. Some seventy thousand priests and nuns were expelled from religious life. Over the next three years, ecclesiastical and religious-order property and lands came on the market, usually at cut-rate prices, and a whole group of middle-class men on the make gained a vested interest in maintaining the Revolution by buying up church assets at bargain-basement prices. A scandalous example of this is the destruction of the magnificent late-medieval buildings of Cluny Abbey, which were bought up by a developer from nearby Mâcon who then used the abbey as a quarry for building materials.

The state now controlled ecclesiastical finances, and the assembly realized that this was a golden opportunity to regularize church-state relationships in its favor. On July 12, 1790, the National Assembly passed the Civil Constitution of the Clergy. It claimed that it affected only the civil aspects of the church, but these were inseparable from its spiritual side. Most of the bishops refused to accept the Civil Constitution and, despite their Gallican leanings, appealed to Pope Pius VI. Their appeal gained further traction with the imposition of an oath of loyalty on the clergy to the Civil Constitution in November 1790; if a bishop or priest refused, he forfeited his salary and position. The clergy were now divided into "jurors" and "nonjurors," those who took the oath and those who didn't. About 50 percent of priests swore the oath, but then many rejected it when Pius VI eventually condemned the Civil Constitution in early 1791. Because a large majority of bishops refused it, Talleyrand had to consecrate a whole new bench of bishops. Priests began joining the émigrés abroad. Clergy were now forced to marry, affecting many people: there were about ninety thousand diocesan clergy and about eighty thousand members of religious orders, including fifty-five thousand nuns. Celibacy was deemed "unnatural" because it prevented men (women were not considered) from fulfilling their natural role: having children to populate the state. The Civil Constitution redrew diocesan boundaries to conform to the borders of the new *départments*, and bishops were to be elected by *citoyens actifs* (active citizens). The pope was merely "notified" of their election. *Curés* were to be elected by the parish. The church was now an arm of the state, which was not all that different from the Gallicanism of the old regime.

Overwhelmed by the sheer speed of the Revolution, especially in Paris, the indecisive Pius VI remained cautious, waiting to see the reaction of the French church. Louis XVI, a genuinely devout man, hesitated, awaiting the pope's decision. Eventually, on March 10, 1791, Pius VI condemned the Civil Constitution as schismatic, suspended priests and bishops who had taken the oath, and denounced the Declaration of the Rights of Man.

By early 1791 the Revolution in France became increasingly radical, anticlerical, and antireligious. The choice was clear: Catholics split between those who supported the Revolution and those who didn't. Religion was declared a private affair, and nonjuring clergy were increasingly identified with émigrés and enemies abroad and threatened with arrest and banishment. Then on the night of June 20, 1791, the king and royal family fled Paris in disguise, heading for the fortress of Montmédy, near the German border, which was controlled by loyal troops. The royal party got to Varennes, within thirty kilometers (eighteen miles) of Montmédy, but were recognized and returned to Paris as prisoners. Radicals called for the abolition of the monarchy, for the establishment of a republic, and for the king to be put on trial.

On September 30, 1791, the National Assembly was dissolved and elections held for a new legislative assembly. This was dominated by the "Left," the Jacobins. In August 1792 the king, who had resisted all legal attacks on the church, was arrested with the royal family and the monarchy abolished. In response, proroyalist insurrections broke out in the Vendée, Brittany, and Dauphiné. The country descended into chaos, with no effective government. By mid-August Paris was in the hands of the local Commune, which was dominated by the Jacobins, led by extremists like Georges-Jacques Danton and Maximilien Robespierre, a lethal fanatic and idealist who could justify the execution of anyone who opposed his vision.

Austria and Prussia had already formed an alliance against France, and in response in April 1792 the French declared war on Austria and invaded the Austrian Netherlands. In turn, Prussia invaded France, and a ragtag French army surrendered at Verdun on September 2, 1792. Panic spread in Paris, which was already suffering serious food shortages. Inflamed by radicals who claimed that the prisons were full of counterrevolutionary priests and nobility, the September Massacres began on September 3, 1792, when 24 priest prisoners were killed by a frenzied mob. A kind of collective insanity spread as fear seized the population. Prisons were invaded. Feelings were so intense that the mob, many of them drunk, massacred defenseless people. Two-thirds of the 1,100 to 1,400 people killed that September were innocent civilians, common criminals, and prostitutes. All told, some 225 priests were killed in this week of madness.

On September 20, 1792, the extremist Jacobins assumed power, and the monarchy and the Christian calendar were abolished and

Year I of the Republic proclaimed. Civil divorce was introduced. By November the French armies were successful on the northern front, and on January 21, 1793, Louis XVI was executed. Present in Paris throughout this period was a young, ambitious army officer, Napoleon Bonaparte.

By early 1793 discontent was seething in France, especially in Paris. The extremist Jacobins and the *sans-culottes* (a mixture of urban poor and lower-middle class) were making common cause. By early April they gained control of the Committee of Public Safety (effectively the acting executive government), and the Reign of Terror began. The most intense period of the terror was in June–July 1794. Some 18,000 people were executed. An anticlerical, anti-Christian campaign began. A revolutionary "cult of reason" was introduced, later modified into the "cult of the supreme being" when Robespierre was dominant. On June 8, 1794, the first "Feast of the Supreme Being" was celebrated. One who witnessed this was Englishwoman Helen Maria Williams, a radical writer who was in Paris until mid-1794. She had little patience for it all. "On the principal church of every town was inscribed 'the temple of reason'; and a tutelary goddess was installed with a ceremony equally pedantic, ridiculous and profane." Describing the installation of the cult in Notre Dame in Paris, she says, "The Goddess of Reason was a fine, blooming damsel of the opera house, and she acted her part in this comedy . . . to the entire satisfaction of her new votaries. . . . Only one universal cry was heard 'no more priests, and no other gods.'"[2]

The Jacobins were overthrown in the Thermidorian Reaction of late July 1794, bringing the terror to an end. Freedom of worship was decreed in February 1795, but persecution of Catholics, especially nonjuring clergy, continued. On November 10, 1799, the now general Napoleon Bonaparte pulled off the *coup d'état* of Brumaire, after which a three-man consulate was set up, with Napoleon himself as first consul and, given his military power, the dominant partner. According to the consulate's "Constitution of the Year VIII," the Revolution was officially over: "The Revolution is established upon the principles which began it; it is ended."

BONAPARTE FIRST BECAME prominent in May 1796 when he took Milan from the Austrians and seized the Legations (the northern part of the Papal States, including Ravenna, Ferrara, and Bologna), the most prosperous part of the papal principality, from the pope. He demanded 21 million crowns in cash, one hundred works of art, and five hundred manuscripts as booty. This was the beginning of his cultural larceny that lasted until his fall. By February 1797 Bonaparte controlled northern Italy, and he forced the pope to sign the Treaty of Tolentino, imposing a further indemnity of 15 million crowns and more artworks. But Bonaparte didn't occupy Rome; he recognized the obstinate soft power of the papacy. After his success in Italy, Bonaparte set off to campaign in Egypt.

By now Pius VI was old and sick. Except for Rome, he had lost the Papal States, and the papal government was fatally weakened. The French stirred up civil strife in Rome, and on February 9, 1798, the pope was deposed and a French-sponsored nonpapal *régime* established. The half-paralyzed pope was bundled out of Rome and across the Alps, eventually dying in Valence. The French government believed that the papacy was finished, and all contemporary evidence certainly pointed in that direction. The year 1799 was probably the lowest point in the history of the papacy. It had faced many difficulties in its long history, not least the corrupt popes and the dominance of the Mafia-like Roman clans in the tenth century and the Great Western Schism of the fourteenth and fifteenth centuries when there were two, then three, claimants to the papal office. But in 1799 it looked as though the *philosophes* were right and the papacy was finally finished.

Despite Catholic belief in Jesus's words that "the gates of hell will not prevail" against Peter and his successors (Matt. 16:18), the situation in September 1799 was dire for the papacy. Two things saved it: First, Pius VI had issued a bull in 1798 giving the cardinal dean, Gian Francesco Albani, the authority to hold the conclave anywhere there was a Catholic ruler and whenever he could get most of the cardinals together. After Pius's death, Albani and the secretary of the conclave, Monsignor Ercole Consalvi, worked hard to get the cardinals together. But the thing that really saved the papacy was an unexpected shift in the strategic situation. In

September 1799 the Neapolitans, assisted by the British navy, expelled the French from Rome. Meanwhile, in northern Italy, the Austrians had regained control of Venice. Although Rome was no longer under French control, several of the cardinals, including Albani, had already found their way to Austrian-controlled Venice. Many of them were penniless refugees, like the Cardinal Duke of York, brother of Bonnie Prince Charlie and sometimes known as King Henry IX, the final Stuart pretender to the British and Scottish thrones. To help him the British government generously granted him a pension. After the death of Pius VI on August 29, 1799, the challenge for Albani and Consalvi and what was left of the papal government was to get as many cardinals as they could to Venice to elect a new pope. Consalvi was very able, and he wrote to all forty-six cardinals and to the Catholic monarchs to inform them that Albani had called for a conclave to be held in Venice. It began on December 1, 1799, and dragged on for more than three months. The cardinals finally elected the Benedictine monk Luigi Barnabà Chiaramonti, who took the style Pius VII (1800–1823). He was a good choice—fifty-eight years old, a gentle, courageous man, neither reactionary nor opposed to democracy. He decided to return to Rome, no matter how dangerous the city might be, eventually arriving there on July 3, 1800.

He was wise to have left Venice because Bonaparte, back in northern Italy, defeated the Austrians at Marengo on June 14, 1800. A realist, Bonaparte knew he had to make peace with the church. He looked at Catholicism "dispassionately and came to the conclusion that it was a force not to be destroyed, but to be enlisted in his support."[3] He later advised his ambassador in Rome in 1801, François Cacault, to "treat the pope as though he had an army of 200,000 men." Even though negotiating from a very weak stance, Pius VII used whatever influence the papacy had left to deal with Bonaparte. He sent Consalvi to Paris as his chief negotiator. It was a good choice.

There were two obstacles to doing a deal. The first issue was the émigré French bishops who wanted their dioceses back. The second was the anti-Catholic revolutionaries who were now courting

Bonaparte. In the end, Consalvi and the pope refused to reappoint the émigré bishops, and Bonaparte ignored the revolutionaries. The Revolution was, after all, "over." The negotiations leading to the Concordat (a diplomatically binding agreement between the Holy See and a government) were complex, with Consalvi and the former bishop Talleyrand as chief negotiators and Bonaparte regularly throwing temper tantrums in the background. After a last-minute crisis engineered by Talleyrand, who tried to slip past Consalvi a different text from the one he had agreed to, the Concordat was signed in Paris on September 10, 1801.[4] Catholicism was recognized as "the religion of the great majority of Frenchmen," but it was no longer the state religion. Freedom of religion was guaranteed, and Catholic worship "shall be public while conforming to such police regulation as the government shall consider necessary to public tranquillity."[5] The number of dioceses was reduced from 136 to 60. The government nominated new bishops, with the pope granting their canonical institution. Only government-approved *curés* were to be appointed to parishes by bishops. Bishops and priests were to be paid by the government, but the pittance of five hundred francs per annum paid to priests was well below the poverty line. Church property required for worship was restored to the church.

Consalvi had gained many concessions but was furious when he discovered that Bonaparte had attached a set of "Organic Articles" to the Concordat. These were police powers that regulated the publication of papal documents in France, required state permission for the establishment of seminaries, forbade public processions in towns where there were "adherents of different creeds," and regulated the boundaries of dioceses, priests' salaries, and clerical dress. The aim was to make the church a department of state. What, in fact, the articles did was to turn the Catholic community away from Gallicanism as they began to resist state interference in church affairs. The articles pointed the French church in the direction of what was later called "ultramontanism." The word comes from the Latin *ultra montes*, "beyond the mountains" (that is, the Alps). This propapalist ideology (it was never a coherent theology) divorced the church from state control and turned it toward the papacy as the central focus of Catholicism. It became the underlying theory for the enhancement of papal power in the church and, as we shall see, is still a basic issue for Catholicism.

While the Concordat and articles may have made the church effectively a department of state, it did nothing for the actual practice of religion. No priests had been ordained since 1790. Thousands of priests had left France; seven thousand of them lived in England between 1792 and 1801, existing on British government pensions. There were many parishes without priests, and the average age of the clergy was high. In Rome opposition to the conciliatory policies of Pius VII and Consalvi, now cardinal secretary of state, was growing among the *zelanti* (Italian for "zealots" or "fanatics") cardinals and officials; they were concerned that the French legal code, the Code Napoleon, which allowed divorce, already operative in the Legations, would be imposed on the rest of the Papal States.

Bonaparte was immensely popular in France and northern Italy, and the upstart Corsican began to think of himself as the "new Charlemagne." He was God's "elect" and felt the time had come for him to join the anointed crowned heads of Europe. His nomination by the Senate as emperor "by the grace of God and the will of the people" was supported by a large majority vote in France. His position strengthened, he wanted a papal coronation in Paris, a backhanded acknowledgment of the pope's traditional influence, even as he demanded the papacy's submission to him. There were serious reservations about this in Rome, but Pius VII decided to attend Bonaparte's coronation on December 2, 1804. One of the conditions of papal attendance was that Joséphine de Beauharnais (the abandoned wife of an aristocrat) and Bonaparte, who were civilly married, be married in the church, which they secretly did before the coronation. The coronation was immortalized by Jacques-Louis David's propaganda masterpiece painting. He shows Bonaparte crowning Joséphine. The eyes of everyone in the scene are on the crown that Bonaparte holds aloft. Napoleon had already crowned himself to avoid acknowledging any form of papal superiority over him. The pope in the painting looks glum, but he enjoyed his time in Paris; he had an easy way with people, and on the journey home-ward people came out to cheer him. A modern, populist papacy was being born.

Relations between Bonaparte and Pius VII degenerated between 1805 and 1808. There were constant French incursions into pa-pal territory, and the pope refused to support Bonaparte's plan to invade Britain. The divorce legislation in the Napoleonic Code transferring marriage into the civil sphere caused further tension. When the pope refused to deport foreign agents from the Papal States, Bonaparte instructed his ambassador (and uncle) Cardinal Joseph Fesch: "Tell them . . . I am Charlemagne, the sword of the church and their emperor. And that I should be treated as such."[6] On February 2, 1808, the French again occupied Rome and the Papal States. Bonaparte declared Rome a "free imperial city" and abolished the papal government. Pius VII responded by excom-municating him. Bonaparte was furious. He wrote, "If the pope preaches revolt . . . he ought to be arrested."[7] The French author-ities in Rome took the order literally, and the pope was kidnapped and taken to Grenoble and then to Savona, on the Italian Medi-terranean coast. The papal government was dissolved and the pa-pal archives taken to France. The Papal States were integrated into the French Empire, and the Napoleonic Code was applied, with its marriage regulations and divorce.

In retaliation Pius VII dug in, refusing from 1809 to 1811 to cooperate with Bonaparte. Around mid-1811 Pius's health began to deteriorate. "He had sharp headaches and a rapid pulse, and be-tween his bouts of excitability, he would stare ahead of him with a vacant, glassy eye."[8] This might have resulted from infection or chronic fatigue, or he might even have been drugged by Napoleon's spies. He gradually recovered, and just after the ill-fated French in-vasion of Russia began in June 1812, the pope was moved from Savona over the Alps to Fontainebleau, near Paris. It was a dreadful journey in a heavy Berlin carriage; Pius was suffering from a uri-nary tract infection. At Fontainebleau the pope recommenced his resistance, and he began to be seen as a "martyr" for his opposition to Bonaparte, especially in Protestant England. After the Russian disaster in December 1812, Bonaparte was no longer seen as invincible. In January 1814 coalition armies entered France, and Paris fell on March 31, 1814. The empire was dissolved, and Bonaparte abdicated on April 4, 1814, and was exiled to the Mediterranean island of Elba. The pope had returned to Rome, entering in triumph on March 24, 1814. The papacy, at one of its lowest ebbs in church history, had survived by managing Napoleon and through support from Protestant Britain.

Bonaparte escaped Elba in March 1815, returned to France, and rallied his army, only to be finally defeated on June 18, 1815, just north of the French-Belgian border at Waterloo by the British, commanded by the Duke of Wellington and the Prussians under Gebhard von Blücher. The always terse Wellington commented that the battle was "the nearest thing you ever saw in your life." Bonaparte was exiled to the island of Saint Helena in the South Atlantic, where he died in 1821.

The astonishing thing is that the papacy survived the death of Pius VI. It is a testimony to its profound roots in European history and tradition and, many Catholics would argue, in Christ's promise to Saint Peter that "the gates of hell would not prevail" against the church (Matt. 16:18). Pius VII was also extraordinarily lucky to have had Napoleon as his interlocutor: the emperor recognized the influence of Catholicism and saw it as the basis of civilization, social and moral order, and good government. While his personal religious sentiments and commitment to Catholicism are difficult to discern, Napoleon's approach to the church was largely utilitarian. He knew he had to negotiate with the pope and keep the church on his side and in that very process enhanced and reinforced the symbolic power of the papacy. Advised and supported by Consalvi (perhaps the greatest of the secretaries of state), Pius VII shrewdly used his position to enhance papal influence.

One of the key foundations upon which the modern papacy is built is ultramontanism, the antithesis of the old Gallican theory of the union of throne and altar. The collapse of the French monarchy opened the way for this papal ideology to emerge. So while the revolutionary and Napoleonic period may have seen the papacy at its weakest, the early nineteenth century laid the seedbed from which modern papal centralism emerged.

———————

THE DEFEAT OF Bonaparte brought the kings back to power, including France's Louis XVIII. By his side was the ever-opportunistic Talleyrand. The "principle of legitimacy," the notion that kings should be restored to their rightful thrones, appealed to the victors, and after twenty-two years of war, everyone was ready for peace. The Catholic powers, particularly Austria, tried to exclude the pope from the peace negotiations at the Congress of Vienna (1814–1815). The Austrians wanted to grab northern Italy, particularly the most prosperous part of the Papal States, the northeastern Legations. But with the support of the British foreign secretary, Viscount Castlereagh, Consalvi secured a place at the table. Consalvi had visited London in June–July 1814, and it was here that he was welcomed and became friendly with Foreign Secretary Castlereagh and was received at court by the prince regent, later George IV, who, to Consalvi's disappointment, insisted on speaking in French rather than English. Given the popularity of Pius VII in England, the English-speaking Anglophile Consalvi secured British support for the restoration of the Papal States. Consalvi, whom Bonaparte called "a lion in sheep's clothing," loved everything English because his patron had been Henry the Cardinal Duke of York, bishop of Frascati and Stuart pretender to the English Crown.[9]

The principle of legitimacy was applied inconsistently at Vienna, and it was a struggle for Consalvi to get the Papal States reinstated against Austrian and French opposition. The sticking point was, as Austrian chancellor Klemens von Metternich reminded Consalvi, that the Papal States had been signed away by Pius VI at the Treaty of Tolentino in 1797. It was only Pius VII's prestige in Europe and the influence of Castlereagh that got the Papal States restored. Consalvi's aim in the restoration was to protect the neutrality of the papacy, and he insisted on retaining the Legations; they were the most economically viable part of the principality. But the problem was that notions of liberalism, democracy, and freedom of the press had already spread through north-central Italy, and under Bonaparte the Legations had been united with Lombardy and the Po plain, which was their natural geographic and economic locus.

The Congress of Vienna eventually restored the "legitimate" ruler of the Papal States to his principality. Consalvi immediately set about reorganizing the papal dominions, restoring the educational system, reforming the finances, setting up a new civil and criminal code, and improving public safety. He also began a major program of public works. Rome, however, remained economically stagnant. Pilgrims began flocking there only after 1850. The papal government was forced to resort to loans, frequently from the Rothschilds, to balance the books.[10] Another problem was the secret societies. As early as 1817, the *Carbonari* (Charcoal Burners), an anticlerical revolutionary secret society possibly of Masonic origin that favored liberal ideals and Italian unification, unsuccessfully revolted against the papacy, and some of their leaders were imprisoned or banished.

Neither Pius VII nor Consalvi wanted to return to the *ancien régime*; their problems were practical, not least the restoration of the papal government. But the reestablishment of the Papal States became a calamity for the church. The principality became a noose around the papal neck. It tied the popes politically and psychologically to a legitimist ideology. They were left running a theocratic principality in which spiritual and temporal were constantly conflated. There was an insistence on traditional ways of doing things and a lack of political common sense. Lay citizens of the Papal States, who had already enjoyed a measure of democracy and responsibility under Bonaparte, certainly didn't want to return to the corrupt and inefficient clericalist regime. Even modest reforms were opposed by intransigent *zelanti* cardinals like Bartolomeo Pacca, and they soon controlled the agenda. Thus, the ministerial interests of the church were sacrificed to the maintenance of a principality that was already moribund, with the popes projecting their problems with democracy, pluralism, freedom of religion, separation of church and state, and free speech in the Papal States onto the universal church. It was a recipe for disaster.

Pius VII and Consalvi also faced a church in chaos across Europe, resulting from war, the abolition of the Holy Roman Empire, and a papal government that had been exiled for sixteen years. To restore order to church-state relationships, Consalvi negotiated concordats with Bavaria (1817), Sardinia (1817), Russia (1818), the Two Sicilies (1818), and Prussia and the Rhineland princes (1821); the French concordat was renewed in 1817 without the Organic Articles. The papacy also recognized the newly independent Latin American republics after 1820 when it broke with Spanish claims to legitimacy and dominance.

One of the first things Pius VII did on return to Rome was to restore the Jesuits on August 7, 1814, after a forty-one-year suppression. They quickly became the foremost defenders of the papacy. Consalvi, whose portrait by Sir Thomas Lawrence is in Windsor Castle, also played a major role in restoring Rome as an archaeological, artistic, and cultural capital. Lawrence, who was in Rome in 1819, commented, "There is now here a general spirit of exertion, both in judicious repairs in preserving the great monuments of antiquity, and by excavations in discovering their foundations and parts . . . that were before hidden from the eye."[11]

However, Pius VII's death on July 20, 1823, marked the end of Consalvi's career as secretary of state. Elected on September 28, 1823, the pious, austere Annibale della Genga took the style Leo XII (1823–1829). The *zelanti* were now in charge. Consalvi's legal reforms were rolled back with the reintroduction of the pre-1800 ecclesiastical courts, laymen were no longer hired by the papal government, the Jews were forced back into the ghetto, criminals and brigands were summarily executed, the *Index of Forbidden Books* and the Roman Inquisition were restored, and Freemasonry and secret societies were forbidden. Petty regulations made the papal *régime* even more resented: low-cut dresses, the public sale of alcohol, and gambling and recreation on Sundays and holy days were all forbidden. The *Sanfidesti*, the Army of the Holy Faith, a kind of papal guerrilla movement begun in 1799, was reactivated to attack the secret societies. Anticlericalism was understandable, and there was resentment against priestly control, especially in the Legations.

The result was predictable: economic stagnation and the alienation of the aristocracy, educated people, and the middle class from the papal government. The modernization that Consalvi encouraged was swept aside, and a police state overrun with scandalmongers, spies, and slackers and dominated by inefficient, incompetent clerics determined to control everyone's lives reemerged, setting up precisely the conditions that encouraged revolution.

Map of Italy in the 1820s, showing the Papal States lying right across the peninsula

Credit: Methuen and Company, Ltd.

2

THE "NEW CONSCIOUSNESS" AND "NEO-ULTRAMONTANISM"

FRANCESCO SAVERIO CASTIGLIONE, the man who was elected pope after the death of Leo XII in March 1829, was a moderate who was sympathetic to the policies of Pius VII and Consalvi. He had just missed out on election in 1823 when he was outmaneuvered by the *zelanti* cardinals. He took the style Pius VIII (1829–1830). He ran a more open regime in the Papal States and retreated somewhat from police-state methods. But he was still very much the product of the narrow parochialism of the Papal States, and his major focus was on pastoral and doctrinal issues. In a grab-bag encyclical letter, he blamed the decline in religious practice on indifference to church doctrine, Protestant Bible societies, and the failure to recognize the sacredness of marriage. His secretary of state, Giuseppe Albani, was a hard-nosed reactionary, totally unsympathetic to the nationalist aspirations of the Catholic Irish, Poles, and Belgians who were oppressed by Protestant and Orthodox regimes. However, the Roman Catholic Relief Act, popularly known as Catholic emancipation, was passed by the British Parliament in April 1829. It repealed the remaining penal laws against Catholics and allowed them to sit in Parliament and join the armed forces. One of the prime movers in this had been Irish leader Daniel O'Connell, who had often been very critical of the papacy because it had done absolutely nothing to support Catholic Ireland against the British. Pius VIII also approved the decrees of the First Provincial Council, held by the US bishops in Baltimore in October 1829.

Never physically strong, Pius VIII died after only twenty months in office. The conclave to elect his successor was a drawn-out affair that was under enormous pressure from Austrian chancellor Klemens von Metternich, who wanted a pope who would favor Austrian interests in northern Italy and not compromise with "the political madness of the age," that is, with liberal trends. Sponsored by Albani and supported by the *zelanti* in the conclave, Camaldolese monk Bartolomeo Cappellari, who took the style Gregory XVI, was finally elected. An austere reactionary, he tried to take the papacy back to the eighteenth century. He was totally out of tune with the postrevolutionary age.

AFTER 1815 EUROPEAN culture faced an entirely new situation. First, a whole new way of working and living emerged for Europe's growing population based on industrialization. Between 1815 and 1914, Europe changed from being a predominantly rural society to a largely urban one, except in Russia. Mechanized industry demanded an around-the-clock workforce that was provided by population increase and growing urbanization. Between 1800 and 1900, the European population more than doubled, from 180 million to 390 million, and this occurred despite the fact that some 40 million Europeans emigrated to the New World. This vast increase in the industrial proletariat, bad working conditions, and the exploitative employment of women and children led to acute social problems and ultimately to a series of revolutions in 1848. This meant that after 1815, the papacy faced an entirely new situation.

At the same time, a new political phenomenon emerged— liberalism. Derived from the thought of John Locke, liberalism says that the source of sovereignty is neither God nor kings, but the people. Liberals embraced democracy, freedom of expression and the press, separation of church and state, and a belief in progress. They saw human history as a constant ascent to a better life based on science and viewed the technical control of nature as a sign of progress. Liberalism believed that the state must be governed by constitutional principles that ensure the freedom of every individual. This appealed strongly to the bourgeoisie. A clash between liberalism and an absolutist church was inevitable.

Linked to industrialization and liberalism was a whole new form of consciousness that was emerging in Europe. The principles of the Revolution—liberty, equality, fraternity, freedom of expression, and democracy—were spread by French military victories. Central to this new consciousness was romanticism. Finding it almost impossible to define, Kenneth Clark comes closest to an explanation when he says, "I feel. Therefore I am."[1] He says that romanticism is a revolt against the symmetry and logic of eighteenth-century classicism with the emergence of an art based on movement and energy and an emphasis on freedom. Beethoven's Third Symphony in E-flat major, *Eroica*, composed in 1803–1804, gives expression to the restless energy and struggle that underpinned romanticism and his opera *Fidelio* to the desire for liberty from political repression. Romanticism's love of nature emerges in English poets William Wordsworth and Samuel Taylor Coleridge, who began writing just prior to the French Revolution.

However, there was a reactionary side to romanticism that particularly influenced Catholicism. Ultramontanism was derived from the antirevolutionary aspects of romanticism and is usually labeled "neo-ultramontanism." While the term was coined by English writer Wilfred Ward, the pioneer of neo-ultramontanism was Viscount François-René Chateaubriand. Chateaubriand, for whom the beef dish is named, was an antirevolutionary whose 1802 book, *Le génie du Christianisme* (*The Genius of Christianity*), argued that Christianity is true because it is beautiful. An elegant if superficial writer, he claimed that Christianity was the most humane, poetical, artistic, and intellectual of all faiths. His aim was to rehabilitate Christianity after the destructive cynicism of the eighteenth-century *philosophes*. He shifted debate from an Enlightenment emphasis on reason to a romantic focus on feeling. Catholicism, he claimed, was guaranteed by the papacy and popes, like kings, are sovereigns, but papal sovereignty is superior to all others. Popes are infallible and have never made a doctrinal error.

Another reactionary group were the traditionalists, antirevolutionary conservatives who claimed that it was only through a "perennial tradition" that truth and social stability could be maintained. They held that there was an indissoluble union between church and monarchy and that revolutions were wrong because they interfered with the transmission of truth. The key traditionalist writer in the neo-ultramontanist context is Joseph de Maistre. Maistre was a political theorist and publicist, not a theologian. His elegant, comic, and mocking style made his two-volume 1819 book, *Du pape* (*Concerning the Pope*), very influential. He saw European history as a vast process that is interrupted at various times by disordered forces that are ultimately destructive of civilization. The eighteenth century was one of those interruptions when the *philosophes* and revolutionaries denied God and attempted to destroy the foundations of Christian civilization. All they offered was a return to the state of nature *à la mode de* Rousseau. Maistre saw the papacy as the major point of cohesion in Western civilization. Without the papacy, there would be no Christianity and therefore no civilization. His focus on the papacy was essentially political. He claimed that subjects are bound to obey sovereign governments, for they must be assumed to be right; they are, in that sense, "infallible." The "practical" infallibility of government transmutes into the "absolute" infallibility of the papacy. Thus, the Catholic Church was the key safeguard of political stability.

While Chateaubriand assimilates the prevailing romantic feelings of his time, Maistre's thought was eccentric and incoherent. It had no theological foundation whatsoever, yet it is the primary source of the neo-ultramontanism that fed straight into the First Vatican Council (1870), which itself is the basis of modern papal power. What is significant is that these distorted pseudotheologies were developed by political thinkers with no theological competence. Their ideas were popularized by journalist Louis-François Veuillot and his daily newspaper *L'Univers*, and Veuillot became the leader of nineteenth-century French neo-ultramontanism.

Not that the reactionaries had the field all to themselves. There were also liberal Catholics who were more in tune with the times, including one of the great figures of nineteenth-century

Catholicism, Hugues-Félicité Robert de Lamennais. Born in Saint-Malo in 1782, he was intelligent and precocious. He was ordained a priest in 1816. An unstable man, his life was characterized by sudden changes of direction, as well as illness and depression. He began as a traditionalist and in the first (1817) of his four-volume *Essai sur l'indifférence en matière de religion* (*Essay on Indifference in Matters of Religion*), he argued that the moral health of a society depends on the doctrine or faith it holds, and he called for the restoration of Catholicism as the religion of the French state.[2] Ecclesiastical authority was essential for right order in society. Like Chateaubriand and Maistre, Lamennais seemed to hanker for an authoritarian order in society, perhaps understandable after the insecurities of the Reign of Terror and two decades of war.

In the mid-1820s, Lamennais's approach began to change. Disillusioned with the monarchical patronage of Catholicism, he argued that for the church to attract unbelievers and skeptics, it had to be separated from the state. The pope alone, he believed, could give leadership in this. Influenced by Maistre, Lamennais became a strong ultramontanist. His argument was as follows: no pope, no church; no church, no Christianity; no Christianity, no religion; no religion, no society. The church and ecclesiastical authority, by creating common moral standards and beliefs, provided unity to humanity, and the pope brought unity to church and society, thus creating a kind of ultramontanist democratic papal theocracy—a contradiction in terms! Leo XII invited him to Rome and wanted to make him a cardinal; Lamennais refused. Young lay disciples began to gather around him, including Count Charles Forbes de Montalembert; Henri Lacordaire, later to become a great Dominican preacher; Prosper Guéranger, later a reformer of the Benedictines in France; economist Charles de Coux; and Frédéric Ozanam, founder of the Saint Vincent de Paul Society. By 1829 Lamennais was calling for the church to free itself from the monarchy and to abandon privilege and its bondage to the state. He also demanded a renewal of theology, particularly seminary theology, which he saw as degenerate scholasticism. These views caused a tremendous stir in France: bishops attacked him in their pastoral letters.

The year 1830 was a time of revolutions in France, Belgium, and Poland. The French revolt was an essentially bourgeois affair in which the Bourbon king, Charles X, was overthrown by his cousin Louis-Philippe, Duke of Orléans. It ushered in a skeptical regime in which religion was scorned by the establishment. Lamennais was unenthusiastic about Louis-Philippe, and in October 1830 he founded the daily newspaper *L'Avenir* (The Future) with his colleagues in which they defended Catholicism against the hostility of the government. They promoted ultramontanism against the remnant Gallicanism of some bishops and clergy. By late 1830 *L'Avenir* was calling for complete religious freedom, separation of church and state, freedom of the press, liberty of association, universal suffrage, and the rights of parents to have their children educated as they wished. The paper strongly supported Belgian, Polish, and Irish Catholics in their struggles for liberation. Perhaps the most radical aspect of Lamennais's program was that he began to gather local groups "for the defence of religious liberty." Here were laypeople organizing themselves in a country in which religious affairs had been dominated by clerics and the state for centuries.

Lamennais and friends were the first truly modern Catholics. *L'Avenir* was now a serious challenge to the establishment, both clerical and lay. The French bishops believed that its ideas of democracy and separation of church and state were undermining their authority, and they were prepared to fight tooth and nail. The irony is that *L'Avenir* was repulsive to the French hierarchy as much for its ultramontanism as for its liberalism. Nevertheless, that didn't stop these same French bishops from putting pressure on Rome to silence the troublesome abbé. The newly elected Gregory XVI was ready to oblige.

In November 1831 the somewhat naive Lamennais, Lacordaire, and Montalembert went to *Rome*, calling themselves "pilgrims of liberty"; they received a cool reception. They can't have been unaware of the ecclesiastical machinations going on around them. They also had to know that the intransigent archreactionary Pope Gregory XVI (1831–1846) had written *The Triumph of the Holy See and the Church Against the Attacks of the Innovators*

(1799), advocating papal infallibility and the maintenance of the Papal States. He had condemned the Catholic Belgians in their revolt against the Protestant king of the Netherlands, and while the "pilgrims" were in Rome he attacked the Catholic Poles for their revolt against the Orthodox czar. Lamennais, Lacordaire, and Montalembert submitted a résumé of their views and waited for seven months. Disillusioned, they left Rome in early July 1832 without any response. It was only when they got to Munich in late August that a rejoinder reached them in the form of an encyclical letter, *Mirari vos* (August 15, 1832). It was directed specifically against Lamennais and *L'Avenir.*

Pope Gregory condemned all forms of Catholic liberalism, especially "the evil smelling spring of indifferentism . . . [from which flows] the erroneous and absurd opinion—or rather derangement—that freedom of conscience must be asserted for everybody." This "most pestilential error," Gregory says, "opens the door to complete and immoderate liberty of opinions" that causes "widespread harm in both church and state."[3] Gregory condemned Lamennais because he couldn't tolerate liberal opinions in the Papal States that in his mind had now become the norm for the whole church. The pope believed that liberalism was rooted in indifference and that God, not the people, was the source of authority and sovereignty.

After the body blow of *Mirari vos,* Lamennais drifted away from the church. In May 1834 he published *Paroles d'un croyant (Words of a Believer),* which was written in simple, straightforward language that any literate person could read. It was a kind of paean of praise for "the people," who he said were close to God and Christ; the law of God is a law of equality. Pope Gregory responded with another encyclical, *Singulari nos* (July 15, 1834), in which he describes the *Paroles* as a book "small in size, but immense in perversity." Lamennais drifted further from the church, and the full tragedy was played out when he died unreconciled in 1854.

Back in the Papal States, Gregory XVI maintained a resolutely antimodern stance: he condemned gas street lighting and railways, opposed Italian nationalism, and maintained a papal army made up of mercenaries who were a drain on the already strained papal treasury. The Papal States were seen by liberals as "the sick man" of Europe. Meanwhile, outside the Papal States, the church was growing apace in free societies like the United States, the United Kingdom, Canada, and Australia. Gregory encouraged what became the greatest missionary expansion in the history of Catholicism. This was strengthened by the foundation of new missionary orders of men and women, reform of older orders, and the establishment of new missions, vicariates, and dioceses. He also encouraged the training of indigenous clergy. He condemned the slave trade, encouraged art and scholarship, and in Rome supported archaeological research.

Despite these positive notes, when Gregory XVI died on June 1, 1846, the Papal States were in a state of near-constant rebellion. He had shown no comprehension whatsoever of the historical forces at play in the nineteenth century. Gregory reinforced the pattern of alienation of the church from modern culture. This deepened in the next papacy that was to be the longest in history.

———————

THE CONCLAVE GATHERED in the Quirinal Palace on June 15, 1846. The cardinals used the Quirinal because the Vatican was in disrepair, and in midsummer it was stiflingly hot. A short two-day conclave elected Giovanni Mastai-Ferretti, bishop of Imola; he was fifty-four. He took the style Pius IX, and *Pio Nono*, the Italian version of Pius IX, became a kind of nickname. When he died on February 7, 1878, Pius IX had been pope for thirty-one years and five months. Twenty years into Pius IX's papacy, English theologian and later cardinal John Henry Newman called his papacy "a climax of tyranny. . . . It is not good for a pope to live 20 years. It is an anomaly and bears no good fruit."[4]

The election of Pius IX was a turning point in the evolution of papal power. It was not only the longevity of the pope but also the fact that he was a man intuitively sympathetic to the most reactionary elements of nineteenth-century culture. He seized on the emerging conservative shift among the bourgeoisie and was in tune with the romantic emphasis on religious feeling. He also exploited the growing empathy among many non-Italian Catholics for the pope's "plight" as the Papal States were increasingly seized by the forces of Italian nationalism. He played the "martyr" to great effect. The level of focused centralization on the papacy that Pius IX achieved was an anticipation of the fascist and communist dictatorships that were to emerge in the twentieth century. In that sense, his papacy was a tyranny because he rejected modern culture, refusing to use his authority to influence modernity and to articulate Christ's message within its context. This is not to suggest that he had a thought-out policy; rather, he simply followed his instincts and tried to dominate the internal life of the church, in the process creating the modern papacy. Catholicism has yet to retreat from the papocentric church that Pius IX largely created.

Pius IX had been popular as bishop in Imola and before that had spent eighteen months in Chile with a papal mission. At first, he was thought to be sympathetic to Italian national aspirations for unification, and enormous expectations built up in Italy that he was a "liberal." On election, he seemed to confirm these hopes when he proclaimed an amnesty for prisoners, allowed limited freedom of the press and assembly, planned for street lighting and railways, and set up a Consultà (a consultative assembly) in October 1847. But he was being swept along by his popularity, and his commitment to Italian nationalism was quickly tested. The year 1848 saw revolutions across Europe, with revolts in France (Louis-Philippe was overthrown), Germany, Austria (Metternich was sidelined), and Naples. King Charles Albert of Sardinia-Piedmont took advantage of Austrian instability to advance into Austrian-occupied Lombardy in what became the First Italian War of Independence. However, he was quickly defeated in mid-1848 by the Austrians under Field Marshal Joseph von Radetzky in whose honor Johann Strauss Sr. wrote the *Radetzky March*. Many Italians felt that things would have been different if Pius IX had supported Italian nationalism.

Meanwhile, in Rome the *Consultà* became increasingly liberal, and Pope Pius IX appointed Count Pellegrino Rossi as his premier. The cautious Rossi slowed down the introduction of democratic reforms in the Papal States, and he was hated by the republicans and secret societies. On November 15, 1848, he was fatally stabbed in the neck by an assassin. This was the signal for revolution. Pius IX fled to Gaeta in Neapolitan territory (November 24, 1848), and the anticlerical nationalist Giuseppe Mazzini arrived in Rome, quickly followed by the mercenary freebooter Giuseppe Garibaldi. They proclaimed a short-lived Roman Republic and "a new religious synthesis of God and the people." Meanwhile, the newly established Second French Republic, dominated by President Louis Napoleon, the nephew of Bonaparte (later Emperor Napoleon III), sent French troops to retake Rome on June 30, 1849.

Pope Pius IX returned to the city in April 1850 a changed man. Profoundly shaken by the seizure of Rome, he had abandoned what superficial liberal tendencies he might have had. He now stood firmly against the modern world with its threats to his temporal power and authority in the church. For Pius IX, the Papal States guaranteed his freedom of action, but this became a noose around his neck. He was not a simple reactionary like his predecessor, Gregory XVI, but a man of feeling and sentiment rather than thought and judgment. Poorly educated theologically, intellectually superficial, obstinate, credulous, and changeable, he took himself too seriously as pope and saw any opposition as betrayal. He was affected in his youth by a type of epilepsy. Historian Roger Aubert says that this left him "with an excessive emotiveness which led him at times into violent fits of temper, or to ill-considered language. . . . This volatility explains . . . his frequent reversals of policy following the last advice he had received."[5] The question of whether his epilepsy was cured remains open, but he was not a stable person and questions have legitimately been asked as to whether he was fully *compos mentis*; he certainly had a deeply narcissistic personality.

He was not helped by lack of competent staff, and he tended to be surrounded by mediocre men who were devoted to him and told him what he wanted to hear. Many were as poorly educated as he, and they lived in an enclosed clerical world. Typical of them was Anglo-Irish monsignor George Talbot de Malahide, who spent many years in Rome, where he acted as papal chamberlain and canon of Saint Peter's Basilica. An early convert from the Oxford Movement, he was ordained a priest after a superficial formation. Emotionally unstable, he died in a mental institution outside Paris in 1886. He gained Pius IX's ear and became his trusted confidant. With absolutely no pastoral experience, he made himself indispensable to the pope and influenced him on all things English. Pio Nono's secretary of state was Giacomo Antonelli, appointed after he had persuaded (then president) Louis Napoleon to send French troops to retake Rome from Mazzini and Garibaldi. Antonelli was calculating and shrewd, "a technocrat more than an ideologue or politician, [who] sought to determine which way the wind was blowing before committing himself to any stance."[6] A good administrator and diplomat, he often absorbed criticisms that should have been directed to Pius IX; he was the stabilizing force in this papacy. He acted as a kind of papal "prime minister," and it was under his administration that the post-1848 Papal States were restored.

However, the pope was not totally out of touch. He correctly intuited the increasingly new conservative attitude of the European bourgeoisie, as many of them returned to Catholicism, embracing what they perceived as the social stability that an absolutist church seemed to offer. He also recognized the shift toward a more feeling-based religiosity that emerged in tandem with romanticism. Severe images of God and Christ as judge and a distrust of popular piety and the miraculous, characteristic of Enlightenment reason, gave way from the 1840s onward to a warmer, more tactile spirituality expressed in images of a more merciful Jesus and an appeal to the intercession of Mary. This found expression in miraculous apparitions of the Blessed Virgin, the most important of which were those at pilgrimage shrines like La Salette (1846) and Lourdes (1858). Pilgrimages to Lourdes with its healing spring became so popular that special trains were provided to carry the pilgrims. These pilgrimage sites appealed especially to women, who often traveled to them in groups, getting them out of the house and briefly freeing them from patriarchal family and domestic duties. For them, pilgrimages were a liberation, giving them a solidarity with other similar women.

In this same Marian vein, Pius IX proposed the definition of the doctrine of the Immaculate Conception in December 1855. This is the notion that Mary was kept free from original sin. This began a century of intense devotion to the Blessed Virgin, leading to a kind of feminization of Catholic piety. In fact, a devotional revolution was occurring that included not only this Marian emphasis but also a focus on the humanity of Jesus, with devotion to the Passion of Christ, the Sacred Heart, and the Blessed Sacrament. These new forms of emotive piety were really revivals of a Romanized, baroque religiosity that also helped spread neo-ultramontanism. Large numbers of active religious orders of sisters, priests, and brothers were founded that focused on one or another of these devotions. Most of them were missionary, educational, nursing, or social welfare in orientation. Roger Aubert comments that this spirituality "had a weak theological foundation." He adds that devotion to the Sacred Heart was also seen by the church as "the best means to protest against the rationalistic and pleasure-seeking trends of [the] time."[7] Papal centralization was strengthened by the fact that these religious orders sought Roman authorization.

The political context of Pius's papacy was the *Risorgimento*—Italian unification. The upper classes, the liberal bourgeoisie, and secret societies—those who had the most to gain—were the leaders in articulating Italian nationalism. It was from this context that figures like Mazzini and Garibaldi emerged, touting their belief in the "world destiny of Italy." A new sense of *italianità* (a consciousness of being Italian) was growing, together with the realization that nationalism would bring Italy a firm economic base with internal borders and customs barriers broken down. A kind of Italian "free trade zone" developed, with standard metric weights and measures and better roads and railways. But this movement remained an elite affair and had little impact on most Italians, whose lives still focused on the regional and local. Italy has always been polycentric, with considerable linguistic diversity. As Metternich said, Italy was more a "geographical expression" than a nation, and it was only in the mid-nineteenth century that the Tuscan dialect as spoken in Florence became standard Italian. Ironically for secularist, anticlerical proponents of unification, the one thing that really united Italians was Catholicism.

By 1850 Italian unification was focused on the Piedmontese monarchy in Turin. Prime Minister Camillo, Count of Cavour, was the ruthless pragmatist who turned *italianità* into the political reality of Italy. Much of the papal opposition to the *Risorgimento* was based on Piedmont's sponsorship of anticlericalism, secular marriage, and nonreligious education. The Second Italian War of Independence broke out in the spring of 1859, with Lombardy, Tuscany, Parma, Modena, and the whole southern half of Italy absorbed into a united Italy under the Piedmontese king. French troops continued to defend Rome. Pius IX was determined not to surrender without a fight. He made Monsignor François Xavier de Mérode armaments minister and was determined to defend the Papal States with a force of about fifteen thousand volunteers who had been raised from across the world. In early September 1860, thirty-five thousand Piedmontese troops invaded papal Umbria and advanced along the coast toward Ancona. After skirmishes a major battle was fought on September 18, 1860, at Castelfidardo, which led to the surrender of the papal troops. All papal territory conquered in 1859–1860 was absorbed into Italy. By the beginning of 1861, all that Pius IX had left was the Patrimonium Petri, a small rectangular region around Rome. But the papal forces survived as an international volunteer army of Papal Zouaves with forty-six hundred men, commanded by German general Hermann Kanzler. They were reinforced by professional French troops whom (now emperor) Napoleon III assigned to defend Rome.

THE LOSS OF all the Papal States except the Patrimonium set the scene for the second half of Pius IX's papacy. The pope became increasingly obsessed with a struggle against three major bugbears. The first was modern culture and the Enlightenment. There were two possible reactions to this for Catholicism: to enter into a soft-power dialogue with modernity and embrace intellectual freedom and to participate critically in contemporary culture, thus influencing what happened, or to retreat into a totally negative stance. Pius IX chose the latter because of his fear of rationalism and liberalism, which he saw as destructive of faith. This set the pattern for Catholicism's next century.

The pope's second bugbear was his fear of Gallicanism. Since the Middle Ages, the papacy had been, and to an extent still is, profoundly afraid of any form of theological or practical challenge to its authority from local churches. Gallicanism is rooted in Conciliarism, the assertion of the superiority of an ecumenical council over the papacy, because a council can, and often did in the past, represent the whole community by having laity and priests as well as bishops present. This theology is in profound continuity with Saint Paul's image of the church as the body of Christ, where the head is part of the body, not separate from it. It is the antithesis of neo-ultramontanism; Conciliarism places the pope within the church, not over and above it.

Pius IX's third bugbear was the *Risorgimento* and its assault on his temporal domains. He saw this as the direct result of an anticlerical culture and modern errors. He was a champion of legitimacy and cast himself in the role of opponent of progress and modernity, a role he embraced with gusto.

His most forceful, focused, and direct response to modernity was the encyclical *Quanta cura* and the *Syllabus of Errors* (December 8, 1864). The immediate occasion of the syllabus was the Catholic Congress at Malines, Belgium, in August 1863. The three thousand people attending were the heirs of Lamennais, and among them was Count Charles Montalembert, who called for *l'église libre dans l'état libre* (a free church in a free state). In another lecture, he directly contradicted Gregory XVI's *Mirari vos* and called for freedom of conscience for Catholics. However, in Rome the lectures were interpreted as an attack on the temporal sovereignty of the pope, which was unfair since Montalembert had supported papal independence. The pope had Secretary of State Antonelli write to him, privately accusing him of disregarding *Mirari vos*. Antonelli also accused Montalembert of arguing that the papacy should adapt itself to the prevailing culture, which, he said, was the equivalent of saying that the church didn't hold the keys to salvation, a complete *non sequitur*.

A parallel congress of Catholic scholars was held in Munich in September 1863, organized by church historian Ignaz von Döllinger. Döllinger's speech at the conference discussed the question of the autonomy of history as an independent science, arguing that historians' conclusions were not subject to ecclesiastical authority or correction. Theology, particularly papal theology, could be improved, he said, if it integrated biblical and historical criticism. Döllinger was already out of favor in Rome because of his criticisms of papal temporal rule. The response from Rome came in the form of a papal brief to Archbishop Gregor von Scherr of Munich. It didn't explicitly condemn Döllinger but insisted that all research work of Catholic scholars be subjected to ecclesiastical authority.

This was the background to *Quanta cura*. What was striking about the encyclical was its apocalyptic tone and hysterical rhetoric. First, it condemns state indifference to religion and, second, the democratic principle that the people are the source of the law, independent of God and the rights of princes. It claims that some people, "utterly neglecting and disregarding the surest principles of sound reason, dare to proclaim that the people's will manifested by what is called public opinion . . . constitutes a supreme law free from all divine and human control." It also adopts a scattergun approach in which a whole range of issues are attacked: it condemns freedom of conscience and worship, assaults on religious orders, the neglect of holy days, loss of church control over education, secret societies, the "fatal error" of communism and socialism, and the "impudence" that subjects "to the will of the civil authority the supreme authority of the church and of this apostolic see given to her by Christ himself." In the midst of "such great perversity of depraved opinions . . . and other impious doctrines . . . [spread] by means of pestilential books, pamphlets and newspapers," *Quanta cura* asserts the independence of the church from civil authority, the right of the church to educate the young, and the fullness of papal power even in the civil sphere.

Attached to the encyclical is a syllabus or list of eighty errors that the pope claimed that various unnamed people held, including belief in rationalism, liberalism, indifferentism, pantheism, latitudinarianism, socialism, and communism; membership in secret societies and Bible societies; and inaccurate notions concerning the church and its rights, civil society and church-state relations, natural and Christian ethics, Christian marriage, and the civil power of the pope. The final error sums it all up: "That the Roman Pontiff can, and ought, to reconcile himself and come to terms with progress, liberalism and modern civilization."[8] The problem was that listing all these "errors" together gave the impression of a complete rejection of the contemporary world. It was an ill-conceived attempt to assert papal hard power by ranting at the world, and it achieved nothing but to alienate the papacy from contemporary culture. Antonelli saw it as a serious lapse of judgment that created misunderstandings and difficulties, especially for Catholics in democratic countries.

THERE IS A real sense in which Pius IX perhaps unconsciously, perhaps consciously, compensated for his loss of political power in the Papal States by proactively enhancing his power within the church. From the early 1860s he became so myopically focused on his position as pope and on the loss of the temporal sovereignty that his view of the broader church became distorted. There is something profoundly narcissistic about his attitude toward himself and his office. It was this self-absorption that Newman was referring to when he said that a long papacy led to "a climax of tyranny." As he got older, Pius's unpredictable mood swings increased, with him frequently castigating people; he often seemed like a bully.

Throughout his papacy, there was an increasing centralization of power in Rome, with the local church becoming little more than a branch of head office. Gallicanism had pretty much evaporated by the 1850s. The emphasis now was on the universal church, with the papacy the symbol of that universalism. The influence of neo-ultramontanism promoted and strengthened this focus. Rome became a pilgrimage center, and modern transportation in the form of railways and regular shipping made it more accessible to the pilgrims who flocked there. Pius IX became the first papal "personality," and people found him attractive, fascinating, and charming. He could be witty and funny, and he was very much in tune with the religious sentiment of the time, with its emphasis on external religious practices and devotions. The number of papal audiences increased, and they were open not just to the elite but to a broad cross-section of people. Increasingly, many saw Pius as a living saint, undergoing a kind of "martyrdom" with the loss of the Papal States to Italian nationalism. He played the role of the victim well, becoming an admired figure, especially in neo-ultramontanist circles. Roman centralization grew, not only bureaucratically, but also through the establishment of national seminaries in Rome, such as the North American College, which opened in 1859. Also, new Polish, Irish, and Latin American colleges were built in Rome, where elite diocesan students for the priesthood were trained and imbibed the *Romanità* (Romanness). Many of these students later became bishops.

The Congregation of Propaganda Fide (now the Congregation for Evangelization) under Cardinal Alessandro Barnabò played an important role in the centralization process. It promoted missionary expansion, established vicariates and dioceses, appointed missionary bishops, settled disputes, and brought the whole missionary enterprise under Roman control. It decided that bishops in mission countries required faculties, authorization to govern and administer their dioceses, which had to be renewed every five or ten years. Here it should be noted that predominantly Protestant countries like the United States, United Kingdom, and Australia were considered "mission countries" and were included under the jurisdiction of Propaganda until the 1950s. This gave it tremendous power over much of the church.

The most important centralizing element was the way in which bishops were appointed. There is no specific point in time when Rome took over the power of appointing the world's bishops, although this power was ratified in the 1917 Code of Canon Law.

In the early church, bishops were directly elected by the local community. By the medieval period, cathedral chapters (that is, senior priests attached to the local cathedral) or lay rulers controlled most appointments. The prevailing norm was that no bishop was appointed against the wishes of the local priests and people. From the late seventeenth century, local recommendations sent to Rome were dealt with by the Consistorial Congregation. Local rulers, cathedral chapters, and provincial synods still largely nominated their bishops, and Rome usually accepted their nominations. This hodgepodge "system" pretty much remained the situation until the nineteenth century. By then secular governments had become uninterested in episcopal appointments, so the papacy increasingly asserted its authority to appoint bishops. The influence of the papal nuncio increased: no longer did he just represent the papacy to a specific government, but he became the one who drew up the *terna*, the list of three priests suitable for appointment as bishops, and sent it to Rome. Needless to say, priests who were lukewarm about neo-ultramontanism were excluded. Cathedral chapters, which previously played an important role in episcopal appointments, decreased in influence. Priests were increasingly ignored in the episcopal selection process; they were now much more under the control of local bishops, and the vast majority of them were in parish appointments, their tenure largely controlled by the bishop. The practice of *ad limina* visits (that is, bishops coming to Rome and reporting on their dioceses every five years) was also introduced, conveying the notion that bishops were branch managers reporting to the head office.

Rome even tried to intervene in the appointment of bishops in the Eastern churches in union with the papacy. These bishops had, like their Orthodox colleagues, always been elected by local synods. Rome's aim was to exclude laymen and lower clergy having a voice in the episcopal election process. The appointment of bishops is the most important power that Rome has taken to itself, because it is the way in which the pope eventually shapes the church by appointing like-minded men. It is an exercise of hard power.

As Pius IX's papacy wore on, the pope made several serious errors of judgment. The syllabus was one. But the kidnappings of two covertly baptized Jewish boys whose families lived in the Papal States were even worse in terms of the injustice to the boys and their families. In 1858 a six-year-old Jewish boy, Edgardo Mortara, was seized from his parents' home in Bologna on the orders of the Inquisition and brought up as a Christian. The claim was that he had been secretly baptized by a Catholic servant girl without his parents' permission. The pope adopted Edgardo and began to see him almost as his own son. In 1864 another Jewish child, Giuseppe Coen, was taken from his family in Rome. Both cases created sensations in the international press and turned many people against the papacy in England, the United States, and France, where Napoleon III was so enraged that he wanted to withdraw his troops from Rome but was prevented by neo-ultramontanist public opinion. After the Coen case, he began a careful, phased withdrawal. Mazzini and Garibaldi also used these cases for propaganda purposes. Pope Pius later told Mortara, who by then had become a priest, "Your case set off a worldwide storm against me. . . . Governments and peoples . . . as well as the journalists—who are truly powerful people in our times—declared war on me. . . . [Yet] no one showed any concern for me, father of all the faithful."[9] This comment is delusional. After 1870 Mortara fled to Austria and finally to Belgium, where he died in 1940 just before the German invasion.

THE MOST IMPORTANT event of this papacy was the First Vatican Council (December 8, 1869–July 18, 1870). This gathering is probably the most important nineteenth-century element in the papal recovery from the near-death experience and abject weakness of 1799. Sure, the popularity of Pius IX with the emerging middle class was part of the process of recovery, but the decrees of Vatican I provided an absolutely essential theoretical basis for the restoration of papal power within the church itself. This cannot be underestimated.

The idea of holding a council first emerged in 1849, but the evolution of the idea cannot be divorced from the prevailing neo-ultramontanist movement. This emphasis on papal authority provided Catholics who needed it with a sense of identity and psychological certainty and security in a rapidly changing world. France was the original home of aggressive neo-ultramontanism, which was "much more politico-social than theological," as Cuthbert Butler says. Its aim was to make almost everything the pope said infallible. Neo-ultramontanes used the popular press, and their views lent themselves to a kind of journalistic "theology" that was typified by *L'Univers*, a newspaper edited by Louis-François Veuillot, a layman who returned to the practice of Catholicism during a visit to Rome. He was a passionate supporter of Pius IX, the temporal power of the pope over Rome, and the Patrimonium Petri, and he wanted the most extreme definition of infallibility. There is something almost idolatrous and blasphemous about his more manic utterances: "We must affirm squarely the authority and omnipotence of the pope, as the source of all authority, spiritual and temporal," or "We all know certainly only one thing, that is that no man knows anything except the Man with whom God is forever, the Man who carries the thought of God. We must unswervingly follow his inspired directions."[10] *L'Univers*, which was widely read among the French clergy, became a battering ram to attack secularists and especially Catholic liberals, whom Veuillot saw as hopelessly compromised by the principles of the Revolution. He stood for a theocratic model of the state and a kind of idolatrous papal cult that turned the pope into a quasi-divine figure. These views were mirrored by many, including Gaspard Mermillod, bishop of Geneva (and later cardinal), who spoke of "the three incarnations of the Son of God." The first was in the womb of the Virgin Mary, the second in the Eucharist, and the third in "the old man in the Vatican." On another occasion, Mermillod said, "We want to give you Jesus Christ here in earth. We have seen him in Bethlehem in the form of a child. We see him today in the form of an old man." In various other places, the pope was referred to as the "Vice-God of mankind" and the "Permanent Word Incarnate." In these absurd blasphemies, Pius IX was identified with Christ, even assuming the place of Christ.[11] He did absolutely nothing to stop or limit this nonsense.

In England most of the bishops were cautious ultramontan-
ists. The exception was Henry Edward Manning, archbishop of
Westminster. A converted Church of England clergyman, Manning was an extreme neo-ultramontane, and he became a leader
of the strongly pro-infallibilist party in the council. He was an un-
attractive, ambitious man who was utterly convinced that he was
right, and the overwhelming absolutism of his views made dialogue
with him almost impossible. Manning was a crusader for infallibility,
and he conceived of it in either-or terms. His personal theologian
was the lay convert William George Ward, who believed that "all
direct doctrinal instructions of all encyclicals, all letters to individual bishops and allocutions published by the popes, are *ex cathedra*
pronouncements and *ipso facto* infallible."[12] Pugnacious, but with
a saving sense of humor, Ward said that "I should like a new papal
bull every morning with my *Times* at breakfast."

Another who popularized the Manning-Ward take on the papacy
was the convert Frederick William Faber, the famous hymn writer.
In a sermon at Brompton Oratory on New Year's Day 1860, he
spoke of Jesus, "leaving us the Pope. The Sovereign Pontiff is a . . .
visible presence of Jesus amongst us. . . . The Pope is the Vicar of
Jesus on earth, and enjoys among the monarchs of the world all the
rights and sovereignties of the Sacred Humanity of Jesus. . . . [O]f
all kings he is the [closest] to the King of kings." Faber further said,
"The Pope is to us in all our conduct what the Blessed Sacrament
is to us in all our adoration. The mystery of His Vicariate is akin to
the mystery of the Blessed Sacrament," adding, "What is done to
the Pope, for him or against him, is done to Jesus Himself."[13] The
scandal is that Pius IX did absolutely nothing to rein in the extrem-
ism of the neo-ultramontanists.

The Jesuits were also important in the neo-ultramontanist onslaught. After the 1814 restoration of the Society of Jesus, Jesuits became increasingly influential in the Vatican, and neo-ultramontanist
theology was spread through Rome's Gregorian University. This
approach was reflected in the Jesuit periodical *La Civiltà Cattolica*,
which claimed that "when the pope thinks, it is God who is thinking
through him." *Civiltà* also called for the declaration of infallibility

by acclamation. Many Jesuits, like Carlo Passaglia, were cautious, but the Society had its extreme neo-ultramontanes, like Clemens Schrader, a theocrat who thought the *Syllabus of Errors* was infallible and who wrote the first version of the council's Dogmatic Constitution on the Church. Schrader maintained his influence despite the fact that he was involved with the scandal of the Sant'Ambrogio convent in Rome, with lesbianism linked to pseudomysticism, threats of poison and murder, as well as affairs and romantic involvements with priests.[14]

It is important to distinguish the "moderate" ultramontanism of Saint Robert Bellarmine (1542–1621) from extreme neo-ultramontanism. In the early seventeenth century, the theory of the divine right of kings was articulated, and it was in this context that Bellarmine articulated his theory of absolute papal monarchy. Christ, he said, is the supreme head of the church, and the pope is his vicar, his ministerial head on earth, and has absolute power to rule the church; he receives these rights and prerogatives *iure divino* (by divine right) and not merely *iure ecclesiastico* (by ecclesiastical right). Bellarmine held that a pope cannot be judged, deposed, or punished by anyone, including a general council of the church, and that such councils can err and the pope must give his confirmation to a council's decrees for them to be genuine. He is the supreme judge in deciding controversies on faith and morals, and what he formally teaches is *ipso facto* infallible. Many bishops followed the Bellarmine thesis, and essentially it was his position that was defined at Vatican I.

However, a sizable minority of bishops at Vatican I opposed the definition of infallibility. There were two groups: the first opposed the definition on theological and historical grounds, and the second argued that the timing was wrong. The first group was small. There were a few moderate Gallicans, such as Bishop Henri Maret, dean of theology at the Sorbonne in Paris; Felix de la Casas, bishop of Constantine in Algeria; and hardworking pastoral bishop Augustin Verot of Savannah, Georgia. Another opponent of Roman centralism was Archbishop Georges Darboy of Paris. Several other bishops had historical objections. The most learned of them was Karl

Josef von Hefele of Rottenburg, who wrote the seven-volume *Conciliengeschichte*, a history of ecumenical councils. He helped with the preparations for the council and was in Rome in the winter of 1868–1869. While Hefele eventually accepted the decision of the council, he had serious doubts about it, and it is very significant that he was the best church historian at Vatican I. The issue of the significance of church history was important in Germany, and many German theologians were horrified by the simplistic vulgarities of the neo-ultramontanists. Among them was Döllinger, who became increasingly suspicious of papal centralist absolutism, and he was appalled by the call for infallibility to be declared by acclamation. He wrote several articles, later published in book form under the title *The Pope and the Council*, using the pseudonym "Janus," attacking the whole institution of the papacy from the Middle Ages onward. Given his immense erudition, Butler says that he constructed an imposing onslaught on the papacy, "probably the most damaging ever compiled."[15] The book caused a sensation in Germany.

Most of the rest of the bishops who opposed the infallibility definition considered it the wrong time to define the doctrine. Many of them lived in non-Catholic countries where Catholics were a minority. They didn't want to create further alienation between the church and culture. Some felt that there was a danger that the papacy would be divorced from the context of the church and ignore the governing and teaching role of bishops within Catholicism. These issues troubled, among others, Cardinals Friedrich von Schwarzenberg of Prague, Joseph Othmar Rauscher of Vienna, and Filippo Maria Guidi of Bologna; several Hungarian bishops; and Archbishop Peter Kenrick of St. Louis, Missouri, who, like many of the US bishops, was concerned about the obstacle that infallibility would create for Protestants. In Ireland Archbishop John MacHale of Tuam and Bishop David Moriarty of Kerry were also concerned about the broader effects on the church of the definition, as were Bishop Félix Dupanloup of Orléans and Bishop Josip Strossmayer of what is now Djakovo, in modern Slovenia. All told, the minority opposed to infallibility amounted to about 140 bishops, out of about 700 bishops who attended the council, a significant group.

The pope announced his intention of calling a council in the bull *Aeterni Patris* (June 26, 1867). There was no mention of infallibility, and the focus was on "what must be done in such disastrous times for the greater glory of God, the integrity of the faith, the betterment of Catholicism and the eternal salvation of humankind." There had been no general council for two centuries since the Council of Trent (1545–1563), which was called in response to the Protestant Reformation. In Catholicism generally, there was little enthusiasm for a council, let alone infallibility. This lack of enthusiasm also infected the Roman Curia, which feared that the council could drag on, impinging on its own power. Antonelli was particularly unenthusiastic. The notion of infallibility was alarming to the French, Italian, and other governments because it seemed to threaten civil power. The nuncio to the court of Bavaria warned Antonelli that there might be schism if infallibility was defined. Catholic monarchs had the expectation that they would be invited to participate. Antonelli got around that problem by telling them that since the excommunicated King Victor Emmanuel II of Italy couldn't be invited, the papacy had decided not to invite any Catholic rulers. Then in a ham-fisted but well-intentioned move, the pope invited the entire Orthodox episcopate to submit to Rome so that they could attend the council. Anglicans and Protestants were also invited to return to Roman unity. From our contemporary ecumenical perspective, these seem like ridiculous moves, and even from the perspective of 1869 they reflect an ignorance of the wider Christian world that is breathtaking.

Vatican I, which up until then was the largest council ever held, began on December 8, 1869. It met in the north or right transept of Saint Peter's Basilica. The average attendance was between 600 and 700. There were 60 Eastern-rite bishops (most from the Near East) and almost 200 from outside Europe, many of them missionary bishops. However, there were no indigenous bishops; all of the missionaries were European. There were 121 bishops from the Americas, including 49 from the United States and 18 from Canada; 41 from India, China, and the Far East; 18 from Oceania, including 10 from Australia; and 9 from the African missions. Despite this broad

geographic spread, this council was an almost totally European affair. Among the Europeans, hierarchs of Mediterranean origin pre-
dominated, with 35 percent (293) of the bishops coming from Italy
alone. Two-thirds of the consulters and experts, all of the secretaries, and all of the presidents were Italian. However, the secretary-
general, Bishop Josef Fessler of St. Pölten, was Austrian. The Italians
and French constituted more than 50 percent of those present. The
German-speaking world was underrepresented, with only 55 bishops from Austria-Hungary and 22 from Germany.[16] As a result,
Döllinger questioned the ecumenicity of the council because of the
preponderance of bishops from Italy and the Francophone world.

VATICAN I PRODUCED only two documents: the Dogmatic Constitution on the Catholic Faith (*Dei Filius*) and the Dogmatic Constitution on the Church (*Pastor aeternus* [*PA*]). A draft of *Dei Filius*
was presented to the council on December 12, 1869, as a schema
(proposed document) on Catholic doctrine against the errors of the
day. It had taken *Quanta cura* and the *Syllabus of Errors* as its models. It was severely criticized by the bishops as "too long and elabo-
rate, too abstract and obscure, and it did not meet the needs of the
times." It was during this debate that Bishop Strossmayer, whose
diocese straddled the Hapsburg and Ottoman Empires, objected to
Protestants being called the source of "all the errors of the day" in
the schema. He said that "there exists in Protestantism . . . a great
crowd of men who love Our Lord Jesus Christ." When the presidents tried to stop him from saying this, Strossmayer complained
about freedom of expression and the council's processes. He was
then shouted down by a mob of about 200 bishops from Catholic
countries with no experience of Protestantism who called him "Lu-
cifer" and "Luther."[17] This is significant because it indicates that
freedom of speech at Vatican I was limited by the council presidents
and a more inclusive theology by the gross ignorance of bishops
from Mediterranean countries with no experience of either Orthodoxy or Protestantism.

A rewritten *Dei Filius* was submitted to the council and debated from March 18 to April 19, 1870. It was passed by the council on April 24. It is a predictable, uninspiring document with all the usual "isms" being condemned, although, thanks to Strossmayer, any direct reference to Protestantism had disappeared. The only passage of long-term significance is hidden away in Chapter 3, where it says that Catholics must believe what is found in scripture and tradition and in addition those teachings that "are proposed by the church as matters . . . divinely revealed, whether by her solemn judgment or in her *ordinary and universal magisterium*."[18] The term *ordinary and universal magisterium* is very modern by historical standards. It was coined by Jesuit Joseph Kleutgen, who was the final redactor of *Dei Filius*, and it was through him that the term passed into the constitution. Aubert comments that "for almost a century . . . [*Dei Filius*] was to be the basis of standard theological textbooks."[19] This explains the stultification of priestly theological training from 1870 to the late 1950s.

The most important document of Vatican I was the constitution, *Pastor aeternus*, on papal primacy and infallibility. Campaigns for and against infallibility were waged through various newspapers. Veuillot's *L'Univers* was strongly pro-infallibilist, while Döllinger, now using the pen name "Quirinus," wrote a series of articles in the *Augsburger Allgemeine Zeitung*, the then leading political daily in Germany. The primary organizer of the minority anti-infallibilists in Rome was English layman Lord John Dalberg-Acton. Acton was born in Naples and married to a Bavarian countess. He had many international connections and was multilingual. He had studied with Döllinger in Munich, had been a member of the House of Commons, and was an intimate friend of Prime Minister William Gladstone. He was later to become Regius Professor of Modern History at Cambridge and founder of *The Cambridge Modern History*. A skilled politician, at Vatican I he organized the minority bishops, made them aware of the scheming of the pro-infallibilists, provided them with historical evidence to support their stance, and made contact with foreign governments that were concerned about the consequences of infallibility for church-state relations. Two petitions had been circulating, one for the inclusion of infallibility in the conciliar deliberations with 450 bishops' signatures and another against with 136 signatures, when on March 1, 1870, Pius IX decided to include a definition of papal infallibility in the draft of the schema on the church. The pope's irritation was growing with those who opposed infallibility. This caused concern among minority bishops and governments that the papacy might interfere in secular affairs, and there were worries that the definition might place Catholics in democratic countries in the position of divided loyalties.

The debate on papal primacy began on June 6, 1870.[20] Primacy refers to the pope's jurisdictional authority and government of the church. While subsequent theological attention has been largely focused on infallibility, in fact papal primacy has become the strongest support for enormously increased papal power in the church and is also the most intractable problem that Catholicism has inherited from Vatican I. The definition of primacy has implications not only for Catholics but also for ecumenical relations. Butler realized this back in 1930 when he said that primacy as defined at Vatican I presents great "obstacles to [a] united Christendom." The basic reason for this was pointed out by many bishops during the debate: the vision of the church underpinning *PA* is defective, inadequate, and incomplete. "Here . . . is a summary of Catholic doctrine on the church," says Butler, "in which there is no account taken of the hierarchy, episcopate, ministry, ecumenical councils," and, he might have added, laity. "Simply church and pope." "*Stupefacti sumus*" (We are astonished), said one bishop.[21]

Central to the problem is the wording of the definition; it claims an all-embracing and unlimited power. It is best summarized in the canon or anathema at the end of Chapter 3:

> If anyone says that the Roman pontiff has merely an office of supervision or guidance, and not the full and supreme power of jurisdiction over the whole church, and this not only in matters of faith and morals, but also in those which concern the discipline and government of the church dispersed throughout the whole world; or that

he has only the principal part, *but not the absolute fullness of this su-preme power*; or that this power of his is not ordinary and immediate both over-all and each of the churches and over-all and each of the pastors and faithful: let [them] be anathema.[22]

There is something almost demented about the repetition of the term *supreme power* and the phrase *the absolute fullness of this su-preme power*. These claims are especially overstated in light of the humility of the crucified Christ who had washed his disciples' feet at the Last Supper. There was no pretense of humility in *PA* nor any aspiration to humble service. This definition is in the best tradition of John Jay McCloy's comment to President John F. Kennedy: "The only thing that matters is power." The ironic thing is that this claim was made on the very eve of the final annihilation of what was left of the Papal States, so popes had nowhere to exercise this absolute power except within the life of the Catholic community, and since 1870 they haven't hesitated to do so. It was a classic case of massive overcompensation.

Certainly, the primacy of the bishop of Rome had been recognized from early Christianity, but it was always contextualized by an ecclesiology of communion in which Rome was the heart of the church and final court of appeal in disciplinary and doctrinal matters. In the debate at Vatican I, the bishops focused on what the terms *ordinary* and *immediate* meant in practice. These are not theological terms but legal words. The word *ordinary* here is used in the canonical sense, meaning "not delegated"; that is, the power of the office comes with the bestowal of the office. You have the power if you have the office. The word *immediate* means that the pope can act directly in any part of the church. He doesn't have to go through another person or structure. So where does this leave the bishops? Are they just branch managers? Can the pope go over their heads and interfere in their dioceses? As successors of the apostles, they also have ordinary jurisdiction, but this definition says that the pope can overrule, ignore, or dismiss them without any process.

Actually, the anathema quoted above originally didn't have the phrase *or that he has only the principal part, but not the absolute full-ness of this supreme power* in it. In what Butler calls "a grave error of judgement," this phrase was added at the last minute in a way that "was clearly irregular."[23] After protests the deputation was ready to withdraw the clause, but the chairman of the deputation, Cardinal Luigi Bilio, was told that Pius IX definitely wanted the clause inserted. It was another example of the restriction of the freedom of the bishops, who accepted this papal *fait accompli*. The core problem with this definition is that scriptural and ecclesiological language is replaced with canonical, legal rhetoric, which gives the impression that the pope owns the church, lock, stock, and barrel.

One of the reasons the bishops didn't focus carefully on primacy was that many wanted to get on to the infallibility debate. This began on June 15 and ended on July 4, 1870. Even though most of the subsequent attention of theologians has been focused on infallibility, it's not as important as primacy, because the infallibility definition was carefully debated and is hedged by tight wording. Two of the most important speeches on infallibility came from Cardinals Joseph Rauscher and Filippo Maria Guidi. Both picked up on the Dominican order's tradition and Saint Thomas Aquinas's teaching that the Roman *church* rather than the pope *personally* is infallible.[24] In his speech Rauscher quoted the view of the Dominican Saint Antoninus, a theologian at the Council of Ferrara-Florence (1438–1439), who said, "The successor of Saint Peter, using the counsel and seeking the help of the universal church, cannot err."[25] Rauscher also emphasized that infallibility cannot be divorced from the indefectibility of the church. This simply refers to the fact that the church will not fail, that it will not abandon the authentic message of Jesus and the Gospel. Guidi argued that the pope was not personally, in and of himself, infallible, but infallible only within the context of the church's belief and only to the extent that his teachings reflected those of the bishops and theologians. He emphasized that it was the definition that was infallible, not the person of the pope. The pope alone could not issue infallible definitions; he had to consult the bishops. Popes had to use what we would call "due diligence." Like Rauscher, Guidi was attempting to keep infallibility within the context of the church.

Guidi was a Dominican and archbishop of Bologna, although, while he was born there, he never received the *regio exequatur* ("permission of the king" of Italy) to reside there as archbishop. Guidi's parentage is unknown, there is no biography, and there are suggestions that he was the illegitimate son of Pius IX.[26] More important than this titillating scandal is the fact that Guidi was personally upbraided by Pius IX on the night of his speech. Guidi argued that he had followed the teachings of Aquinas and Bellarmine. Pius accused him of saying that before exercising infallibility, "the pope is obliged to investigate first the tradition of the church. . . . [T]his is an error." Guidi responded that it was not an error. The pope said vehemently, "Yes, it is an error, for I, I am the tradition, I am the church." This is an extraordinary statement.[27] Not only was Pius IX talking nonsense—and probably heresy—but he was also interfering with the freedom of the council. In response to Guidi and Rauscher, the pro-infallibilist Cardinal Paul Cullen of Dublin stressed the specific and unique authority conferred on Peter by Christ, arguing against the necessity of the pope consulting the bishops or the church.

Throughout the debate, many bishops gave long-winded speeches (there were no time limits) supporting the personal infallibility of the pope, but the minority still argued that papal authority must remain within the context of the church. Archbishop Thomas Connolly of Halifax, Canada, put the question bluntly: Is the pope infallible in and of himself, or does he need, as Saint Antoninus said, the counsel and assistance of the church? Connolly opted for Antoninus's position.

By now the pressure on those who opposed infallibility was considerable. This was true especially of missionary bishops subject to the Propaganda Congregation and dependent upon it for financial support. Using the Congregation's stranglehold over these bishops, Cardinal Prefect Barnabò was accused of putting undue pressure on them, especially Eastern-rite bishops and even prelates from North America like Archbishops Connolly and Kenrick of St. Louis. Again, this dangerously infringed upon the freedom of the council. By July 4 the summer heat and the endless speechifying had left everyone exhausted, and the presidents foreclosed the debate. The amendments went back to the deputation. In the end, the problem focused on whether papal infallibility was personal, separate, and absolute or had to be contained within the context of the church. The deputation opted for the personal notion of infallibility because they were determined to exclude the Gallican position, which argued that the pope was infallible only if the bishops and the church subsequently accepted his teaching. The Gallican position is clearly different from that of Saint Antoninus, Rauscher, Guidi, and Connolly. These bishops argued for the need for consultation *before* any definition, while Gallicanism argued for a postdefinition acceptance. But the deputation didn't seem to grasp that distinction. The reason for that is simple: the neo-ultramontanes on the deputation were utterly determined to define the personal infallibility of the pope. On July 11 Prince-Bishop Gasser of Brixen, Austria, reported back from the deputation, saying that infallibility didn't belong to the pope personally, but only as bishop of Rome and successor of Saint Peter. This in no way excludes the participation of the church in discerning its belief. The neo-ultramontanes were deeply disappointed with this more nuanced, hedged-in definition. Equally, the moderates wanted infallibility placed much more firmly within the context of the church. Two days after Gasser's speech, there was an indicative vote. Of 601 bishops voting, 451 voted *placet* (yes) to the schema as explained by Gasser, 88 voted *non placet* (no), and 62 voted *placet juxta modum* (yes, but with modifications). It was now clear that infallibility would be passed, so many of the minority began to leave Rome so as not to vote no publicly in the council.

Monday, July 18, 1870, was the day of the vote. The day "dawned with rain after a night of thunder and lightning." Proceedings began at 9:00 a.m. in the presence of the pope. After the Litany of the Saints and the singing of the hymn *Veni Creator, PA* was read aloud from the ambo. As the vote was being taken, a storm broke out, "which had been threatening all morning." It burst out, according to the *Times* of London correspondent Anglican priest Thomas Mozley, "with the utmost violence, and to many a superstitious mind might have conveyed the idea that it was the expression of divine wrath."[28] Only two of the minority stayed to vote *non placet*: Edward Fitzgerald of Little Rock, Arkansas, and Luigi

Riccio of Caiazzo, just north of Naples. Fitzgerald was a tall, Irish-born American who was the wonderfully pastoral bishop of Little Rock for forty years. His concern with infallibility was that the vote would be an obstacle to evangelization in the United States, and he later told a priest friend that he didn't go all the way to Rome not to follow his conscience. It is less clear why Riccio voted against the definition.

So what had actually been defined? The text of *Pastor aeternus* says:

> We teach and define . . . that when the Roman Pontiff speaks *ex cathedra*, that is, when, in the exercise of his office as shepherd and teacher of all Christians, in virtue of his supreme apostolic authority, he defines a doctrine concerning faith or morals to be held by the whole church, he possesses . . . that infallibility which the divine Redeemer willed his church to enjoy in defining doctrine concerning faith or morals. Therefore, such definitions of the Roman Pontiff are of themselves, and not by the consent of the church, irreformable.[29]

Because there had been a lot of debate, the council ended up with a definition that was reasonably moderate and represented the mainstream ultramontanism of Bellarmine. The extreme neo-ultramontanes had been defeated. The one problem with the definition lies in the last sentence and particularly in the words *not by the consent of the church*. This phrase was intended to exclude the Gallican position and was inserted after the debate by the deputation. This may have been an innocent action, but it seemed to go back to implying that the pope didn't need to consult the bishops and suggested that somehow the pope could act arbitrarily. It opened the way to the kind of creeping infallibility that still compromises Catholicism today.

Eventually, all the minority bishops accepted infallibility as defined, no doubt many of them with personal mental reservations. Small groups in Germany, Austria, and the Netherlands, known as "Old Catholics," refused to accept the definition. They later formed a loose confederation with the Anglican Church. Of all the German bishops, it was Hefele who had the greatest difficulty with the doctrine. He accepted, but his problem was the insufficient attention devoted to history during the council. Döllinger refused infallibility and was formally excommunicated.

However, Döllinger and Hefele have subsequently been vindicated, for what Döllinger said in *The Pope and the Council* has been shown by subsequent research to be historically correct. He said that for thirteen centuries, papal infallibility was never mentioned in church tradition. "To prove the dogma of Papal Infallibility from Church History," Döllinger said, "nothing less is required than a complete falsification of it." This has now been confirmed by the work of Brian Tierney in *The Origins of Papal Infallibility*. Tierney has shown that generally up until the twelfth century, canonists held that the pope could and did err and that it was the church, the *congregatio fidelium*, not the papacy, that could not err. Tierney says that the doctrine of infallibility was "invented in the first place by a few dissident Franciscans because it suited their convenience to invent it." At first the popes resisted infallibility because they realized that they would be bound by the decisions of their predecessors, and it was only finally "accepted by the papacy because it suited the convenience of the popes to accept it."[30]

Pius IX got what he wanted with *Pastor aeternus*. In theory, the bishops were to return to their dioceses and then reconvene the council and resume the debate on the schema on bishops. For strategic reasons, it didn't work out that way, and no doubt the pope was relieved that it didn't. In the end, the council was suspended *sine die* (without a date being set for resumption) on October 20, 1870.

———

MEANWHILE, INTERNATIONAL AFFAIRS were moving swiftly. The Franco-Prussian War went badly for the French and Napoleon III, and he finally withdrew his four thousand French troops from Rome in early August 1870. This emboldened the Italian government, which informed other European powers that the "Roman question" had to be solved to fulfill the "legitimate aspirations" of the Italian people to have their capital in Rome. On September 11,

1870, Italy invaded the Patrimonium Petri. The papal policy was to withdraw to the Vatican and put up a token resistance to cast the Italians as aggressors. By September 19 Italian troops encircled Rome. The break came on September 20 at the Porta Pia, near the top of the present Via Nomentana, when the Italian invaders shelled the Aurelian Wall. In what was not exactly Italy's greatest military victory, volunteer Papal Zouaves made a strong stand, some fifteen of them were killed, and, despite surrendering, undisciplined Italian troops rushed in, killing several more Zouaves. There was no further resistance, and by nightfall the city was occupied.

Pius IX was now infallible and the absolute ruler of the church, but he had completely lost the Papal States. The Italian government offered him the so-called Law of Guarantees in May 1871, which ensured his independence as a sovereign and gave him an annual endowment and possession of the Leonine City, that is, the whole of the present-day Vatican as well as the Castel Sant'Angelo. In addition, the Italians offered the Lateran Palace, and the villa of Castel Gandolfo, outside Rome. Pius IX refused. He retired to the Vatican, casting himself as a "prisoner" of the Italian state. In September 1874 the Sacred Penitentiary issued the decree *Non expedit*, which banned Italian Catholics from participating in elections and in Italian political life, as it could be interpreted as approving the seizure of the Papal States. It was intended to snub anticlerical Italy, but it only succeeded in preventing Catholics from participating in and influencing Italian political life until the end of World War I. Pio Nono's last years were spent in his self-imposed "prison" in the Vatican, his narcissism deepened by increasing senility. He died on February 7, 1878. There have been continuous attempts to have him declared a saint, and he was beatified in 2000.

His papacy was one of the most momentous in church history. Throughout the second half of the nineteenth century, Catholicism underwent a spiritual renewal. New religious orders devoted to practical ministry enhanced the church's work in education, health care, social work, and especially foreign missions. As a result, the church expanded enormously. In 1800 there were about 106 million Catholics worldwide; by 1910 there were about 291 million. Clergy were better trained, even if they were increasingly clerical in their attitudes. As a result of ultramontanism, Catholics were devoted to the papacy, which magnified a kind of papalism whereby the church became identified in the popular mind with the pope. Despite Vatican I's relatively cautious definition, a kind of "creeping infallibility" infected Catholicism, whereby everything the pope said was taken as "infallible." Between 1800 and 1900, a real revolution in Catholicism had occurred.

The shock of the church's near-death experience during the French Revolution and its aftermath, the pressure of militant secular liberalism, the loss of the Papal States to the *Risorgimento*, and the revolutionary and communist threats to destroy the church completely all conspired to force Catholicism back onto itself to create a kind of worldwide ghetto, a sectarian Catholicism. All the opposition confirmed Pius IX's worst fears about the modern world. A more creative, intelligent pope might have responded positively to influence events, but instead Pius worked, both personally and institutionally, to enhance papal power and to turn the church inward. Within the church discipline and conformity were enforced by hard power. Having claimed "the absolute fullness of supreme power," the popes following Pius IX largely turned inward in a defensive stance, claiming that the church was a "perfect society" that had no need of the wider world and could learn nothing from it. Catholicism was "the one, true church."

Ultramontanism provided an overarching ideological theory for papal centralism, while modern communication provided the means for that to take root worldwide. As a result, "an entirely new phenomenon emerged in the church—the omnipresent papacy." The problem is that this could all too easily devolve into "a personality cult, a form of manipulative demagoguery. It seems to be precisely for this reason that Jesus was so careful of avoiding it."[31] Church history has been reinterpreted to claim that the papacy was always like this, when in reality neo-ultramontanism was a radical break with the past.

It was not until John XXIII in 1958 that the church's windows were opened again to let the fresh air in and let the people see out. It was a long eighty-year wait.

PART II

FROM "SUPREME POWER" TO SUPREME PONTIFF

3

TACKLING A WHOLE NEW WORLD

THE EVENTS OF 1799 provided the papacy with a real near-death experience. The integrity and stubbornness of Pius VII in his dealings with Napoleon restored something of the papacy's reputation, and the diplomatic skill of Consalvi at the 1815 Congress of Vienna recovered the pope's temporal power. The three nondescript successors of Pius VII achieved nothing except to bog down the papacy in the parochial politics of Italy and the Papal States. What Pius IX did was to create a new populist model of the papacy, almost a new way of being pope. But in contrast to Pius VII and Consalvi, his focus was inward, on the restoration of papal power and centralized authority within the church. In the process of achieving this, he distorted the traditional theological balance in Catholicism between the head and members, the center and the periphery. By the late nineteenth century, Catholicism had become an extraordinarily centralized institution that had no precedent in Christian history. Sure, a few medieval popes like Boniface VIII (1294–1303) had made outrageous claims, but under Pius IX and his successors the church became identified with the papacy in the minds of Catholics and non-Catholics alike, and papal power was enormously enhanced. In one sense, it was a remarkable achievement; in another, it led to a totally distorted notion of the church. The disjunction that occurred then still deeply affects us today.

At the same time that he was enhancing his own authority, Pius IX repudiated the modern world and turned the papacy into an inward-looking, claustrophobic institution. In doing so, he had irresponsibly allowed a massive social and cultural change to occur in which the papacy played no part, except to issue condemnations like the *Syllabus of Errors*. True, much of that new world was ugly because by the 1880s, the problems and injustices that flowed from the population explosion, the enclosure of rural lands that forced the dispossessed into the cities, unfettered capitalism, industrialization, and the factory system couldn't be avoided.

Industrialization had begun in England in the late eighteenth century, and it was there that the economic philosophy emerged that underpinned it. Based on the theories of Adam Smith, the Manchester School was developed by Richard Cobden and John Bright, and was an agglomeration of ideas based on the notion that free trade, free competition, and liberalism would lead to a more equitable society; it had much in common with so-called modern "trickle-down" economics. Manchester was a center of manufacturing, and most of the proponents of this school were practical men rather than theorists. The notion of economic "freedom" expressed itself through seeing labor as a commodity to be bought at the lowest price (that is, rock-bottom wages), while selling food staples, like grain, at the highest price. Accommodation was also a service to be bought at inflated rents for low-standard housing. Manufactured goods should be sold at the highest possible price. This led to appalling working conditions and exploitation of men, women, and children.

The great visionary William Blake's poem "*Jerusalem,*" composed in 1804, was one of the first protests against the consequences of rampant industrial capitalism. The poem is based on the medieval legend, associated with Glastonbury Abbey, that Christ might have spent some of his "hidden years" before his public ministry in England: "And did those feet in ancient time / Walk upon England's mountains green?"

But by Blake's time, the green landscape was fast disappearing "Among these dark Satanic mills" and the ever-growing urban ugliness. Blake sees his prophetic task as restoring the "mountains green" and calling people to liberation:

> *I will not cease from Mental Fight,*
> *Nor shall my sword sleep in my hand:*

Till we have built Jerusalem,
In England's green & pleasant Land.

The poem is an early, prophetic Christian critique of the way industrial capitalism oppressed and exploited the poor, forcing women
and children to work in dangerous conditions, while businessmen
made themselves wealthy by espousing economic liberalism. Industrialization, based on free trade, soon spread from England to France,
Germany, and Belgium in the early to mid-nineteenth century.

By the death of Pius IX in 1878, the worst effects of industrialization were impacting right across Europe, including Italy, which
was one of the last European countries to be industrialized. Perhaps
this explains papal tardiness in tackling the social justice problems
embedded in industrialization. Various solutions were proposed.
At first the Protestant and Anglican churches proposed a kind of
philanthropy by caring for the "deserving poor" while throwing the
"undeserving poor" into the workhouse. In contrast, Marxism and
communism called for a radical solution that involved proletarian
revolution, leading to the overthrow of capitalism and the imposition of state socialism. Pius IX had contributed virtually nothing to
the debate except to condemn socialism and communism, but the
papacy could not avoid this issue forever.

Before another pope could tackle these problems, however, he
had to be elected. The cardinals first had to decide on a location
for the conclave because the new Italian king, Umberto I, now occupied the Quirinal Palace. The papacy was literally homeless; the
pope still had the Vatican, but only on sufferance of the Italian government. Malta was proposed as a possible location, but in the end
the Vatican was chosen. After extensive work to prepare the area
around the Sistine Chapel, the conclave met, but Cardinal John
McCloskey of New York arrived too late to participate. Of the sixty
voting cardinals who entered the conclave on February 19, 1878,
only twenty-five were non-Italian.

The only serious rival to Gioacchino Pecci, bishop of Perugia,
was Luigi Bilio. However, most electors felt a need for change,
and Pecci, who was perceived as somewhat open to modernity, was

elected at the third scrutiny on February 20, 1878, taking the style Leo XIII. Because Pecci was sixty-eight and in poor health, the cardinals thought they were electing a transitional pope, but he survived to ninety-three and was pope for twenty-five years and five months. Physically very different from Pius IX, who was a short, portly man of the people, Leo XIII was tall, thin, ascetic, and aloof, although pictures sometimes show a gentle smile breaking through. Nevertheless, even a casual walk in the Vatican gardens turned into a solemn procession, with everyone falling to their knees as the pope passed. Even in private audiences Leo carried on conversations with visitors still on their knees. Whereas Pius was emotional and instinctual, Leo was intellectual, and as he aged he seemed to become almost disincarnated from the material world. What these popes had in common was that both were deeply ultramontane, and Leo continued the centralizing tendencies inherited from Pius. While hostile to Catholics entering into involvement with Italian politics, Leo XIII had a more open attitude. From 1887 he was ably assisted by Cardinal Mariano Rampolla del Tindaro as secretary of state.

At first Leo took an antagonistic stance toward modernity and promoted an idealized image of medieval Christianity as the norm for Catholicism. He had no comprehension of the changes that Europe was undergoing, and, as theologian Bruce Duncan says, "there was little awareness in the papacy of the sociological changes pressing secularization forward."[1] Nevertheless, Pope Leo believed that the church should play an active role in society. He was committed to the abolition of slavery, promoted the role of the Catholicism providing social welfare, and supported the arts and sciences and the development of the papal social justice tradition. He instinctively understood how to use social justice as a way of influencing society and addressing issues of profound social concern.

It was not a particularly friendly world that Leo faced, especially close to home in Italy. Until 1929 the Vatican refused to acknowledge the existence of Italy via the *Non expedit* decree (1874), which is understandable, given the anti-Catholic behavior of the Italian state. Historian Denis Mack Smith says that this approach was "sterile in fact, but quite valid in theory," because the papacy had to protest against the seizure of Rome.[2] Posing as the "prisoner of the Vatican" struck many contemporaries as melodramatic, but the popes between 1870 and the 1920s saw no other option. Once Rome became the Italian capital, there was an influx of Piedmontese bureaucrats, and property speculation became rampant. The *prati* (meadows) abutting the Castel Sant'Angelo and the Vatican were sold off to those working in the government ministries that were moving into the area, and the whole district became a place for anticlericals to thumb their noses at the Vatican. Relations were tense after an anticlerical mob tried unsuccessfully to toss the body of Pius IX into the Tiber when it was being transferred in July 1881 to the Basilica of San Lorenzo fuori le Mura.

Nevertheless, Pope Leo made attempts to reconcile with Italy, even though the Italian government really represented only a tiny proportion of the population due to a limited franchise and rigged electoral system. In May 1887 the pope approached the newly elected prime minister, Francesco Crispi, who replied brusquely that the 1871 Law of Guarantees, in which Italy ensured papal independence by offering the papacy an area slightly larger than what is now Vatican City, was still on the table, so there was nothing to discuss. The pope retreated to demanding restoration of the Papal States. By 1900 both Catholics and secularists realized that the whole situation in Italy was intolerable.

Outside Italy there were also problems for the papacy, especially in Germany and France. In Germany Leo worked to resolve the *Kulturkampf*, the anti-Catholic "culture battle." The *Kulturkampf* originated after the Franco-Prussian War (1870), during Otto von Bismarck's formation of the Second Reich on a Prussian model, with its liberal state bureaucracy determined to rein in the historical privileges of Catholicism. The Protestant Bismarck didn't trust Catholics, and this was reinforced by the syllabus and the infallibility decree of Vatican I. Bismarck was opposed by the *Zentrumspartei*, the Catholic Center Party. The party gave the German laity genuine political power beyond clerical control, in contrast to Italy, where the laity was denied a political voice by the *Non expedit* decree. The focus of Bismarck's attack on Catholicism from July 1871 was education, with church schools being subjected to inspection by state authorities and a pulpit law that forbade criticism of government by the clergy. In June 1872 the Jesuits and later other religious orders were expelled from Germany, and diplomatic relations with the Vatican were broken. In 1873 the May Laws of Culture Minister Adalbert Falk were passed, giving the state control over internal church affairs. In 1875 civil marriage was imposed on Germany. The intention was to turn Catholicism into a state church under government control, like the Lutheran Church. It was a direct result of the May Laws that five Franciscan nuns expelled from Germany drowned when their ship foundered on the English east coast. Gerard Manley Hopkins immortalized them in the great poem "*The Wreck of the Deutschland.*"

However, Bismarck's *Kulturkampf*, rather than weakening German Catholics, united them, despite the fact that many church personnel were exiled and church assets stripped. Eventually, Bismarck needed *Zentrumspartei* support in the *Reichstag* against the left-leaning Social Democrats, so his hard-line attitudes toward Catholicism began to soften. In response, Leo XIII took a conciliatory line. He hoped that if he was reasonable, Bismarck would support him in dealing with the Italians. Slowly, the anti-Catholic measures were withdrawn, and the German church emerged from the struggle with an enhanced sense of identity and cohesion, much of it due to the lay leadership that the *Zentrumspartei* represented.

In France church-state relations were particularly toxic. Philosopher Charles Péguy commented that in France, "*Tout commence en la mystique et tout finit en la politique*" (Everything begins in mysticism [perhaps "ideology" is a better translation] and everything ends up political). This might be a Frenchman taking himself too seriously, but the tragedy of this period is that everyone was caught up in a quasi-ideological cross-fire that made negotiated settlements impossible. After defeat in the Franco-Prussian War in 1870 and the rise and fall of the Paris Commune (in which almost forty thousand people died, including Paris archbishop Georges Darboy), France was left bitterly divided. Things became steadily worse after the establishment of the Third Republic in 1875. In

1882 anticlerical Freemason and a supporter of *laïcité* (militant secularism) Education Minister Jules Ferry introduced a law that broke church control of grade schools by introducing free compulsory secular education. Accompanying these changes were a whole series of anticlerical decrees expelling the Jesuits and other male religious orders. Ferry said that his aim was "to organize humanity without God and without kings." The underlying issue in this was the question of the disestablishment of the church and the separation of church and state. Pope Leo, who had been to Paris, spoke fluent French, was very attracted to French culture, and had a particular interest in France, made no public protest over Ferry's secularist legislation. The reason was that Leo was slowly distancing himself from the intransigent policies of Pius IX. In the encyclical *Immortale Dei* (1885), for instance, after a long catalog of "modern errors," he conceded that "if judged dispassionately, no one of the several forms of government is in itself condemned. . . . Neither is it blameworthy . . . for the people to have a share . . . in government." This was a real departure from the *Syllabus of Errors.* The encyclical *Libertas* (1888) also maintains something of the old dogmatism, while still making openings for a more nuanced approach. "It is not of itself wrong to prefer a democratic form of government, if only the Catholic doctrine be maintained. . . . Of the various forms of government, the Church does not reject any that are fitted to procure the welfare of the subject." This is a big advance on the syllabus. It is not that Leo XIII particularly liked the Third Republic, but he was determined to try to secure the position of the church by achieving a *modus vivendi* with republicanism.

But he also faced the dichotomy outlined by Péguy. It was succinctly expressed by social reformer, aristocrat, and Catholic antirepublican Albert de Mun: "Either the church must kill the revolution, or the revolution will kill the church."[3] While anticlerical republicans were problematic enough, conservative Catholic royalists were even more of a nuisance to the papal program. Like all conservatives, French Catholics were only too happy to pick and choose what papal teachings and emphases they followed. Leo's attempts to build a theological basis for reconciliation between church and state led to newspapers like *L'Univers* and the *Journal de Rome* negatively contrasting Leo's actions to the "achievements" of Pius IX's papacy.

Pope Leo and Secretary Rampolla were determined that the French church reconcile itself with the Republic while, at the same time, trying to get the government to refrain from hostility toward Catholicism. This was the policy of the *Ralliement*, the "winning over" of French Catholics to the Republic. This was easier said than done because of the vicious animosity between monarchist-conservative Catholics and secularist republicans. France became one place where papal soft power didn't work. French life was increasingly poisoned by the infamous Dreyfus affair, in which many right-wing Catholics took an openly anti-Semitic stance. Captain Alfred Dreyfus was a Jewish army officer falsely accused of treason. He was convicted in December 1894 of selling military secrets to the Germans and sentenced to life imprisonment at the notorious prison on Devil's Island, in French Guiana. By 1896 it was clear that the real traitor was a Major Ferdinand Esterhazy. This led to novelist Emile Zola's open letter, *J'Accuse*, which split France apart. Nationalists, anti-Semites, and conservative Catholics stuck by the army; republicans, anticlericals, and socialists supported Dreyfus. Dreyfus's conviction was eventually overturned in 1906. By then the *Ralliement* had failed completely.

———

LEO XIII BEGAN his papacy as a conservative who slowly began to broaden out as he dealt with the complexity of the issues he faced. This is not to suggest that he became "liberal"; he never shifted one iota from his fundamental conviction that a centralizing papal monarchy was a key element in church governance. Much of his political maneuvering was focused on the ultimate restoration of the Papal States in some form or another. Given this, Leo had little sympathy for moderate Italian Catholics who felt that the time had come for reconciliation with the Italian state. This became an explosive issue in 1877 when the Jesuit founder of *La Civiltà Cattolica*, Carlo Curci, called for an acceptance of the loss of the Papal States and for reconciliation with the Kingdom of Italy. Curci was dismissed from the Jesuits and suspended *a divinis,* that is, from practicing as a priest. Nevertheless, in the latter part of Leo's papacy, increasing numbers of moderate Catholics called for an abandonment of claims for the restoration of the Papal States and for reconciliation with Italy, including priests like Romolo Murri (who later became a major figure in Italian Catholicism) and the bishop of Cremona Gerema Bonomelli. An anonymously published pamphlet of Bonomelli proposed that the pope be given a small territory roughly the equivalent of the present-day Vatican City State. Leo was furious, and in April 1889 he placed the pamphlet on the *Index of Forbidden Books* and demanded that the bishop read out a retraction of his views in his own cathedral. It was a ruthless application of papal hard power.

While never favoring democracy, Leo tolerated it as a way of keeping revolutionary socialist impulses under control. His early encyclical on socialism, *Quod apostolici muneris* (1878), attacks "that sect of men who are called socialists, communists, or nihilists who . . . strive to bring to [bring about] the overthrow of "various orders" [that is, class war] in civil society." Leo's mental horizons were profoundly hierarchical, and he favored a paternalistic monarchical government working in league with the church. He had a strong sense of the papacy's long history, and one of the medieval notions he emphasized was of the church as a *societas perfecta,* a perfect society. This notion finds its origins in Saint Augustine and was used by Leo and his successors to protect the rights of the church against secularist governments. In *Immortale Dei* Leo asserts that "the Church no less than the State itself is a society perfect in its own nature . . . and those who exercise sovereignty ought not . . . act to compel the Church to become subservient or subject to them, or to hamper her liberty in the management of her own affairs." While secular states attempted to reduce religion to the merely private sphere, Leo claims that the church was "far superior" to the state, because its function and goal were "sublime" and "perfect," not in need of reform, and entirely independent of the state.

Leo's medievalism was also expressed in his determination that the theology of Saint Thomas Aquinas (ca. 1225–1274) be normative in all Catholic tertiary institutions, particularly in seminaries. His encyclical *Aeterni Patris* (1879) specifically recommended the use of Aquinas's theology, particularly Thomas's emphasis on the compatibility of faith and reason. For Leo XIII, this was the basis upon which a whole new approach to the modern world could be developed. This caused a stir, as there were still many in the church deeply opposed to Thomism.

Pope Leo gave expression to his sense of history in his "Letter on Historical Studies" (1883). He insisted that historians return critically to the original sources, and he opened the Vatican Secret Archives to selected scholars, such as the leading historian of the popes, Ludwig von Pastor. But he also maintained that historical research had an apologetic function: to strengthen Catholicism against attacks by anticlerical historians. Aware of the work Protestant scholars had already done, he encouraged the use of critical methods in biblical research, although the encyclical *Providentissimus Deus* (1893) warned of dangers in "higher criticism." By this Leo was referring to the critical method whereby the origins, authorship, and literary structure of the various books of the Bible were established. In 1902 he set up the Pontifical Biblical Commission to guide and assist biblical scholars.

He was also something of an Anglophile. He was aware of the work of John Henry Newman, and he proposed that the English theologian be made a cardinal. Despite pettifogging interference from Manning in Westminster, Newman was created a cardinal deacon on May 12, 1879. The pope also wrote the apostolic letter *Ad Anglos* (1895), addressed to "the illustrious English race," inviting them to return to union with Rome after their "sad defection" at the Reformation. In the letter he nevertheless manages to ignore the Church of England completely. He also set up a committee to examine the validity of Anglican orders, but, after machinations by Benedictine monk (later cardinal) Francis Aidan Gasquet, the pope decreed in the bull *Apostolicae curae* (1896) that "ordinations carried out according to the Anglican rite are absolutely null and utterly void." No equivocation there!

BY THE TIME of Leo's election in 1878, European expansionism had been in full swing for 450 years. A complex process, it went through several stages and involved in varying proportions national pride, adventure, exploration, cultural conquest, trading, robbery, piracy, and settlement. It didn't always involve seafaring; it could be across landmasses. Russia's expansion into central Asia and the westward thrust of the United States are also examples of expansionism. After 1815 new economic forces drove colonial expansion, and in the mid-nineteenth century the word imperialism was invented to describe what was happening. J. A. Hobson claimed that "the economic taproot of imperialism . . . [was] excessive capitalism in search of investment." This seems an overly economic interpretation, although, as historian David Thomson says, "whatever political, religious, or more idealistic excuses might be made, the real impulse was always one of capitalistic greed for cheap raw materials, advantageous markets, good investments and fresh fields of exploitation," and, one might add, new markets for the sale of manufactured goods.[4]

Missionary expansion usually went along with and often preceded European imperialism. Sometimes, as in the case of some French missionaries, it was hard to discern the borders between evangelization and cultural nationalism. In many situations missionaries penetrated territory well before the imperialists arrived. Nowadays, missionaries are often blamed for destroying local cultures with the imposition of Eurocentrism. They are accused of being the "right arm" of imperialism. Of course, there is some truth to this, but it is also true that the religious orders brought health care, literacy, education, and often a chance to break out of tribal and clan structures that were dehumanizing. At times the very survival of indigenous people depended on the protection that the missionaries offered. The missionary impulse ran strongly through the nineteenth century, and, as we have seen, Catholicism was blessed with a large number of new missionary religious orders of both men and women, most founded in France, but also with a good number from Germany, Ireland, Italy, and Spain. This missionary expansion of the church outside Europe continued strongly during Leo's papacy, with 248 new dioceses being established across the world.

Linked to this missionary expansion was the growth of the church in the New World of North America and the South Pacific. Emigration from Europe to the United States, Canada, Australia, and New Zealand led to the growth of the church in the New World. Here Catholicism prospered in democratic and secular regimes, and to an extent Leo XIII recognized this. But as the church expanded, Roman power and micromanagement increased. As we saw, the Congregation of Propaganda Fide, the Roman department that supervised missionary countries (which included North America and Australasia), still appointed all bishops in these countries and forced them to apply for delegated faculties or permission to exercise even the minutiae of their offices. The fullness of supreme power was making itself felt at the local level.

The most egregious example of Roman interference in the affairs of a New World church is the unfortunate condemnation of so-called "Americanism," which is the theological response of US Catholics to life and ministry as they made sense of their faith in a democratic context. The underlying issue in Americanism is ecclesiological, focusing on the nature of the church. New World Catholics understood that the church is incarnated within specific sociocultural contexts, and they knew that theirs was very different from those of Europe. Historian James Hennesey says that among American Catholics, "there was a deeply rooted conviction of the basic harmony of American democratic ways with Catholicism."[5] While this optimism involves a certain amount of naïveté, there is also something creative and optimistic about the US enthusiasm for democracy and the separation of church and state in contrast to musty European debates about papal sovereignty and the union between throne and altar, liberalism and church. Given Leo XIII's high papalism, conflict with the Americans was inevitable.

The source of Americanism was Isaac Thomas Hecker. Born in New York City in 1819, he was the son of German Protestant immigrants. He converted to Catholicism after a period with utopian transcendentalist communities in Massachusetts. After ordination he founded his own religious order, devoted to the conversion of America, the Missionary Society of Saint Paul, or the Paulists.

He believed that Catholicism had much to offer in finding a balance between the American tradition of rugged individualism and the need for community. A saintly man, he gradually developed a uniquely American spirituality. A seeker throughout his life, Hecker's spirituality focused on the action of the Holy Spirit in each person's experience. He believed that the world could be transformed if people were more attentive to God's Spirit in their lives. His ideas gained traction among powerful Catholics, including Archbishop John Ireland of St. Paul; Monsignor Denis O'Connell, first rector of Rome's North American College; Cardinal James Gibbons of Baltimore; Peoria bishop John Lancaster Spalding; and Bishop John J. Keane, first rector of the Catholic University of America in Washington, DC. O'Connell and Keane developed the notion of the US separation of church and state as a model for the rest of the church; they were strongly ecumenical and open to Protestants. O'Connell noted the incompatibility of canon law with the common-law tradition. Ireland went so far as to write: "Let there be individual initiative, layman need not wait for priest, nor priest for bishop, nor bishop for pope."[6] Needless to say, such ideas raised opposition among other bishops, including New York archbishop Michael Corrigan, Bishop Bernard McQuaid of Rochester, and several German American bishops from the Midwest.

In mid-1892 Ireland visited France, where he was undiplomatic enough to tell the French clergy that they needed to come down from their ivory towers and learn from the American experience. "The people is king now," Ireland said.[7] These views were quickly reported to Rome, which sent Italian archbishop Francesco Satolli to the United States to report discreetly to Rome on American affairs. On January 14, 1893, Satolli was appointed first apostolic delegate to the United States, giving him direct power over internal church affairs. The US hierarchy was unhappy with this appointment because they had not been consulted. Two midwestern bishops (Spalding and James Ryan, from Alton, now Springfield in Illinois) described the apostolic delegation as a "foreign intrusion." Many bishops felt that the US church was unjustly feeling the force of direct Roman intervention.

The Americanist crisis came to a head in France. Hecker had died in 1888, and an 1891 biography by Walter Elliott, a Paulist priest, was published. It was translated into French in 1897. Hecker's ideas about democracy and Catholicism as a religion of seekers conflicted with the notion of Catholicism as the repository of all truth. When these notions spread in France in the midst of the *Ralliement*, trouble quickly brewed, especially after they were picked up by liberal Catholics. Conservative French Catholics, who coined the term *Americanism*, were mightily offended that anyone would think that they had anything to learn from American "Anglo-Saxons"; Hecker was tagged a "heresiarch." The final blow came with the encyclical *Testem benevolentiae* (January 22, 1899), addressed to Baltimore's Cardinal Gibbons. In it Pope Leo says that the biography of Hecker is a problem because it promotes an "underlying principle" that "in order to more easily attract those who differ from her, the Church should shape her teachings more in accord with the spirit of the age and relax some of her ancient severity and make some concessions to new opinions." Essentially, Leo couldn't get his head around the issue of cultural difference and get past the dominant Eurocentrism of Catholicism. US theologian Margaret Mary Reher says that Leo viewed "the situation from his own perspective" and saw US Catholicism from "a paternalistic, parochially Italian" point of view.[8] Fortunately, *Testem benevolentiae* did little to halt the growth of the US church. Whether any of the Americans even held the theological views attributed to them by Leo XIII is highly debatable. In the end, the condemnation was silly and ill-informed, based as it was on French misinterpretations, misunderstandings, and deliberate lies. It revealed that Rome still had no understanding of the church's relationship with the democratic governments and the separation of church and state that characterized the English-speaking world. The most important aspect of the whole episode is the seemingly limitless expansion of papal interference in the affairs of local churches. This was "absolute power" in practice.

———

POPE LEO'S PAPACY began as the long-term effects of industrialization were being experienced across Europe. Blake's "dark Satanic mills" had spread from the United Kingdom to France, Belgium, Germany, Spain, and finally Italy, which was one of the last European countries to be industrialized. Pope Leo soon realized that the papacy couldn't ignore industrialization, the factory system, and the condition of the working classes. The socialists were offering a radical collectivist solution, and ruthless laissez-faire capitalism was espousing radical individualism; both were viewed as serious threats by the pope. In the process of responding, he began the tradition of papal social teaching, one of the papacy's most important contributions to social justice and human welfare. But some significant Catholics had gone before him.

Pope Leo built on a Catholic tradition that reached back to the 1830s as the effects of the Industrial Revolution began to be felt in continental Europe. The group *L'Avenir* was the first to see the treatment of the poor as an issue of justice. The key figure here was Frédéric Ozanam, the founder of the Saint Vincent de Paul Society. Ozanam, a committed democrat, called for a living wage and said that the poor deserved not just charity but justice. In 1833 in Paris he founded the society that today still serves the poor and is present in 140 countries, with an estimated membership of eight hundred thousand volunteers. After the 1848 revolutions, French Catholicism became increasingly bourgeois and paternalistic. This was the period when some argue that the French working class turned to socialism. However, in the second half of the nineteenth century, it was hard for a faith whose founder was born a homeless refugee to ignore the shocking conditions under which working people lived. At the time of his election, Leo XIII had some knowledge of the social question, but it tended to be in terms of asserting the rights of private property, condemning socialism, and paternalistically encouraging workers to form associations under religious patronage. It was in Germany, England, and the United States that Catholics began to confront issues of social justice.

In Germany the key figure was Wilhelm von Ketteler, bishop of Mainz. He had been a public servant before he became a priest and was aware of the threat that rampant industrialization posed to the Christian ideal of human dignity when workers were used as pawns in the factory system. Ketteler, a tall, outspoken man of action, believed that the social question was the central issue of the century and that the church could not be satisfied with charitable window dressing. He considered that private property and wealth were not absolute; they came with restrictions, specifically that they must be used for the common good. Ketteler attacked Manchester liberalism as much as he did communism. After initial hesitation, he conceded that "the State must play a major role in social reform . . . by increasing wages, reducing working hours, allowing Sunday rest and prohibiting women and children from working in factories."[9] He approved of strikes. He died in 1877 of cholera.

The significant figure in Catholic social justice in England was Cardinal Henry Edward Manning, archbishop of Westminster. We met him at Vatican I as a nasty ecclesiastical schemer and extreme ultramontanist, but he also has an impressive record on the social question. He had practical knowledge of working conditions in England, and he knew that exploitation of workers was widespread, despite a series of Factory Acts between 1819 and 1878 that eventually prohibited children under ten from working and limited women's work to sixty hours per week. Manning supported democracy and was happy to cooperate with both governmental and nongovernmental agencies like the Salvation Army in alleviating poverty. He opposed slavery, supported unions, and encouraged state intervention to protect workers from rapacious employers and inhumane working conditions. He intervened decisively in the London Dock Strike of 1889. Manning's views influenced Leo XIII in the composition of what would be the most durable and influential encyclical of his papacy.

In the United States, there were a number of important voices, including priest Edward McGlynn.[10] Born in New York City in 1837, McGlynn was a spellbinding orator with a theology doctorate from Rome. He was appointed pastor of Saint Stephen's Church on East Twenty-Eighth Street in Manhattan, and he championed the cause of Irish independence. At home he called for state intervention in social and economic issues to protect the rights of

workers from the ravages of rampant capitalism. He opposed parochial schools and urged parents to send their children to public
schools. He was a strong supporter of the views of Henry George,
who advocated a "single tax" on land. What appealed to McGlynn
was that George was trying to make all land the common property of everyone. Land, George argued, is a product of nature, and
it cannot be owned or possessed by any individual. This sense of
common access reflects the early Christian community as described
in the Acts of the Apostles: "All who believed were together and
had all things in common" (2:44). McGlynn ran into trouble with
New York archbishop Michael Corrigan, who suspended him from
priestly duties in 1886. After a protracted dispute, which included
accusations that George's views were socialist and communist, Mc-
Glynn was summoned to Rome, but he refused to go. This particularly annoyed Leo XIII, and it was this refusal that led in the
end to McGlynn's excommunication in 1888. He cofounded the
Anti-Poverty Society in 1887 and was restored to the priesthood in
1892 after nothing was found in his writings that was contrary to
church doctrine.

———————

IT WAS WITHIN this context that Leo XIII issued on May 15, 1891,
the encyclical *Rerum novarum* (*RN*). This letter provides the foundation upon which papal and Catholic social teaching has been built
over the past 125 years and is probably the most important papal
use of soft-power influence in the modern world. Although written
in the usual pompous papal style, *RN* is a revolutionary document.
It focuses on three major themes: first, the absolute centrality of the
common good, for God gives the earth and its fruits to all; second,
the need for equity between capital and labor; and third, the central
role of the state in regulating these relationships.

Leo unequivocally blames the capitalist system for the condition
of the working class, and he speaks of "rapacious usury" (exploitative interest rates) and of the fact that "the hiring of labor and
the conduct of trade are in the hands of comparatively few, so that
a small number of very rich men have been able to lay upon the

teeming masses of the labouring poor a yoke little better than that of slavery itself." In this context, he is supportive of trade unions. Catholicism has always been ambivalent about capitalism, and Leo XIII's and subsequent papal social teaching reflects this. While the pope accepts private ownership as an inherent right, he also argues that this must be balanced by the demands of the common good. This notion originates in Aristotle, but more important it is emphasized by the Hebrew prophets and in Jesus's constant concern for the poor and marginalized. The notion of the common good is much more than the utilitarian "greatest good for the greatest number." It embraces all: the poor, the destitute, the exploited, and those most despised in society. It is based on God's all-embracing love and demands that those with the most share with those with the least. "Whoever has received from the divine bounty a large share of temporal blessings, whether they be external and material, or gifts of the mind, has received them for the purpose of using them . . . as the steward of God's providence, for the benefit of others." In *RN* Leo also articulates what nowadays we call "the preferential option for the poor": "When there is question of defending the rights of individuals," he says, "the poor . . . have a claim to especial consideration." While the wealthy can "shield themselves," the poor often have to "depend upon the state," and they should be "specially cared for and protected by the government."

The second basic issue in *Rerum novarum* focuses on the need for equity between capital and labor. From the start Leo admits, "It is no easy matter to define the relative rights and mutual duties of the rich and of the poor, of capital and of labor." He sees them as interdependent. "Each needs the other: capital cannot do without labor, nor labor without capital," and constant conflict between them "produces confusion and savage barbarity." He had no time for class warfare. After outlining the respective duties of workers and employers, he emphasizes that wages must be free agreements between worker and employer and must meet the basic needs of workers and their families. The pope says that the state has a clear role to play in maintaining the balance between labor and capital. Its function is to ensure the well-being of all members of society, but especially the poor. Government must serve the common good.

"The more that is done for the benefit of the working classes by the general laws of the country, the less need will there be to seek for special means to relieve them." However, government must know its limits: "The State must not absorb the individual or the family; both should be allowed free and untrammelled action so far as is consistent with the common good and the interest of others."

Leo the pragmatist admits that inequalities are inevitable, but he says that class war is wrong. While the Catholic position is closer to socialism, the popes have always been critical of the godless, secular socialism that leads to communism. True human worth, Leo says, lies not in wealth or poverty but, like Christ, in nobility of life, generosity of spirit, and a commitment to morality. The church has a key role to play in social questions by influencing people's consciences so that they act according to duty. He concludes by saying that "the condition of the working classes is the pressing question of the hour, and nothing can be of higher interest to all classes of the State than that it should be rightly and reasonably settled." He clearly intended that social justice be a top priority for the church.

LEO XIII DIED on July 20, 1903. His papacy of twenty-five years and five months after Pius's thirty-one years and seven months meant there had only been two popes in fifty-seven years. The average length of a papacy in church history is about seven years. While Leo XIII tried to reconcile the church with the contemporary world, the disjunction between himself and Pius IX should not be exaggerated. Leo continued Pius's policy of centralization in the church and refused to negotiate with the Kingdom of Italy, maintaining an obsession with the recovery of the Papal States, while continuing to play the "prisoner in the Vatican" charade. But his diplomacy—along with that of Cardinal Rampolla—had restored the international reputation of the Vatican, and it had recovered some of the prestige that it had lost. Leo XIII made the papacy an international player again.

4

"GOD AND THE REVOLVER!"

ALTHOUGH IT TOOK the popes a long time to realize it, the loss of the Papal States did them an enormous favor. Now that they were no longer burdened with running a princedom—often badly—papal attention could be focused on pastoral, spiritual, and faith matters as well as Catholicism's role in the world. In fact, their prestige and influence increased precisely because their focus shifted away from maintaining their temporal power in the Papal States. The years after 1870 had also been a transitional time for Europe. In this period there was a retreat from what had been called "the concert of Europe," a kind of international balance of power that prevented any general war on the Continent since 1815. While international relations and contacts remained strong, the European powers had been rearming, and Germany was looking for ways to challenge British maritime supremacy. Disputes over overseas colonies had been largely settled, but the real powder keg lay in the Balkans, where nationalism was on the rise and anarchists, the precursor to today's terrorists, were only too willing to use nationalist tensions to assassinate royalty and leaders.

The papacy was also changing. It had begun the nineteenth century in survival mode, just hanging on through one of the weakest periods in its history. As the twentieth century dawned, it had not only survived but with Leo XIII had begun to become a player again in European and world affairs. This had been largely achieved by an intelligent application of a soft-power approach to culture and society and through a willingness to open up and participate again in a reasonable way in diplomatic negotiations. The church's moral authority had been enhanced by people like Frédéric Oza- nam and the Saint Vincent de Paul Society, Bishop von Kettler in Germany, and Cardinal Manning in London. Pope Leo's *Rerum novarum* was one of the most important encyclicals ever issued by any pope, and it began a tradition of papal involvement in moral and economic debates over social justice issues that has continued right up until the present.

There had also been a pattern in the nineteenth century of a "diplomatic" pope being succeeded by a "pastoral" one. Leo XIII had been the diplomat *par excellence*, so there was a feeling among many of the sixty-two cardinals who entered the conclave on July 30, 1903, that they needed to elect a pastor. With a ten-day interregnum between the death of a pope and the beginning of the conclave to elect his successor, Cardinal Patrick Moran of Sydney, Australia, was (literally) still at sea when the conclave began, and he arrived too late to vote. But Baltimore's Cardinal James Gibbons just happened to be in Rome when Leo died, so he was able to en- ter the conclave and became the first American to vote for a pope.

The cardinals were divided on several issues. Some wanted to continue the Leo XIII papacy and therefore favored Rampolla. But Rampolla's problem was that his French policy had collapsed, and he was also perceived as opposed to the interests of Austria- Hungary. Another group wanted reconciliation with Italy. Others wanted a pastoral pope who would focus on faith issues and oppose liberal trends in theology and biblical interpretation. These empha- ses were not mutually exclusive, and there was considerable overlap all around. A key factor was that the European powers were again interested in the papacy and its influence in world affairs, in contrast to the hands-off attitude taken in the 1878 conclave.

The conclave lasted three and a half days, with Austrian emperor Franz Josef, influenced by Cardinal Jan Puzyna of Kraków, present- ing an imperial veto against Rampolla. The Austrian emperor had a traditional right to veto a cardinal's election as pope. Rampolla was vetoed because he had abandoned the Catholic Poles and supported Russian policy. Puzyna seems to have been the real actor here rather than the Austrian government. In fact, Rampolla's chances were probably already finished before the veto, with votes already flowing to Giuseppe Sarto of Venice. He was elected on the morning of August 4, 1903, and took the style Pius to honor Pius IX. Calling himself "Pius" indicated that he wanted to return to and emphasize the priorities of the Mastai-Ferretti papacy. Son of a postman from the Veneto region, Pius X was a devout man with an iron will; he lacked flexibility, and his outlook was parochially Italian. He had no real intellectual formation, and his interests were in the inner life of the church and pastoral care. He was pessimistic, resolutely reactionary, and intent on restoring a traditional Catholic social order. "If Leo XIII's papacy had been a cautious attempt to come to terms with the modern world, then Pius X's was a repudiation of it. . . . This papacy belongs to the nineteenth century rather than to the twentieth."[1]

Nevertheless, some of Europe's social problems seem to have penetrated the Vatican. Pope Pius's deep pessimism was obvious in his first encyclical, *E supremi* (October 4, 1903). He said he was "terrified . . . by the disastrous state of human society today." Things were so bad as to be apocalyptic: "There is good reason to fear lest this great perversity may be . . . a foretaste and perhaps the beginning of those evils which are reserved for the last days." To counter this disastrous state, he said his aim was "to lead mankind back under the dominion of Christ," and he took as his motto "To restore all things in Christ." Resolutely antidemocratic, his rejection of Leo XIII and Rampolla's willingness to become politically involved and to use diplomatic soft power to enhance the pastoral work of the church and bring about reconciliation in society meant that the papacy withdrew from involvement in the wider culture. He was supported by his secretary of state, Rafael Merry del Val, a pious, moralistic, inexperienced, and intransigent thirty-eight-year-old son of a Spanish diplomat who spent his early life in England.

Right from his election, Pius X had to deal with France. Rampolla had had some diplomatic success, but the Dreyfus affair aroused terrible bitterness, with anticlericalism the default position of French secularists. Prime Minister Émile Combes's anti-Catholic government (1903–1905) enforced the law against religious orders, and some twenty thousand priests and other religious were expelled from France, many to the United Kingdom. Schools were closed and church property confiscated. But the virulently anti-Catholic Combes, a former student for the priesthood, didn't have the numbers to force the complete separation of church and state. His successor, Aristide Briand, did have the numbers in the National Assembly, and he forced through the Law of Separation of church and state on December 9, 1905. This led to "a war between two Frances," secular France, guided by *laïcité*, and conservative France, guided by Catholicism. Pius X described the separation as "a most pernicious error" and a "negation of the supernatural order," but the breakdown was really a symptom of Pius and Merry del Val's diplomatic inexperience and intransigence.

Portugal also experienced church-state conflicts. An anticlerical republic was established in 1910, and separation of church and state was decreed on April 20, 1911. The papal response was the encyclical *Iamdudum*, which claimed that the republican government was imbued with "the most implacable hatred of the Catholic religion." It was a fruitless attempt at a show of force that accomplished nothing. Given that Portugal remained a strongly Catholic country, a diplomatic approach might have achieved much more. All that Pius X succeeded in doing was to keep the local church at loggerheads with the republic until a military coup established the right-wing António Salazar regime in May 1926.

Pius X is fondly remembered in Catholicism for his encouragement of the regular reception of Communion. By the nineteenth century, the practice of frequent Communion at Mass had almost disappeared, and in a radical move in December 1905 Pius called for weekly, even daily, Communion for all Catholics, including children. As long as a person had the right dispositions and had confessed serious mortal sin, they could receive the Eucharist. A new attitude to the Eucharist emerged in the church, and without doubt this was Pius's most important achievement. Closely associated with this was his promotion of a catechetical renewal. This was directed as much to adults as to children. His emphasis was on basic instruction in the faith, but this led indirectly to the evolution of a whole new approach to catechesis in the German- and English-speaking worlds. In the following decades, the link between formation in faith and liturgy was emphasized by theologians like Josef Andreas Jungmann, Johannes Hofinger, and Francis Drinkwater. Pope Pius also wanted to get rid of the orchestral and operatic elements in church music that were particularly prevalent in Italy, in which virtuoso performance supplanted worship. He recommended Gregorian chant and classical polyphony and prohibited women singers. Fortunately, this last requirement was largely ignored. His reforms didn't impact popular hymn singing, which was the staple of parish worship. The most important thing is that the modern liturgical reform movement gained momentum in this papacy and laid the foundations for Vatican II.

Linked to the Eucharistic reforms was Pius X's attempt to improve the education and spiritual formation of priests. Above all, he wanted obedient, clerical priests who could cope with parochial ministry. To achieve this, he decided to reform seminaries. However, the real problems of priestly formation were much deeper: the seminary system worldwide was inadequate to prepare candidates for ministry in the world because it took candidates into a quasi-monastic, all-male environment with a theological formation that varied in quality from the ordinary to the very bad. As we shall see, this problem was compounded by the modernist condemnation that drove the best, most creative minds in Catholicism out of seminaries and theological formation and sometimes right out of the church.

Pius X came to Rome as an experienced diocesan administrator, and he found the Roman Curia in disarray. Designed to govern both the church and the Papal States, there had been desultory attempts to reform the central administration, but by 1900 the whole structure was a mess of conflicting, crisscrossing, and incompatible responsibilities, rights, and vested interests. In 1907 reform of the curia was entrusted to a committee of cardinals under the close supervision of the pope. What was achieved was a compromise, a rejigging rather than a reform. Administration was more clearly separated from judicial functions, which were now handed over to three tribunals that administered justice in both the external and the internal forums. Administration was entrusted to eleven congregations (what in English we would call "departments") and five offices and secretariats. But little had really changed. Parochial Italian bureaucrats lacking pastoral experience were still in place. All that was achieved was a further centralization of power in Rome.

Perhaps the most significant change was that the Roman Inquisition now became the Supreme Sacred Congregation of the Holy Office, "supreme" because the pope was now its prefect. Its tasks remained "the defence of the doctrine of the faith and morals, processes against heresy, as well as other offenses that created a suspicion of heresy . . . solicitation *ad turpia* [that is, soliciting sexual favors] by a priest in confession, divination, witchcraft, casting spells . . . and all matters pertaining to indulgences."[2] When the Code of Canon Law was later published, all discernment of truth or error in the church was handed over to the Holy Office. This was a radical centralizing of decision making. Up until the nineteenth and twentieth centuries, the papacy was seen by the church as "a doctrinal court of final appeal," that is, you appealed to Rome for a decision on theology and doctrine only when all other processes had been exhausted. From the early twentieth century, the papacy became, as theologian Richard R. Gaillardetz says, "the chief expositor and arbiter of doctrinal orthodoxy."[3] In other words, this bureaucratic body replaced the traditional role of bishops, theologians, and the belief of the faithful in deciding what was genuine Catholic theology and belief. Power to decide truth and error was completely centralized in Rome. This radical reduction of theological pluralism and minority opinion is a complete distortion of the traditional way, whereby the church discerns its belief. With the Holy Office, the Vatican had introduced a form of thought control that limited the theological diversity that had always been a characteristic of Catholicism.

The pope also began the process of the codification of canon law and adaptation of church law to the decrees of Vatican I and its concept of absolute power. Reaching back to earliest Christian times, the corpus of church law was vast. Several attempts to codify these laws and decrees had been made by individuals, of which the most important was that of John Gratian around 1140. His *Decretum Gratianum*, an enormous collection of some four thousand canonical rulings, remained the definitive text until the early twentieth century. Despite Gratian, church law remained an inaccessible, confused jumble, except to experts. To simplify this Pius X established a commission of cardinals and lawyers to compile a code along the lines of Napoleon's legal code. Monsignor (later Cardinal) Pietro Gasparri was appointed secretary of the commission and together with a committee set about the task of codification, which was not completed until 1917. Parts of the code were issued at various times, such as the decree *Ne temere* (August 2, 1907), which required Catholics to marry before an authorized priest and two witnesses and declared *invalid* any marriage contracted by a Catholic outside the Catholic Church. This again was an arbitrary restriction of the freedom of Catholics.

What the Holy Office, the Code of Canon Law, and administrative changes in the Vatican achieved was an ultracentralizing of the church. Here was the papacy seizing more and more direct authority in the internal life of Catholicism. Pius X focused power in the church in a way that had never been attempted before and was completely out of synchronicity with previous tradition. What had begun at Vatican I was now bearing fruit, and "the absolute fullness of supreme power" was becoming reality. There was a real sense that in the years after 1870, the curia was shifting from being the court of an absolute monarch to the bureaucracy of an ecclesiastical dictator. In the letter *Vehementer nos* (February 11, 1906), Pius X projected an image of the church as "an *unequal* [emphasis added] society, that is, a society comprising two categories of persons, the Pastors and the flock, those who occupy a rank in . . . the hierarchy and the multitude of the faithful. . . . [T]he one duty of the multitude is to allow themselves to be led, and, like a docile flock, to follow the Pastors." Centralized microcontrol was reinforced by the Italianization of the curia. Italians always vastly outnumbered non-Italians. But perhaps more important was the way in which the whole place worked; its processes, procedures, and attitudes were entirely Italianate and culturally Latin. Being a *straniero* (foreigner)

put you at a distinct disadvantage. And the most foreign of all for-
eigners were the "Anglo-Saxons," which pretty much meant the
entire English-speaking world. Roman parochialism increased an
inward-looking approach, and Italian curalists were convinced they
had the uniquely right attitudes and values to govern Catholicism.
It was a completely incestuous world.

If Leo XIII's papacy was a cautious opening to contemporary developments in cultural and intellectual life, Pius X's was a wholesale
rejection of modernity. Roger Aubert says that the pope "instinctively mistrusted progressive endeavours."[4] While he was genuinely
open to the pastoral renewal of the church, Pius X's intellectual nar-
rowness closed off a theological response to modern culture. This
led to a stunted theology that divorced official Catholicism from
contemporary cultural currents, setting up a separation between
church and world that was toxic for believers.

An example of his complete insensitivity to the modern world
and to other Christians was the encyclical *Editae saepe* (May 29,
1910) on Saint Charles Borromeo, bishop of Milan who died in
1584. Drafted by reactionary Spanish cardinal Vives y Tuto and
Monsignor Umberto Benigni, the encyclical was utterly insulting
to Protestants, who were described as "proud and rebellious" and
"enemies of the cross of Christ." Breaking with the papacy, "they
pandered to the whims of the dissolute princes and people." They
called "themselves reformers. . . . In reality they were corrupters."
In typical fashion, the Vatican had not thought about the effect of
the encyclical on anyone outside ecclesiastical Rome. It caused such
offense that a formal apology had to be issued to the Prussian ambassador, and Pius X was substantially forced to withdraw it completely. He was equally unsympathetic to the Orthodox Church and
was unyielding on the question of cultural adaptation in the missionary work of Catholicism in the developing world. The church
remained tied to the colonial powers and to a European style of
faith that was imposed on the new churches. It was the syllabus all
over again, and it came to a head in the so-called modernist crisis.

THEOLOGICAL MODERNISM, AS distinct from the *very* different artistic movement of the same name, was a phenomenon entirely invented by Pius X and the Holy Office. It was the papal rejection of the attempt of theologians and philosophers, both lay and clerical, from France, Germany, Italy, and England, who called for freedom of inquiry in order to articulate Catholic faith within the context of modern culture. These thinkers applied literary and critical methods to the Bible and historical studies and tried to explain belief in terms of contemporary philosophy; they firmly believed that Catholicism was compatible with modern democratic politics and religious pluralism. They were also convinced that the neoscholastic theology and philosophy taught in the Roman ecclesiastical universities and in seminaries worldwide—which had little to do with the genuine thought of Aquinas—were totally insufficient to confront the philosophical questions of the day articulated by thinkers like Schopenhauer, Nietzsche, Bergson, Hegel, Spencer, and Darwin. Neoscholasticism was an aridly rationalistic theology and largely ignored the deeper spiritual, more dynamic, personal aspects of faith. Modernism, in contrast, tried to take these more mystic aspects of belief seriously. More an orientation or tendency than a movement as such, the modernists realized that a new approach to faith was needed, one derived not from church dogma but from experience of life itself. Like Döllinger and Acton thirty years before, they argued that modern scholarship needed freedom from church authority.

Here I am focusing particularly on several of the major modernists because they are forerunners and precursors of Vatican II and the contemporary church. If the papacy had listened to them instead of rejecting what they had to say, Catholicism might well be in a better position today.

In Germany modernism was called "reform Catholicism." It gave expression to a renewed energy in the German church, and theologians emphasized dialogue with the world rather than a rejection of it. Catholics, they said, needed to break out of a ghetto mentality. One of the most important of them was Herman Schell. He wanted an "openness and intellectual honesty on the part of

Catholics and . . . the training of a mature and responsible laity."
He challenged both the church "and his fellow German Catholics
to engage themselves energetically in the social and political fab-
ric of their country." He developed a theological rationale for that
engagement. Catholics, he said, should not be "mental eunuchs."[5]
Schell's writing is now recognized as fundamental to modern theology and Vatican II, but his work was placed by the Holy Office on
the *Index of Forbidden Books.*

In France the influence of German Protestant biblical scholarship began to have a real impact in the 1890s, especially on better-
educated clergy. Prominent among biblical scholars was Dominican
Marie-Joseph Lagrange, who founded the École Biblique in 1890
in Jerusalem, the first Catholic institution devoted to biblical
study and archaeological research. In 1892 he established the still-
published *Revue Biblique*. Lagrange's parallel in church history was
Monsignor Louis Duchesne, who applied critical methods to early
church history, and his edition of the *Liber pontificalis* (biographies
of the early popes) is still the standard. From 1895 until 1922 he
was the director of the École Française in Rome. His important
three-volume *Early History of the Christian Church* was considered
"semimodernist" and placed on the *Index* in 1912 by the Holy Office after it was translated into Italian.

The epicenter of the modernist crisis in France was biblical
scholar, writer, and priest Alfred Loisy. A talented writer with a critical intelligence, he argued that the Bible should be interpreted like
any historical book. He questioned the traditional literalist interpretation of the Bible, especially the Pentateuch (Genesis, Exodus,
Leviticus, Numbers, and Deuteronomy). He also debated questions
concerning biblical inspiration (that is, God's role in the composition of scripture) and biblical inerrancy (that is, the historical truth
or otherwise of biblical facts and events), while also focusing critically on the life and miracles of Jesus. Loisy argued that the Bible
should be studied like any literary work and that scholars, rather
than the church's teaching authority, should be the final interpret-
ers of the text. More populist and less cautious than scholars like
Lagrange, Loisy's 1902 book, *L'Évangile et l'église* (*The Gospel and*

the Church), argued that Jesus announced a dynamic kingdom of God, but what resulted was an institutional church. His 1903 answer to his critics was a more radical book, *Autour d'un petit livre* (*About a Little Book*). He argues that all human expressions of truth are relative to their historical contexts, that revelation is our consciousness of our relationship with God, and that church dogma is a way of expressing the inexpressible in human words that become poetic symbols of what is beyond understanding. "Though the dogmas may be Divine in origin and substance," Loisy says, "they are human in structure and composition."[6] While some clergy and a few bishops had sympathy with his views, any suggestion of doctrinal development or historical change in church structure and teaching was treated with paranoid suspicion by Rome. The Holy Office placed his books on the *Index* in 1903, and he was excommunicated in 1908. Loisy was probably the only scholar who comes near to fulfilling Pius X's definition of a "modernist."

The rest of those who suffered from the modernist reaction were genuine Catholics trying to take a creative approach to theology and its relationship to culture. Priest Henri Bremond, a spiritual writer, historian, stylist, and member of the Académie Française, used literature and psychology to describe religious experience. He also spread Newman's notion of development of doctrine in France. Newman had argued that the church's understanding of its faith was a dynamic and progressive thing. It only gradually teased out and brought to consciousness the inner meaning of its beliefs. So, for Newman, doctrine was not static and propositional but involved a developing and evolving understanding of what it believed. Related to this, French layman Maurice Blondel argued for the need to develop an apologetic, by which he meant the articulation of a humane and reasonable basis for belief. Blondel argued that on the deepest level, we are always searching for and seeking something that is indispensable for meaning in life but that is, at the same time, profoundly inaccessible.

But these more dynamic approaches to belief led to a counter-reaction. "With every day that passes," Blondel commented, "the conflict between tendencies which set Catholic against Catholic in every order—social, political, philosophical—is revealed as sharper and more general. . . . [T]here are now two quite incompatible 'Catholic mentalities,' particularly in France."[7] But not just in France.

In Italy Catholics have always had to struggle to disentangle themselves from ecclesiastical power structures and shift the emphasis to the church as community. Catholic intellectual life stagnated in the second half of the nineteenth century and began to revive only in the latter part of Leo XIII's papacy. The aim of more liberal Italian Catholics was to deepen the religious culture and education of the average Catholic; their approach was more pastoral than rationalist, with a strong sociopolitical emphasis. All of the Italian modernists had a deep interest in ways of helping people grow in faith rather than the academic and philosophical approach favored by the French. An example of this is church historian Ernesto Buonaiuti. His interests were historical and theological, and he focused on the evolution of doctrine and the early church. Born in Rome and ordained priest there, Buonaiuti tried to get beyond a religion of external, servile discipline and develop a transformation of the spirit to get in touch with the unconscious forces of transcendence within us. There is a real sense in which he was using the categories of modern psychology, and his work has Jungian overtones.

The international nature of the modernist movement is well illustrated by Baron Friedrich von Hügel. Son of an Austrian botanist, traveler (who had visited northern India and Australia in the 1830s), and diplomat and a Scottish mother, he was born in Florence in 1852, but he lived most of his life in London, becoming a British subject in 1914. Hügel always emphasized that scholarship must be rooted in a sincere attachment to Catholicism and a strong sense of history. His major work, *The Mystical Element of Religion* (1908), argued that a deep spirituality and a strong faith commitment must underpin any critical approach to Catholicism. "I try to do everything I can," he says, "to make my old church intellectually as acceptable as possible, not because reason is the most important thing in religion, but rather because my church already possesses all the knowledge necessary to guide spiritual life." He also wants to bring "wounded and embittered Catholics who have fallen, or about to fall away from the faith," back to the church.[8]

If Hügel was the international contact person of modernism, its major prophet was Anglo-Irishman George Tyrrell. Born in Ireland in 1861 and a convert to Catholicism, he joined the English Jesuits. Very much in tune with contemporary attitudes, he was in contact with and influenced many leading scientists, intellectuals, and members of the British government. His interests focused particularly on fundamental theology, biblical studies, apologetics, and religious experience, and he was a spiritual writer of depth and sensitivity. By 1900 he was well known as a writer and was critical of the static notion of doctrine held by the neoscholastics, particularly their identification of a medieval expression of faith as normative. He was critical of a kind of historicism that implies that the church and its teaching do not change and develop. He believed that faith and doctrine needed to be approached through spirituality and mysticism and that Christ came not as a teacher of orthodoxy but as someone who brought divine love to the earth. Thus, he believed that the church should not be a despotic system of imposed truth, but a place where people discovered the fullness of God's life. It is precisely in this sense that he was a direct precursor of Vatican II. Tyrrell was warm, impulsive, boyish, highly intelligent, and questioning by nature, but he could be difficult and sarcastic to people he felt were ignorant. This made his life as a Jesuit difficult. He suffered from Bright's disease (nephritis, an inflammation of the kidneys) and died at the early age of forty-eight.

While Tyrrell was generally supported by the English Jesuits, the then general of the order, Luís Martín, a sex-obsessed, self-tortured man, totally lacking any understanding of the world outside his own extremely narrow Spanish background, was already suspicious of the English Jesuits and unsympathetic to Tyrrell.[9] Martín was convinced that Tyrrell was imbued with "Americanism" and "liberalism." Another player in this tangled Roman web was Merry del Val (before he became secretary of state), who was convinced that English Catholics who accepted liberalism needed to be confronted. He hatched a plot to have the English bishops issue a pastoral letter attacking liberalism, but because he felt they were too "soft," the pastoral would be written in Rome and imposed on them. Discussing the causes of the "problems" in England, Merry del Val mentioned "the evil effects upon Catholics of living in a Protestant and rationalistic atmosphere where almost in spite of themselves they must gradually assimilate so much that is wrong."[10]

With views like these dominating the Roman scene, there was little hope for Tyrrell, whose aim was to try to develop an apologetic that helped make sense of Catholicism for Protestants and skeptics in England. In 1903 Tyrrell produced *The Church and the Future*, a radical book that he published anonymously, in which he criticizes the papacy's preoccupation with power. He is particularly critical of the theologians of the Roman universities, whom he describes, somewhat snobbishly, as "men mostly from the uneducated classes" who have been trained "almost exclusively on [a] windy metaphysical diet with little or no corrective in the way of positive knowledge, scientific or historic." The papacy depended on these theologians, and they put forward their conclusions "as the oracles of God," constituting "one of the worst intellectual tyrannies the world has even known." All this led to a situation in which the papacy and curia "arrogate to themselves the functions of the Holy Spirit working through the entire organism of the Church." Speaking of church government, he says that "there is no convincing evidence in the Gospels for the idea that Christ exercised and conferred upon his Church a juridical power over souls. . . . The direct heir of Christ's Spirit is the whole multitude of the faithful." He emphasizes the *sensus fidelium*, which he describes as "informal, unofficial *Ecclesia docens*" (teaching church).[11] These were not ideas that would have endeared him to either Martín or the Roman authorities, and by early 1905, after his authorship became known, there were discussions about expelling Tyrrell from the Jesuits.

Tyrrell's conflict with the Jesuit general came to a head in January 1906, and he was dismissed from the society. Tyrrell accepted that conflict was inevitable, and he assured Martín that he held no "personal rancour or resentment." He blamed "a collision of systems and tendencies rather than persons."[12] Tyrrell could no longer act as a priest, but he could receive Communion. The person who stood by Tyrrell was his friend Maude Dominica Petre (pronounced "Peter"). She took him into her home in Storrington in West Sussex and financially supported him. As a young woman, Petre went to Rome to study the philosophy of Aquinas. This led one of her aunts to tell a friend, "Maude has gone to Rome to study for the priesthood!" There is a real sense in which Petre's whole life was a spiritual and theological journey, and her thought reflected this. Nowadays she is seen as being as important as Tyrrell and von Hügel, and many of her theological views foreshadow Vatican II. She befriended Tyrrell until his death and remained his champion all her life.

IN EARLY 1907 there was a sense of crisis among the most reactionary cardinals in the Vatican, including Merry del Val. The concern was with thinkers who Pius X said "profess and disseminate in a subtle form monstrous errors" that constitute "the compendium and poison of all the heresies."[13] So the conviction grew in Rome that the time for action had come.

On July 3, 1907, the Roman Inquisition issued a list of sixty-five "errors of the modernists" in the decree *Lamentabili sane exitu* (With sad results). *Lamentabili* claimed that modernism was "a synthesis of all heresies," but some of the decree's propositions were so badly formulated that it's clear that the Roman assessors had no idea what they were talking about. This was followed on September 8, 1907, by Pius X's encyclical *Pascendi Dominici gregis* (Feeding the Lord's flock). What the pope claimed to have discovered were "enemies of the cross of Christ . . . who are striving by arts, entirely new and full of subtlety, to destroy the vital energy of the Church, and, if they can, to overthrow utterly Christ's kingdom itself." But these villains are not the church's external enemies but "in her very bosom and heart." These Catholic quislings were dubbed "modernists," and the pope ascribes to them the worst possible motives. "None," he says, "is more skillful, none more astute than they, in the employment of a thousand noxious arts"; they are deceivers who rely on a "false conscience"; they are "arrogant," "proud," and "obstinate," and they "disdain all authority." Oddly, though, he says they possess "a reputation for the strictest morality." They "put themselves forward as reformers of the church," but they are, in fact, "thoroughly imbued with the poisonous doctrines taught by the enemies of the church." In order to tackle them, he will "bring their teachings together" and "prescribe remedies for averting their errors."[14] But all that *Pascendi* does is construct and demolish a straw man, a caricature. It is confusing, repetitive, and hectoring. While it was signed by Pius X, Joseph Lemius was the draftsman of the theological section, and in it he achieves a synthesis of modernist theology that the modernists themselves never attained. Catalan cardinal José Vives y Tuto prepared the disciplinary section.[15] His nickname in the Vatican was *Vives Fa Tuto* (Vives Does Everything). A prolific neoscholastic textbook writer and compulsive worker with no comprehension of contemporary culture, he had a number of nervous breakdowns that resulted in eventual madness.

Pascendi claims that the modernists believe that "religious consciousness is . . . the universal rule, to be put on an equal footing with revelation, and to which all must submit, even the supreme authority of the church." Essentially, this is claiming that Catholicism is placed on the same level as other faiths and is not the only true revelation of God. Turning to dogma, *Pascendi* says that the modernists argue that since all reality is evolving, dogmas don't "express absolute truth." They are "symbols . . . images of truth . . . and are . . . liable to change." As a consequence, "the way is open to the intrinsic evolution of dogma." This, *Pascendi* says, "ruins and destroys all religion." On the Bible the modernists are said to claim that God is not really the author of scripture and that divine inspiration does not extend to the whole Bible. The job of the biblical scholar, *Pascendi* claims, is to interpret the text just like any human document. In the end, Lemius has, as Gabriel Daly says, "contrived a synthesis of contemporary theological trends which would satisfy the scholastic mind."[16]

The final disciplinary section of *Pascendi* constitutes an extraordinary personal attack on modernists: "It is pride which fills Modernists with confidence in themselves and leads them to hold themselves up as the rule for all, pride which puffs them up with that vainglory which allows them to regard themselves as the sole possessors of knowledge, and makes them say, inflated with presumption, *We are not as the rest of men*, and . . . leads them to embrace all kinds of the most absurd novelties; it is pride . . . [that] begets their absolute want of respect for authority, not excepting the supreme authority."

The last part of the document deals with the "remedies" needed to discipline those suspected of modernism. *Pascendi* says that scholastic philosophy must be studied in seminaries and Catholic universities as a basis for theology, and anyone not subscribing to it will be automatically suspect. Suspected modernist staff in seminaries and universities must be "excluded without compunction" and, if already employed, sacked forthwith. Even those who "favor" modernism by showing "a love of novelty in history, archaeology, biblical exegesis, and . . . those who neglect the sacred sciences or appear to prefer to them the profane," or who extol "the Modernists or [excuse] their culpable conduct, by criticising scholasticism, the Holy Father, or by refusing obedience to ecclesiastical authority in any of its depositaries," are also to be fired. No one is to be ordained who "loves novelty" or who is "proud and obstinate," and no one is to receive a doctorate from a Catholic university if they have not done scholastic philosophy. Clerics must avoid attending secular universities. *Pascendi* instructs bishops that they are to drive "pernicious books" out of their dioceses and to make sure that Catholic booksellers don't "put on sale unsound books." To nip the problem in the bud, bishops are also told to make sure that "bad books" are not even published. Official censors are to be appointed in each diocese to check all religious books by Catholics before publication, and all Catholics are required to get a *Nihil obstat* (Nothing stands in the way) and *Imprimatur* (Let it be printed) before publication. Bishops are to set up "councils of vigilance" to "watch most carefully for every trace and sign of Modernism both in publications and in teaching."

As a further measure of enforcement, an antimodernist oath was imposed by the Motu proprio *Sacrorum antistites* (September 1,

1910) on all ordinands, as well as when priests and bishops assumed any pastoral office. (A Motu proprio is an official document like a bull or encyclical.) They had to swear to the *Latin* text of the oath so that any form of equivocation in another language was impossible. The person had to swear that they agreed "to all the condemnations, declarations and prescriptions contained in the Encyclical Letter *Pascendi* and the Decree *Lamentabili* and especially in the matter of what is called the history of dogma."[17] This oath remained in force until 1966.

SO WHERE DID all this leave the modernists? The vast majority of modernist scholars accepted the encyclical because they didn't see anything of their own views condemned in *Pascendi*. Loisy was probably the only person whose opinions *Pascendi* even remotely described, and he was already on his way out of the church. Perhaps the most telling criticism was that *Pascendi* was concerned only with condemnations and didn't address the deeper underlying causes that stimulated modernism in the first place. There were also criticisms of the very oppressive practical measures *Pascendi* placed on academic freedom and research, particularly from the German-speaking church, which correctly saw these measures as an assertion of Roman power. The problem was, however, that *Pascendi* was so vague that it could trap any scholar, as subsequent events were to show.

One man stands out as a victim of *Pascendi*: George Tyrrell. He certainly set himself up for trouble because of his outspokenness. Less than a month after the encyclical was published, he wrote in *The Times* of London that *Pascendi* "tries to show the Modernist that he is no Catholic; it mostly succeeds in showing he is no scholastic." Tyrrell rightly diagnosed that the Roman obsession with power and obedience was the real problem facing the church. In December 1907 he told a French colleague, "The root error was 1870 [Vatican I]. Condense all power in the hands of one man, who may be a fool or a knave, and what can you expect?"[18] Tyrrell understood that papal power was the root cause of the church's troubles, especially when this power was in the hands of narrow-minded, fearful men of circumscribed experience like Pius X and Merry del Val.

Already suspended from the priesthood as a result of his expulsion from the Jesuits, on October 22, 1907, Tyrrell was informed that he had been excommunicated by the bishop of Southwark, the Gibraltar-born Peter Amigo, for his criticism of *Pascendi* in *The Times*. Then in early 1908 Belgian cardinal Désiré-Joseph Mercier of Malines issued a Lenten Pastoral Letter on *Pascendi*, claiming that the person most "deeply imbued" with the spirit of modernism was "the English priest Tyrrell." This, Mercier informed his readers, didn't surprise him, because "Tyrrell is a convert whose early education was Protestant."[19] In a devastating response to Mercier in his 1908 book, *Medievalism*, Tyrrell systematically takes apart the Lenten Pastoral Letter's accusations against him. The cardinal had claimed that he had learned "immanentism" from Kant and Protestantism. Tyrrell simply says: "I learned the 'method of immanentism' not from Kant . . . nor from Protestantism, but solely from the Spiritual Exercises of the founder of the Jesuits." He points out that Saint Ignatius Loyola himself had "derived it [his spirituality] from the great masters of that mystical method which the encyclical *Pascendi* has swept away in the confusion of its onslaught against modernism."[20]

Tyrrell died on the morning of July 15, 1909, in the company of Maude Petre, Hügel, Henri Bremond, and several others. Almost immediately, Amigo informed Petre that a Catholic burial was out of the question unless Tyrrell had recanted. This was an act of complete bastardy, and Tyrrell was eventually buried in the Anglican cemetery at Storrington in Sussex. Bremond read prayers and gave a eulogy. Within three days Bremond himself was suspended by Amigo, who was just a weak patsy acting on the orders of Rome. Nowadays Tyrrell has been vindicated: As Gabriel Daly says, he was "a stimulating, pastorally inspired and inspiring theologian . . . whose only fault was to have anticipated the reforms of Vatican II."[21]

The Tyrrell case was just the beginning of the Roman reaction. What followed was one of the most disgraceful affairs in modern papal history: the antimodernist "crusade." Despite the fact that modernism was very much in decline after 1907, concern among reactionary Catholics grew about an imagined vast modernist conspiracy encircling Catholicism. *Pascendi* let loose the forces of integralist reaction, where the word *integralism*, from the French *intégrisme*, describes the position of those who claimed to defend Catholicism in its full integrity. The word also refers to those who rejected modern democracy and contemporary culture and any attempt by Catholics to be reconciled with secular reality. Convinced that modernist errors still abounded, the integralists began the hunt for "semimodernists," or those with "modernistic tendencies" or the "modernist mentality." In the end, anyone who disagreed with the Roman line was a modernist.

The integralists were ignorant of biblical and critical historical studies. They lacked any notion of historical development of doctrine in the sense in which Newman, for instance, conceived the idea. They were caught up in a totalistic vision in which profound mysteries of faith can be expressed only within the neoscholastic tradition that they saw as beyond the realities of history. Therefore, those who espoused any form of historical critique of these dogmas were, by definition, heretical and modernist. Without scruple, the integralists used anonymous denunciation and underhanded methods, and they didn't hesitate to spy on scholars of complete integrity, accusing them of being "semimodernists." There was also a strong vein of anti-Semitism among integralists.

Exactly what role did the papacy play in the reaction against modernism? Pius X supported integralism to the hilt. It is clear that he believed the church was under siege, and he became neurotically anxious about an insidious kind of omnipresent semimodernism. The attack on perceived "deviant" theologians reached its peak in 1912–1913. Orthodoxy was identified with obedience and loyalty to the papacy. On May 27, 1914, the pope told a group of newly appointed cardinals that "devout sons of the pope are only those who obey his words and follow him in everything." David G. Schultenover is right when he says that Italian clerics like Pius X were dominated by a "Mediterranean mentality," by which he means they were so immersed in their own closed Latin world that they had no ability to comprehend what was happening in the rest of the Western world. They were culturally blocked by their projection of their own social and familial social structures onto the broader church. This Mediterranean mentality has been a toxic influence in the church for centuries. The result is a breakdown of understanding between two very different perceptions of our place in the world. "To the Mediterranean ecclesiastical mind," Schultenover says, "requirements of group loyalty militate against individuality and freedom of thought and expression."[22] For Anglo-Saxons and northern Europeans, precisely the opposite is true. Here the emphasis is on individual conscience and freedom of thought. For Pius X, this was not only anathema; it was literally incomprehensible. His attitude was that anything was justified to protect the interests of the family, that is, the church.

This meant that there were many integralist heresy hunters during this papacy. Clerics on the up-and-up were only too happy to accuse their colleagues of "semimodernism" if it helped their career prospects. The most infamous of them was Monsignor Umberto Benigni. What is interesting about him is that he was the first person in papal employment to understand the importance of the media. From early in his priestly career until his death, he edited newspapers and news sheets, and in 1907 he set up a kind of news bulletin, *Corrispondenza di Roma*, which was sent to supporters and sympathetic journalists and in which he leaked information about those suspected of "heresy." In 1912 he began a press bureau, International Agency Roma. He was convinced that all Italy's and Catholicism's troubles could be traced to anticlericalism, socialism, liberalism, Freemasonry, and eventually to the Jews; he was a virulent anti-Semite. Trained as a church historian, he rose rapidly in the curia, becoming secretary of the Congregation for Extraordinary Ecclesiastical Affairs (the papal foreign office) in 1906. Benigni worked there until 1914, when he was pushed aside by the new pope, Benedict XIV.

Benigni divided everyone into two classes, clericals and anticlericals. He was opposed to all forms of Christian democracy, Catholic liberalism, socialism, and anything remotely suggestive of modernism. "There is now only one choice," he said, "God and the revolver!"[23] Historian Émile Poulat calls him *intraitable* (impossible or intractable). He was a "culture warrior" through and through. His in-group, the *Sodalitium Pianum* (the Sodality of Pope Pius V), remained small, never more than fifty Europe-wide. The *Sodalitium* was known by the code name *La Sapinière* (meaning "fir wood" or "plantation"), and his work was well known to Pius X and partly financed by him. His circle used a set of 726 code words and was obsessed with secrecy. Material passed on to journalists could never be sourced back to him.

We know about the secrecy because a cache of the *Sodalitium*'s secret documents was discovered in an almost John Le Carré twist in the Netherlands by German military intelligence during the First World War and was eventually published. Essentially, what the *Sodalitium* did was to seek out and hunt down scholars, bishops, and priests in any way suspected of modernism, semimodernism, or being too soft toward those under suspicion. The word *scholar* was almost synonymous with modernism. It "spreads and organizes," according to the then reactionary Paris newspaper *La Croix*, "by means of the malice of some and by the naiveté and carelessness of others."[24] Once someone was targeted, the clandestine network would undermine their reputation and plant articles in right-wing magazines and periodicals, denouncing them and calling for their firing. This even included cardinals: Andrea Ferrari of Milan, Pietro Maffi of Pisa, Léon-Adolfe Amete of Paris, and Anton Fischer of Cologne were all suspected of being soft on modernism. The target was "thought crime," and an innocuous comment, a mild criticism, a word out of place could lead to trouble.

The Ferrari case is interesting. As a truly pastoral bishop—he has now been beatified—his Milan seminary was criticized by a Venice newspaper as being a nest of modernists. Ferrari defended the seminary and addressed the students. An integralist student on the make sent a copy of Ferrari's comments to Rome, and Pius X reprimanded the cardinal and placed the seminary under an apostolic visitor. It was a clerical tempest in a teacup, but if a distinguished and saintly cardinal could get into this much trouble on the say-so of an unordained, on-the-make student, you can imagine the fear it infused in ordinary mortals.

Benigni ended up an ecclesiastical outcast and a fascist spy. He died in 1934. He had done enormous damage, but he would not have been able to do it without Pius X.

So who were these "semimodernists" that Benigni and his ilk pursued? The answer is perfectly orthodox people like Marie-Joseph Lagrange. Described as a dangerous radical, he was accused of using the historico-critical method of biblical analysis and of being an undercover "reformer," that is, a modernist. Seminarians were forbidden to read his books, and he was briefly removed from the editorship of *Revue Biblique*, forbidden to publish, and exiled for a period from the École Biblique. He was never formally condemned and remained profoundly Catholic, but his orthodoxy remained under a cloud for years. Another who suffered a similar fate was historian Louis Duchesne. A man with a caustic tongue, the story is told that he was in Egypt in late 1912 when he met a friend from Paris. Asked what he was doing in Egypt, he replied, "I'm waiting for the death of King Herod!" (that is, Pius X). Pierre Batiffol, a theologian and historian trained by Duchesne, was very much on the conservative side of those who applied historical scholarship to theology. He was highly critical of Loisy and was a disciple of Newman. But the integralists saw anyone who advocated a historical treatment of dogma as a modernist, and in July 1907 his book on the Eucharist and the real presence was put on the *Index* by the Holy Office. Henri Bremond was also in trouble. His 1912 book, *Sainte Chantal, 1572–1641*, was placed on the *Index* because Bremond's treatment of Saint Jeanne de Chantal as a spiritual theologian was accused of placing too much emphasis on subjective religious experience.

In Italy the most prominent victim was historian Ernesto Buonaiuti. A seminary classmate of Angelo Roncalli (later Pope John XXIII), Buonaiuti assisted Roncalli at his first Mass in 1904. He taught history at the Seminario Romano but was dismissed from his teaching post after a visit to Alfred Loisy in 1906, suspended from the priesthood in 1916, and excommunicated in 1921. He was again excommunicated in 1925, and this remained in force until he died in 1946. Nevertheless, he remained a faithful Catholic until his death, and John XXIII said that he prayed "for Ernesto every evening and every night. Perhaps the last word has not been said."[25] Like Tyrrell, Buonaiuti is now seen as a prophet of Vatican II.

Other victims of the purge were Christian democracy movements in Italy and France that were denounced as "social modernism." Italian priest Romolo Murri, who promoted the idea of Christian democracy in the latter part of Leo XIII's papacy, began to apply the principles of the Gospel to secular and political life, including issues like just wages, reasonable housing, and the right to strike. In Italy with the 1874 *Non expedit* decree still in operation, Catholics, particularly priests, were expected to focus on the fate of the papacy rather than on sociopolitical issues. Nevertheless, Murri and his disciple Luigi Sturzo argued that Christian democracy aimed, as Sturzo put it, "to form in the people, together with their religious conscience, a social conscience."[26] Murri founded the *Lega Democratica Nazionale* (National Democratic League). It was independent of the hierarchy and is the precursor of Sturzo's *Partito Popolare Italiano* (Italian Popular Party), which eventually became in 1945 the Christian Democratic Party, which governed Italy for much of the postwar period. A thoroughgoing democrat, in 1902 Murri called for church reform and for Catholicism to return to Gospel values and abandon "warmed-over semi-heathen customs, the juridic concepts derived from Roman law, the decadent monastic institutions that are incapable of rejuvenation, and the abstract categories that kill like the letter of the law."[27] He became increasingly radical, which led quickly to ecclesiastical penalties. He was suspended in 1907 and excommunicated in 1909. In a deplorable comment, Pius X said that Murri "is better off out of the church."[28] That same year Murri was elected to the Italian Chamber of Deputies.

A parallel democratic development was occurring in France. Here *Le Sillon* (the Furrow), founded and led by Marc Sangnier, a committed Catholic and sincere Republican, took the lead in the development of a democratic Christian approach to politics. *Le Sillon*'s aim was to prepare Catholics to participate fully in the politico-economic life of the republic, especially after the 1905 separation of church and state. Many young people and priests were attracted to *Le Sillon*, which at one stage had almost a half-million members. The movement maintained independence of the hierarchy and tried to create a broad-based political movement, including Protestants and non-Christians, which would evolve into a mainstream political party. This was a recipe for confrontation with the hierarchy and Pius X. In his letter *Notre charge apostolique* (1910) to the French bishops, Pius X claimed that he "loved the leaders" of *Le Sillon*, but that "they were not adequately equipped with historical knowledge, sound philosophy, and solid theology to tackle without danger the difficult social problems in which their work and their inclinations were involving them. They . . . [didn't] guard against the penetration of liberal and Protestant concepts on doctrine and obedience." The letter constantly uses the word *heterodox* to describe *Le Sillon* and predicts that "the end result of this developing promiscuousness . . . can only be a Democracy which will be neither Catholic, nor Protestant, nor Jewish. It will be a religion."[29] The letter is over the top to the point of absurdity. Sillonist influence continued right through until the fall of the Third Republic in 1940. A mass movement, it had had enormous influence.

THE FIRST WORLD War broke out on August 3, 1914. Pius X died seventeen days later, on August 20, 1914, not of a broken heart, as some have suggested, but of pneumonia. *The Oxford Dictionary of Popes* describes Pius X as "one of the most constructive reforming popes" and goes on to praise "his transparent goodness and humility."[30] Certainly, his encouragement of frequent Communion transformed Eucharistic spirituality, which, in turn, encouraged the start of the liturgical movement. However, in my view, this papacy was an absolute disaster. Pius X set a pattern that turned the church inward for another fifty years, and he was not interested in continuing Leo XIII's policy of building bridges with the wider world. The use of hard power within the church to stamp out even the most legitimate theological development showed that Pius X lacked any comprehension of what was actually at stake in the modernist crisis. In a cautious judgment, Roger Aubert says that in light of the merciless treatment of theologians and the fear of scholarship that was engendered among the clergy resulting from the antimodernist reaction, Pius X "must be assessed negatively. . . . Many men loyal to the church were mercilessly banned. . . . The gap between the church and modern culture widened. The solution of fundamental problems was postponed and . . . harm was done."[31]

His attempt to streamline the Roman Curia and the central administration of the church continued the centralizing tendencies that had begun under Pius IX and further enhanced the power of the pope. The codification of canon law that he began also exaggerated the centralizing tendencies of the modern papacy.

Perhaps the most damning assessment of Pius X came from Cardinal Pietro Gasparri, who from 1914 to 1931 was secretary of state. When Pius X's cause was introduced for beatification, Gasparri commented, "Pope Pius X approved, blessed, and encouraged a secret espionage association [the Benigni *Sodalitium*] outside and above the hierarchy, which spied on members of the hierarchy itself, even on their Eminences the Cardinals; in short, he approved, blessed and encouraged a sort of freemasonry in the Church, something unheard of in ecclesiastical history."[32]

That about sums it up.

5

"OBBEDIRE, OBEY"

THE CONCLAVE TO elect the next pope began on August 31, 1914, less than a month after the outbreak of the First World War. Europe had literally stumbled into war primarily because of the assassination of the Austrian archduke and heir to the Austrian throne, Franz Ferdinand, and his wife, Sophie, in Sarajevo by Serb terrorist Gavrilo Princip on June 28, 1914. An increasingly paranoid and aggressive Austrian government miscalculated the situation badly and failed to separate decisively their problems with nationalism in the Balkans from the general European-wide alliance system. No one seemed to perceive what was really happening as a rolling escalation of threats and counterthreats led to Austria declaring war on Bosnia, with Austria's ally Germany also declaring war. To protect Orthodox Serbs in Bosnia, Russia mobilized, and in response Germany declared war on Russia and thus on its ally France. Britain became involved because of Germany's invasion of neutral Belgium. By August 3, 1914, Europe had stumbled into a general war, and as the British foreign secretary, Sir Edward Grey, said, "The lamps are going out all over Europe; we shall not see them lit again in our lifetime."

With Pius X dying and preoccupied with the antimodernist crusade, Secretary of State Merry del Val, like many others in Europe, didn't realize the seriousness of the developing situation and the danger of escalation toward war. The Secretariat of State was poorly informed, and the papacy had lost its international leverage and soft-power influence under Pius X, so whatever the pope said or did would not have cut much ice with the great powers. In the face of the crisis, the Vatican seemed impotent. By the time the conclave met, the French and Germans in northern France were already locked into fruitless trench warfare, sealed by the Battle of the Marne in September 1914. Trench warfare was to last for the next four years. On the eastern front the Battle of Tannenberg in East Prussia had already occurred before the conclave met—it lasted from August 23 to 28—with fifty thousand casualties and an entire Russian army wiped out.

Fortunately for the cardinals, Italy was still neutral, but the war certainly provided the context for the election. There were fifty-seven electors. Six cardinals, including two Americans, William O'Connell of Boston and James Gibbons of Baltimore, couldn't get to Rome in time. The cardinals from the warring sides maintained their distance, and there was tension between Cardinals Desiré Mercier of Mechelen-Brussels and Felix von Hartmann of Cologne. Merry del Val quickly emerged as a great elector—the most influential cardinal—but at forty-eight he was too young to be elected himself. He pushed for a pope in the Pius X mold, but the feeling was that the international situation demanded a diplomat pope. Many also wanted to break with integralism, and two candidates emerged: Pietro Maffi, archbishop of Pisa, and Giacomo Della Chiesa, an experienced diplomat trained by Rampolla and for seven years archbishop of Bologna. His biographer John F. Pollard says Della Chiesa "was a front runner from the start" because he had "the best mix of the curial, diplomatic and pastoral experience required of a pope facing the horrors of a general European war."[1] Curial cardinals, loyal to Pius X, opposed Della Chiesa to the bitter end. Close to Rampolla, he had been exiled to Bologna after the diplomat-cardinal's fall and had been appointed cardinal himself just three months before the death of Pius X.

Elected on September 3, 1914, Della Chiesa chose the style Benedict XV, after Saint Benedict, patron saint of Europe. He had been born prematurely and was unusually short and physically frail; when sitting in ornate chairs, his feet often didn't touch the ground. He was calm and withdrawn, a cautious, matter-of-fact man who could be impatient and bad tempered. Pictures show him to have had a somewhat prissy appearance, leading many to think of him as a bureaucrat. While history has neglected him, nowadays he is emerging as a more important pope and his qualities as a statesman are being reassessed. His background in the Secretariat of State meant he had an appreciation of the persuasive soft-power role of the papacy, especially in the cause of peace.

Benedict begins the papal transition from the nineteenth to the twentieth centuries. He couldn't avoid confronting the modern world with the war raging around him. He gradually retreated from the integralism of the Sarto papacy and attempted to rein in the modernist heresy hunt. He recognized in his first encyclical, *Ad beatissimi* (November 1, 1914), that there is "room for divergent [theological] opinions in the absence of any authoritative intervention of the Apostolic See." He also said that Catholics can freely defend their views without their ideas being labeled with "the stigma of disloyalty to faith or discipline." His appointments also signified a shift away from hard-nosed integralism: Merry del Val was removed as secretary of state to a minor role, as were a number of the old guard, including Benigni, although his secret movement, *La Sapinière*, survived underground and, unknown to Benedict, continued hunting "modernists" until after the war. The new secretary of state was Cardinal Pietro Gasparri, secretary of the commission working on the codification of Canon Law. The son of a farmer, Gasparri was nicknamed *Il Contadino*, the "country bumpkin." He was short in stature, rotund, friendly with a genuine sense of humor, and politically shrewd. He had lectured on canon law at the *Institut Catholique* in Paris for twenty-eight years, so he was sympathetic to French interests. He also spent two years as apostolic delegate to Peru, Bolivia, and Ecuador, giving him much broader international experience than was generally the case in the Roman Curia at this time.

Benedict's encyclical *Ad beatissimi* was given a very cool reception by both warring sides. Reflecting on the causes of the war, he speaks of it in almost apocalyptic tones: "The end of civilization would seem to be at hand," he says. The main cause of the war, he said, was the abandonment of Christian principles, class warfare, liberal individualism, materialism, and anticlericalism. He asserts that egalitarian democracy, "race hatred," divisions within and between nations, "the burning envy of class against class," and "self-love" have all contributed to break down civilization. He is critical of the "proletariat and the workers," who are "inflamed with hatred and envy."

Given the war situation, Benedict XV decided that the papacy would maintain strict neutrality. He argued that Christ died for all, so the pope as Vicar of Christ must care for all beyond race and nationality. His position was further complicated by the fact that there were about 64 million Catholics in Germany and Austria-Hungary and about 124 million in France, the United Kingdom, and the British Empire, and he felt it was his duty to support Catholics on both sides. Both sides brought pressure to bear to get him to condemn the other, and both accused him of favoring the other. French Republicans like Georges Clemenceau and the French press often referred to him as the *Pape boche* (German pope), while the Germans called him the *Französischer Papst* (French pope). Certainly, the weight of evidence points to Benedict personally being strictly neutral and not favoring either side, although some have tried to argue that he was at heart pro-German.

While the pope personally remained strictly neutral, it is true that there was more sympathy among Vatican personnel and the Italian clergy for the Triple Alliance of Germany, Austria-Hungary, and Italy, later joined by the Ottoman Empire and Bulgaria—after 1914 the Central Powers—than for the Triple Entente of Britain and the empire, France, and Russia, later joined by Italy and the United States. This is entirely natural, as Austria-Hungary and Italy were Catholic countries and Germany was almost half Catholic, whereas Britain was seen by Italians as predominantly Protestant, the French government was overtly anticlerical, and Russia was Orthodox and oppressive of Catholics, especially in Poland. Also, Austria and Germany (represented by two ambassadors in the Vatican—one each for Prussia and Bavaria) had always maintained close contact with the Vatican. With the outbreak of war, Britain shrewdly appointed Sir Michael Howard as "envoy extraordinary" to the Holy See to influence the papacy and to get access to the information that flowed through the Vatican from the worldwide church.

Part of the papacy's powerlessness derived from the fact that it had no official status because of the failure to resolve the Roman Question and clarify the international position of the Holy See in relationship to the Kingdom of Italy. It existed in a kind of diplomatic limbo, and this became a key issue with the outbreak of the war. The question: What role could the papacy play as a nonstate actor? From 1870 onward, "the Holy See subsisted as a *sui generis* power that had the right to enter into diplomatic relations with individual states. . . . [T]he right was derived from its spiritual sovereignty." This meant that the pope's influence rested not on military power, "but on the moral prestige and religious authority of the papacy."[2] Thus, the pope's only option was persuasion with an emphasis on love and mercy, rather than force and authority. If people felt that soft power was weakness in a war situation, then Benedict was willing to accept that. Neither side had God "on board"; neither side was fighting a "just" war. Both sides accused the other of war crimes. The most the pope could do was to maintain neutrality so he could help victims of the war. That became the focus of his efforts. This neutrality was tested by German atrocities in Belgium and during the Armenian genocide, when one and a half million Christian Armenians (both Orthodox and Catholic) were slaughtered by the Ottoman Turks.

Benedict XV and Gasparri worked hard to bring the warring sides together. Their situation was made more complicated when, in an act of sheer opportunism, Italy entered the war. From 1881 Italy had been a member of the Triple Alliance but, unprepared for war, promised Austria benevolent neutrality. By early 1915 the conservative Italian prime minister, Antonio Salandra, was secretly negotiating with the British. He was fishing for the best deal he could get from either side to fulfill Italy's territorial ambitions. Salandra intensified covert negotiations with London, and this led to the secret Treaty of London (April 26, 1915), which committed Italy to entering the war. "Salandra . . . deceived [his] own cabinet, and none of the ministers and military leaders knew that these secret negotiations were proceeding at London." The actual text of the treaty was revealed only after the war. There was little enthusiasm for war in Italy, although the Salandra government used firebrands like protofascist Gabriele D'Annunzio to stir up nationalistic fervor. "After long years of national humiliation," D'Annunzio said, "God has been pleased to grant us proof of our privileged blood. . . . Blessed are those young men who hunger and thirst for glory, for they shall be filled."[3]

A key article in the Treaty of London was that the papacy be excluded from any peace conference after the war. "France, Great Britain and Russia shall support such opposition as Italy may make to any proposal . . . [to introduce] a representative of the Holy See in any peace negotiations or negotiations for the settlement of questions raised by the present war."[4] The Salandra government feared the internationalization of the Roman Question and the threat to the geographical integrity of Italy, with territory being handed back to the pope in recompense for the loss of the Papal States. Benedict and Gasparri found out about the London treaty provision eleven months after it was signed. They had strongly opposed Italy's entry into the war, which made their situation more isolated. The Central Powers' diplomatic representatives had to retreat from Rome to Lugarno in Switzerland, but lines of communication remained open. The Vatican's relationship with the state of Italy throughout this period remained tense; from Benedict's perspective, the Law of Guarantees guaranteed very little. The pope didn't even own Saint Peter's and the Vatican palaces and buildings; he just "enjoyed" them. The Italian government even attempted to call up clerical and lay Vatican staff for army service, including senior prelates, and many Italian priests served in the army.

Benedict was almost a pacifist, a very unpopular stance in wartime, and he never mentioned the just-war theory. Theologian Ronald G. Musto says that Benedict was "as close to an absolute pacifist as any pope. . . . [He] opposed war in any form and rejected the theory of the just war as historically outmoded." Benedict was very active in defending "the rights of prisoners, the wounded, and non-combatants, in organizing relief work, or arranging truces, or

reducing unnecessary violence." He protested a whole series of out-
rages: the German "rape" of Belgium, the use of poison gas, the
sinking of the *Lusitania*, bombing attacks on civilians, and taking
of hostages. "He diverted huge amounts of church funds for the
relief of war victims both during and after the war, emptying the
Vatican treasury so that on his death there was barely enough money
left to hold the conclave that elected his successor."[5] The Vatican
undertook a vast program of relief work that included the welfare
of prisoners of war (POWs), tracing missing persons and soldiers,
repatriation of sick and wounded prisoners to Switzerland, and the
difficult business of exchanging prisoners. Benedict intervened with
Germany to stop the deportation of Belgian civilians and tried to
help starving populations in Ottoman territory. He also spoke out
on behalf of Christians in the Middle East, especially the Armenians.
He was also asked to speak on behalf of Jews suffering under Russian
domination in Poland and elsewhere. His work was "comparable in
extent to [that] . . . of the International Red Cross."[6]

BENEDICT'S MOST IMPORTANT attempt to achieve peace was his
seven-point *Peace Note* of August 1917. Morally cogent and well
argued, it failed to deliver peace because politicians on both sides
were so mediocre and besotted with self-importance and crass nationalism that they were prepared to pay any price in other people's
lives to win a war that was now essentially a stalemate. The *Peace
Note* also failed because the papacy was still living with the consequences of its failure to engage with modernity, especially under
Pius X.

When Austrian emperor Franz Josef died on November 21,
1916, after almost sixty-eight years on the throne, his successor,
Karl I, began secret negotiations with the French. Parallel with
this the German chancellor, Leopold von Bethmann-Hollweg, offered the Allies peace negotiations with no specific preconditions.
Bethmann-Hollweg was afraid of US intervention in the war, and
the offer of peace was a way of trying to forestall US action. Lacking

specifics, Benedict XV didn't support the German plan. Perhaps the papacy realized that Bethmann-Hollweg's influence was already in decline and that the German High Command under Paul von Hindenburg and Erich Ludendorff was becoming a de facto military dictatorship. In the United Kingdom, hard-liner David Lloyd George replaced Herbert Asquith as prime minister in December 1916; he declared that "an acceptable peace could only come with the outright defeat of Germany." The German declaration of unrestricted submarine warfare by Admiral Alfred von Tirpitz in January 1917 completely scuttled Bethmann-Hollweg's peace initiatives. In late 1917 the combative Georges Clemenceau became premier of France. Victory rather than peace was on the minds of politicians.

The broader background to the papal *Peace Note* was the fall of the czarist government in Russia and the entry of the United States into the war. Czar Nicholas II abdicated on March 15, 1917, and while the Provisional Government struggled on with the war until the Bolshevik takeover in October 1917, Russia was now in chaos. On April 2, 1917, President Woodrow Wilson told Congress that "the world must be made safe for democracy" and that entering the war was a "new crusade." Wilson, a Presbyterian, was profoundly aware of what he was doing in taking the United States to war. "My message today," he told his longtime Catholic private secretary, Joseph Tumulty, "was a message of death for our young men."[7] Nevertheless, in the summer of 1917 there were indications that Benedict's peace proposals might gain some traction. Eugenio Pacelli (later Pius XII), the recently appointed nuncio to Bavaria, was sent to Berlin to prepare the ground with the German government for the *Peace Note* and met with some encouragement. There was also continuing interest in peace proposals in Austria-Hungary. They had suffered appalling losses of 375,000 men on the eastern front in the Brusilov offensive of June–August 1917; the Russians lost 500,000.

In writing to "the Leaders of the Belligerent Peoples" on August 7, 1917, Benedict asked: "Is Europe, so glorious and flourishing, to rush into the abyss as if stricken by a universal madness, and commit suicide?" To prevent this, he proposed a seven-point plan

that could lead to "a just and durable peace." He called for immediate cessation of all hostilities, the reduction of armaments on all
sides, a system of international arbitration, freedom of navigation,
elimination of punitive reparations and damages imposed on any
nation, return of occupied territories, and resolution of conflict by
negotiation.[8] After some initial mild enthusiasm in Germany and
Austria-Hungary, Benedict's proposals received a cool reception in
Russia, the United States, and France. Essentially, the *Peace Note*
called for a return to the prewar frontiers without annexations or
indemnities. Writing through his secretary of state, Robert Lansing,
Wilson told the pope that he "was touched by this moving appeal"
and felt "the dignity and force of the humane and generous motives
which prompted it," but warned it would be folly to try to pursue
the peace plan with Germany, which he described as "a vast military
establishment controlled by an irresponsible government which . . .
secretly planned to dominate the world."[9] Wilson, descended from
Northern Irish Presbyterians, had little sympathy for the papacy.
The president issued his own fourteen-point peace plan just five
months later, in January 1918.

Britain's Foreign Office used the *Peace Note* to instruct Sir Michael Howard to ask the Germans what they intended to do regarding Belgium. Howard forwarded this message to Berlin through
Gasparri. This led to secret negotiations through the Holy See over
the next few months, but they fizzled out because Lloyd George
was interested only in complete military victory, the naval defeat of
Germany, and the triumph of sterling as the leading world currency.
Benedict was deeply disappointed at the failure of the *Peace Note*,
particularly its rejection by Wilson, who, by now, had emerged as a
world leader.

Benedict's relationship with Italy came back into focus after
the Italian defeat by Austria-Hungary and Germany at Caporetto
in November 1917. The Italians lost all of their territory at the
northern end of the Adriatic, stretching from just north of Venice
around to just north of Trieste and inland to the Alps. Benedict was
pestered with requests for information about sons and relatives by
the very Italian politicians who had most obstructed his previous

attempts to help prisoners. Despite the efforts of the clergy and Catholic people to support Italy, the anticlerical political elite and press turned on the pope and blamed his *Peace Note* for the rout, which, they claimed, spread defeatism among the troops. In fact, as Pollard says, "Benedict and Gasparri showed considerable sympathy towards Italy throughout the conflict," even abandoning their policy of impartiality "for the sake of Italy."[10]

By early 1918 the stalemate on the western front deepened. The Treaty of Brest-Litovsk (March 3, 1918) had taken Russia out of the war, so Germany was no longer fighting on two fronts. But the entry of the Americans had tipped the balance; they poured money into France's and Britain's coffers, they provided equipment and food, and, above all, they brought fresh troops to the front line. Germany lost 1 million men between March and July 1918. When eventually the German front line collapsed and the Bulgarians separately sued for peace, Ludendorff persuaded Kaiser Wilhelm II to seek an armistice, which was negotiated for November 11, 1918. By then Austria, Turkey, and Bulgaria were defeated. The kaiser abdicated.

The statistics of the war are staggering: Britain and the empire lost 956,000 killed, France 1.4 million, Russia 1.7 million, and Italy more than 500,000. Germany lost 2 million killed, Austria-Hungary 1.2 million, and Turkey 350,000. Then, in the fall of 1918, the worst pandemic in modern history hit the world, the influenza epidemic of 1918–1919. Stanford University estimates that between 20 and 40 million people died.[11]

―――――――

ALL THAT WAS left to do now was to create a new world out of the destruction of the old. The peace conference gathered at Versailles in January 1919, but the Italians were determined to exclude the papacy from the conference, using Article 15 of the Treaty of London. This turned out to be a blessing. By not being invited, the papacy avoided being associated with what became the failed and vindictive Versailles Treaty imposed on Germany. The Holy See also avoided being caught up with other arrangements that resulted from the conference that could have compromised it or placed the church in an impossible position.

Despite Wilson's idealism in promoting world peace and the League of Nations, much of what happened at Paris was pragmatism, national self-interest, and straight-out revenge. The French got on with the task of exacting its maximum pound of flesh from Germany, trying to make sure the Germans never lifted their heads again. Britain continued to build its mercantile empire, and Italy, Serbia, and Romania demanded territorial concessions. The result was a mess of weak more or less democratic states based loosely on "national self-determination" and the dismemberment of the Russian, Ottoman, and Austro-Hungarian Empires that left many embittered. Essentially, the position of the Vatican was that the creation of states based on nationality was no better—and probably worse—than multiethnic dynastic empires like Austria-Hungary. Given the chronic instability of the Balkans, one is inclined to agree. Gasparri feared that these small states would be vulnerable to Bolshevik takeover. The creation of Yugoslavia out of Slovenia, Croatia, Serbia, and Bosnia-Herzegovina led Benedict to criticize the absorption of Catholic Croats and Slovenes into a country controlled by Orthodox Serbs.

Gasparri sent an experienced diplomat, Archbishop Bonaventura Cerretti to the peace conference to work behind the scenes to secure the interests of the Holy See. Cerretti had worked in the nunciature in Mexico and the apostolic delegation in Washington, DC (1906–1914), and he was an apostolic delegate to Australia and New Zealand (1914–1917). Diplomatic relations with France were restored in 1921 after the canonization of Joan of Arc in 1920, and Cerretti was appointed nuncio to Paris.

Woodrow Wilson arrived in Europe in mid-December 1918 before the peace conference and undertook an almost triumphal journey across the Continent, with cheering crowds greeting him everywhere. Due to the groundwork laid by Baltimore's Cardinal Gibbons, Wilson visited the Vatican on January 4, 1919. He was shrewdly aware of the growing influence of immigrant Catholics in the US Democratic Party, so political calculus at home was part of his motivation in meeting Pope Benedict. The Italian government did its best to disperse any cheering crowds around Wilson's visit to the Vatican, and Italian paranoia reached a fever pitch, fearing the president would promote the presence of the Holy See at the peace conference and discuss the Roman Question with the pope. Neither happened. They talked about prisoners of war and the prospects for lasting peace. The visit went off reasonably well, despite the prickly Protestant president asking for a clarification about the papal blessing offered by the pope. Benedict tried to explain that God blesses everyone, but in front of the pope Wilson bluntly asked his party, "Are there any Catholics here?" presumably wanting to push them forward to get the blessing. So while the Catholics knelt, Wilson stood back, head bowed.[12] Benedict's attitude to the Wilson-proposed League of Nations was ambivalent. Traditionally, the Vatican saw itself as a key player in international disputes, and it saw the league as inserting itself into something that had been its preserve. Benedict was concerned that the league was not based on explicitly Christian principles, and it came in for harsh criticism in *La Civiltà Cattolica*, with some Catholics characterizing it as socialist or Masonic in inspiration.

One area where Benedict did influence events was in the crisis over several hundred thousand refugee children in the former Austria-Hungary. This occurred during the severe winter of 1919–1920 at the height of the influenza pandemic. Enormous efforts were made to care for these children, and in Britain in 1919 Eglantyne Jebb and her sister founded the Save the Children Fund. Clearly, Pope Benedict knew of this because he mentions the fund twice in his encyclical *Annus iam plenus* (December 1, 1920) on the conditions of children in Eastern Europe. "We cannot desist from offering a public tribute of praise," he says, "to the society entitled the 'Save the Children Fund,' which has exerted all possible care and diligence in the collection of money, clothing, and food." This was typical of his strong social justice approach.

———

THE PEACE CONFERENCE imposed five treaties on the defeated countries. The Treaty of Versailles with Germany imposed draconian terms that reflected the French need for revenge over its defeat in the Franco-Prussian War of 1870 and its determination to prevent Germany from ever rising again against France. Its principal achievement was to establish the preconditions for the rise of Hitler's Nazis. In an apostolic exhortation on the first anniversary of the outbreak of the war (July 15, 1915) that was a passionate call for reconciliation and peace, Pope Benedict made a prediction that was to come true in World War II. "Remember that Nations do not die," he said. "Humbled and oppressed, they chafe under the yoke imposed upon them . . . passing down from generation to generation a mournful heritage of hatred and revenge." This is exactly what happened in Germany as a result of the Treaty of Versailles.

Throughout the war Benedict had seen Austria-Hungary as a bulwark against Russian Orthodoxy. The Treaty of Saint Germain (September 10, 1919) dismembered the Hapsburg Empire, creating the independent nations of Austria, Czechoslovakia, Poland, Hungary, and the Kingdom of the Croats, Slovenes, and Serbs (later called "Yugoslavia"). The papacy now had to deal with these newly independent states, including a now united and strongly Catholic Poland. There is a sense in which Poland became the new bastion against Russia. In mid-1918 Monsignor Achille Ratti was sent from the Vatican Library to Warsaw as an apostolic visitor; he became nuncio to a united Poland a year later. Ratti won much praise when during the Soviet invasion of Poland in August 1920 he very publicly stayed on in Warsaw while the Bolsheviks were in the suburbs of the city. Never really trusted by the nationalistic Polish hierarchy, Ratti was recalled by Pope Benedict and made archbishop of Milan and cardinal in 1920.

While Benedict and Gasparri were busy with Poland, they were more circumspect in supporting the independence of Catholic Ireland. The hands-off papal approach mirrored that of the Irish bishops who gave little support to either the 1916 Easter Rising against the British or the guerrilla war that broke out in early 1919, masterminded by Michael Collins and waged by the Irish Republican

Army. In contrast to the hierarchy, the Irish clergy was supportive of independence and the IRA, including the Irish clerical Mafia in Rome, centering on Monsignor John Hagan at the Pontifical Irish College. There was also strong support for independence from Irish diaspora communities.

The Lloyd George government in London was convinced that they could defeat the IRA and the ever-elusive Collins. But to achieve this they felt they needed a condemnation of IRA violence against the British from the pope. British influence in Rome at this time was considerable. Merry del Val, English curial cardinal Aidan Gasquet, and Count de Salis, the British minister, all argued the government's position against IRA violence. The power of this clique was considerable, and it looked as though a papal condemnation would be forthcoming. But Irish Australian archbishop Patrick Clune of Perth arrived in Rome in the nick of time to tell the pope bluntly that "such a pronouncement would be a disaster for the Church, not only in Ireland but in every country where there were descendants of the Irish race." Clune's outspokenness and firsthand experience of Ireland made "a great impression on His Holiness," and talk of condemnation was abandoned.[13] But there was still no positive support for Ireland.

Soon afterward another Irish Australian archbishop, Daniel Mannix of Melbourne, arrived in Rome, on April 1, 1921. Like Clune, he had adopted a typically Australian outspokenness. Clune had already apprised Benedict and Gasparri of the appallingly violent behavior of the Black and Tans, an ill-disciplined auxiliary police force, in Ireland. Mannix reinforced Clune's message and bluntly told the pope that Irish Catholics felt that he was unsympathetic to their independence struggle. He suggested that Benedict send a letter of sympathy to the Irish people and a donation to help victims of civil strife. Benedict agreed and asked Mannix to draft the letter. Adopting most of the Mannix text, Benedict wrote to the Irish bishops on April 27, 1921. He also sent a sizable gift of two hundred thousand lire to relieve distress in Ireland. He acknowledged Ireland's "devotion to the ancient faith . . . and reverence for the Holy See." The letter is critical of all violence, but the emphasis seems to be on that perpetrated by the Black and Tans when he speaks of "property and homes being ruthlessly and disgracefully laid waste . . . villages and farmsteads being set aflame . . . resulting in the death of unarmed people." As Mannix biographer Brenda Niall points out, "Rather than presenting the Irish as rebels, as the British did, [Benedict] called the conflict a war," thus putting the English and the Irish on equal terms.[14] The letter came at a good time because English public opinion was already shifting against the Lloyd George government policy in Ireland; a truce was arranged on July 11, 1921, and the Anglo-Irish Treaty was signed in London by Michael Collins and Arthur Griffith on December 6 that year. The great tragedy is that the treaty led straight to a civil war, in which Collins was eventually murdered.

Benedict's papacy also became embroiled in the complex politics of the Middle East. The World War I victors had attempted to carve up Ottoman territory in the Treaty of Sèvres (August 1920) that established British and French spheres of influence in the Middle East. Essentially, the British gained mandates over Palestine (which the pope and Gasparri favored), Transjordan (a smaller version of present-day Jordan), and oil-rich Iraq and the French over Lebanon and Syria. Christian Armenia was recognized as a separate state. The papacy's deepest concern was access to the holy places in Palestine and the protection of the region's Christians. Access to the holy places under Ottoman rule had been generally good, and the French exercised a kind of "protectorate" over these sites; after 1918 even anticlerical French governments attempted to maintain this system. The situation was complicated by the 1917 "Balfour Declaration" that pledged British support for forming a "Jewish homeland" in Palestine, while still protecting the rights of the region's Arab population. Reflecting something of the inherent anti-Semitism of most Europeans of the period, Benedict and Gasparri tended to associate Jews with Bolshevism, and they feared that the declaration was a recipe for a Jewish takeover of Palestine and the exclusion of Christians. It was in this context that Benedict said that he was "especially anxious" about the holy places, which, he said, must remain under the control of Christians. It would be "a terrible grief for us," he said, "if infidels were placed in a privileged and prominent position," threatening Christian access.[15] While Zionism was certainly an issue, one cannot underestimate a kind of accepted Catholic anti-Semitism current at this time. Gasparri preferred to have Jerusalem internationalized rather than handing it over to a potential Jewish state. Benedict returned to the dangers of Zionism in June 1921 when he said that Jewish rights should be respected but not above those of Christians.

In the postwar years Italy became increasingly unstable. The war had left the country deeply divided. The anticlerical liberals who had controlled parliament since 1870 and who had taken an ill-prepared Italy into the war on the side of the Allies were left deeply disappointed by the postwar settlement. Prime Minister Vittorio Orlando was humiliated at the Peace Conference when Italy was not given the enclave of Fiume on the Dalmatian coast; he publicly burst into tears and withdrew the Italian delegation. After the war unemployment and inflation became serious problems, and by 1919 Italy was very unstable, economically, politically, and socially. Parallel with this was the emergence of three new political forces: the *Partito Populare Italiano*, the Socialists, and the Fascists of Benito Mussolini.

From the papacy's point of view, the PPI was the most important new force. It was founded by Sicilian priest Luigi Sturzo. Pastoral experience in Sicily and southern Italy taught him that the church had little to offer the poor, and he was influenced by the ideas of his friend Romolo Murri that Catholics needed both a religious and a social conscience. Both felt that the Italian church was too preoccupied with the fate of the papacy rather than the fate of the people, and they planned a popular political party that would promote Catholic social teaching. Murri was impatient and antagonized the intransigent Pius X and was excommunicated. Sturzo was more cautious; he bided his time. Formed in 1918–1919, the PPI, with a strong social justice agenda, leaned leftward, demanding proportional representation, votes for women, the division of big estates, and support for trade unions and agrarian workers' strikes. Sturzo correctly judged that the 1919 elections would be the PPI's moment. He was shrewd enough to see that Benedict was not Pius X, and he was wise enough to know that the time had come for a different approach. In December 1918 Sturzo consulted Gasparri, who indicated that the Vatican would raise no objection to a PPI not directly linked to the church, because then the church wouldn't have to take responsibility for it if it failed. He also knew that Sturzo was no firebrand like Murri. Just four days before the general election on November 16, 1919, Benedict lifted the *Non expedit* decree. Catholics were free to vote.

About half of those Italians eligible actually voted, and the result returned an unworkable chamber. Out of 508 seats, various combinations of the deeply divided Liberals gained 252 seats, the PPI 100 seats, and on the Left the Socialists 156 seats. There were no Fascists.[16] The problem the PPI faced was that "they spoke with no single voice." Their main rivals were Socialists, whose strength lay in the northern industrial cities. The Socialists lacked leadership and in a very Italian way replaced concerted action with high-sounding rhetoric and, as historian Denis Mack Smith says, "made a right-wing victory almost inevitable."[17] The Italian government had been embarrassed by the egregious Gabriele D'Annunzio seizing the city of Fiume in September 1919, despite its being given to Yugoslavia by the Peace Conference. The absurd musical-comedy "state" of Fiume signified contempt for ordered government on the part of many elements in Italian society that actively supported D'Annunzio, and it provided a model for the Fascists to seize power. Throughout 1920 and 1921 the Italian government struggled on toward an almost inevitable conclusion: dictatorship.

Meanwhile, the Vatican was building strong relationships with the new nations of the postwar world. Ambassadors were exchanged, and during the Benedict papacy the Holy See began to recover diplomatic influence because of the pope's influential role during the war and in the postwar settlement. By September 1914 there were seventeen states with diplomatic relations with the Holy See and seven papal nuncios representing the papacy abroad. In January 1922 twenty-seven states had diplomatic relations with the Holy See and twenty-four papal nuncios abroad.[18] Britain continued its representation, and in June 1919 Germany established diplomatic relations because the Vatican was seen as sympathetic. On April 20, 1920, Diego von Bergen became German ambassador to the Holy See, and Eugenio Pacelli, then nuncio to Bavaria, was appointed to Berlin. One of the issues of immediate concern to both Germany and the Vatican was the territories that were separated from the Reich as a result of the Versailles Treaty. Several of the eastern territories and almost all of the western territories lost to Germany, as well as the demilitarized Rhineland, had significant majorities of Catholics. "The total population of the lost territories was 5,517,270 of which 3,625,682 were Catholics; Alsace-Lorraine alone had 1.6 million Catholics."[19] The Holy See also sent apostolic delegates (who represented the pope without actual diplomatic status) to countries like the United States, Canada, and Australia that then didn't exchange ambassadors with the Vatican.

During the war Pollard estimates that the Vatican lost "nearly 40% of its capital" and that Peter's Pence (a collection revived in 1871 by Pius IX made up of small contributions from Catholics all over the world) covered about half of the shortfall. Much of this came from US Catholics. Benedict XV had generously spent his own money and that of the Holy See to assist the victims of the war. After the war, the Vatican's financial affairs were in poor shape. Several historians have asserted that the Holy See was almost broke when Benedict died and that Gasparri had to raise a loan from the Rothschilds' bank to finance the 1922 conclave. Pollard repudiates this, saying that Gasparri faced "more of a short-term cash flow problem" than near bankruptcy.[20]

BENEDICT HAD SPENT much of his papacy trying to deal with war and peace as the situation evolved around him. However, in 1917 he turned his attention to intrachurch affairs and to the promulgation of the Code of Canon Law. While the code brought some order, it also enormously enhanced overcentralization and emphasized the juridical and legal aspects of the Latin church. Significantly, it "failed to make reference to the Holy Scriptures or the Church Fathers in contrast to the ancient canonical collections."[21] It conflates solemn (infallible) and ordinary (noninfallible) church teaching and identifies error with formal heresy. The fundamental problem is that it shifts the emphasis in the church's practice from the ministerial to the legal. This is a profoundly significant change, and the practical result has been that in pastoral care the most important question is not what will enhance Christian love, life, and commitment, but how is the law to be applied? While organizations need laws, the code seems to upend Saint Paul's teaching that "where the Spirit of the Lord is, there is freedom" (2 Cor. 3:17) and the fact that Christians "are called to freedom . . . For the whole law is summed up in a single commandment, 'You shall love your neighbour as yourself'" (Gal. 5:13–14). Rubbing it in, Paul says that Christians are "discharged from the Law" and are no longer "slaves to the old written code" but free in the Spirit (Rom. 7:6).

However, Benedict reflected none of the mean-spirited claustrophobia of the previous papacy. His vision of the church was outward looking, more concerned about mission and ministry than rigid orthodoxy. The nineteenth-century missionary thrust of Catholicism followed, and sometimes preceded, European expansion into Asia, Africa, and the Pacific. It was often a form of cultural colonization; the style and model of church imposed on new converts were European and Roman. But World War I effectively broke the link between colonization and missionary expansion, thus freeing the church's missionary work from colonialism. The time had come for a renewed approach to mission, and Benedict XV provided it in his apostolic letter *Maximum illud* (November 30, 1919).

Benedict's greatest concern was for the development of local clergy, and *Maximum illud* strongly supported the training of indigenous priests in local seminaries and the admittance of indigenous women into religious orders of sisters. He told bishops that they must "make it [their] special concern to secure and train local candidates," because "the local priest, one with his people by birth . . . is remarkably effective in appealing to their mentality and thus attracting them to the Faith. . . . [H]e often has easy access to places where a foreign priest would not be tolerated." These priests must be well trained and educated, with "the same kind of education for the priesthood that a European would receive." They were not just second-class clergy who acted "as the assistants of foreign priests."[22] He wanted the church to be what today we call "inculturated," an ugly neologism that means that the church is not alien but culturally integrated into the countries where missionaries work. Also, they must be thoroughly trained for their work and must be proficient in local languages. Significantly, the pope also praises the work of missionary sisters and "the work that is being done by women . . . since the very earliest days of the Church." He says that the whole aim of missionary activity is the proclamation of the Gospel, not the promotion of the imperialist ideology of the colonizing country.

An example of a missionary church freeing itself from European cultural dominance can be seen most clearly in China. The first missionaries in China were the Jesuits, and their pioneering work there was led by mathematician, astronomer, and linguist Matteo Ricci, who entered China in 1582, eventually reaching the imperial court in Peking in 1601. The Jesuits' whole approach involved an adaptation of Christianity as far as possible to Chinese cultural conditions, but they were later accused by Dominican and Franciscan missionaries who entered China in the wake of the Jesuits of compromising Christianity by allowing Chinese customs. The other orders insisted on imposing a Roman form of Catholicism on Chinese converts. Eventually, Catholic missionaries were all expelled from China in 1724 by the Yongzheng Emperor and Catholicism proscribed. Missionaries returned with European economic penetration of China in the nineteenth century. None of the new missionaries showed the wisdom of the Jesuits, and Catholicism was very much a Euro-centric affair, especially as promoted by French missionaries. They looked down on Chinese culture and civilization, treated their converts as children, and kept Chinese priests in subordinate positions. The missionaries remained dependent on the foreign powers, particularly France, to protect them.

The person who broke this cultural dominance was the extraordinary Belgian missionary in China Father Frédéric-Vincent Lebbe.

A member of the Vincentians, a French religious order, Lebbe adopted a Chinese name, Lei Ming-yuan ("Thunder rolling in the distance"), wore the cotton outfit preferred by the Chinese clergy, partially shaved his head, and grew a Chinese-style pigtail. He walked everywhere or rode a bicycle. He completely mastered spoken Chinese, read the classics, gave lectures to Chinese intellectuals, and began publishing newspapers. This soon led to conflict with his French superiors. But he was already part of a small group of Chinese and foreign priests who eventually wrote to the Propaganda Congregation in Rome, the department covering mission countries, arguing that while foreign interests dominated the church in China, Catholicism would never really take root. Cardinal Willem van Rossum, the prefect of Propaganda, was impressed by the letter, and Lebbe's ideas about Chinese leadership of the church found expression in *Maximum illud*. Here Benedict XV was particularly critical of situations that "could easily give rise to the conviction that the Christian religion is the national religion of some foreign people and that anyone converted to it is abandoning his loyalty to his own people and submitting to the pretensions and domination of a foreign power." This is precisely the point that Lebbe was trying to make. But resistance to Chinese leadership of the church continued, and it was not until 1926 that the first six Chinese-born bishops were ordained.

Pope Benedict was also concerned about Catholicism's relationship to the Eastern Orthodox churches, with whom he canvassed the possibility of reunion. He established the Congregation for the Oriental Churches with the task of administering the non-Latin churches in union with Rome as well as the Pontifical Oriental Institute as a study center focusing on the Eastern churches; both were established in 1917. In *Maximum illud* he says that the institute will prepare priests and others with "fluency in Eastern languages and an intimate acquaintance with Eastern ways, along with a thorough mastery of various other skills that will be of use to them." The aim was to build bridges with the Orthodox.

In 1920 Benedict issued the encyclical *Spiritus Paraclitus* on biblical studies to commemorate the work of fourth-century biblical scholar Saint Jerome. The encyclical asserts that divine inspiration guarantees the historicity (that is, the historical accuracy) and the "absolute immunity of Scripture from error." This, he says, is incompatible with the notion that the scripture writers were historically bound to their particular cultural contexts and therefore reflected them. In other words, he had little sympathy with literary forms and historical context. What apparently troubled Benedict was an increased emphasis on evolution, with the ideas of Charles Darwin and Thomas Huxley slowly penetrating Italy with vigorous debate around evolutionary theory and creationism at this time, with *La Civiltà Cattolica* publishing several articles on evolution in 1919 and 1920.

As the Benedict papacy came to an end, Italy began descending into the civil strife that led to Mussolini and the Fascists. The pope unexpectedly died on January 22, 1922, from a bronchitis attack that developed into pneumonia. He was sixty-seven. He remains a much underestimated pope who strengthened the church's reputation and influence in the world. To some extent he healed the divisions created by Pius X over modernism, but he didn't rein in the power of the Holy Office that dominated the church theologically until Vatican II. While conventionally pious in an old-fashioned sense and often irascible, he always maintained a ministerial approach to the issues that faced him. Where this pope's strength lay was in his extraordinary generosity to those in need during the war and his constant efforts for peace. He was outward looking in his attitude, especially in terms of the church's missionary activity. While no revolutionary, he left the church "a stronger and more prestigious institution in the world than he had found it."[23] He is undoubtedly the first pope of the twentieth century.

JANUARY–FEBRUARY 1922 WERE key months for Italy. After the indecisive elections of 1919, the country descended into chaos, with a maelstrom of strikes, civil unrest, and breakdown of stable government. Mussolini's Fascists had not done well in the 1919 elections, and *Il Duce* "was in serious danger of ending up as just a confused and egocentric demagogue with a talent for histrionics."[24] A braggart and a bully with an unerring feeling for what ordinary Italians felt, Mussolini really believed he was the new Julius Caesar, *Il Duce*, the Leader or "Boss." D'Annunzio's seizure of Fiume gave Mussolini a model, and he instinctively knew that his real chance to gain power lay in fostering anarchy so that he could inject himself as savior. Elections were held in May 1921, and the Fascists gained 37 seats in the Chamber of Deputies. The PPI increased its vote and won 108 seats and the Socialists 123 seats. But a coalition of Liberals formed a government, and they brought the Fascists in, with Prime Minster Giovanni Giolitti hoping to "tame" them. But this government quickly collapsed, as did the next, and throughout February 1922 there was no government. During the especially hot summer of 1922, Italy was on the verge of collapse. King Victor Emmanuel III (1900–1946) was weak and afraid of the Fascists, and Queen Mother Margherita was an avowed supporter of Mussolini. With the country in chaos, the king should have declared martial law to bring the Fascists to heel, but instead on October 29, 1922, he asked Mussolini to form a government.

It was within the political context that the conclave to elect Benedict XV's successor met. It began on February 2, 1922, with fifty-three of the fifty-nine cardinals present. Four cardinals from the Americas arrived too late to be admitted. Boston's Cardinal William O'Connell, who had missed out on the 1914 conclave, arrived just as the election finished. Absolutely furious, he demanded that the interregnum be extended from ten to fifteen days.

In the conclave, Merry del Val and Gasparri were the early runners, but it was soon clear that they wouldn't get the required two-thirds majority. It was then that Cardinal Ambrogio Achille Ratti of Milan emerged as a compromise candidate. Out of the running, Merry del Val broke the conclave rules by negotiating together with Cardinal Gaetano De Lai to offer Ratti his votes if Ratti promised *not* to appoint Gasparri secretary of state. Ratti refused. If true, Merry del Val and De Lai incurred excommunications *latae sententiae* (automatic) for breaking conclave rules. However, with Gasparri's quiet support, the sixty-five-year-old Ratti gained the requisite majority on February 6, 1922. He chose the style Pius XI and immediately appointed Gasparri secretary of state. A first-class linguist and polymath, Ratti had spent most of his life as a scholar, working first in the Ambrosian Library in Milan and then the Vatican Library, where he became an adviser of Benedict XV. He was a surprise appointment as apostolic visitor to Poland and Lithuania in 1918, where he negotiated the release of many POWs from the Bolsheviks. He was certainly courageous, but in his last year in Warsaw he became embroiled in a dispute in Upper Silesia, where German cardinal Adolf Bertram of Breslau (then in Germany, now Wrocław in Poland) was trying to curtail the outspoken nationalism of Polish priests in his diocese. The Polish press denounced Ratti for not tackling Bertram. In May 1921 he was rescued from the Polish quagmire by Benedict XV by being appointed archbishop of Milan.

Before election he had been a famous mountain climber, having climbed Mont Blanc (4,809 meters [15,781 feet]), the Matterhorn (4,478 meters [14,692 feet]), and the Monte Rosa peak (4,634 meters [15,203 feet]). A careful planner and always well equipped, he often spent nights in the open.[25] Understandably, he felt cramped by the small world of the Vatican; he missed the mountains, fresh air, and physical activity. A voracious reader, he constantly quoted books he had read and once lectured Mussolini on his duties from Manzoni's novel *I promessi sposi* (*The Betrothed*). He was also a keen reader of Mark Twain. A short, balding man with a large head and an unsmiling face, his penetrating eyes were framed by gold-rimmed glasses. An excellent climber he may have been, but he was also a martinet who ran the Vatican in an almost despotic fashion. Belgian ambassador Baron Eugene Beyens said, "After he became pope there was only one word on every tongue, *obbedire*, obey."[26] He was a forceful, passionate, and outspoken character who was much given to shouting at cardinals and other underlings and slamming his fist on tables. While he continued many of the policies of Benedict XV, he immediately broke with the tradition of newly elected popes giving their first *urbi et orbi* blessing (to the city and to the world) within the confines of Saint Peter's Basilica as a sign of their disapproval of the Italian state. Pope Pius gave his blessing from the loggia, the open front balcony facing the Piazza of Saint Peter's. "Pope of the world, he wished to show that his benediction was given *urbi et orbi*."[27]

Pope Pius's first encyclical, *Ubi arcano Dei* (December 23, 1922), was an outline of his priorities as pope. Placing himself squarely in line with Benedict XV, he says that the "belligerents of yesterday have laid down their arms, but on the heels of this we encounter new horrors and new threats of war . . . [all] because men have forsaken God and Jesus Christ, [and] have sunk to the depths of evil." All this is "a species of moral, legal, and social modernism which we condemn, no less decidedly than we condemn theological modernism." Like Benedict XV, he was no antimodernist in the Pius X sense, but because of reactionaries like Merry del Val, who was now prefect of the Holy Office, he seems to have needed to demonstrate his orthodoxy. The phrase *peace of Christ* recurs seventeen times in this encyclical, and he took "the peace of Christ in the Kingdom of Christ" as a kind of official motto of his papacy. He also introduced the notion of "Catholic Action," a form of lay participation in the work of the church, but always directly under the control of the hierarchy and ultimately of the pope. The Catholic Action theme runs right through this papacy.

But before anything else, he had to deal with Mussolini. The man who saw exactly what Mussolini represented was Sturzo. As his biographer John Molony says, "Sturzo had a concept of politics that transcended the power struggle in which the country was then immersed and he looked to a future in which men might come to realize that true power implied human and individual responsibility."[28] But Sturzo was a genuine democrat, and he was prepared to work with the Socialists to counter the Fascists. For Pius XI and many Italians, working with the godless Socialists was anathema. They longed for the order that the Fascists promised, ironic given that it was the Fascists themselves who were fomenting the violence and riots that created disorder. The word *obbedire* (obey) really sums up the Pius papacy. He longed for an ordered church in an ordered state.

So a democrat like Sturzo was in the wrong place at the wrong time. In early 1923 the Vatican ordered Sturzo to resign his leadership of the PPI. As a result, when the April 1924 elections came around, Italian Catholics were deeply divided. A Nationalist-Liberal-Fascist group led by Mussolini gained 60.1 percent of the vote and assumed government. Like Napoleon, Mussolini realized that he would have to deal with the church. In his youth, he was nicknamed *Mangiaprete*, "Priest Eater." He had published an anticlerical novel entitled *Claudia Particella, l'amante del cardinale*, later published in the United States as *The Cardinal's Mistress*. Leaving that behind, he quickly made overtures to the church and got his children baptized and regularized his marriage. On January 20, 1923, Gasparri and Mussolini began secret negotiations about the relationship of the Italian state to the church. The *Duce* brought the crucifix back into schoolrooms and courthouses, he increased state stipends paid to priests, reintroduced religious education into primary schools, abolished Freemasonry, gave clergy and seminarians an exemption from military service, and promised to rescue the financially strapped Banco di Roma, in which the Vatican had a financial interest. Acting with his usual shrewdness and playing hard to get, but still willing to offer a sweetener to the Fascists, Gasparri suggested that the papacy might sacrifice the PPI and Sturzo. Pius XI was already deeply suspicious of any form of democratic politics and had no time for priests and parties that supported the autonomy of lay action. He believed that the laity must be firmly under the control of the hierarchy before they could participate in the apostolate. Also, the pope's major priority was the settlement of the Roman Question, and Mussolini rather than Sturzo looked like the man to achieve this.

The treatment of Sturzo was appalling, and it demonstrates the way the papacy used power. Here was the PPI, deeply inspired by Catholicism, led by a cultured, pastoral priest, but democratic and not controlled by the hierarchy. This was anathema to Pius XI, who was sure the church was better off with a stable, all-powerful secular ruler than the apparent instability of democracy. He felt he could do business with a deplorable bully like Mussolini rather than a democratic party dedicated to social justice and led by a committed priest. Pius XI was projecting his fear of communism onto the political chaos of Italy and the Italian Socialists with whom Sturzo and the PPI were proposing a coalition to exclude the Fascists.

The pope knew that without Sturzo, the PPI was finished. On February 1, 1924, Pius decreed that priests must withdraw from politics and membership of political parties. Sturzo resigned from the PPI, and the Vatican advised him to leave Italy. In November 1924 he went to London and then in 1940 to the United States and didn't return to Italy until after the Second World War. His departure was terminal for the PPI and led to the collapse of Catholic political influence in Italy, clearing the way for the Fascists to control civil society. Pius XI observed all this "with relative equanimity," historian John Pollard says, "because at least what remained . . . could be brought firmly under the control of the church hierarchy via Italian Catholic Action."[29]

The person he appointed to run *Azione Cattolica* in Italy was Monsignor Giuseppe Pizzardo, the *sostituto* (undersecretary of state). Pizzardo was a clerico-fascist, and as head of Italian Catholic Action he gained microcontrol over all lay activity in the Italian church. This suited the hierarchical and clerical understanding of the church held by Pope Pius, who used papal power to eliminate committed Catholics from public life because they didn't fit his image of the church or, perhaps more accurately, his hierarchical ideology. What is "Catholic Action"? Pizzardo defines it as "the part taken by the organized laity in the apostolate of the hierarchy." There is no sense that the baptized laity have an apostolate (nowadays we would call it "ministry") of their own. The primary apostolate belongs to the hierarchy, "to whom alone the power and grace of Christ is entrusted." Basically, laypeople are at best the "helpmates" of the clergy: "Since the church requires help, the laity provide it; let them be well organized and devoted to the hierarchy." Pizzardo says the church needs "militant" laity, but the hierarchy retains the "central authority" to control and coordinate them.[30] This view dominated papal thinking until Vatican II.

One of the really creative manifestations of Catholic Action that transcended Pizzardo's definitions was the *Jeunesse Ouvrière Chrétienne* (JOC), founded by Belgian priest (later cardinal) Joseph

Cardijn in 1925. The movement quickly spread to the English-speaking world, where it was known as the Young Christian Workers (YCW). The JOC was lay led, and it took Catholic Action into the modern industrial milieu. It later had a strong influence on Latin American liberation theology.

The Pizzardo notion of Catholic Action soon led to conflict with the Fascist regime. Having eliminated the PPI, the papacy now confronted *Il Duce* alone. Fascism saw itself not so much as an ideology as a faith. As historian George L. Mosse says, "Italian Fascism, seeking to rival the church, became increasingly the religion of the state."[31] It resembled Catholicism in its emphasis on a hierarchy of power under the absolute guidance of one leader. It expressed itself through a kind of civil liturgy featuring Mussolini as *Il Duce*. Its teaching emphasized the importance of the family and reproduction to build up the population. It disdained democracy, with its emphasis on the importance of the community over the individual and the absolute authority of the government. Some Fascist theoreticians associated the mission of the party with that of the church. According to Alfredo Rocco, "Italy cannot exist as a state without a world mission—and this mission cannot be anything but Roman and Catholic. Signor Mussolini is the greatest instrument in the hand of God since Charlemagne."[32] Pius XI saw this as caesaro-papism, the blatant use of Catholicism for political ends. In the June 29, 1931, encyclical, *Non abbiamo bisogno*, Pius XI criticized the attempt by the Fascist regime "to monopolize completely the young, from their tenderest years up to manhood and womanhood, for the exclusive advantage of a party and of a regime based on an ideology which clearly resolves itself into a true, a real pagan worship of the State." The encyclical focuses on Catholic Action in Italy and the attempts of the Fascist youth movement to seduce adolescents and young people away from the church by offering them good sporting facilities, colorful uniforms, mass rallies, and organized activities.

WHILE THESE DISAGREEMENTS made negotiations between Gasparri and Mussolini difficult, in the end they didn't stymie agreement about the status of the Holy See in relationship to Italy because it was in the interests of both sides to reach a settlement. Formal negotiations began in December 1926, as Mussolini worked to establish his government by making peace with the dominant forces in Italian society, the church being the most important of these. At first negotiations were carried out by proxies. Profascist Jesuit Pietro Tacchi-Venturi became one of the regular backdoor contacts between Mussolini and the Vatican. In the middle of these negotiations, Tacchi-Venturi claimed that an attempt had been made on his life by an anonymous assailant. But it was seemingly not the assassination plot Tacchi-Venturi claimed but rather attempted revenge on him by a gay lover or abused youth who was never caught. American historian David I. Kertzer has pointed out that a number of Fascist priest-spies worked in the Vatican, together with several priest child abusers, including Monsignor (later Cardinal) Camillo Caccia Dominioni, master of the papal household from 1921, and Colombia's Monsignor Ricardo Sanz de Samper, majordomo and prefect of the Papal Palace. Both worked to undermine Gasparri, and their crimes of abuse were well known to Italian police. Samper was suddenly dismissed in 1926, but Caccia, a colleague of Pius XI from Milan, was never dealt with but sent to the Sydney Eucharistic Congress in 1928 and made a cardinal in 1935.[33] Recruited in 1927, the most notorious of the Fascist spies was the handsome Monsignor Enrico Pucci, editor of the Catholic newspaper *Il Corriere d'Italia*. *Time* reported that he "had a great fondness for food, drink and cards . . . and he liked money," and he acted as a "tipster" for foreign correspondents, especially Americans in Rome.[34] He was a close friend of the then monsignor Francis Spellman, later archbishop of New York.

Given this background, the initial negotiations with Mussolini were anything but smooth. In 1926 there were conflicts over Catholic youth groups, with the government trying to absorb them into the Fascist youth movement. There were arguments over scanty gym clothes and female modesty and the dangers of the cinema and of the young becoming "Americanized." There were disagreements over religious education in secondary schools, with some Fascists saying the church was insufficiently focused on scientific education. On two separate occasions, negotiations were suspended for months. Gasparri was a stubborn interlocutor. He believed that the Italian state had more to gain from a settlement than the Holy See; he was concerned that the pope would lose the image of being "the prisoner in the Vatican" and with it world Catholic sympathy. From the *Duce*'s perspective, Gasparri's intransigence and ability to use popular Italian cultural concerns about hallowed ceremonies like blessing flags and saying Mass at the Tomb of the Unknown Soldier meant that Italy ended up making too many concessions. Profascist elements tried to get Gasparri sidelined from the talks, and Fascist spy Monsignor Umberto Benigni (of modernism fame) tried to mount a defamation campaign against him. At various stages Mussolini tried to drive a wedge between Gasparri and the pope. Pius XI wanted everything tied up in one agreement, and in the end he got his way.

After four years of negotiations, the *Conciliazione* (Reconciliation) was signed on February 11, 1929, by Mussolini for the Italian state and Gasparri for the Holy See in the palazzo adjoining the Saint John Lateran Basilica. The agreement had three elements. First was the Lateran Treaty, which established an independent Vatican City State by recognizing "the sovereignty of the Holy See in the international world." In addition to the 44-hectare (108.7-acre) area around Saint Peter's Basilica, the treaty also guaranteed other extraterritorial Vatican property in Rome (churches, offices, colleges, palaces) and the papal residence at Castel Gandolfo, outside Rome. Italy guaranteed a water supply and a (now disused) rail link, as well as connections with other countries via "telephonic, wireless, broadcasting and postal services." The "person of the Supreme Pontiff as sacred and inviolable" was guaranteed, and "public insults and offenses made on Italian territory against the person of the Supreme Pontiff by speech, act, or writing will be punished." The treaty recognized that Catholicism was "the only state religion" in Italy.

Second, there was an agreement on compensation for the loss of the Papal States. This proved to be a difficult negotiation because Italy was financially impoverished and struggling, and while it was agreed that the compensation was "greatly inferior in value" to the amount that should have been paid, Italy handed over 750 million lire (in 2017 value approximately US$3.54 billion) in cash and 1 billion lire in shares and bonds (in 2017 value approximately US$4.7 billion). It is on the basis of this compensation that the Vatican has subsequently consolidated its complex financial arrangements. An *Amministrazione Speciale* (Special Administration) was set up in June 1929 to administer the compensation under the guidance of another Milanese, Bernardino Nogara. The Special Administration is now APSA, the Administration of the Patrimony of the Apostolic See. Nogara invested much of the money in Switzerland, the United Kingdom, France, and the United States. Nowadays APSA has 680.7 million euros under management, with accounts and deposits in many central banks (for example, the Bank of England and the US Federal Reserve), and invests in financial markets and real estate in France, the United Kingdom, and Switzerland.

Third, there was a concordat with the state of Italy. This guaranteed Catholicism "the free exercise of spiritual power . . . [and] worship." It granted an exemption for clerics from military service, freedom of appointment by the Holy See of Italian bishops, and an adjustment of diocesan boundaries to conform to civil administration, and it recognized "the civil effects of the sacrament of marriage as laid down by Canon Law."

To celebrate the *Conciliazione*, Mussolini planned a wide boulevard, the Via della Conciliazione, that ran from the Tiber through the ancient Borgo district of Rome to the Piazza of Saint Peter's. Between 1936 and 1950, some twenty-two medieval and Renaissance buildings and streets were destroyed to make way for what is now a speedway for Roman drivers dodging wide-eyed tourists.

The Lateran Treaty provided the political and territorial foundation for the modern papacy by creating the Vatican City State. This is a tiny sovereign state from which the Holy See, as the government of the universal Catholic Church, operates. Both are recognized under international law.[35] Ambassadors are accredited to the Holy See, not to the Vatican City State, and papal nuncios represent the Holy See. This means that the Holy See as the ecclesiological organ of government in the church has a unique status with no equivalent anywhere in the world. But there is a fundamental theological problem with this kind of diplomatic and legal definition. It strongly reinforces the emphasis on papal power.

Just a year after signing the *Conciliazione*, Gasparri resigned as secretary of state. It is clear that he didn't go willingly, even though he was eighty. In some ways, his success made him almost equal to Pius XI, who felt Gasparri was getting too big for his boots. The cardinal later described Pius XI "as cold as marble." Gasparri's favored successor was Bonaventura Cerretti. But Cerretti was perceived as being too sympathetic to democracy and the PPI; he had, after all, been in Washington and Australia before going to Paris. The pope instead appointed Eugenio Pacelli, who had just been made a cardinal. Pacelli, as secretary of state and then pope, was to dominate Catholicism for the next twenty-eight years.

———

THE MOTTO OF the Pius XI papacy was "Christ's peace in Christ's kingdom." He saw Christ as king of the world and introduced the Feast of Christ the King in the encyclical *Quas primas* (1925). What the encyclical did was to identify the rule of Christ over the world with the authority of the church. The introduction of a problematic concept like kingship when Jesus himself had told Pontius Pilate "My kingdom is not from this world" (John 18:36) shows complete insensitivity to what was happening in broader society, let alone to the Gospel. Michael Walsh has shown that this feast was promoted in the nineteenth century by French legitimists who supported the restoration of the monarchy.[36] In the encyclical *Quadragesimo anno* (1931), the pope says that modern society is so corrupt and individualism so rampant that society needs to return to a kind of corporatist state modeled on the medieval period. This encyclical was issued during the Great Depression and reaffirmed the social teaching of Leo XIII, rejecting "capitalism in an even more vigorous fashion than *Rerum novarum*" and also asserting that "no one can be a . . . sincere Catholic and a true Socialist," which completely ignores the experience of moderate socialism in countries like the United Kingdom, Canada, and Australia.[37]

As a scholar Pius XI moderated to some extent antimodernist tensions, encouraged science and especially astronomy through the Vatican Observatory, and established the Pontifical Academy of Science (1936), nominating leading international scientists to its membership. He also expanded and modernized the Vatican Library and established the Pontifical Institute of Christian Archaeology. As part of promoting the kingdom of Christ, Pope Pius established Vatican Radio on February 12, 1931. It was a farsighted move that was to have enormous repercussions for papal influence. Guglielmo Marconi, inventor of radio, prophetically announced that this was the first time the pope's voice would be heard "simultaneously in all parts of the world." Quoting from the prophet Isaiah (49:1), Pius XI said: "Listen to me . . . pay attention you peoples from far away," and he continued, "Listen and hear my voice; pay attention and hear my speech" (28:23).[38] These were farsighted words, as radio and later other electronic media were to give subsequent popes an extraordinarily potent means of projecting their influence outward to the entire world.

On moral issues he maintained the established papal line. The encyclical *Casti conubii* (1930) on Christian marriage was a response to an imagined declining European birthrate and to the Lambeth Conference of Anglican Bishops, which had cautiously approved the limited use of contraception. The encyclical condemned modern conceptions of marriage and declared any form of contraception a grave sin. This was an exercise of power over the most intimate aspects of the lives of Catholics, but the encyclical did concede that there was a "secondary" purpose in marriage: "the cultivating of mutual love," or building intimacy between the couple. Unremarkable as this seems today, it was a revolution in papal teaching at the time.

Following the lead of Benedict XV, Pope Pius also strongly promoted local churches and encouraged the ordination of indigenous bishops and clergy. He continued the work of Vincent Lebbe by appointing Archbishop (later Cardinal) Celso Constantini as the apostolic delegate in China. It was Constantini who took six Chinese priests to Rome with him to be ordained as bishops by Pius XI, thus beginning the transition of the hierarchy from European dominated to Chinese. Pius XI supported the Malines Conversations (1921–1926) between Catholics and Anglicans, led by Belgian cardinal Mercier and Anglican Lord Halifax. But he was opposed to a broader ecumenism, accusing it in the encyclical *Mortalium animos* (1928) of indifferentism, relativism, and assuming equality, "yet you will find none at all to whom it ever occurs to submit to and obey the Vicar of Jesus Christ either in His capacity as a teacher or as a governor."

Despite backward-looking notions like kingship, Pius XI still had to engage with contemporary reality. The toxic situation in France between church and state had been exacerbated by Pius X's intransigence. The key issue was the seizure of church property by the state in the 1905 Law of Separation. In the early 1920s the Raymond Poincaré government wanted to allow church property to be administered by *associations diocésaines* under the control of bishops and clergy, thus finally settling the property conflict. In the encyclical *Maximam gravissimamque* (1924), Pope Pius attempted to pull recalcitrant French bishops into line by instructing them to accept this offer regarding ownership of church property. This gave the church the use of its buildings, while the state paid for their upkeep. But the Catholic intellectual right in France was still wedded to promonarchist movements like *Action Française*, which was enormously influential and emphasized the role of Catholicism in French culture, but was antirepublican, antimodern, antidemocratic, anti-Semitic, and anti-German. It was founded by the completely deaf, royalist nonbeliever Charles Maurras. A prolific writer, he is often seen as the spiritual father of corporatism and fascism. Many French bishops and clergy supported *Action Française*. However, the pope couldn't ignore the movement's essential paganism and its virulent anti-Semitic and anti-German attitudes, especially when the papacy was trying to reconcile Germany and France and ease the burden of postwar reparations. Several of Maurras's works were placed on the *Index* (1926) and Catholics forbidden to read the movement's paper. Jesuit neoscholastic theologian and cardinal Louis Billot was forced by Pius XI to resign as cardinal because of his sympathy with *Action Française*. The condemnation of *Action Française* did much to reconcile the Third Republic with the church.

A situation arose in Malta between 1927 and 1930 that vividly illustrated the way in which Italian parochialism distorted papal attitudes. The problem centered on the strategic island of Malta in the middle of *Mare Nostrum*, "Our Mediterranean," as Mussolini saw it. The Maltese people had democratically elected Lord Gerald Strickland, a British Maltese and practicing Catholic, as prime minister. The sticking point became the use of Italian in Maltese education and cultural life, which an interfering Mussolini, supported by the Vatican, promoted. With Valetta Harbor a strategic British naval base, the question of the use of Italian was employed as a Fascist political wedge that challenged British dominance in the Mediterranean. The Strickland government said that all education was to be in Maltese and English. This led to conflict with interfering clergy and superiors of religious orders, most of whom were Italian speaking. Strickland, a blunt man who had spent many years in Australia, responded, attacking the Vatican and the pope. Pius XI was seriously peeved. Things escalated, and the pope, an obstinate martinet, was determined to bring Strickland to heel, despite Gasparri's caution. The local archbishop, Mauro Caruana, issued a pastoral letter, saying it was a mortal sin to vote for Strickland's party. In response, the British government threatened to break off relations with the Holy See, abrogated the Maltese constitution, suspended elections, and demanded that the pastoral be withdrawn. Caruana, supported by Pius XI, refused. Strickland offered to apologize for any "offence to the ecclesiastical authorities in Malta or Rome."[39] The pope refused again, and in the end Strickland had to apologize humbly to Caruana. The pastoral was withdrawn and elections held. But this incident, which in the end was not about any fundamental principle except the interference of the clergy in politics, tells you everything about the way in which the popes were still the captives of the Italian cultural ethos and how Pius XI took himself far too seriously when he demanded an abject apology from a democratically elected Catholic prime minister.

Malta was an example of the papacy increasingly extending its influence beyond continental Europe. We have already seen this in its interventions in the Middle East after the 1914–1918 war. This was a symptom of the interconnected world that was emerging, and one of the most complex situations that Pius XI faced was in Mexico, the Mexico of Graham Greene's powerful novel *The Power and the Glory* (1940). Mexico had been unstable for the first two decades of the twentieth century. Anticlerical republicans gained increasing power, and the 1917 constitution effectively eliminated the corporate existence of the church altogether. However, these measures were not fully applied until 1924, with the election of Plutarco Elías Calles, a rabid anti-Catholic. In response, the bishops imposed an interdict on Mexico, suspending all celebration of Mass and the sacraments. However, the popular caricature that this was a conflict between a reactionary church and a progressive state is wrong. It was actually a deliberate attempt to destroy Catholicism's influence in Mexican society by a radical, nationalistic, bourgeois-Hispanic élite. The interdict led to the outbreak of the Cristero revolt in which the rural peasantry defended both their rights and their religion; they were traditionalist, but not counterrevolutionary. Priests particularly were targeted by the Calles regime. The most famous priest-martyr was Jesuit Miguel Pro, who was executed by a firing squad shouting the rallying cry of the Cristero revolutionaries, *Viva Christo Rey*, "Long Live Christ the King." The Mexican situation was complex, with divisions in the hierarchy between hard-liners and moderates who were willing to negotiate with the government, middle-class lay Catholics in the National Defence League for Religious Liberty, and the Cristeros. Under US influence a limited compromise was reached in 1929, but the church was still subject to draconian regulations. Protesting strongly in the encyclical *Acerba animi* (1932), Pius XI nevertheless realized that he had to accept what was on offer from the Mexicans under pressure from the United States, "so that, by the maintenance of divine worship . . . the light of faith . . . may not be extinguished."

A similar situation developed in Spain a decade later. Here church influence was oppressive and corruption endemic. The close link between the church and the monarchy meant that in Spain, as in other revolutions, the church was seen as the enemy along with the monarchy. After 1918 socialists and more extreme anarcho-syndicalist revolutionaries began to emerge who attacked the church-state alliance. The monarchy had been dominated by a series of military dictators, and in April 1931 the then dictator, Primo de Rivera, re-signed. Following this King Alphonso XIII abdicated, and a repub-lic was declared. A socialist government led by Mánuel Azaña y Diaz was elected. This government passed a series of antichurch mea-sures, declaring that Spain was no longer Catholic. Recognizing re-ality, Pius XI took a moderate approach. His encyclical *Dilectissima nobis* (May 1933) cautiously conceded that "the Catholic Church is never bound to one form of government more than to another, provided the divine rights of God and of Christian consciences are safe." So, while condemning the expropriation of church property, schools, and even liturgical paraphernalia, he didn't attack the re-publican government. However, the local church was strongly op-posed to the Republic, except in the independence-prone Basque region, where many Catholics and priests supported republicanism.

A Catholic political party soon emerged, but it was attacked as "sacrilegious" by promonarchist bishops, including the fiercely in-dependent Cardinal Pedro Segura y Saenz of Toledo. Segura was exiled, and the early 1936 general elections produced a Cortes with a Left majority, even though the Right gained more votes nation-ally. But things turned violent when Azaña's Popular Front govern-ment lost control of the situation and anarcho-syndicalists began burning churches and killing priests, nuns, and religious. Thirteen bishops, 4,172 secular priests, 2,365 religious priests, and 283 nuns were killed. Many were subjected to shocking torture and often dreadful deaths. The worst period was from mid-July 1936 to early 1937 when the priesthood as a profession was targeted. Most of the killers were anarchists aided by other radicals, and they looked forward to a "spiritually-free society. . . . In many places killing the cleric became a sort of revolutionary obligation. . . . [M]ost priests were killed because they were priests." An anticlerical ethos had bred the notion that the church was a parasitical entity, and repub-licans were battling "an apocalyptic monster . . . its three heads representing the three sworn enemies of the people—the rich, the military and the clergy."[40]

A military uprising against the Republican government began in July 1936 when the army in Morocco revolted and Generalissimo Francesco Franco took command. Revolts by the army all across

Spain followed, and soon Franco's army was on the Spanish main-
land. But contrary to the caricature that the Vatican was in Franco's
pocket, it was by no means a supporter. In mid-September 1936
Pius XI gave a speech condemning "the truly satanic hatred against
God . . . and all that concerns religion and the Catholic Church,"
but he admitted that beyond the appalling brutality was the "frat-
ricidal carnage" that was the reality of civil war.[41] While condemning the persecution, he didn't take sides. This was reinforced by an
article in *Osservatore Romano* (October 21, 1937), which said that
"the church does not belong to any political or social camp. It is
not a combatant, but a martyr."[42] While the local church was supportive of Franco—although not uncritically so—the simple fact is
that the Vatican did not support Franco's Falange and maintained
diplomatic relations with the Republican government throughout
the Spanish Civil War. Pius XI was especially worried about the involvement of Hitler and the Nazis on the side of Franco. Even after Franco's victory in 1939, the Generalissimo had his difficulties
with the church. While he was able to force every newly consecrated
bishop to take an oath of allegiance to the state, he didn't control
episcopal nominations.

In contrast, the situation in Portugal was benign. The anticlerical Republican regime was overthrown in a military coup in 1926,
and by 1932 the country was under the control of António Salazar,
an authoritarian academic who favored Catholicism and who followed papal social teaching.

DEMOCRACY WAS ON the wane in 1930s Europe, as the Continent
faced two totalitarian ideologies: on the Right fascism and Nazism
and on the Left communism. Pius XI had to deal with both. The
papacy certainly saw communism as the most threatening of the
two, but in the mid-1930s Nazi racism became the most immediate
problem. Communism was the first on the scene.

The Bolsheviks seized power from the provisional government
in Russia in October 1917. They struggled to survive through a
civil war and then in 1921–1923 had to cope with a famine in the

Volga River region in which about 5 million people died. In July 1921 a request came from Russian Orthodox patriarch Tikhon, begging Benedict XV for help "in the name of God." A Papal Relief Mission was quickly established, headed by US Jesuit Edmund A. Walsh. By mid-1923 the papal mission was feeding 158,000 people each day. But the Bolsheviks made sure that the mission was confined to relief work and didn't proselytize. However, Pius XI was interested in getting a Catholic foothold in Russia, while planning to invite the Orthodox to return to Roman unity. However, the papal mission was withdrawn in November 1923 after show trials and executions of local Orthodox and Catholic clergy and laity by the Soviet government.

By the mid-1920s the small Catholic Church in the Soviet Union had been all but destroyed by the communists. But Pius XI had not given up, and secret negotiations began in early 1925 through the Berlin Nunciature between Pacelli and the Soviet Foreign Ministry. By December 1927 these negotiations had collapsed, and with all bishops eliminated, Catholicism in Russia was literally "decapitated." Meanwhile, in 1926 the pope had the enigmatic French Jesuit and Russian scholar Michel d'Herbigny secretly consecrated a bishop by Pacelli in Berlin and covertly sent on two trips into western Russia and Moscow to contact any remaining priests and consecrate four of them as bishops. However, the secret police, the OGPU, were fully aware of d'Herbigny's activities, and all he achieved was to compromise those he contacted, who were quickly imprisoned.

After 1929 and the Soviet's "godless campaigns," Pius XI's attitudes hardened. This may have been influenced by persecution in Mexico and Spain or just the departure of the moderating influence of Gasparri as secretary of state. Pius, of course, had seen Bolshevism in action when he was in Warsaw, and as he made clear in the encyclical *Quadragesimo anno*, "no one can be a true socialist and a good Catholic." By 1936 Catholicism in the Soviet Union had been eliminated, and Pius XI decided to raise "a solemn protest" against communism. In the encyclical *Divini Redemptoris* (March 19, 1937), he presents communism as a pseudoreligion. It is "a collectivity with no other hierarchy than that of the economic system. It would have only one mission: the production of material things by means of collective labor, so that the goods of this world might be enjoyed in a paradise . . . [inaugurating] a new era and a new civilization which is the result of blind evolutionary forces culminating in a humanity without God." Thus, by its very nature it was anti-Christian and undermined all that Catholicism represents. Pius XI says that communism is imposed by "terrorism," and it is significant that the encyclical parallels Stalin's 1936–1938 "show trials." An emphasis on anticommunism was to dominate Catholic political thinking for the next three decades.

Pius XI was, however, facing another, more immediate, threat: Nazism. As we saw in the 1920s, Vatican sympathies tended to favor Germany. Traditionally, the *Länder* (states) controlled religious and educational issues in Germany, but the postwar constitution of the Reich inclined toward centralization, and there were initial discussions about a concordat with the national government. But the church achieved what it wanted regarding church-state relations and questions surrounding education from the *Länder* through concordats with Bavaria (1924), Prussia (1929), and Baden-Baden (1932). The then papal nuncio Pacelli strongly believed that concordats, diplomatically negotiated, were the answer to securing the position of the church.

Germany had been crippled by the financial crash and Great Depression of 1929–1932. As the Nazis gained influence, some Catholic theologians like Karl Adam reacted naively, accepting Hitler's grand vision uncritically, while ignoring Nazi racism and violence. The bishops took a tougher line, denying party members the sacraments and church burial while excoriating them in the Catholic press. Between 1930 and mid-1932, the Catholic *Zentrumspartei* (Center Party) was in government, with the Nazis the second-largest party in the Reichstag. Led by a devout Catholic chancellor, Heinrich Brüning, the Center Party government faced an impossible task, with 4.5 million people unemployed. Germany was caught up in rampant inflation, the banks were in trouble, and there was the ever-present threat of Nazi violence. Visiting Rome on August 8,

1931, Brüning met with Secretary of State Pacelli. He reports in his *Memoirs* that the cardinal demanded that he seek Nazi support for his minority government rather than that of the left-leaning Social Democrats. Brüning responded that the Nazis were untrustworthy, and he refused to compromise with them. A heated discussion followed. Reflecting afterward, Brüning wrote, "All successes [Pacelli believed] could only be attained by papal diplomacy. The system of concordats led him and the Vatican to despise democracy and the parliamentary system. . . . Rigid governments, rigid centralization and rigid treaties were supposed to introduce an era of stable order . . . of peace and quiet."[43] The problem was that Pacelli—like Pius XI—was obsessed with the authoritarian, hierarchical approach that dominated the church after Vatican I. The Nazi opposition to Bolshevism was the other factor that persuaded Pacelli to show leniency toward Hitler. After Hitler was appointed chancellor in late January 1933 and the Nazi victory in the early March elections, the German bishops lifted their ban on membership of the Nazi Party. Widespread attacks on the Jews began. Despite strong protests from Brüning, the *Zentrumspartei*, now under the influence of Pacelli's confidant Monsignor Ludwig Hass, supported the enabling legislation that gave the Nazis supreme power; the Social Democrats alone bravely opposed the legislation. Finally, on July 4, 1933, the *Zentrumspartei* dissolved itself.

Right from early 1933 Hitler wanted a concordat with the Holy See because that would give him international respectability; he knew he could always ignore clauses that didn't suit him afterward. Recent archival research has shown that there is no evidence that at the time Pius XI and Pacelli were actively seeking a concordat with Hitler before the idea was suggested to them by the Germans in early April 1933. They responded positively because they felt that a concordat would protect the institutional church from the brutal regime. Negotiations for the *Reichskonkordat* began almost immediately, and it was signed on July 20, 1933, in Rome by Pacelli and Franz von Papen for Germany. It erected what Hubert Wolf has called "a forward defensive wall" that protected Catholicism as "the only large-scale institution in Germany that Hitler never managed to co-opt."[44] But it was essentially about protecting ec- clesiastical institutions, and it effectively silenced the church in pro- phetic terms; in other words, the church surrendered its right to speak out against what was to become the appalling brutality of the Nazi regime. It reduced German Catholicism to an otherworldly organization, solely concerned with the religious and sacramental realm. Any protests the church did make were diplomatic and con- fidential. As a result, German Catholics were left speechless when a prophetic naming of evil was called for, especially in the treatment of the Jews.

By 1937 Pius XI's patience with the Nazis was exhausted, and the shape of the Third Reich was clear. Racist, virulently anti- Semitic, and neopagan, the Nazis were proposing a clear alternative to Christianity. Between 1933 and 1936, there had been thirty-four ineffective protests from the church over Hitler's contempt for the terms of the *Reichskonkordat*. The German bishops, with a couple of exceptions, had been ineffective, and their leader, Cardinal Ad- olf Bertram of Breslau, was weak. Pacelli called the five German cardinals to Rome in January 1937. Pius XI was sick, but it was decided to issue an encyclical—which became *Mit brennenen Sorge* (*With Burning Anxiety*)—on the church situation in Germany. A draft was written by Cardinal Michael von Faulhaber of Munich. The tone of this encyclical was pastoral and moderate—some might say "weak"—and the only thing it condemned was Nazi faith in a "national God." Part of this was due to Pacelli protecting his *Reichskonkordat*; he also claimed that "the pope does not wish to exclude the hope, small as it may be, that the situation may im- prove."[45] The encyclical was smuggled into Germany and was read at all Masses on Palm Sunday (1937). It harps on the way the Nazis "emasculated the terms of the [concordat]" and condemns those who follow "that so-called pre-Christian Germanic conception of substituting a dark and impersonal destiny for the personal God." But it never names the Nazis, let alone Nazi anti-Semitism. It infu- riated the Nazis, who were completely blindsided by it, but it was nowhere near as condemnatory as *Divini Redemptoris* was of com- munism, which was issued just a week later.

By 1938 Pius XI became increasingly sensitive to the appalling treatment of the Jews and of the need to condemn anti-Semitism in Germany, Poland, and Hungary. Evidence for this emerged in 1972 when Jim Castelli of the *National Catholic Reporter* discovered a proposed encyclical provisionally entitled "*Humani generis unitas*" (Unity of the human race) on racism and anti-Semitism.[46] The encyclical was drafted in secret between June and December 1938 on the instructions of the pope by US Jesuit John LaFarge and two other Jesuits, Gustav Gundlach and Gustave Desbuquois. The only other person who knew about it was the general of the Jesuits, Pole Wlodimir Ledóchowski, to whom the draft encyclical was entrusted to be passed on to Pius XI. Hubert Wolf thinks that in the last year of his life, Pius XI wanted to address the issue of anti-Semitism, which Pacelli was not "prepared to countenance." So the pope secretly commissioned the encyclical. He died on February 10, 1939, possibly without even having seen the draft, which Ledóchowski seems not to have delivered. Wolf has shown that "Pius XI had resolved . . . [in 1938] to intervene more decisively against National Socialism, its racial ideology and the persecution of the Jews." In response to Fascist adoption of racist laws, the pope told Belgian pilgrims in September 1938 that anti-Semitism is "a repulsive movement with which we Christians have nothing in common. . . . Spiritually," he said, "we are Semites."[47] Pius XI also unsuccessfully tried to get the Canadian and Australian governments to take Jewish immigrants.

What is clear is that at the end of his papacy, this pope was prepared to act prophetically and confront the evils of Nazism and anti-Semitism. The tragedy is that it came just before his death on February 10, 1939. His successor quickly relegated the proposed encyclical to the secret archives.

6

PONTIFICATING ON EVERYTHING

JUST OVER FOUR months before Pius XI died, British prime minister Neville Chamberlain landed at Heston Airport, very close to
the present Heathrow, aboard a British Airways flight from Munich. Standing beside the plane, he held up in the wind a piece of
paper signed by Hitler and himself, saying that the two countries
would "never go to war with each other again." By the time he got
to Downing Street, he was proclaiming "peace in our time." Like
others, including the pope, he had been deceived by the führer,
and Czechoslovakia had been betrayed. Eleven months later, on
September 1, 1939, the Wehrmacht rolled into Poland, and the
Second World War began.

So the conclave that gathered on March 2, 1939, to elect a new
pope did so in an atmosphere of crisis. It was the shortest conclave
of modern history, and Eugenio Pacelli was elected the next day
on the third ballot. He took the style Pius XII to honor his predecessor. Aged sixty-three, he was Pius XI's choice as successor,
and he came to the papacy with ability and experience. An excellent
linguist, he had twelve years as nuncio in Germany and had visited
Britain, France, Argentina, Hungary, and the United States and had
a good knowledge of the wider world. Tall and thin, he was a Roman born and bred, offspring of the black nobility (Roman nobles
who remained loyal to the papacy), a sensitive, taciturn mama's boy
who had not even experienced the boarding-school atmosphere
of the seminary; sickly, he had studied from home. As a priest, he
had virtually no pastoral experience whatsoever, as his entire career had been spent in ecclesiastical politics, and his diplomatic

training drained any sense of the prophetic from him. Given this background, it is understandable that his vision of the church was profoundly institutional.

The new pope faced an immediate challenge—the looming Second World War. He also had to deal with a fascist government in Italy that was now an ally of Nazi Germany, but at least he now had his own territory in the Vatican. But he was also handicapped by his own history of compromise with Nazi Germany and his conviction that diplomacy rather than a prophetic condemnation of the evils of anti-Semitism and Hitler's aggression was what Christian faith and Catholic morality demanded. He appointed the Paris nuncio, Luigi Maglione, as secretary of state, but he made all the key decisions himself, particularly those relating to Germany. Just six months after his election, the Wehrmacht overran western Poland, the Soviets invaded the eastern part of the country, and according to a secret protocol in the Molotov-Ribbentrop Pact between Germany and the Soviet Union, Poland was divided between the Nazi and Soviet power blocs, while the area bordering Germany was annexed to the German Reich.

From the start of the Second World War, Pius XII was perceived as pro-German. The Polish and French ambassadors to the Holy See were furious that he was unwilling to make a public statement about the impending German invasion of Poland. When France was invaded in June 1940, he again remained silent. The diplomat in Pius XII took a stance of public neutrality, no matter what his private feelings might have been. Throughout the war he constantly called for peace, and he adopted a nonpartisan position of diplomatic "impartiality" and neutrality. He took this stance so that he could not be used by any side in the conflict. In his tediously long, hectoring first encyclical, *Summi pontificatus* (October 20, 1939), he makes only passing reference to the war, although he obliquely refers to the treatment of the Jews when he quotes a passage from the Letter to the Colossians, which he claimed reflected the church's teaching: "There is neither Gentile nor Jew, circumcision nor un-circumcision, barbarian nor Scythian, bond nor free. But Christ is all and in all" (3:10–11). But the reference was so oblique that only ecclesiastical insiders would have picked up on its meaning.

This failure to speak publicly is especially focused by the Shoah, the Hebrew word for the catastrophe of the Holocaust. Since the release of much of the Holy See's documentary evidence concerning the Second World War in an eleven-volume set between 1965 and 1981, we are now in a better position to assess the pope's response to the Holocaust.[1] Certainly, the portrayal of Pius XII in Rolf Hochhuth's 1963 play, *The Deputy*, which started much of the modern excoriation of Pius XII, can now be dismissed as a caricature. Part of the problem with judging this papacy is "the incessant partisanship of the so-called Pius War" that replaces "a reasoned assessment of what he did or did not do—and why."[2] But many historians are still highly critical of the pope, and nagging doubts remain: Given that he knew what was happening to the Jews, why didn't he do more?

Was he anti-Semitic? Or, as the title of John Cornwell's book title suggests, was he "Hitler's pope"? The answer is a cautious no, because it's clear that he didn't support Hitler and that he tried to assist the Jews. Canadian historian Jacques Kornberg talks about the pope's "calculated acquiescence" in the Shoah and says, "The pope allowed these crimes to happen because of his own priorities and responsibilities as head of the Roman Catholic Church, but he was in no sense an accomplice to policies he deplored."[3] Kornberg says that a judgment of the Pacelli papacy must take into account the way in which Pius XII saw his duty as pope, and he should be judged on his own terms and by his own values. This again forces us to confront the question of papal authority and power. Pius XII felt he had to do what he thought was best for the papacy, and as a "universal father" he had to juggle protection of the institutional church in Germany and occupied Europe with the fate of the Jews. Benedict XV and Pius XI acted in a similar way. In their own minds, these three popes identified the institutional church with themselves. So prophecy—by which I mean speaking out as Christ did—was beyond them. Pius XI came closest to a prophetic stand on racism at the end of his life, but he died before anything was achieved.

Certainly, Pius XII worked very hard for prisoners of war, refugees, missing persons, and Jews. From mid-1942 he certainly knew that the Holocaust was under way, following the decision of the Wannsee Conference (January 20, 1942) to actuate the *Endlosung*, the "Final Solution" of the Jewish question. Dreadful things had happened prior to Wannsee, and the concentration camps were already fully operative. But from 1942 the focus shifted to the extermination camps such as Birkenau, adjoining Auschwitz. Information about this was flowing into the Vatican from bishops, nuncios, and even Italian military chaplains on the eastern front.

There was also pressure on Pius XII from the Allies who had already issued a Joint Declaration (December 17, 1942) on Hitler's "oft-repeated" determination to exterminate the Jews. But all they got from Pius XII's long 1942 Christmas broadcast was a generalized reference to "the hundreds of thousands of persons who, without any fault on their part, sometimes only because of their nationality or race, have been consigned to death or to a slow decline." But in the same broadcast, he also mentioned Allied carpet bombing of Germany that killed "many thousands of non-combatants . . . . without discrimination," including destroying "houses of prayer."[4] He was clearly determined to maintain his neutrality and felt that if he denounced the Nazis, he would also have to condemn the Allied bombing and the crimes of Soviet forces in Eastern Europe. This could harm the church on both sides, and so he tried to be completely evenhanded.

It was a terrible dilemma, and Pius XII makes no sense unless we place him within his context. One who does this is Carlo Falconi, who probably comes closest to explaining the pope's behavior.[5] Falconi says the pope was worried above all about Soviet communism, especially from early 1943, when the war turned against the Germans on the eastern front. He felt that a condemnation of Nazism would weaken the Hitler regime, which might leave the way open to Soviet tyranny across Europe. He also feared for the fate of the church. What would a grand gesture achieve? Although, ironically, he later became the master of grand gestures, Pius XII's diplomatic training made him suspicious of grandstanding, and his institutional ecclesiology paralyzed him; he felt it was his duty to God to save the church's sacramental ministry at all costs. Falconi suggests that at the psychological and spiritual level, Pius was caught in an appalling moral dilemma that was heightened by his personal faith. He says that Pius's ecclesiology derived from a dogmatic and juridical conception of the church rather than from a mystical and prophetic stance. This institutionalism paralyzed him so that he was unable to risk speaking out for fear of harming the church. This was reinforced by his spirituality. It was otherworldly and focused on an interior life by seeking perfection through mortification. It encouraged a piety that stood in opposition to the profane and engendered a kind of spiritual split in the pope's personality between personal holiness and the ethics demanded of a churchman in the world, which in the end was morally crippling. Falconi says bluntly that the cardinals elected the wrong man in March 1939. They felt the church needed a diplomat, but in fact that was the last thing Catholicism needed. The Nazis despised diplomacy. In fact, the church needed a papal prophet who was willing to risk everything in terms of the institution in order to make a stand against the Hitler regime. But papal prophets are few and far between, and Pacelli was certainly not one of them.

Another who argues along these lines is historian Paul O'Shea. He sees Pius XII, correctly in my view, as someone caught up in the miasma of institutional Roman theology and the parochialism of the Vatican. Despite his travels, this pope lived in a very narrow world. O'Shea says, "His blindness was not that of willful ignorance or of not wanting to know; it was the fervently held belief that the mission of Universal Pastor . . . entrusted to him by Almighty God Himself, made him accountable to God for the preservation and salvation of the Catholic Church. . . . Nothing, not even the death of millions, could be allowed to stand between the Pope and his God-given task."[6]

In addition, O'Shea believes that Pius XII was convinced that communism was the real enemy, and, like his predecessor, he felt the papacy could find a *modus vivendi* with fascism, as demonstrated by the Lateran pacts. Given the pope's hierarchical ecclesiology, the

Fuhrerprinzip (supreme-leader principle) applied in both church and state. O'Shea says Pius also imbibed the long tradition of Christian anti-Judaism. Essentially, this is religious rather than racist, although it could easily modulate into anti-Semitism. Pius also believed the supersessionist myth, the notion that the Jews were no longer the chosen people and that Catholicism had replaced them as the "new Israel."

IN JULY 1943 the situation in Italy changed radically when Mussolini was overthrown and arrested and the new Italian government negotiated to surrender to the Allies. By late September 1943 the Allies held all of southern Italy, up to the German Gustav line, north of Naples and across to near Pescara on the Adriatic coast and just south of the monastery of Monte Cassino. Rome had already been bombed by the US Air Force on July 19, 1943, when in an attack on the San Lorenzo freight yards and steelworks, the ancient Basilica of San Lorenzo was badly damaged and some fifteen hundred civilians were killed. The pope rushed to bombing sites and stood with the injured and openly begged both the Germans and the Allies to declare Rome an "open city" so that it would be saved from bombing and street-by-street fighting. The pope, in contrast to his usual supercool diplomacy, was passionate in his defense of Rome, which many Allied diplomats saw as hypocrisy. But Pius XII's actions sprang "from his conception of Rome as the light and center of civilization, and his belief that the authority and prestige of the papacy was a dam against encroaching godlessness in the form of National Socialism, Communism, socialism and secular liberalism."[7] The Allies were ruthless about what they bombed. Between February and May 1944, in an act of sheer barbarism, the historical Benedictine abbey of Monte Cassino was completely destroyed, including its library and archives. The orders were issued by British general Harold Alexander, even though German commander Field-Marshal Albert Kesselring ordered that German troops *not* occupy the abbey—and they didn't. So the pope's stance regarding the untrustworthiness of the Allies was justified because by this stage they were besotted with aerial bombardment as a way of defeating the Germans.

After the fall of Mussolini, Rome was occupied by the Germans on September 10, 1943. At the time, there were about 7,700 Jews living in the city. A ransom was levied on the community by the SD (the intelligence arm of the SS), and it was paid. Despite this, the Germans began the *razzia*, the rounding up of Jews, and the deportations began in mid-October. At one stage 1,259 Jews (252 were later released) were held in the *Collegio Militare*, abutting the Leonine Wall of the Vatican, and the pope did nothing. O'Shea believes that his failure to intervene to save these Roman Jews is unforgivable and that he didn't speak "because he did not want to." O'Shea says that his actions up to this date "are defensible. After October 1943, they are not." He argues that the church's "fatal flaw lay in the centuries-old fear and hatred of Jews and Judaism."[8] While the papacy was silent, there was local Roman resistance to the *razzia*, and the Jews had time to go into hiding. Actually, 85 percent of Italian Jews survived because ordinary Italians and hundreds of convents, religious houses, and monasteries sheltered them all across the country. There were also communist partisans in the city, and it was their killing of 33 SS troops that led to the massacre of 335 men at the Ardeatine Caves, on the edge of Rome. Some were Italian political prisoners, and others were Jewish civilians. Knowing it was communist partisans who were responsible, the pope blamed them for the massacre and let the Germans off the hook.

On June 4, 1944, the Americans entered Rome, and the Germans withdrew after complex negotiations between Pius XII, German ambassador Ernst von Weizsäcker, Kesselring, Churchill, Roosevelt, and perhaps even Hitler. Rome was declared an "open city" (that is, the city was undefended and didn't need to be attacked) because of its cultural and historical value. The Germans accepted this, but at first the Allies did not; their only concern was military advantage. The Germans certainly gained tactical advantage by withdrawing from Rome and consolidating their forces farther north; it was not worthwhile holding the city. According to von

Weizsäcker, the peaceful handover was due to "the ceaseless quiet activity of the Pope" as well as "the wise instructions given by Kesselring for the withdrawal." Ever the opportunist, "Hitler . . . later made propaganda capital out of the part played by the Germans in the sparing of Rome."[9]

More recent research by Mark Riebling in *Church of Spies* (2015) has shown that Pius XII was deeply and decisively involved with the Catholic and broader anti-Hitler underground in Germany. This creates another perspective from which to view the pope's silence. Pius XII was the key link between the (mainly military) plotters in Germany and the British and American authorities on whose goodwill any replacement German government would have to rely after Hitler was gone. Pius was at the center of a complex network that involved the Abwehr (German military intelligence) and its anti-Nazi boss, Admiral Wilhelm Canaris; Sir D'Arcy Osborne, the British minister to the Vatican; and a web of conspirators, including high-ranking German officers, couriers like Dr. Josef Müller (the hero of Riebling's book), enigmatic Jesuit Robert Leiber, and many others. There were really two stages in the pope's involvement. The first went from the invasion of Poland in September 1939 to the invasion of France in May 1940. In that period, two failed attempts were made on Hitler's life, and the British lost interest in maintaining contact through the pope with anti-Nazi Germans by early 1940. It was after the Germans became bogged down in Russia that the plotters got a second wind, and Pius XII again became involved as an intermediary. It was partly this involvement that dissuaded the pope from making any outspoken condemnations of the Shoah. After the war Müller said unequivocally that the German plotters "had always been very insistent that the Pope should refrain from making any public statement singling out the Nazis and specifically condemning them." Since the plotters were planning to assassinate Hitler, long discussions involving the pope were held, debating the circumstances in which tyrannicide was justified in Catholic moral theology. While this, to an extent, explains Pius's silence, Riebling doesn't let the pope off the hook so easily: "Judging Pius by what he did not say," Riebling writes, "one can only damn him. . . . [D]uring the world's greatest moral crisis, its greatest moral leader seemed at a loss for words."[10]

So what are we to make of the pope's stance during the war? In my view, it can't be understood outside Pius XII's view of himself as the "universal pastor" of the church. For him, the maintenance of the sacramental life of the church, its institutional structure, and papal authority was central. His notion of himself as the one primarily responsible for the church meant that everything else must be subsumed to that priority. He certainly saw Nazism as a threat to the church, but it was a threat that should be dealt with quietly and diplomatically. He feared that outspokenness would lead the Nazis to attack the institutional church, close down its sacramental ministry, and even attack the papacy itself. Deeply embedded in this attitude was the feeling that papal authority could never be compromised. Mentally, he had identified himself with the church, and everything else was jettisoned to maintain that identity. Of course he knew what was happening to the Jews, and of course it constituted a terrible moral dilemma for him. But in the end, he was responsible for the survival of institutional Catholicism, and that must be his first priority. He seemingly separated the church's institutional structure from the its moral responsibility to speak out against the Holocaust. He saw his primary responsibility as safeguarding the institutional church. Everything else, even the greatest moral challenge of the twentieth century, was secondary.

———

THE "PIUS WARS" have for too long dominated all judgment of Pius XII. He was pope for thirteen years after the war, he wasn't closed to modern developments, and to some extent he broke out of the theological and intellectual paralysis that had afflicted the papacy since the modernist crisis. He was interested in science and technology, and he strongly encouraged the Pontifical Academy of Science. He was something of a scientific geek and had a particular interest in the big bang theory of the origin of the universe, articulated by Father Georges Lemaître of the Catholic University of

Leuven, Belgium. The pope's aim was "to transform [modernity], to sanctify and ready it for its redemption."[11] However, he left untouched the stultifying dominance of the Holy Office in theology.

Despite the viciousness of the attacks on it, the church's intellectual life was not destroyed by the modernist crisis. At least in terms of liturgy, Pius X had even accidentally encouraged renewal with his emphasis on pastoral issues. A tradition of historico-liturgical studies began in the late nineteenth century, well before Pius X, and it continued through the first half of the twentieth century. The first phase of liturgical renewal was monastic, beginning in France and then moving on to England, Germany, Belgium, and later the United States. Its beginnings can be traced to the Abbey of Solesmes and Abbot Prosper Guéranger, who began as a disciple of Lamennais. Pioneering historical work on the liturgy was also done in England by the convert layman Edmund Bishop, who worked at Downside Abbey, as did another pioneer, Australian-born monk Hugh Connolly. Anglican scholar Gregory Dix was the third important English liturgical historian. The most important continental scholar was Lambert Beauduin, monk of Mont César in Belgium, who shifted the focus from historical studies to the theological and pastoral aspects of worship.

The revival of liturgy went hand in hand with the revival of ecclesiology, the theology of the church. In contrast to Rome's complete preoccupation with power, German theology since the early nineteenth century had focused on the more mystical and sacramental, less institutional, aspect of the church. The fount of this ecclesiology was Johan Adam Möhler. For the deeply ecumenical Möhler, the church was a living community that symbolized Christ's presence in the world. These ideas were adopted and adapted in the first half of the twentieth century by German monk Odo Casel, from Maria Laach Abbey, who recovered the notion conveyed by the Greek theological word *mysterion* (mystery) as being at the heart of Christian faith. The primary mystery is the incarnation of Christ, to which Christians are joined through his body, the church. Casel saw worship as the process whereby believers entered into the transforming presence and living reality of Christ. Italian-born German theologian Romano Guardini also saw the church as Jesus Christ alive, especially in the liturgy, and it was in worship that the believer primarily experienced Christ. The American Benedictines at Saint John's Abbey at Collegeville, Minnesota, spread these ideas to English speakers. The key person here was Vigil Michel. He succeeded in translating European ideas into the Anglo-American world and related liturgy to the practical life of Catholics. In this way, the relationship with Christ was also linked to responsibility for the world, thus linking worship with social justice. These ideas spread and were popularized among priests and informed Catholics through the periodical *Worship*. All this signified a distinct movement away from a purely institutional, authoritarian view of the church that was typical of Vatican I. There were soon calls for the use of the vernacular in worship and for a general reform of the church's worship. The first fruit of this was the reform of the Easter Triduum (Holy Thursday, Good Friday, and Easter Saturday), announced by Pius XII in 1953. Needless to say, all this led to a conservative institutional backlash, with many pressing Rome, even during the war, to suppress the liturgical movement.

By 1943 Pius XII decided it was time to intervene in the controversies swirling around liturgy and ecclesiology. This was an extraordinary moment to seize the initiate, virtually holed up as he was in the Vatican and Rome. It certainly indicates that he had been following developments in theology and still had very good advice. He saw that ecclesiology was basic, and his encyclical *Mystici corporis* (June 29, 1943) confirmed the developments that began with Möhler. The encyclical draws mainly on the work of Belgian Jesuit Emile Mersch, tragically killed in 1940 in the German advance into France. Mersch, like Möhler, bases his theology on patristic and biblical images of the church, and his *Theology of the Mystical Body* reflects Paul's emphasis on the body of Christ as a model of the way in which the church works (1 Cor. 12:12–30). This personal, dynamic, community-oriented image is more in keeping with the New Testament than an institutional, static model. Although *Mystici corporis* emphasizes the juridical aspects of the church, it also focuses on the presence of Christ in the community and aims to show how the two are united in Catholicism. The pope also highlights the role of the laity, but he remains enmeshed in the hierarchical clericalism of the time. In a creative surge, three months later Pius XII also issued the encyclical *Divino afflante Spiritu* (September 30, 1943), on biblical studies. Given that this was a focus of the modernist controversy, the pope showed his openness by cautiously approving developments in modern biblical theology. This surprised many, and it laid the foundation for the modern Catholic biblical movement and the critical use of the Bible at Vatican II, and it was perhaps the greatest intellectual achievement of the Pacelli papacy.

His third important encyclical was *Mediator Dei* (November 20, 1947), on the liturgy. It praises the historical and theological scholarship of the previous century and gives a definition of the liturgy that has become normative: "The sacred liturgy is the public worship which our Redeemer, the Head of the Church, offers to the heavenly Father, and which the community of Christ's faithful pays to its Founder and through Him to the Eternal Father. . . . [I]t is the whole public worship of the Mystical Body of Jesus Christ, Head and Members."

This integrates Christ with God and the community with Christ and through him with God. The encyclical discusses the theological, pastoral, and juridical aspects of the liturgy, the relations between public and private prayer and liturgical art. While not excluding the use of the vernacular, *Mediator Dei* emphasizes papal authority governing every aspect of the liturgy. He certainly didn't allow room for "local adaptations." The pope was evenhanded about modern liturgical developments, so those opposing the movement saw the "innovations" they criticized condemned, while liturgical reformers tended to see encouragement and approval. Pius XII also later modified the fasting rule before receiving Communion and introduced the idea of an evening Mass, which made it easier for working people to get to Mass. Another practical step forward was that many laity now used missals that translated worship texts into the local languages. This explains the great success of *My Sunday Missal* (first published in 1944 in the United States) and similar publications across the English-speaking world. These three encyclicals laid the foundations for much of the theological work that led to Vatican II. They reflect a pope in tune with what was happening in theology and open to new developments.

———————

BUT THESE ENCYCLICALS should not lead us into thinking that Pius XII had retreated from his conviction that he was the focus of Catholicism and that by divine law he alone exercised absolute power throughout the church. The war didn't prevent a media mystique beginning to be built around him. This began in 1942 when he commissioned the film *Pastor angelicus*, which told his life story and explained his daily routine, personal holiness, and the indestructibility of the papacy. The war was hardly mentioned. Perhaps this was a hedge against the danger of a Nazi "invasion" of the Vatican to seize and imprison him and actually smacks of unconscious anxiety about the papacy caught up in the middle of Axis territory and with the war going badly for Italy. *Pastor angelicus* was not shown in the United States until 1946, with the title *Story of the Pope*. In 1947 another film cast Pius XII as the defender of civilization, *Guerra alla guerra* (War to war). The pope was presented as a living saint who guided people toward peace by his teaching.

The postwar world was the era of the ever-increasingly pervasive presence of electronic media—first films, then radio, and in the 1950s television. So in the decade before his death in 1958, several more documentaries were made about him. Like most major institutions, including the British monarchy and Queen Elizabeth II, the Vatican saw the potential for promoting the papacy, and in Pius XII they had a real "personality." The Vatican was quickly learning about the soft-power use of modern media, which turned the pope into an almost omniscient figure with whom Catholicism was intimately identified. A tall, dignified man who somehow appeared indefinably exalted, Pius XII swept into papal audiences almost as though his feet didn't touch the ground. He didn't walk; he processed, surrounded by clerical and lay flunkies opening doors, walking backward, bowing, genuflecting, kneeling. A lonely, complex man, he apparently related to people but always remained aloof on a pedestal, surrounded by an extraordinarily kitschy kind of worship, even idolatry. For sure, the same applied to Leo XIII and to a lesser extent to the popes up to 1939, but Pius XII took the papal mystique to a new level. In 1950 he proclaimed a holy year in which he invited Catholics to come to Rome to gain a plenary indulgence, further enhancing the cult of the papacy through pilgrimages. John Cornwell correctly says that the pope's "attempts to revitalize Catholic spirituality focused on a hybrid of popular piety and the autocracy of the papal office."[12]

Linked to the holy year was the infallible definition of the doctrine of the Assumption of Mary. Having consulted the bishops of the world by letter, 98 percent of whom affirmed the doctrine, the pope declared on November 1, 1950, that "the Immaculate Mother of God, the ever Virgin Mary, having completed the course of her earthly life, was assumed body and soul into heavenly glory." This is the only occasion on which any doctrine has been declared infallibly since Vatican I. It reflects Pius XII's deep devotion to Mary and particularly to Our Lady of Fatima, a series of visions and prophecies of the Blessed Virgin to a group of peasant children in Portugal in May to October 1917. Two of the children died in the influenza epidemic in 1919 and 1920, but one survived as a nun, Sister Lúcia Santos, until 2005. The Virgin is supposed to have entrusted three secrets to the children, and in 1941 Sister Lúcia revealed two of the secrets: One was a terrible vision of hell. The other was double-edged: World War I would end, but if people did not repent another world war would break out and that if Russia were not converted to Catholicism, there would be endless wars and persecutions. The key thing here is not so much the prophecies or their accuracy, but that the Fatima cult became linked to anticommunism, and this linkage became prominent in the Cold War years. It was the mention of the conversion of Russia in the second Fatima secret that Pius XI and Pius XII latched on to, and Pius XI commanded that the vernacular prayers at the end of Mass that were introduced by Leo XIII be now specifically dedicated to the conversion of Russia. Unlike the cult of Our Lady of Lourdes, which was always linked to curing the sick, the Fatima message became political and was linked to anticommunism. We shall return to the Fatima cult with John Paul II.

In the 1950s, Pius XII's distinctly odd relationship with Sister Pascalina Lehnert, "La Popessa," gained some prominence. This Bavarian sister was Pius XII's housekeeper, cook, soul mate, and a kind of substitute mother. Pius XI had a similar "housekeeper," Signora Linda Banfi, who, despite the *Signora*, was probably a spinster. Pascalina was also the only one who could deal with Pius XII's neurasthenia, his vague nervous debility from overwork and anxiety that became worse as he aged. While the 1983 book *La Popessa* is based on the fascinating relationship between the two, it is gossipy and unreliable. Nevertheless, Pascalina exercised considerable influence over the pope and was resented by many powerful men in the curia, especially the bearded French linguist and scholar Cardinal Eugène Tisserant. According to one account, Sister Pascalina actually slapped the cardinal across the face.[13]

Much of the curial opposition originated in Pius XII's increasing isolation. He cut himself off from the cardinals and, especially from about 1948, ruled in splendid isolation. Maglione had died in 1944, and Pius effectively acted as his own secretary of state, working through the *sostituti* (deputy secretaries) Monsignors Domenico Tardini and Giovanni Battista Montini (later Milan archbishop and Pope Paul VI), who acted as the pope's agents. It was not a good arrangement because it meant that Pacelli had no independent advice.

The first eight years of this papacy were the most theologically open. By about 1948 the Holy Office began investigating what was then derisively known as *la nouvelle théologie* (the new theology), which, in fact, was far more traditional and ancient than the neoscholasticism touted in Rome. The *nouvelle théologie* had emerged as Jesuit and Dominican scholars searched for a culturally relevant theology in the 1930s and during the Second World War when many priests and theologians served in the various armies and were held as prisoners of war. These war experiences confronted them with human, moral, and theological problems that were inconceivable in the isolated and academic theology of the Roman universities. Based on the more dynamic philosophy of Maurice Blondel, Emanuel Mounier, Joseph Maréchal, and later German philosopher Martin Heidegger, these theologians moved beyond ecclesiastical neoscholasticism by returning to biblical, patristic, and medieval sources. This is known in French as *ressourcement*, a return to the sources of Christian faith. These theologians emphasized reengaging the laity with theology and ministry. They were also explicitly ecumenical, and they realized that theology and doctrine divorced from historical context made no sense at all in modern intellectual culture.

Jesuit Henri de Lubac and Dominican Yves Congar were key figures in the *nouvelle théologie*. Lubac was also prominent in the Catholic resistance to French fascism, and during the German occupation he spoke out against anti-Semitism and was under Gestapo surveillance. Together with Jean Daniélou, he began *Sources chrétiennes* in 1942 to provide the church with critical editions of patristic authors. Congar spent five years as a prisoner of war in Germany, and he was a Catholic pioneer in the ecumenical movement who always maintained close contact with practical ministry. Austrian Jesuit Karl Rahner, perhaps the most important Catholic theologian of the twentieth century, was not strictly identified with the *nouvelle théologie*, but no treatment of modern theology would be complete without him.

Lurking behind the *nouvelle théologie* was French Jesuit paleontologist, thinker, and poet Pierre Teilhard de Chardin. His contribution to modern theology and Catholic thinking is enormous.[14] He argues that matter matters because it is imbued with purposive, spiritual energy that moves toward ever greater complexity and reaches its apogee in Christ. His strength is that he addressed what is arguably the most important theological issue facing contemporary Christians: the reintegration of the material and spiritual and the jettisoning of the dualistic separation of body and soul. Teilhard is like his fellow Jesuit George Tyrrell in that he was a radical thinker whose work from early on was suspect for church authorities. Even in the late 1940s, Teilhard was denied permission to publish his seminal work, *The Phenomenon of Man*. It was not published in French until 1955, the year of his death.

The whole renewal movement was deeply suspect in the Vatican's Holy Office, and in the late 1940s a mini modernist crisis blew up. The result was the encyclical *Humani generis* of August 12, 1950, which tragically paralyzed Catholic theology for another decade and negated much of the good that had been achieved in the first part of Pius XII's papacy. Nowadays this encyclical is seen primarily as a Holy Office–inspired attempt to reassert its control of theology, because it was largely drafted by French Dominican Reginald Garrigou-Lagrange, and it certainly reflected his views. He was a supporter of *Action Française* and the Vichy regime. A rigid neoscholastic, totally lacking any historico-critical perspective, he caricatured the *nouvelle théologie* as attacking the foundations of Christian culture. In the encyclical theologians were told that that papal teaching was the proximate and universal norm of truth, that a decision by the pope in controversial questions was final and binding, and that the task of theology was to show how the doctrine of the magisterium was found in the sources. That is, theology became a kind of papal apologetics. The encyclical condemns "the fictitious tenets of evolution which repudiate all that is absolute, firm and immutable," and it warns that immanentism, idealism, and pragmatism have "now assumed the name of existentialism, since it concerns itself only with existence of individual things and neglects all consideration of their immutable essences." Then there is the problem of "a certain historicism which, attributing value only to the events of man's life, overthrows the foundation of all truth and absolute law, both on the level of philosophical speculations and especially to Christian dogmas." Another problem is pantheism, when many "audaciously support the monistic and pantheistic opinion that the world is in continual evolution." In a clear shot at Teilhard, "polygenism" is condemned; polygenism says that the human race is not descended from a single pair, Adam and Eve.

The tragic results of *Humani generis* were that Lubac and Congar and several others were silenced and lost their teaching positions, and the French Dominican and Jesuit provincials lost their jobs for tolerating the *nouvelle théologie*. It is hard to square the encyclical and its consequences with the pope's interest in science and evolution; perhaps it is a symptom that he was going somewhat psychotic. He certainly seems to have suffered from hallucinations, and he was retreating more and more into himself. The encyclical is also a particularly nasty example of Holy Office overkill.

BY 1950 THE Roman Curia was in a state of *immobilismo*—complete stultification. Patronage was rife, and with no retiring age curial cardinals held on until they dropped. Even Jesuit preacher, anticommunist crusader, and founder of the Better World Movement Riccardo Lombardi—he was known as *il microfono di Dio* (the microphone of God)—who was close to the Vatican, spoke of the need for reform. In May 1948, he bluntly told Pius XII that the church was in crisis and that the curia, bishops, clergy, religious orders, and even the laity needed renewal. Commissioned by the pope and Jesuit general John Baptist Janssens, Lombardi produced a report, suggesting a series of reforms that would eventually lead to a general council. Despite *immobilismo*, the curial reaction was swift. Curial heads were not going to accept reforms that put time limits on their careers, did away with careerism and bureaucracy, or de-Italianized and internationalized the curia. Neither were they in love with ecumenism, the reorganization of seminaries, or rejigging the borders of Italian dioceses. Enough was enough, and Pius XII backed off, hanging Lombardi out to dry.[15] However, Pius XII expanded the College of Cardinals and internationalized it, but his isolated style meant that he simply ignored the cardinals.

For the last decade of his life, the pope seemed besotted with the necessity of pontificating on everything, and he became preoccupied with studying issues in encyclopedias and books about which he had previously known nothing, so that he could speak about them as though he were an expert. It was as though he could not bear to think there was anything upon which he could not pontificate authoritatively. The extraordinary range of topics he covered is recorded in the volumes of the Vatican yearbook, the *Acta Apostolicae Sedis* for 1940 to 1958 on the Holy See website. Examples of the groups he addressed are as diverse as scientists, analgesia specialists, bankers, engineers, architects, the Roman Rota, university graduates, foundry technicians, cardinals, accountants, the Food and Agricultural Organization, Catholic young women (on the need for female modesty), priests, students, academics, Bavarian hoteliers, artists from the Comédie Française, and, perhaps most famous of all, Italian midwives, whom he lectured at length on periodic abstinence—what we now call the Ogino-Knaus, or rhythm, method—of avoiding conception. The method, which was nicknamed "Vatican roulette," limited intercourse to times when the wife was infertile, and it was the first time a pope broached the connection between intercourse and the possibility of conception. *Tablet* editor Douglas Woodruff says that he wanted to "address every organized calling before he died; among the last were book-stall keepers, bee-keepers and plastic surgeons."[16]

No pope up to that time had ever been as influential, especially within the church, as Pius XII. It was not only what he said that was important but also the image he projected. "He was the first pope of television," Douglas Woodruff comments, "when all the techniques of modern journalism lent themselves to concentration on a single figure."[17] Visually, Pius XII and Catholicism were identical; he was Catholicism personified.

A flawed but gifted man, as his life came to an end, his almost theatrical persona began to disintegrate. He seemed to retreat more and more into himself, as if his earthly life ended several years before he actually died. He was sick and confused; there was talk of apparitions, visions, and hallucinations, which may have resulted from the controversial cellular rejuvenation treatment he underwent in 1954. He underwent this treatment—which involves being injected with the mashed-up organs of sheep fetuses taken from recently killed mothers—to deal with exhausting hiccup spasms. The cause of these spasms is unknown, but they can be a symptom of kidney failure, pleurisy, pneumonia, or intestinal disorders. Pius XII was personally cared for by Swiss proponent of cellular rejuvenation Dr. Paul Niehans, whom the pope subsequently appointed to the Pontifical Academy of Science. This therapy was treated with suspicion by medical specialists in the 1950s and still is. Perhaps the pope was somewhat mentally disturbed by this stage; he was certainly ill, but his exhaustion was much more likely to have been the result of believing that he represented God on earth and that the entire weight of absolute papal power rested on his shoulders.

This sense of exhaustion was shared by active Catholics across the world: for instance, in a left-wing Italian Catholic newspaper, priest Primo Massolari said before Pius XII died, "We are weary of too much learning, too much power, we are weary of greatness, prestige . . . words."[18] So when he finally died at Castel Gandolfo on October 9, 1958, there was a palpable sense of relief within Catholicism. The church was ready for change.

Part III

ROLLING OUT AND ROLLING BACK VATICAN II

7

GOOD POPE JOHN

IF THE CHURCH had been pretty much at a standstill for the last years of Pius XII from about 1950 onward, the wider world was moving quickly. This was the first decade of the Cold War, with Stalin dying in 1953, to be succeeded by Malenkov, then Bulganin, and later Nikita Khrushchev in 1956. In the United States, Dwight D. Eisenhower was president, and Anthony Eden, having succeeded Churchill, led Britain into the Suez Crisis. De Gaulle had been elected president of France, and the European Economic Community was established. By the mid-1950s, the process of desegregation was beginning in the southern United States, the Berlin Wall was erected, the Americans planned to put a man on the moon, and the Vietnam War began. In 1953 Watson, Crick, Wilkins, and Franklin worked out the structure of DNA, and the integrated circuit, or microchip, was commercialized in the late 1950s. The Beatles formed in 1960, a symptom of the growing influence of pop culture and mass media and rapidly changing cultural, social, and moral standards. It was a revolutionary world of change.

But the papacy had stagnated. This is the problem with an absolutist system, especially with a sick and ailing ruler; the whole system goes into a state of suspended animation. In the 1950s power in the Vatican had devolved into the hands of a self-serving clique of career cardinals like Alfredo Ottaviani at the Holy Office, Giuseppe Pizzardo at the Congregation of Seminaries, and Grégoire-Pierre XV Agagianian at the Propaganda Congregation. For these men, *immobilismo* had become an art form. So, in late October 1958, Catholicism was ready for change. Surprisingly, this was articulated by someone you would expect to be ultraconservative: Monsignor Antonio Bacci, the Vatican's Latin-language expert, who preached the sermon *pro eligendo pontifice* before the cardinals entered the conclave to choose the new pontiff. He spoke of the need for a pope who embraced the Eastern and Western branches of the church, who belonged to all peoples (especially those who were persecuted and poor), who consulted the bishops, and who was not caught up in subtle principles and diplomacy. It was a clarion call for someone very different from Pius XII.

Fifty-one cardinals entered the conclave on the hot, sticky afternoon of October 25, 1958. Cardinals Stepinac (Yugoslavia) and Mindszenty (Hungary) were prevented by their communist governments from attending. Cardinals from North and South Americas and Australia arrived in time because of international air travel; the conclave began just two days before the first Boeing 707 jetliner flew from New York to London. We don't know the details, but the conclave lasted three days and there were eleven ballots, so clearly there was horse-trading and a number of candidates. The three obvious choices were the Armenian Agagianian, who had been in Rome since 1921 and was more Roman than the Romans; Angelo Giuseppe Roncalli of Venice; and Genoa archbishop Giuseppe Siri. There was even talk of a noncardinal being elected, Archbishop Montini of Milan. But Montini was never a real candidate, and the curia's man, Siri, at fifty-two, was too young. By October 28, 1958, Roncalli had the votes needed, and at age seventy-six he was clearly elected as a transitional pope. He chose the style John XXIII, indicating that the previous Pope John XXIII, a freebooter and a thug, elected by the Council of Pisa in 1410 during the Great Western Schism, was considered an antipope.

Pope John was the antithesis of Pius XII. He was jovial and friendly, a smoker and social drinker, and very portly; the papal tailor, Annibale Gamarelli, had to fix his first papal cassock immediately after his election with safety pins. In his first speech from the balcony of Saint Peter's, he expressed "concern for reunion with separated Christians and for world peace." He made it clear that he would be a pastoral pope, since "all other human gifts and accomplishments—learning, practical experience, diplomatic finesse—can broaden and enrich pastoral work, but they cannot replace it."¹ There were neither condemnations nor hectoring. He was such a change from his predecessors that the world fell in love with him.

Roncalli was born in rural poverty on November 25, 1881. Tutored by the local priest, he studied in the diocesan seminary and then in Rome, where he was taught church history by the antimodernist fanatic Umberto Benigni. After military training, he was ordained in 1904. Appointed secretary to the socially minded Bishop Radini-Tedeschi of Bergamo, he also taught church history and patristics in the local seminary. In 1915 he became a military chaplain and medical orderly, grew a mustache, and served in the Italian army until 1918. Before the war he had begun archival work in the pastoral ministry of Milan archbishop Saint Charles Borromeo (1538–1584) and really enjoyed historical research. But this was the height of the modernist crisis, and Roncalli was suspected of having "modernist tendencies" because of passing remarks he made in his seminary lectures. He was also a loyal friend of Ernesto Buonaiuti, who was fired from teaching and the priesthood and finally excommunicated in 1927. Roncalli maintained contact with him until his death. On a visit to the Holy Office in 1958, the new Pope John asked to see his own file. On a postcard sent to him by Buonaiuti (it had been torn into four pieces and then pasted together again and sent to Rome by an ecclesiastical spy in Roncalli's household), someone had written "suspected of heresy." Angry, he wrote, "I, John XXIII, pope, say that I was *never* a modernist."²

Called to Rome by Benedict XV to head up the Italian Propagation of the Faith, which raised money to support the foreign missions, in April 1925 Roncalli was appointed apostolic visitor to Bulgaria by Pius XI to explore the possibilities for reunion with the Bulgarian Orthodox Church. He traveled reluctantly to Sofia on the Orient Express. Bulgaria proved a hard apprenticeship for Roncalli. He had to deal with an autocephalous (locally governed) Orthodox Church, a "Uniate" group of Slav Catholics in union with Rome who followed Orthodox liturgy and customs, and a community of

Latin-rite Catholics. He had been sent to explore the possibility of reunion of the Bulgarian church with Rome, so he had to learn quickly the basics of the kind of ecumenism that was to later characterize his papacy. In this he was influenced by his lifelong friend Belgian Benedictine Lambert Beauduin, a pioneer of Catholic ecumenism. Roncalli also met the ecumenical patriarch of Constantinople, Basil III, who said he would "go to the pope of Rome" so they could protect the persecuted church and "together . . . fight the Anti-Christ"—communism.[3] Pius XI was not interested; the encyclical *Mortalium animos* (1928) denounced ecumenical gatherings "at which all without distinction are invited to join in the discussion." It was not until Roncalli became pope that this kind of sectarian approach was jettisoned.

In Bulgaria Roncalli encountered the complexities of Orthodoxy, but he was unable to convey the reality of independent churches like the Bulgarian to closed minds in Rome. A major ecumenical issue arose with the 1930 marriage of King Boris III of Bulgaria to Princess Giovanna, daughter of Victor Emmanuel III of Italy. The princess was a Catholic, and Boris, a man of considerable integrity, had been born Catholic, but had embraced Orthodoxy to be united with the majority of his subjects. Boris committed to marrying Giovanna in a Catholic ceremony and promised to bring up the children as Catholics. They married in Assisi, but then went through the ceremony again in Sofia's Orthodox cathedral. Pius XI was furious, an anger that deepened when the first child was baptized Orthodox. Roncalli had to convey Pope Pius's petulance to king and government. As always, he was careful to moderate the pope's harshness and was himself severely criticized in the Vatican because he was too "soft." He denied this, but there is something naive about Roncalli during his time in Bulgaria and later in Turkey. He saw the good in people and accepted it at face value without taking into account human hypocrisy, dissimulation, and dishonesty. He was much more pastoral than diplomatic, and this was to stand him in good stead when he became pope.

In November 1934, after ten long years in Bulgaria, he was appointed apostolic delegate to Greece and Turkey, an even more

difficult and sensitive post. In Turkey he was not officially accredited to the government, and, as in Bulgaria, he more or less ran
the local church, which kept him very much in touch with pastoral issues. There were only tiny groups of Catholics in Turkey and
Greece, and neither government was particularly friendly toward
Catholicism. Nevertheless, in Istanbul he began building close personal contacts with other Christian leaders, particularly Anglicans
and Orthodox. Here he experienced a state and a leader, Mustafa
Kemal Atatürk, who was professedly nonreligious and identified
modernization with Western secularism. To break the power of
Islam, Atatürk had privatized religion. But privatization was also
applied to other religions, including Catholicism. Roncalli happily
adjusted to a low-key ministry and wore lay dress, as required.

Although instructed by the Vatican to devote himself more to
Greece than Turkey, he found the situation there utterly frustrat-
ing. The Greeks were unwilling to concede an inch to the "Franks"
(as in medieval crusaders), as they called the Latin Church. The
Greek government was understandably suspicious of all Italians,
even if they claimed to represent the pope, and it was made much
worse by Mussolini's annexation of Albania and Italian behavior
in the Mediterranean. The Italians invaded Greece from Albania
in October 1940. They were driven back, but this forced the Germans to intervene and occupy Greece in April 1941. The German
invasion led to a terrible famine. Working with the Greek Orthodox
archbishop, Roncalli negotiated a partial lift of the British blockade
of Greece, but much of the famine was due to German exactions
and up to 13 percent of the Greek population died in the war period, most due to starvation.

World War II also made Roncalli's role in Istanbul more important. The Vatican maintained strict neutrality, but in Turkey Roncalli
had to deal with a shrewd and wily German ambassador, Franz von
Papen, whom Roncalli described to the Vatican as "a sincere and
good Catholic." He had been conned by Papen, and when Roncalli's first report arrived at the Secretariat of State, Tardini (later to
be his secretary of state) tartly commented, "This fellow [Roncalli]
has understood nothing." That may be so, but Istanbul became a

spy capital, and here the warring sides could talk and Roncalli was in the midst of it. His great strength was that he talked to everyone, including the Russians. Much of his work involved tracing prisoners of war in cooperation with the Red Cross. He also helped refugees, especially Jews trying to get through to Palestine. He continued to assist Bulgaria's King Boris, who did much to protect the Jews until he died in 1943 on a flight from Germany, where he had seen Hitler; it is assumed that he was murdered because the Nazis felt he was unreliable. It was said that he died of a heart attack or was poisoned. Roncalli also passed on a request from the Jerusalem-based Jewish Agency, asking Vatican Radio to broadcast that helping the Jews was a good deed for Christians. However, Secretary of State Maglione showed appalling parochialism, arguing that the Holy See felt that too many Jews in Palestine might endanger Christian access to the holy sites. Papen also worked to save Jews, and Roncalli later wrote to the Nazi War Crime Tribunal that the German "gave me the chance to save the lives of 24,000 Jews."[4]

Turkey became a workshop for Roncalli in understanding the use of soft power for peace, refugees, and prisoners. In fact, the priorities of the Roncalli papacy had begun to emerge: a genuine openness to the world and to people of all faiths and none, a profound respect for other Christian churches grounded in a sincere ecumenism, and a broad universalism that far transcended his parochial Italian background. Roncalli grew personally through his diplomatic-pastoral work: always humble and jovial, he was an optimist whose naïveté evolved into a shrewd simplicity; he was a man of traditional religiosity that masked a profound spirituality. He always remained humane and gentle, as his spiritual diary, *Journal of a Soul*, illustrates. He says of himself: "My own temperament inclines me towards compliance and a readiness to appreciate the good side of people and things, rather than to criticize and pronounce harsh judgments."[5]

———

THIS WAS ALL to stand him in good stead when on December 6, 1944, he was appointed nuncio to France; he was to remain there until 1953. The Free French had entered Paris on August 25, 1944, and Charles de Gaulle's provisional government immediately attempted to restore unity to France and deal with the collaborators, among them twenty-five bishops, including three cardinals, who were seen as cooperating with the Pétain administration. The de Gaulle government had also suggested the names of "good" priests and bishops who might be promoted. This was Gallicanism "lite," although de Gaulle himself respected the papacy. One of the cardinals the government wanted fired was Emmanuel Suhard of Paris, who had spoken out in 1942 against the deportation of the Jews, but de Gaulle disliked him. At the same time, negotiations were under way for the appointment of philosopher Jacques Maritain as ambassador to the Holy See. At first, he was unacceptable to Rome because he was seen as too "liberal," but he was eventually accredited and together with Tardini took over negotiations regarding collaborationist bishops. Eventually, seven were discreetly removed, but Roncalli was completely ignored in the negotiations. Pius XII used nuncios as he saw fit, and when it suited him, he bypassed them.

Two major crises arose while Roncalli was nuncio: the attack on the *nouvelle théologie* and the worker-priest movement. We have already seen the hard-power treatment of theologians by the Holy Office. Roncalli listened carefully to what the *nouvelle théologie* theologians were saying but did little to intervene; in France he was considered anti-intellectual rather than reactionary. The other contentious issue focused on the worker priests. During and after the war, the conviction grew that working-class France was a *pays de mission* (mission country), and to try to reach the workers Cardinal Suhard allowed several specially chosen priests to work in factories. They took part in union activities and inevitably became involved with the French Communist Party. Roncalli probably didn't support the experiment, but he advised Rome not to condemn it because it had the support of the majority of the French hierarchy. In the long term, Suhard and the worker-priest movement influenced Roncalli. Suhard was a remarkable bishop who was open to the world and believed in dialogue with all people of goodwill, including communists. He felt that the church was in deep need of renewal through an active laity and more involvement of the priesthood in everyday life.

Rome condemned the movement in June 1953 after Roncalli left Paris. It is clear that Rome was unhappy with its Paris nuncio, and Pius XII complained that Roncalli was often "away" when needed, that he went "out" walking too much (Pius thought this "undignified" for a nuncio), and his warm, friendly, humane style was not popular in the curia. He met with a wide range of people and was never narrowly ecclesiastical. He was particularly popular on the diplomatic circuit, where, as nuncio, he was the dean of the corps. There is a famous story told about his attendance at diplomatic receptions: "During a dinner party in Paris he was asked, 'Aren't you embarrassed, *Monseigneur*, when there are women present who wear very low-cut dresses? It's often a scandal.' 'A scandal? Why no,' Roncalli replied. 'When there's a woman with a plunging neckline, they don't look at her. They look at the apostolic nuncio to see how he's taking it.'"[6]

Roncalli finally left Paris in January 1953. He had been created cardinal and appointed patriarch of Venice. Here he found his true *métier* in full-time pastoral work. While his episcopal style had a paternalistic streak, he was never authoritarian or dogmatic. He was friendly and never pretentious. He kept out of Italian politics, and, to the chagrin of the Vatican and the Catholic Right, he welcomed the Italian socialists to Venice in 1957.[7] He encouraged art, music, filmmakers, and writers and supported the cultural and art extravaganza the Venice Biennale. He continued his research work on Saint Charles Borromeo. Only five years younger than Pius XII when he died on October 9, 1958, Roncalli left Venice for Rome with a return ticket, fully expecting to end his days as patriarch of the *Serenissima*.

———

JOHN XXIII'S PAPACY (1958–1963) corresponded to the height of the Cold War and paralleled the Berlin crisis (1958–1961), the Russian shooting down of a U2 spy plane (1960), the Bay of Pigs invasion (1961), and the Cuban missile crisis (1962). Pope John needed and skillfully deployed his soft-power influence in all these crises. It was his intervention in the Cuban missile crisis that broke the stalemate and brought Kennedy and Khrushchev together and saved the world from nuclear war.

But Pope John had to deal first with intramural affairs. He appointed Domenico Tardini secretary of state and reconfirmed in office the leftover curial cardinals from the previous papacy, many of whom were unenthusiastic about his election. Most were career Italians of limited competence and minimal pastoral experience. Throughout his career Pope John had little patience with the highly bureaucratic, controlling way the Roman Curia and the Vatican operated. "Pope John was not a curial man," Monsignor Ignio Cardinale told Peter Hebblethwaite in 1980. "He didn't know too much about the curia, and what he did know, he didn't like."[8]

People discerned in John XXIII something deeply human. He confessed that sometimes he forgot he was pope but always remembered that he was a bishop and that bishops cared for and visited their people. On his first Christmas Day as pope, he visited two hospitals, including one for children with polio; the next day he visited Rome's Regina Coeli prison, which caused a sensation in the world press. In his first Holy Week, he deleted the reference in the Good Friday prayer *pro perfidis Judaeis* (for the unbelieving Jews). "I am your brother," he told a group of American Jews in October 1960. He also reached out to the press. This was the beginning of a "love affair" with the media that lasted throughout his papacy. What John XXIII seemed to understand, almost instinctively, was that much more would be achieved by reaching out to people rather than hectoring them. He set up a pattern of engagement with the world that brought the influence of the papacy to bear on a whole range of important issues. It was a shrewd use of the bully pulpit that the papacy provides. He wasn't interested in reviving an imaginary Christendom headed up by the pope. Rather, he wanted a church that was listening to the world and learning from it, but also offering it a critique based, above all, on the teachings of Christ.

On December 15, 1958, Pope John appointed a batch of new cardinals, breaking the rule of Sixtus V (1585–1590) that the number be limited to seventy. To the fifty-three at the death of Pius XII, he added twenty-three more, including two from the United States. The College of Cardinals was becoming increasingly international:

among the rest of the appointments were thirteen from Italy, two from France, and one each from Mexico, Uruguay, England, Spain, Austria, and Germany. A year later, he created eight more. Although the group was international in scope, representing Italy (three), the United States (two), and Spain, Germany, and Scotland (one each), only one of them, Albert Meyer of Chicago, was a diocesan bishop. In three more consistories, he appointed another twenty-one cardinals, representing Italy, Japan, France, the Netherlands, Philippines, Tanganyika, the United States, Venezuela, Belgium, Peru, and Chile. Of these, eleven were members of the Roman Curia; through these appointments he began to fulfill another of his aims, to internationalize the Vatican and the Roman Curia. Nevertheless, while he was breaking the Italian stranglehold of the curia, many of his new international appointees ultimately turned out to be more Roman than the Romans, which, of course, defeated his purpose. In subsequent papacies this has continued to be a problem, with many of the international appointments to the curia becoming more inward looking, bureaucratic, and controlling than the Italians.

Pope John also began getting rid of pretentious papal rhetoric, especially in the Vatican City daily newspaper, *L'Osservatore Romano*, and customs like kneeling in his presence. However, he still liked big ceremonies with all the papal paraphernalia: the *sedia gestatoria* (portable chair), the papal tiara (triple crown), the fan-shaped *flabella* (ostrich plumes), and the *camauro* (an ermine-trimmed red wool bonnet), which he sometimes wore. In one sense, these were just silly Old World accidentals, but they did give expression to Roncalli's traditionalism.

But he was also a church historian. This is important in understanding him; he was familiar with historical change, the mutability of human affairs, and the relativity of things. He knew that the church had to adapt its pastoral methods, attitudes, structures, and teaching to changed societies. To those brought up in an imagined unchanging, immutable church, this was anathema. The word Pope John used to sum up this need for change was *aggiornamento*, which meant putting the church in touch with modernity, renewing a moribund ecclesiastical structure, and rethinking theology and pastoral practice in a contemporary cultural context. He first used *aggiornamento* in his speech announcing the council, where he spoke of "the desired and expected *aggiornamento* of the *Codex Iuris Canonici*" (Code of Canon Law).[9] This word opened a can of worms for horrified traditionalists. They tried to rein in the meaning of the word to a mere streamlining of the old ways. Later interpretations of *aggiornamento* by theologians like Hans Urs von Balthasar and Joseph Ratzinger also tried to water down the meaning of the word by maintaining that it was wrongly interpreted as a facile identification with the attitudes of the world, excluding the need for inner renewal. This was a fatuous attempt to shift the focus and deny just how radical Pope John really was, a radicalism based in his historical approach to faith and church, something entirely lacking in Ratzinger and Balthasar's theology.

In a way, this difference gives expression to an important dividing line in contemporary Catholicism and one that reaches back through all of the theological debates outlined in this book. This is the difference between a theology that is rooted in and contextualized by history and one that ignores or bypasses historical context and simply sees church teaching as a kind of timeless, abstract exercise without roots and context in a particular age and place. Once you develop a genuine historical sense and understand theology and doctrine in context, you realize that church teaching really makes sense only in its own time and place and that it must be constantly reinterpreted in each era for it to make sense within a new cultural context. This is what Ratzinger and Balthasar and many other theologians, lacking a feeling for history, simply don't get; they live in an abstract world in which articulated belief is divorced from time and space. They don't understand that the church is constantly in process, that doctrine is not something merely "handed down" in an antiquarian sense, but something "handed over" in a transformative sense. This implies a process of dynamic and creative change that is nevertheless rooted in an ongoing tradition.

It is precisely this difference of approach—which is rooted in different psychologies and in the human need for varying levels of security—that was to become the central issue at the Second Vatican Council.

THE MOST IMPORTANT act of any pope in the past two centuries was the calling of the Second Vatican Council. Pope John had been in office for only three months when he announced his intention of calling a council to a group of largely curial cardinals in the chapter house of the monastery of Saint Paul's Outside the Walls on January 25, 1959, the feast of the Conversion of Saint Paul. After a pessimistic analysis of the modern world, he said, "Venerable brothers . . . trembling with emotion, but simultaneously humbly determined, I announce to you a double celebration: a diocesan synod for the City [Rome] and an ecumenical council for the universal church." He said that the council would respond to the spiritual needs of the contemporary world, and he invited the cardinals to send him "a note of confidential reply to assure me of your pleasure." He then extended "a loving and renewed invitation for all our brothers of the separated churches to participate with us in this convocation of grace and fraternity." As Giancarlo Zizola points out, in the published text the word *churches* became *communities*, for the Roman bureaucrats, Catholicism alone was the "church." The pope got no immediate response from the cardinals, who probably thought that councils were redundant since everything had already been settled at Vatican I. What quickly became clear was that many felt Pope John had made a bad mistake in calling a council, but they realized that if it couldn't be prevented, then at least they could control and "manage" it. Overall preparation was placed in the hands of Secretary of State Tardini through his presidency of the antepreparatory commission. The Roman aim—as distinct from the pope's—was an in-house council approving, but not debating, documents previously put together by the curia. It was incomprehensible to them that they didn't have the answers; they had nothing to learn from the worldwide church. This led the blunt-speaking French theologian Yves Congar to comment that the curia "produced a bottomless paternalism and stupidity." Congar felt that John XXIII's failure to get rid of Pius XII's "old guard" meant the danger was that "the council was to be mastered, dominated, emasculated [by them] as soon as it had been born."[10]

Central to the curia was the Supreme Sacred Congregation of the Holy Office. The secretary was Cardinal Alfredo Ottaviani. A gruff baker's son from Rome's Trastevere neighborhood, he had been Holy Office assessor since 1935 and secretary since 1953. His cardinal's motto was *Semper idem* (Always the same), which tells you everything. He was determined that this would not be a council of renewal, as the pope intended, but rather one that attacked the kinds of modern "errors" outlined in Pius XII's 1950 encyclical *Humani generis*. As far as Ottaviani and the egregious Giuseppe Pizzardo at the Congregation for Seminaries and Universities were concerned, there were enough modern errors around to have their work cut out for them. Congar later bluntly described Pizzardo as "an imbecile, sub-human . . . a wretched freak, [a] sub-mediocrity."[11] Both Pizzardo and Ottaviani had been involved in discussions about a proposed council under Pius XII in 1948, but that pope quickly convinced himself that he didn't need advice from anyone, let alone a council.

Aware of his age (in November 1960 he turned seventy-nine), John XXIII wanted to get things launched. So after a year of preparation, he held the Synod for the Diocese of Rome (January 24–31, 1960) that he had announced along with the council. If he felt it was a success, many thought otherwise. As J. Oscar Beozzo points out, "The diocese . . . was unprepared and was in a state of centuries-old disintegration. . . . [It] was not attuned to the pope's intentions and the synod . . . was in need of adaptation."[12] To forestall the usual long-winded speeches by Italian clerics, the synod consisted of reading preprepared synodal regulations, inviting written responses from the clergy present. This gave the impression that it was a rubber-stamp exercise, and many feared that this is what would happen at the council. The synodal regulations were meant as a kind of guide for Christian life rather than laws that must be obeyed. Most applied only to minor issues, like priests wearing the cassock in public, not attending the races or opera, showing respect to the police, obeying traffic regulations, not getting into public spats with anticlericals, and, interestingly, caring for "priests labouring under censure or other penalty, or who have perhaps unhappily left the church," that is, ex-priests, who at that time were the ultimate pariahs.[13] This had been explicitly included by Pope John.

John XXIII had studied the archives on Pius XII's proposal for a council in 1948, but he wanted a different type of assembly altogether. He focused on one that would work toward Christian unity, and in German Jesuit and biblical scholar Augustin Bea he found the man to assist him in this endeavor. As rector of Rome's Pontifical Biblical Institute, consulter of several Roman congregations, and confessor of Pius XII, Bea had much influence on the composition of Pius XII's encyclical on biblical studies, *Divino afflante Spiritu*, and his breadth of learning matched his experience of the curia. He was the ideal man to lead the Secretariat of Christian Unity, set up in March 1960. Otherwise, Pope John allowed the preconciliar dynamics to sort themselves out. While he was aware of the politics, he realized that the wider church had yet to get its head around what he proposed. Gradually, bishops, theologians, and laypeople latched on to the idea of a council, and slowly consciousness and expectation grew. Congar, who understood immediately what the pope was proposing, said he was endeavoring "to urge public opinion to expect and ask for a great deal. . . . Christian public opinion must force the council . . . to achieve something."[14]

Those who supported the pope's expectations for the council were surprised when on February 22, 1962, he issued the Apostolic Constitution *Veterum sapientia* (Ancient wisdom) on the use of Latin in seminaries. The background to this was the preconciliar debate about the use of vernacular languages in the liturgy, and the pope appeared to be going along with traditionalist elements who wanted to use *Veterum sapientia* as a preemptive strike against the provernacular push. The underlying argument here was the relationship between the local and universal churches. Latin was a symbol of universalism and the vernacular a symbol of local culture. Latin was also considered central in maintaining "unchangeable" church doctrine by traditionalists. Essentially, this was an attempt by curial traditionalists to keep control of the preparatory process, and to an extent they were successful, although they were unprepared for what would happen when the council met.

In his *Journal of the Council*, Congar reveals that he thought that "from the theological point of view and above all from that of ecumenism it would seem that the council has come twenty-five years too soon."[15] He felt that only the youngest bishops had imbibed the renewed theological, historical, and scriptural studies that underpinned the council's documents. There was also a smug sense that the papacy had nothing to learn and had a pathological fear of Conciliarism, the notion that a council threatened the papacy and was in fact superior to it. Pope John shared none of these fears. Conscious of his age, he pushed ahead with preparations for the council, confident that the bishops would seize the initiative when they met. The first session of the council opened on October 11, 1962. The most important gathering of bishops in Catholicism's second millennium began.

AN EVENT OCCURRED in 1962 that showed vividly the radical change in the status, power, and influence of the papacy in comparison to 1799, or even to 1914. The context was that the world had come to the brink of nuclear war and destruction in the Cuban missile crisis of October 1962, and world leaders had turned to John XXIII to help them resolve that crisis. This was an excellent example of the new soft-power role that the papacy could play.

The US-Soviet confrontation occurred when a U2 spy plane overflying Cuba on October 14, 1962, pictured Soviet short- and long-range missiles in Castro's Cuba, placing the whole continental United States within range. The United States immediately clamped a US naval blockade on the island, and the crisis escalated when a convoy of Russian ships with more missiles sailed toward the blockade. Historian and special assistant to President Kennedy Arthur Schlesinger Jr. says that by late October, things were "beyond the realm of tactical manoeuvre: all roads led to the abyss."[16] President Kennedy moved the US defense-readiness scale to DEFCON 2, defined as high readiness, with troops on a six-hour deployment notice. The Cuban missile crisis was the only time in the past sixty years that the United States has gotten to this level of readiness for war.

The one positive was that both Kennedy and Khrushchev realized the danger and were looking for a way out. The background to eventual peace negotiations was provided through a meeting of the Dartmouth Conference, which met annually, with Russian and US strategic thinkers fortuitously gathered for discussions in Phillips Academy in Andover, Massachusetts. The conference agreed that there needed to be intervention by an influential neutral agent whom both leaders trusted. A priest participant at the conference suggested John XXIII. The conference agreed and contacted the White House. Kennedy, a Catholic, quickly recognized his enormous influence and the fact that he was trusted worldwide, accepted the suggestion, and very quietly approached the pope. There had also been negotiations behind the scenes between the Vatican and the Soviets, and Khrushchev also trusted the pope. After secret three-cornered negotiations, John XXIII issued a passionate call for peace on Vatican Radio, begging world leaders to "keep the horrors of war from the world—a war whose horrible consequences no one can foresee." It worked. The papal call gave both Kennedy and Khrushchev an honorable escape route. Kennedy promised not to invade Cuba and secretly agreed to withdraw US missiles from Turkey, and Khrushchev agreed to dismantle the Russian missiles in Cuba. Negotiations began for the Nuclear Test Ban Treaty (1963).[17]

Pope John had already begun a policy of reconciliation with the communist world. The first result was the release in January 1963 of Ukrainian archbishop Josyf Slipyj, metropolitan archbishop of Lvov, who had spent eighteen years in a Soviet prison. Then in March 1963, Nikita Khrushchev's daughter Rada and son-in-law Alexi Adzhubei, editor of the newspaper *Izvestia*, were welcomed to the Vatican by the pope. This willingness to talk to communists was a decisive break with Pius XII.

During his papacy John issued eight encyclicals, two of which are primary documents for the development of Catholic social thought and for an understanding of the relationship of Catholicism to the world. The first encyclical was *Mater et magistra* (Mother and teacher), published on May 15, 1961. Pope John acknowledged that a new world had emerged in culture, science, technology, economics, social structures, and politics. At the core of his argument was the centrality of the human person, but he acknowledged a growing gap between rich and poor and "scientific discoveries, technical inventions and economic resources being used to provide terrible instruments of ruin and death." The only solution was one that envisaged "the social and economic progress of individuals and the whole of human society, and which respects and promotes true human values." Wealth must be distributed, and "economic progress must be accompanied by a corresponding social progress." To develop this kind of social progress, he refers to a formula for discerning what the Christian should do in concrete social situations. It was first articulated by Belgian priest (later cardinal) Joseph Cardijn, the founder of the Young Christian Workers. The formula was simple: "see, judge, act." Pope John explains it this way: "First, one reviews the concrete situation; secondly, one forms a judgment in the light of these same principles; thirdly, one decides what in the circumstances can and should be done to implement these principles." While the encyclical confirms his predecessors' ideas, John's approach is different: he doesn't lecture, hector, or condemn but is open to democracy, the welfare state, and even socialism.

These themes were further developed in *Pacem in terris* (Peace on earth), published on April 11, 1963. The Cuban missile crisis formed the context for *Pacem in terris*. It is addressed not just to Catholics but to everyone "of good will." Its primary theological premise is "the marvellous order [that] predominates in the world of living beings and . . . nature," which is a testimony "to the infinite greatness of God, who created both humankind and the universe." On the basis of this natural theology, he argues that humankind should reflect the order of nature. Almost in a parallel to the 1948 UN *Declaration on Human Rights*, he says that men and women have a right to worship "according to . . . conscience" and a right "to choose for themselves the kind of life which appeals to them." In the family, he says both "man and woman enjoy equal rights and duties," probably the first time the *equal* rights of women have been recognized by a pope. He outlines a range of other rights that are summed up in "the conviction . . . that all are equal in natural dignity." He then outlines how individuals live out these rights within the context of society and argues that the primary duty of government is to maintain the common good. Just as there is human equality, so too there is equality among nations that need to build relationships and cooperate. He challenges Catholics "to take an active part in public life, and to work together for the benefit of the whole human race, as well as for their own political communities." One of his most striking comments is when he speaks of women's role in political life and of "an increasing awareness of their natural dignity. Far from being content with a purely passive role or allowing themselves to be regarded as a kind of instrument, they are demanding both in domestic and in public life the rights and duties which belong to them as human persons." He also speaks of equality among nations, the need to protect "political refugees," and the arms race that involves "a vast outlay of intellectual and material resources, with the result that people . . . are saddled with a great burden, while other countries lack the help they need for their economic and social development. . . . True and lasting peace among nations cannot consist in the possession of an equal supply of armaments, but only in mutual trust."

This encyclical marks several basic turning points. It is written in direct language, far from the hectoring, moralizing, verbose rhetoric typical of previous papal encyclicals. The emphasis on the rights of women is a profound turning point from which the papacy has seriously retreated since 1963. It signifies a shift in the papal use of power in relationship to secularity. Previously, the church's role was to influence the state to use political authority for the good of society and especially the church. However, John XXIII and Vatican II subtlety shifted the emphasis "from a church-state to a church-society focus" to a situation in which there was "more stress on the need to shape the societal conditions that determine how that power will be used."[18] In other words, papal social theory moved beyond a church-state dualism, a ruler-to-ruler relationship, to a recognition of the role of society operating within the context of a democratic polity. This is a clear move in the recognition of the importance of soft power by the papacy.

Pope John already knew in early 1963 that he had inoperable stomach cancer and that he had only a few months to live. *Pacem in terris* is his last testament. John XXIII died on June 3, 1963, just fifty-three days after *Pacem in terris* was issued and between the first and second sessions of Vatican II. Not only was his papacy a key to the future of Catholicism, but it also showed that a pope open to contemporary reality could use soft power for the good of the world and church.

He was, without a doubt, by far the most important pope of the twentieth century and probably the most important since the Reformation.

8

"THROWING OPEN THE WINDOWS"

UNFORTUNATELY, JOHN XXIII probably never said that he wanted "to throw open the windows of the church to let in fresh air," which is sad because it is such a vivid image. In preparing for the council, the pope had taken a hands-off attitude, and curial traditionalists exploited it. In mid-1962 Ottaviani told Italian television that the council would be condemning dissident theologians, and many felt that the pope had lost interest in the conciliar idea. Cardinal Paul-Émile Léger of Canada wrote to John XXIII, asking him to intervene against the curial-traditionalist agenda, and Cardinal Giovanni Battista Montini visited him personally, making the same request.

It was not until his opening speech to the council on October 11, 1962, that Pope John showed his true colors. "Mother Church rejoices," he said, because "led by the light of the Council we are confident that the church . . . will bravely look to the future . . . by updating herself where required." There was no golden age in church history, he said, that needed to be restored. "Errors," he said, "often vanish like fog before the sun," and he hoped the church "will look to the future without fear." He was particularly critical of pessimistic people, lacking "discretion and prudence," who come to him complaining about "ruin and calamity . . . in human society." They constantly say things are "getting worse" and talk as though they have learned nothing from history, which is full of ups and downs, and the church has weathered them all. Ottaviani, Pizzardo, and their ilk would have known precisely to whom he was referring. For Pope John, God is leading us "to a new order of human relationships for the greater good of the church." He could not resist upending the statement of Gregory XVI, who preferred to "employ the rod" with dissident Catholics and everyone else with whom he disagreed. In contrast, Pope John sketched a vision of hope, saying that the church today "prefers to use the medicine of mercy . . . rather than condemnation."[1] The pope was not setting out a program but articulating an attitude for the bishops to adopt.

Traditionalists from the curia and Roman universities largely controlled conciliar preparations by dominating the eleven commissions preparing the initial *schemata* (documents). The most important of these were the theological and liturgical commissions. Speaking of the theological commission in July 1960, Congar said, "It really is very slanted in one direction," toward traditionalist theology.[2] People wanted the pope to be more proactive in forcing the preparatory commissions to embrace his vision. He was certainly aware that many were critical of the chaos, exclusion of certain theologians and laypeople, and antagonism to ecumenism. Also, while the pope wanted an "open" council, no press office was set up until just before the council began, and even then information was scarce, given the curia's obsession with secrecy. Even insiders often didn't know what was happening outside their own bailiwick.

Outside Rome things were different, with interest in the council growing. For most people, it was popular religious journals, like the *Tablet* (United Kingdom), *Herder Korrespondenz* (Germany), and *La Croix* and *Informations Catholique Internationales* (France) that informed them. Theological journals influenced the better-educated bishops, clergy, and laity. Books of popular, accessible theology also played a major role. The most important book was by a young Swiss theologian at Germany's Tübingen University, Hans Küng. *The Council, Reform and Reunion* appeared in German in 1960 and English in 1962. Küng articulated an alternative agenda that was extraordinarily prophetic. He called for reform of Catholicism, leading to reunion with other Christians; an emphasis on the use of the Bible in worship and theology; a vernacular liturgy; a focus on the universal priesthood of all believers; dialogue with other cultures and religions; reform of the Roman Curia; the depoliticization of the papacy; and the abolition of the *Index of Forbidden Books*. The book and Küng's lectures all over the world enjoyed enormous publicity and offered a viable alternative to the traditionalist agenda.

Several influential bishops also began embracing a new vision. Among them were Cardinals Joseph Frings (Cologne), Franz König (Vienna), Paul-Émile Léger (Montreal), Achille Liénart (Lille), Julius Döpfner (Munich), Giovanni Battista Montini (Milan), Giacomo Lercaro (Bologna), Marcel Dubois (Besançon), Bernard Alfrink (Utrecht), and Léon-Joseph Suenens (Mechelen-Brussels). The Dutch bishops issued a pastoral letter in late 1961 that was largely written by theologian Edward Schillebeeckx, calling for liturgical reform, collegiality of bishops, the enhancement of the role of the laity, and ecumenism. Ottaviani tried to get them to withdraw it but succeeded only in forcing the bishops to retract an Italian translation. Theologians and bishops embraced the foundations of an ecclesiological vision that had been laid, often at great personal cost, by theologians over the previous fifty years.

The council opened with a seven-hour ceremony on October 11, 1962, in Saint Peter's. Congar left at one in the afternoon, saying, "I could not take any more. . . . I was overcome by this *seigneurial* [feudal], Renaissance set-up." The triumphalism reminded him of Pius IX.[3] Austrian liturgical historian Josef Andreas Jungmann was also disappointed. He liked the music, but "the whole conception was in the style of Leo XIII."[4] Most Italians thought it was wonderful. The bishops sat on tiered stands along both sides of the nave of Saint Peter's, according to seniority of rank and episcopal ordination. This meant that they often sat with others from totally different parts of the world. This internationalized them, as they learned from their neighbors the kinds of issues they faced as well as common problems. It was by far the largest council in church history: numbers varied, but all told about 2,640 participated, the vast majority of them bishops. Superiors general of clerical religious orders also attended. At the opening session, there were 1,041 Europeans, 956 from the Americas, 300 from Asia and Oceania, and 279 Africans. The numerical superiority of the Italians, who had dominated Vatican I, was gone. Each day began with Mass and then debate in Latin. Because of their lack of familiarity with Latin, most speakers were reduced to reading from prepared texts, which made for boring speeches. Cardinal Richard Cushing of Boston offered to pay for simultaneous translation (which was provided for the non-Catholic observers), but this was not adopted and Cushing returned to Boston. Bishops were given eight minutes to speak, but that didn't prevent boring speakers from driving people to Bar Jonah (as in Simon bar Jonah, Saint Peter's Aramaic name), the coffee bar set up in the basilica.

The World Council of Churches, the Anglican Church, Protestant churches, and the Coptic, Syrian, Russian, Ethiopian, and Armenian Orthodox Churches were represented among the approximately fifty non-Catholic observers. There was no representative of the Orthodox patriarch of Constantinople. Other Christians were now "separated brethren," and their presence and psychological influence constantly reminded the council that Catholicism didn't exhaust Christianity and that Christian unity was a priority. There were also some 225 official *periti* (experts) present; 137 of them (61 percent) came from either the curia or Roman universities. To counter this, many (mainly European) theologians came to Rome, some as official *periti*, others as theologians advising bishops' conferences or individual bishops. After lunch and a siesta, the late afternoons and evenings were increasingly occupied with conferences and lectures from theologians, as bishops tried to get themselves up to speed on the major issues.

The first working session began on October 13, 1962. The curia immediately tried to stampede the bishops into accepting its lists of members of conciliar commissions, just as they had at Vatican I. Since these commissions were going to adapt and rewrite the council documents, a broad membership was vitally important. After protests by Liénart and Frings, Pope John ordered that election for these commissions be put off for three days. This gave the emerging leadership group of cardinals like Frings and Liénart time to organize sympathetic candidates for the commissions. As a result, the commissions were more broadly representative. This was the first move in a struggle for control of the council, and the traditionalist Giuseppe Siri, archbishop of Genoa and regular failed candidate in papal elections, was certain that the devil was responsible for Liénart and Frings's action. He was also convinced that only Italians had the necessary calm detachment to govern the church. He considered that "the northerners," by which he meant the French and the Germans, were too influenced by Protestantism and were the heirs of "a mistake-ridden history."[5]

Nevertheless, it is not correct to see the council in terms of traditionalists versus everyone else. Yes, there were a "pastoral" majority and a "traditionalist" minority, but these were not impermeable divisions. The real struggle was more complex, with coalitions forming around different issues. Several pressure groups formed, including the *Coetus Internationalis Partrum* (International Group of Fathers), a disciplined alliance of reactionary bishops of whom the most prominent were Luigi Carli, bishop of Segni, and Cardinals Ernesto Ruffini (Palermo), a scriptural scholar, and Giuseppe Siri. Council votes showed that the hard-core minority were, at most, several hundred, but their influence far outweighed their numbers. They could also count on support from the council's secretary-general, Archbishop Pericle Felici, and many in the curia; through them they could put pressure on the pope.

The first session, from October 13 to December 8, 1962, debated liturgy, revelation, church unity, ecclesiology, and communications. Ottaviani presented the *schemata* that had all been prepared by the traditionalist-dominated theological commission. The document on the church, *Lumen gentium*, was criticized by a succession of speakers, who said it reduced the church to a set of laws; was theologically superficial, triumphal, and juridical; ignored the role of laypeople; had too much on primacy and infallibility and not enough on bishops; and wasn't ecumenical. The majority position was forcefully expressed by Bishop Emile de Smedt (Bruges, Belgium), who said *LG* smacked of "Romanism," triumphalism, clericalism, juridicism, and an assumption that the papacy "owned" the church. He emphasized the importance of rethinking *LG* within an ecumenical context. In response, Carli gave voice to the reservations of some bishops in Italy, Spain, and Portugal about the ecumenical emphasis. In these countries Catholics were the majority, and separated brethren were rare birds indeed.

Debate on the worship schema focused on the use of vernacular languages in the Mass and sacraments, Communion under both kinds, concelebration of Mass (that is, when a number of priests or bishops, or a combination, celebrate Mass together), and, most important for episcopal authority, whether local conferences of bishops could decide on liturgical changes for their own cultures with only general reference to Rome. No decisions were made at this session, and the schema went back to the commission for rewriting.

The first session concluded on December 8, 1962, having achieved very little. But the bishops had begun to think for themselves and make their own decisions; the council had gained its own momentum and asserted itself. The curial traditionalists were no longer in control.

———

BETWEEN THE TWO sessions an enormous amount of work was done in rewriting the schemata in accordance with the criticisms of the council. The second session began on September 29, 1963, and the newly elected Pope Paul VI (John XXIII had died on June 3, 1963) set several major tasks for the succeeding sessions: a doctrinal presentation of the nature of the church that placed *LG* as a central focus and the importance of the collegiality of bishops in sharing with the pope the government of the worldwide church. He also emphasized an inner, spiritual renewal of the church, the importance of Christian unity, and a broadened ecumenism through open dialogue with the contemporary world.

The revised *LG* was presented to the council by the irrepressible Ottaviani and dour Irish Dominican cardinal Michael Browne. It had four chapters, the first on the hierarchical structure of the church, followed by the laity as the people of God. Cardinal Joseph Frings of Cologne, who also quickly emerged as a leader of the majority (it was Frings who brought Joseph Ratzinger to the council as his expert theologian), moved to have the people of God put first before the hierarchy. This was followed by a fierce debate over the question of the collegiality of bishops. For a minority, the idea that the pope share his authority with the bishops was anathema. They

saw this as an encroachment on papal primacy and denied that collegiality was based in scripture or tradition. This was self-interested,
of course, because many of those who most strongly opposed collegiality worked in the Vatican and thus shared in papal power.
Most bishops saw it for what it was: a self-interested maintenance
of personal power. To ease the tension, discussion moved on to the
notion of a married diaconate; a minority saw this as a "threat" to
priestly celibacy.

It was a natural progression to the role of the laity. There was
only one Catholic layman invited to the first session of the council,
French Catholic intellectual Jean Guitton. At the second session
Paul VI invited three more men (two Italians and a Pole) to join
Guitton as Catholic lay auditors; the group was gradually expanded.
Cardinal Léon-Joseph Suenens of Belgium commented on the
complete absence of women at the council and suggested that they
join the small group of male Catholic lay auditors. The right-wing
press jeered Suenens for promoting women, and snide references
were made to "His Feminance." The Rome-based reactionary rag *Il
Borghese* on October 31, 1963, pretentiously described him as "the
paladin of ecclesiastical neo-feminism." Suenens emphasized that
the gifts of God were given to all and not just to the hierarchy, and
it was on the basis of this theology of gift that the lay ministry was
based. Gradually, this idea gained traction, and eventually fifteen
women joined the male auditors. Over the next three sessions the
group had a lot of influence, and eventually two men addressed the
council on world poverty and the role of the laity. Despite pressure
to allow economist Barbara Ward to address the council, it was decided it would be too much for the traditionalists to allow a woman
to speak!

Intimately connected with collegiality was *Christus Dominus*, the
schema on the pastoral office of bishops and government of dioceses. Cardinal Paolo Marella, who presented *CD* to the council,
claimed that the curia had an intimate knowledge of every diocese
and always respected local uniqueness. This was greeted by the bishops with open ridicule. They had long experience of the petty, centralized bureaucratic control exercised by curial departments over

every aspect of church life. *CD* was attacked as juridical and disjointed, with too much insistence on the power of the papacy and too little on episcopal authority in the government of the church. It was during this discussion that the idea of a Synod of Bishops was suggested. The idea also gained traction that the curia needed radical reform to make it the servant of the church, not its master.

By November the council was bogged down, nerves were frayed, and the curia alone benefited from the situation. They hoped that bishops would get sick of it all and go home, leaving them in charge. Not surprisingly, one of the real "scenes" of Vatican II occurred in this period. On November 8, 1963, Frings attacked the Holy Office, accusing it of acting inquisitorially by condemning people without a hearing, without clear charges, and without giving them an opportunity to defend themselves. He spoke of "procedures in many respects no longer suited to our age [that] harm the church and [are] scandalous to many."[6] This was greeted by long, loud applause, which was forbidden. Ottaviani angrily responded. *Ego altissime protestor*, he said, literally, "I protest to high heaven." He said that such attacks were "ignorant," and to attack the Holy Office was to attack the pope because he is its prefect. It was over the top, but he was supported by Cardinals Browne and Ruffini, who warned of the dangers of collegiality. That afternoon Ottaviani tried to get the support of Paul VI but was rebuffed. There was talk of the cardinal resigning. As though the council "scene" that morning was not enough, that evening the Holy Office sponsored the showing of the movie *The Cardinal*, which Henri Fesquet described in *Le Monde* as "a puerile but readable enough novel" that had been made into a film "that is not only stupid, but in dubious taste. Nothing is lacking, not even a love-affair between the ecclesiastical hero and a young girl with tender eyes."[7] Many bishops were furious with Ottaviani. *CD* was passed back to the commission for complete rewriting.

On November 18 the schema on ecumenism was introduced. Much of the early debate on it focused on two chapters: the relationship of Judaism to Catholicism and the question of religious liberty. Augustin Bea spoke of the lineal continuity between ancient Israel and the church, of the terrible consequences of anti-Semitism, and of the fact that contemporary Jews could not be blamed for the treatment of Christ two thousand years ago. His focus was theological, and he tried to distance it from the relationship of Israel to the Palestinians. Nevertheless, this was precisely the issue on which many bishops focused!

The chapter on religious liberty was introduced by Bishop de Smedt. He stated the core teaching of the chapter unequivocally: Every person who follows their conscience in religious matters has the right to authentic religious freedom. No person or institution can take the place of a free judgment of individual conscience. These ideas had been developed by French philosopher Jacques Maritain and American Jesuit theologian John Courtney Murray. Catholicism had a tradition of claiming religious freedom for itself, but when it had power and influence in a country, it was unwilling to grant it to others. De Smedt quoted the encyclical of Pius IX *Quanta cura* (1864), where freedom of conscience and religion is described as *deliriamentum* (madness, delirium). In contrast to Pius IX, when the union of church and state was the norm, de Smedt presented religious liberty to the council in terms of modern pluralist, democratic experience. A counterattack on these two chapters was soon mounted, and the council seemed to be grinding to a halt again. Bishops whose dioceses were in predominantly Arab Muslim countries were concerned with Israel and the Palestinian question, and many bishops saw religious liberty as an American and Western European issue. Some promoters of ecumenism began to feel that these two questions needed to be separated from the ecumenical schema. This was complicated by the stranglehold that the curia traditionalists still had on the machinery of the council, especially through the council secretary, Archbishop Pericle Felici. The two problem chapters went into a temporary limbo.

Meanwhile, some work had been brought to a conclusion. The council formally adopted the *Constitution on the Liturgy* on December 4, 1963. The liturgy constitution laid the foundation for the most radical and far-reaching reform of church worship in history. For most Catholics, the introduction of the vernacular at Mass and sacraments, together with full participation in the church's worship, was the most tangible effect of Vatican II.

The closing address by Pope Paul VI conceded that there had been problems and that the council was not corresponding to all expectations. Another session was scheduled. He announced he was traveling to Jerusalem in January 1964 to meet the patriarch of Orthodoxy, Athenagoras I of Constantinople. This strengthened the ecumenical thrust of the council.

THE THIRD SESSION lasted from September 14 to November 21, 1964. The coordinating commission had outlined in advance the areas for consideration:

- the nature of the church
- revelation
- episcopal office
- ecumenism
- Jews and religious liberty
- lay apostolate
- the church in the modern world

The issue of the church and world was a new one, generated by Paul VI's concern for dialogue with modernity. Significantly, in his opening speech, the pope spoke of the relationship of papal primacy to the episcopacy. He quoted Pope Gregory I (590–604), saying, "My honor is the strength of my brothers." He continued, "It is not our intention to deprive you of the authority which belongs to you. . . . [I am] the first to respect that sacred authority."[8] That was a clear signal to the opponents of collegiality to back down. They didn't.

Debate was reopened on the revised *LG*. The paragraphs on collegiality were still the stumbling blocks, although sample votes indicated that no more than 328 (out of 2,247) bishops opposed collegiality. The reintroduction of *Christus Dominus*, the schema on bishops, also ran into difficulties. Firebrand, reactionary Italian bishop Luigi Carli insisted that bishops were not competent to share with the pope government of the universal church. The text was sent back to the commission for revision. Religious liberty and the Jewish question were also still causing trouble. The fundamental question regarding religious liberty was freedom of conscience. Ruffini asked, how can the Catholic Church, believing itself to be the true church, allow people the freedom to ignore, abandon, reject, or even attack it? Toleration of error was permissible; allowing error to thrive was not. It was the American cardinals Albert Meyer (Chicago) and Joseph Ritter (St. Louis), supported by Archbishop Karol Wojtyła (Kraków), who defended religious freedom and conscience. *The Declaration on the Jews* had by now become a largely political issue, and the stumbling block was Arab rejection of the state of Israel. Again, the document was returned to the commission for rewriting.

The important schema *Gaudium et spes* (*GS*) on the church in the modern world was introduced in mid-October. Paul VI was one of the prime movers of it, and he was determined to see it through. It had far-reaching implications, shifting the church's focus outward to the world as the context of ministry. Discussion ranged across many modern issues, including contraception, social justice, sexuality, population, and nuclear weapons.

However, dissatisfaction with Secretary-General Felici's manipulation of the council on behalf of the reactionary minority had been simmering for weeks. Feelings reached a crisis in mid-November when the revised *LG* was returned to the bishops. Felici informed them that a "superior authority"—presumed to be Paul VI—had imposed a *nota explicativa praevia* (explicative note) to the chapter on collegiality to preclude any encroachment on papal primacy. Confusion reigned. Was the *nota* part of the text? No, said Felici. What was its purpose then? Felici said the bishops had to understand the text in terms of the *nota*. Why? The pope had been under pressure from the reactionaries; he wanted moral unanimity when the text was voted on, and he knew the minority would never agree unless the *nota* were imposed. The majority bishops were furious and asked, did the pope have the right to determine the interpretation of the text in advance? A gloomy council adopted *LG* on November 21, 1964. Decisions on declarations on religious liberty and the Jews were put off until the next session. After the final Mass, Pope Paul's face was grim as he was carried out of the basilica through row upon row of bishops who applauded perfunctorily or, in some cases, not at all. Nevertheless, an enormous amount of work had to be done before the fourth session.

The bishops returned to Rome on September 14, 1965. Already Paul VI announced that he would reform the Roman Curia, set up a Synod of Bishops, and revise canon law. This session was largely fought out in the commissions framing the schemata rather than in Saint Peter's. *The Declaration on Religious Liberty* was first up. Its core assertion was that no human power could command conscience. With concerted opposition from the reactionary *Coetus Internationalis Partrum* (the small but powerful international group of ultraconservative bishops), the *Declaration* didn't pass until the second-to-last day of the council. The document on the Jews was now expanded into *The Declaration on Non-Christian Religions*, but it too ran into heavy weather, with bishops saying it implied recognition of Israel, despite its being addressed to the other great religious traditions as well as to the Jews.

The last big issue for the council was *GS*. Despite enormous work by subcommittees, there were still many problems when it was submitted to the council. There was a long discussion of marriage and sexuality, but birth control was avoided, on Paul VI's command. More than 450 bishops said *GS* was too soft on atheism and communism. The Vietnam War was escalating, and nuclear war and deterrence were fully debated. World population was also mentioned. *GS* was finally approved on December 7, 1965. That same day Paul VI and Patriarch Athenagoras I "consigned to oblivion" the mutual excommunications that had poisoned Catholic-Orthodox relationships since the schism of 1054. The council closed the next day.

Even though it was the most important council in the second millennium of the history of the church and surpasses even the sixteenth-century Council of Trent in importance, Vatican II was still a mixed blessing. In order to get the major decrees through the council, compromises had to be made. Some of the reforms have been enormously successful, such as the vernacular liturgy, which has given Catholics a sense of participation in the public prayer of the church. However, some of the compromises have had deleterious results. For instance, as a result of the Constitution on the Church, *Lumen gentium*, two mutually exclusive models of the church are left sitting side by side, and in the long term they are incompatible. These models have proved corrosive and mutually exclusive, and Catholicism has lived with the consequences now for almost fifty years.

The council's work was not over when it closed. It now remained for Vatican II to be implemented. The key figure in that task was Paul VI. Here we will briefly backtrack two and a half years to his election to the papacy soon after the end of the first session.

———————

JOHN XXIII DIED in June 1963, and the eighty cardinals who entered the conclave on June 20 that year were in for high drama. Given the Cold War context, this was the first conclave in which the Central Intelligence Agency (CIA) and other intelligence services were seriously interested. Media scrutiny was intense. Who was elected was vitally important, because the new pope would have to decide if the council continued.

Montini of Milan was the moderate, middle-of-the-road candidate, but despite his intelligence and politico-cultural contacts across Europe, he was intensely disliked by many curial cardinals. The pastoral-progressive candidate was Giacomo Lercaro of Bologna, and those opposed to the council and many of the curial cardinals supported Ildebrando Antoniutti, the former nuncio to Spain. By the third ballot, Montini had fifty votes after the Lercaro group went over to him, but he was opposed by a significant curial minority, who seemingly weren't going to budge. Then the moderate curial cardinal Gustavo Testa, an old friend of John XXIII, broke the conclave rules and openly accused the Antoniutti faction of obstruction. Siri of Genoa counterattacked and loudly complained about Testa's violation of the rules, and then Montini, who was always much given to indecision and fearful of being a cause of division, was getting to his feet to renounce his candidacy, but Cardinal Giovanni Urbani of Venice literally grabbed him by the arm and dragged him back into his seat, muttering, "*Eminenza, Lei stia zitto!*" (Eminence, shut up!). By the next morning, the curalists were reconciled to voting for Montini as less "radical" than Lercaro, and on the sixth ballot he was elected.[9] Montini took the style Paul VI and immediately announced the continuation of the council.

Most of Montini's career had been in the Secretariat of State, but he was moved from the curia to Milan in 1954 by Pius XII. Congar describes him as "an extremely intelligent and well-informed person," but felt he would "want to decide things on the basis of ideas" rather than "letting things evolve by themselves."[10] Some saw an indecisiveness, an inability to make up his mind. Even John XXIII called him *Amleto*; he certainly had a Hamlet-like tendency that made him excessively cautious and stymied action. This is true, but the other key factor for him would have been maintaining moral unanimity in the council. From 1963 to 1965, he was preoccupied with Vatican II, and while his sympathy was with the majority, he often capitulated to traditionalist pressure in order to hold the gathering together. The work of Vatican II didn't finish on December 8, 1965. It continued through the implementation of practical reforms across the life of the church: worship, ecumenical relations, episcopal conferences, rejigging the curia, and revision of canon law. But the compromises that had been made in the council and the failure of Paul VI to reform the Vatican thoroughly meant that there were always opportunities for those who wished to maintain the old attitudes and structures.

LG is seen as the theological highlight of the council, but unresolved problems in the text still cause difficulties. It set out to rebalance the church inherited from Vatican I that had defined Catholicism in terms of papal central control and power. All authority was focused in the pope through papal primacy and all teaching authority through infallibility and ordinary magisterium. In contrast to this purely hierarchical view, Chapters 1 and 2 of *LG* develop images of the church as a sacramental mystery, as a communion, and as the people of God. In this model, authority arises from the base.

Karl Rahner calls the church *ursakrament* (the prime or basic sacrament).[11] In other words, the church is a symbol that God is active in the world to save and fulfill those who hunger for justice, work for integrity, and seek the meaning of human existence through commitment to Christ. *LG* sees the church primarily located in the local community, drawn together by God's Spirit. The emphasis is no longer on hierarchical power but focuses on a people on the pilgrimage of life. These chapters reflect a bottom-up church rather than a top-down model that begins with the pope. But the third chapter of *LG* presents the church as a hierarchy, almost as though the two previous chapters didn't exist. The conventional argument is that these two models—hierarchy and community—are complementary, except that in practice they are diametrically different ways of operating. Yes, this might just work if popes, bishops, and priests always acted as Christlike leaders, respecting the community. But they don't, and Catholics experience the disjunction between their internalized image of the church as a participative community and their actual experience of a hierarchical and arbitrary institution. This has been very corrosive for the faith of a lot of Catholics.

Another challenge to absolute papal power is collegiality. Collegiality means that bishops are not just local branch managers representing head office. They are successors of the apostles who share in the government of the whole church with the pope, who himself is a member of the College of Bishops. Collegiality also means that bishops of national churches should work together in episcopal conferences and that these conferences should take responsibility for the church in the region on a whole range of local issues, especially liturgy. The reality is, however, that the types of bishops appointed since John Paul II's election in 1978 have failed dismally to take the initiative in assuming responsibility for the local church. Bishops' conferences still look slavishly to Rome and allow the Vatican a stranglehold over decisions they should make themselves. Their constant excuse, even when dealing with the most ordinary issues, is "This is beyond our competence."

At the international level, Paul VI tried to make collegiality real by instituting the Synod of Bishops, and a couple of the early synods worked well, especially the one on evangelization in 1974. But the synod began as a papal concession and has subsequently become a toothless tiger. The pope calls it at his discretion, presides over it, determines its agenda, and decides what its results are and how they will be communicated. While Paul VI made desultory attempts to make it work, John Paul II turned it into a caricature. Theologian René Laurentin speaks of "the unbelievable accumulation of restrictions" placed on the synod and "the ancient fear . . . [of] any organs of a democratic type which might limit papal power." Laurentin says that Paul VI was fearful of anything that "might interfere with papal power and papal psychology. . . . [H]e barricaded his power."[12]

It was probably also "papal psychology" that prevented Paul VI from taking an ax to the curia. His Apostolic Constitution *Regimini ecclesiae universae* (1967) attempted a reform, but it was really just a rejigging and was entrusted to those who had a vested interest in maintaining the old structure. Certainly, the pope was trying to keep the traditionalists onside, but his caution meant that he never really tackled issues head-on and failed to act decisively. His reform of the curia was "like asking the Mafia to reform the Mafia," Leuven University scholar Monsignor Charles Moeller, undersecretary of the Holy Office from 1966 to 1973, commented after trying to change attitudes in the congregation. The only significant alteration in the Paul VI rejigging was that the Secretariat of State emerged as the central body of the Vatican; it became a duplicate curia within the curia, with the secretary of state becoming, in effect, the papal prime minister. In 1969 Cardinal Jean Villot of France succeeded the aging Amleto Cicognani as secretary of state, but the key officials were the *sostituti* (substitutes), Archbishops Giovanni Benelli, who dealt with internal church affairs, and Agostino Casaroli, who dealt with foreign affairs, including *Ostpolitik*, the attempt to negotiate agreements with the communist regimes of Eastern Europe. The aim was to alleviate the oppression and persecution of Catholics throughout the Soviet bloc and to provide for pastoral care and episcopal appointments in countries behind the Iron Curtain. It was a retreat from the belligerent anticommunism of Pius XII and was strongly opposed by traditionalist Catholics, who embraced anticommunism almost as an article of faith.

The old curia remained pretty much the same, with a certain amount of tinkering and renaming. The Holy Office became the Congregation for the Doctrine of the Faith (CDF), and the Congregation of Propaganda Fide became the Congregation for Evangelization of Peoples. A number of new bodies were set up: the Secretariats for Christian Unity (1960), Non-Believers (1965), and the Pontifical Council for Justice and Peace (1967); several more have subsequently been added. Vatican officials now had to offer their resignation at age seventy-five, and cardinals lost their vote in papal elections after they turned eighty, much to the chagrin of several octogenarians. There was a significant increase in the number of curial officials: in 1900 there were fewer than 200; by 1978 there were around 3,000. These new offices brought even more aspects of church life under centralized control and enhanced papal power. Ultimately, this exercise did nothing to change the perception that the papacy "owns" the church. However, Paul VI did continue the internationalization of the College of Cardinals. He appointed 143 cardinals, literally from all over the world, especially the developing world. The percentage of Italians declined sharply.

There is a sense in which tremendous expectations had been built up by Vatican II that a renewed church, much more open to modern life and its demands, was emerging. People were prepared to commit energy to bringing that about. So when renewal slowly ground to a halt in the 1970s, people became disappointed and alienated. Many Catholics and competent priests left the church and ministry in frustration. Post–Vatican II enthusiasm turned to a sense of betrayal by church leadership. Novelist Morris West has spoken of "the deep hurt and division . . . within the post–Vatican II generation who . . . see the fading of the hopes they had invested in the updating and renewal of the church."[13]

POPE PAUL'S BIOGRAPHER Peter Hebblethwaite calls him "the first modern pope."[14] This is true, especially in terms of ecumenism, to which he was deeply committed. He was determined that all Christians "may be one": he met with Anglican archbishops Michael Ramsey and Donald Coggan, Patriarch Athenagoras I first in Jerusalem, then Istanbul, and finally in Rome, and Coptic patriarch Shenouda III of Alexandria, and he encouraged theological dialogues with Lutherans, Anglicans, Reformed churches, and Methodists.

He was also the first pope in history to use international travel as a way of projecting papal power outward, both to local churches and to the countries he visited. While these trips were pastoral in intention, *de facto* they enhanced the prestige of the papacy and made the pope the center of attention and primary symbol of Catholicism. Travel also promoted the pope as a celebrity, although this never happened to Pope Paul because of his shyness and humility. In the first six years of his papacy, Paul VI visited Jordan and Israel (1964), Lebanon and India (1964), and the United States and the United Nations (1965). At the UN, he made the plea, "Never again war, never again war! It is peace, peace that has to guide the destiny of the nations." He also visited Colombia (1968), Uganda (1969), and, his longest trip, in November–December 1970, was to Iran, East Pakistan (Bangladesh), the Philippines, Samoa, Australia, Indonesia, Hong Kong, and Sri Lanka. Another important trip was to Geneva, where he addressed the International Labor Organization and the World Council of Churches.

Paul VI's most important encyclical was *Populorum progressio* (1967), probably the most radical of all papal social justice documents. It deals fundamentally with the North-South divide, the gap between rich and poor. This, the pope claimed, will be resolved only by the full human development of all. He speaks of a world where everyone, "no matter what their race, religion or nationality, can live a fully human life . . . where the poor man Lazarus can sit down with the rich man." He highlights the social responsibility of wealth and ownership, criticizes neorationalist economics and the dominance of market forces, and focuses on the need for foreign aid programs, higher prices for the exports of developing countries, and a more generous approach to loan repayments. For the first time, a pope recognizes that there is a world population problem: "There is no denying that the accelerated rate of population growth brings many added difficulties to the problems of development where the size of the population grows more rapidly than the quantity of available resources to such a degree that things seem to have reached an impasse." But then, after a few words on procreation and marriage, he dismisses the issue. Development, Pope Paul says, "is a new name for peace . . . which implies a more perfect form of justice among [people]." He also emphasizes the notion that "God intended the use of the earth and all it contains for . . . every human being. . . . All other rights whatsoever, including those of property and free commerce, are to be subordinated to this principle." That's all well and good, but the problem is that the earth's resources are not infinite, and that is where his easy dismissal of the population problem is a serious failure. This issue continues to be ignored by papal social teaching and by the churches generally.

Also in 1967 Pope Paul issued *Sacerdotalis caelibatus*, strongly defending priestly celibacy. He had withdrawn this issue from the consideration of the council, and the encyclical appeared just as large numbers of priests began leaving the ministry to marry. If he thought the encyclical would stem the flow, he was wrong. Paul VI had also withdrawn the contraception question from the council. In 1930 Pius XI's encyclical *Casti conubii* held that the primary purpose of marriage was procreation, and any form of contraception was forbidden. Access to oral contraceptives in the early 1960s shifted the focus of discussion, and some Catholic moralists argued that the pill was not a direct physical intervention against conception. Catholic couples for whom this was not a theoretical issue began to use the pill. In the debate on *GS* at the council, Cardinal Suenens of Belgium warned of the danger of another "Galileo case" over birth control. The outspoken Melchite patriarch of Antioch, Maximos IV Saigh, linked it with the question of world population, and he called for "the official position of the church in this matter to be revised."[15] Paul VI intervened and withdrew the birth control issue from the council and reserved the question of the morality of contraception to himself. He was probably against approval of the pill from the beginning, and he unsuccessfully tried to get the last session of the council to condemn the pill because "he obviously thought that in this question the binding tradition of the church was at stake."[16] But the problem he faced was that the majority of the fifty-eight-member birth control commission that he himself had established saw no moral problem with the pill; only four of the twenty-four priests on the commission considered its use immoral. In April 1966 he appointed sixteen cardinals and bishops, to whom the commission reported, but a majority of them also recommended approval of oral contraceptives. This was leaked to the US-based *National Catholic Reporter* and to the *Tablet* in London. Now the issue was out in the open. Caught by the publicity, Paul VI set up another secret committee, headed by Ottaviani, which quickly concocted a minority report that recommended that the pope maintain the Pius XI line, because any change would gravely weaken the consistency of papal teaching authority and endanger the confidence of the faithful.

After months of agonizing doubt, Pope Paul began working on an encyclical with Gustave Martelet, a French Jesuit. The result was *Humanae vitae* (*HV*), issued on July 25, 1968. It was addressed to Catholics and "all men [*sic*] of good will" and contained many admirable reflections on marriage and fidelity. But it also argued that conception was the natural result of intercourse, and the processes of nature could not be artificially vitiated. Thus, every act of intercourse must be open to the transmission of life, and every contraceptive act was "intrinsically evil." All must give internal, conscientious assent to this papal teaching. Paul VI admitted that many would not agree with him, but he wanted them to obey nevertheless. This was interpreted as hypocrisy and showed how out of touch he was with contemporary life. *HV* is not an infallible document; it is an exercise of the ordinary magisterium and therefore can be changed. That, however, did not prevent some bishops and priests from presenting it as "almost infallible," and some used it as a line in the sand. Archbishop Thomas Cahill of Canberra-Goulburn, Australia, said it bluntly: "You can't belong to the church if you refuse to obey the pope."[17]

HV is the most disastrous papal statement of modern times, the "Galileo case" that Suenens predicted. The argumentation is based on a theory of natural law and on erroneous and outdated Aristotelian biology. Certainly, Pope Paul was a pastoral man who genuinely understood the burden he was placing on couples. This was not just some abstract theological conundrum that could be dismissed as irrelevant; it touched people's lives at their most intimate level. The encyclical took no account of how marriage was lived in the modern world, and well-informed Catholics knew that it was not about pastoral care, but about maintaining the consistency of papal power. People saw it as hypocritical, and many Catholics left the church, never to return. If the pope had been more honest and admitted that he couldn't change because he was bound by the decision of Pius XI but had had the courage to emphasize the priority of conscience, then the damage might have been contained. But unconvincing arguments from natural law persuaded no one, except traditionalists. The tragedy was that everything was sacrificed to preserve papal power. *HV* was an act of papal arrogance.

The reaction to *HV* was a firestorm of negativity. It created an enormous problem of conscience for many Catholics. The response of episcopal conferences ran the gamut from praise to careful qualification. Bishops' conferences in Canada, Belgium, the Netherlands, France, Scandinavia, and Italy told people that the pope had proposed a high ideal, but if they could not live up to it, they should not consider themselves excluded from the church. The Belgian bishops said that "someone . . . may, after serious examination before God come to other conclusions" than those of the encyclical. The Canadian bishops told Catholics who dissented from *HV* that they "should not be considered, or consider themselves, shut off from the body of the faithful." As Bishop Derek Warlock of Portsmouth, England, wisely said, *HV* was "not the acid test of Christianity."[18] Hundreds of theologians from across the world issued dissenting statements. The central issue became that of individual conscience, and perhaps one good result of *HV* was that it brought many Catholics to moral maturity in one step: they assumed responsibility for their own conscientious decisions. No longer would they ask the church to decide what was right and wrong. The vast majority of fertile Catholics in the developed countries nowadays use contraception, and it simply would not enter the minds of young people to think that contraception is a moral issue. The long-term result of *HV* is that church teaching on sexuality has become even more irrelevant to people's lives.

Theologically, rather than strengthening the papacy, *HV* has confronted the church with the question of the status of a non-infallible papal teaching that is largely ignored by the very people to whom it is directed. This was the argument used by Cardinal Basil Hume of Westminster and Archbishop John Quinn of San Francisco at the 1982 World Synod of Bishops on the family. They argued that the church cannot possibly maintain that all Catholics using artificial contraception are in bad faith. Many of them are the best people in local parish communities who have decided in conscience that their fertility is their own affair. So the church today is confronted by a series of basic questions not about contraception but about the papal magisterium (teaching power). English bishop Christopher Butler, who attended all four sessions of the council, argues that *HV* has simply not been "accepted" by the church, which, in fact, invalidates it.

———

HV CAST A shadow over the rest of the Paul VI papacy. It is clear that the negative response to *HV* astonished him, and for the next decade he said very little. However, one ongoing issue he could not avoid was the loss of many priests from ministry. According to French theologian Christian Duquoc, the council's document on priestly ministry and life created a conflict between the theology of a cultic, celibate priesthood and a ministry that consists in "openness to non-believers . . . profound involvement in everyday life . . . and service of the poor."[19] This placed the priest, Duquoc argues, in an irreconcilable bind between the demands of modern ministry and an outdated theology of the priesthood. The other reality was that it was primarily priests as leaders of local communities who faced the massive process of adjustment and change since Vatican II. Not least of the issues they had to face was voluntary disempowerment as they handed over to the laity aspects of their former role. They have also had to face the departure of many of their friends and colleagues from the active priestly ministry. Another part of the problem was that the pressures of the cultural revolution of the 1960s–1970s inevitably influenced them. The sexual revolution exacerbated the difficulties of celibacy, which was further compounded by a training that kept them immature and out of contact with the real world. And then there is the sexual abuse crisis, which I will deal with later in the book. What has become increasingly clear is that the priesthood is now facing a profound crisis, as it struggles with celibacy, sexual abuse, clericalism, and identity.

Another issue that surfaced in Paul VI's time was the ever-deepening schism promoted by rebel French archbishop Marcel Lefebvre and his ultratraditionalist revolt against Vatican II. This was dressed up as a protest against the liturgical reforms, but it was really a revolt of integralists, who actually wanted to live in a nineteenth-century church that had not really come to terms with the reality and principles of the French Revolution. They still believed in the union of throne and altar, church and state.

Scandals surrounding the Vatican Bank also came to the surface in the latter years of Paul VI. What is colloquially called the "Vatican Bank," which was set up in 1942 by Pius XII as the *Istituto per le Opere di Religione* (IOR, the Institute of Religious Works), was originally intended to take deposits from international religious orders, church-related agencies, and private individuals working for or associated with the Vatican. Because the Vatican was territorially independent of Italy, the Vatican Bank could operate independent of Italian currency laws and the Italian tax system. In the 1960s, it began to be used as a conduit to launder Mafia money out of Italy. In this period Paul VI's financial advisers, particularly Chicago-born archbishop Paul Marcinkus, allowed themselves to become caught up with some of the most notorious thieves and con men of the twentieth century. When questioned about the propriety of the church running a bank, Cicero-born Marcinkus—Al Capone came from the same neighborhood—replied, "You can't run the church on Hail Marys." Highly centralized and secretive administrations like the Vatican are especially vulnerable to scams and con men because there are insufficient checks and balances and no accountability.

As a result, the Vatican got caught first in the clutches of Mafia banker Michele Sindona. In his early days at the bank, Marcinkus looked for friends to guide him in the world of finance, and he found one in Sindona, a Sicilian then resident in Milan who had close Mafia ties both in Italy and in the United States. Sindona used the bank to launder money out of Italy. Eventually, his whole edifice crashed, and he was first imprisoned in the United States and then extradited to Italy, where, within three weeks of arrival, he was poisoned in jail. It is uncertain if it was murder or suicide, but most likely it was murder.

Having not learned his lesson with Sindona, Marcinkus then got caught up with the greatest con man of the twentieth century, Roberto Calvi. The Vatican and Marcinkus saw him as *un uomo di fiducia* (a man of trust). But that was the last thing he was, even though he was chairman of the Catholic-run *Banco Ambrosiano* in Milan. What he was not telling Marcinkus was that he was tied up with some of the worst right-wing, neofascist people in Italy, all associated with the notorious Masonic lodge *Propaganda Due* (P2). Calvi's *modus operandi* was to own or get control of a bank, like the *Ambrosiano*, and then rob it by stripping its assets, while using the Vatican Bank as a way of laundering his ill-gotten gains out of Italy. Also, his association with the Vatican gave him respectability and clout in financial circles. Eventually, his empire collapsed, and he was found hanged under London's Blackfriars Bridge. He had been murdered by the Sicilian Mafia, either under instructions from or in association with P2.

Near the end of his life, Paul VI was also impacted by homegrown terrorism. This was the time of the *Brigate Rosse*, the Italian Red Brigades, a Marxist-Leninist, far-left-wing terrorist group determined to force Italy out of the North Atlantic Treaty Organization and eventually to overthrow the Italian state. Pope Paul was deeply upset by the kidnapping in central Rome on March 16, 1978, and murder in early May of his lifelong friend Christian

Democratic statesman Aldo Moro by the *Brigate Rosse*. The pope was furious that the Italian political establishment did nothing to rescue the kidnapped politician and may have even deliberately abandoned him to the *Brigate Rosse*. Moro was snatched as he traveled to a meeting to try to negotiate a "historic compromise" between the Christian Democratic Party, of which he was leader, and the Italian Communist Party. The full truth of this assassination has never been revealed, and it now seems certain that the CIA, the KGB (the Soviet State Security Committee), and the highest levels of the Italian state were involved in Moro's kidnapping. Paul VI's anger at the complete failure of the Italian authorities to rescue Moro seems increasingly justified.

The murder of Moro was the last straw for Pope Paul, who celebrated his friend's funeral Mass and soon afterward himself died of a heart attack on August 6, 1978, at Castel Gandolfo. In a way, he really was a kind of Hamlet, a man who could never bring himself to act decisively. He was involved in endless compromises, and on the one occasion he did act on contraception after two years of dithering, it was a disaster. He even asked himself, "Am I Hamlet or Don Quixote?" He saw his task as steering the "old" church of Vatican I through the difficult transformational period into the "new" church of Vatican II without causing a schism. He constantly compromised to keep the traditionalists onside, and certainly on contraception his sympathies lay with them. He was also shy, reserved, and somewhat snobbish, and he was constantly compared unfavorably in the media to "good Pope John." Probably, for him, it was a relief that "Pope Hamlet" was at last at rest.

9

THE POLISH COLOSSUS

THE 1970S BROUGHT humankind a mixed bag of significant events. The world population passed 4 billion; in 1978 when Paul VI died, it was 4.3 billion. The Middle East oil crisis increased the price of fuel worldwide. In the United States, it went from thirty-six cents per gallon in 1970 to eighty-six cents in 1979. Forty-three nations signed the Nuclear Non-Proliferation Treaty in 1970, and the Boeing 747 made its first commercial flight across the Atlantic. The first microprocessor was built in 1971, the Supreme Court case *Roe v. Wade* made abortion constitutional in 1973, President Richard M. Nixon resigned in disgrace after the Watergate scandal in 1974, and the Vietnam War ended in 1975 with the communist capture of Saigon. Besides the papal elections, the other major event of 1978 was the signing of the Camp David Accords between Israel and Egypt.

On the papal front, one significant thing that Paul VI had done was to expand the College of Cardinals. The number of cardinals in the college was limited to 70 in the reforms of Sixtus V in 1586. John XXIII had broken that rule and expanded the number, but it was Paul VI who had doubled the size of the college to 120. But he also decreed that from January 1, 1971, cardinals over eighty were excluded from future conclaves and lost their vote to elect the pope. Many older cardinals were furious with this decision; they claimed that they had not lost touch with the wider church and were not rigid in their thinking. When he died there were 130 cardinals, with 15 over eighty. Of those eligible, 111 cardinals (1 had died and 3 were too sick to attend) entered the conclave to elect Paul's successor on a stiflingly hot day, August 25, 1978. Only a quarter of them were Italian. With the expanded number of electors, there had been a twenty-day delay in getting the Borgia Apartments ready for the conclave, and this gave the 15 cardinals aged over eighty a chance to challenge their exclusion. They were unsuccessful.

London bookmaker Ladbrokes offered odds on possible popes: Italians Sergio Pignedoli was at five to two, Sebastino Baggio and Ugo Poletti were seven to two, and Giovanni Benelli was four to one; Dutchman Jan Willebrands was eight to one. Ladbrokes was completely wrong. The short-odds cardinals were never in the race. In the first scrutiny, the ultratraditionalist Giuseppe Siri of Genoa had about twenty-five votes and Albino Luciani, patriarch of Venice, twenty-three. There was a determined, well-organized effort by progressive cardinals, led by Léon-Joseph Suenens of Mechelen-Brussels, to exclude Siri. As a result, Luciani probably had enough votes by the third scrutiny but insisted on a fourth, in which he received ninety-six votes. He took the unusual style John Paul.

From a poor, working-class background in northern Italy, he was an entirely new style of pope, completely unconnected to the curia, but with many years of pastoral experience. A laughing, smiling, warm man with a genuine sense of humor and a whimsical writer, he charmed people, including more than eight hundred journalists in a press conference. Totally unostentatious, he replaced the papal coronation with an installation Mass in Saint Peter's Piazza, and rather than being crowned with the triple tiara, he was invested with the pallium, the symbol of episcopal office. He got rid of much of the detritus surrounding the papal office like the *sedia gestatoria* (the portable chair carried by six men), dropped the royal *we*, and was a man of genuine faith who liked being with people. It was as though "morning had broken" in the church and it was John XXIII all over again.

But we never got a chance to know him better, for after just thirty-three days in office, at about eleven o'clock on the night of September 28, 1978, he died. He was discovered early the next morning by Sister Vincenza, who had come with him from Venice and who always brought him a morning coffee. Things were badly mishandled after his death. There was a rushed decision to follow papal tradition and not have an autopsy after what was a sudden and unexpected death. With no postmortem, the Vatican doctor who examined the body said he *might* have died from a heart attack. The media were then told that he was found by his priest-secretary, not by Sister Vincenza; it was felt having a woman in the pope's bedroom early in the morning was scandalous, even if she was just bringing him coffee. The Vatican also claimed that he was reading a book of piety, *The Imitation of Christ*, not his own notes.

All this gave conspiracy theorists enough material to construct a vast plot based on assumptions that he was going to reverse *Humanae vitae*, clean up the Vatican Bank, and fire a whole crowd of curial diehards. Theories also included an assassination orchestrated by Secretary of State Jean Villot and sundry other villains, including Archbishop Marcinkus. David Yallop's *In God's Name* creates a risible fictional conspiracy that has been repudiated, pretty much point by point, by John Cornwell's book *A Thief in the Night*. Cornwell plausibly argues that Luciani was a sick man before he was elected pope and that his priest-secretaries were careless with his health after his election and that he died of a pulmonary aneurysm. The curious behavior of Villot can be explained by the fact that he was completely shocked at the sudden death of the pope and was afraid of "scandal," something the Vatican fears more than anything else.

There is also absolutely no evidence whatsoever that Pope Luciani was a closet "radical" who was going to turn things upside down in Catholicism. Everything points to his being a moderate whose emphasis would have been on pastoral care, humble service, and making collegiality actually work through the Synod of Bishops and consultation with the worldwide episcopate. Other than that, we have no idea what he might have done as pope.

————

ONE HUNDRED AND eleven shell-shocked cardinals returned to Rome in early October 1978 to elect another pope. They knew that they had to find a man who, like Pope Luciani, could captivate people and draw them to faith and the church. They were also still looking for someone with pastoral experience but also with robust, good health. Some cardinals entered the conclave feeling that God was trying to say something to them through John Paul's death. They felt that Luciani's sudden death might somehow be a signal that the time for a non-Italian candidate had now arrived. The most influential great elector was Cardinal Franz König of Vienna, who came to Rome determined that a non-Italian be elected, and his nominee was Cardinal Karol Wojtyła of Kraków. Again, Siri of Genoa was the conservative favorite, but he badly damaged his reputation with an interview in the Turin-based *Gazzetta del Populo* the day before the conclave began in which he attacked John XXIII, Paul VI, Vatican II, and the collegiality of bishops, which he called a "disaster." The other Italian and more middle-of-the-road candidate was Giovanni Benelli, who had spent many years in the curia before becoming archbishop of Florence.

Vote counts for this conclave are unclear; the secrecy was well observed, and we're not even sure how many ballots were held, most likely eight. The conclave began in the late afternoon of October 14, 1978. It seems that Siri was an early favorite, and by the fourth ballot he had seventy votes, five short of the required number. Benelli, who had surged early, fell back. The five votes Siri needed proved hard to get. A couple of cardinals, including John Carberry of St. Louis, said there was a "drama" of some sort around the sixth scrutiny, but no one knows exactly what happened. It may have been that an offer was made to Siri that if he would guarantee that Benelli was appointed secretary of state, the needed votes would be forthcoming. He apparently angrily rejected this clear contravention of the conclave rules, and he never got the votes. With the Italians now out of the running, König stepped in to break the impasse and, supported by Polish American John Krol of Philadelphia, promoted Karol Wojtyła of Kraków. He quickly garnered votes and was most probably elected on the eighth ballot, and he took the style John Paul II, in honor of his predecessor. He was fifty-eight, spoke fluent Italian, and quickly charmed the Roman crowd in the Piazza of Saint Peter's. If the pastorally progressive König later regretted promoting Wojtyła's election, he never said so; he simply commented, "You must remember he's a Polish Pope and we are all fashioned by the country we come from, the Catholicism we come from."[1]

The Polish-background experience is absolutely central to understanding Karol Wojtyła. A Slavic nation, Poland's religious roots have much in common with Eastern Orthodoxy. Wedged as Poland is between Germany and Russia, its Catholicism gives Polish culture a distinct marker, a point of difference, and links the nation with Western Europe. This was especially important during the 125 years until 1918 when Poland didn't exist as a political entity, divided as it was between Russia, Prussia, and Austria. Poles learned to distinguish between the nation as a cultural entity, which they embraced with gusto, and as a political entity, which was denied to them. This sense of cultural identity became the dominant motif in Poland, and poets like Adam Mickiewicz pictured the partition in terms of the suffering servant of the prophet Isaiah, which later interpretation identifies with the crucified Christ. In this messianic vision, Poland, after being tested by suffering, will be, like Christ, the source of salvation for the corrupt West. Wojtyła's favorite poet, Cyprian Norwid, also stressed the redemptive value of suffering as part of Poland's role in history.

BEFORE DEALING WITH his ministry as pope, I am going to detail something of John Paul II's intellectual development, because that is central to his conception of his role as pope. Also, no pope has been as influential and powerful as John Paul II. He is the apogee of papal power. None of his predecessors reached his level of celebrity, which makes him a central person in a book subtitled *How the Pope Became the Most Influential Man in the World.* He took absolute power to its outer limits.

Born in south-central Poland in the small town of Wadowice on May 18, 1922, Karol Józef Wojtyła grew up in the part of Poland that had been dominated until 1918 by the Austro-Hungarian Empire. This paternalistic empire promoted itself as a tolerant polity bestowing the advantages of Western civilization on its multiethnic subjects, in contrast to imperial Russian "barbarism." Wojtyła imbibed something of this Pan-European sense in that he didn't really believe in frontiers or nationalistic states, but he had faith in nations and peoples. This was why as pope he was more interested in the people than in rulers, politicians, or conventional political processes. Political leaders come and go; the people are permanent.

His mother, Emilia, died when Karol was nine, and four years later his older brother, Edmund, a medical doctor, died of scarlet fever that he contracted from a patient. This left Karol alone with his father, and their relationship was strong. Known as "the Captain" around Wadowice, Karol Wojtyła Sr. had served in both the Austro-Hungarian and the Polish armies. Karol was educated in local state schools, he was a good sport, and as an accomplished actor he seems to have contemplated entering the theater professionally. In 1938 father and son moved to Kraków, and Wojtyła entered the historic Jagiellonian University to study Polish language and literature. A year later, Germany invaded Poland. Not only did the Nazi extermination machine eliminate almost all of Poland's 3 million Jews, but it also massacred an equal number of Poles. The terror was directed especially against intellectuals and clergy, the aim being to eliminate any form of leadership that could offer resistance. Schools and universities were closed, but, as Wojtyła's experience shows, underground networks of students and even an underground theater, in which he acted in several plays, continued to operate. He also worked as a laborer in the quarry of the Solway chemical works. His father died in 1941 when he was twenty-one, and later that year he joined an underground seminary in the residence of Archbishop Adam Sapieha. He had also come under the influence of an extraordinary lay mystic, Jan Tyranowski, whose ministry with young people partly replaced that of local priests who had been sent to the concentration camps. Tyranowski introduced Wojtyła to the sixteenth-century Spanish Carmelite Saint John of the Cross, one of the church's greatest mystics. The German occupation was very dangerous for a young man like Wojtyła; he could have easily been picked up on the street and drafted into a labor battalion or suffered an even worse fate if his underground activities were discovered.

With the retreat of the Nazis and the reopening of the Jagiellonian in January 1945, Wojtyła returned to theology, graduating in August 1946. He was ordained on November 1, 1946, and was sent to Rome, where he completed a doctorate on Saint John of the Cross at the Dominican Angelicum University. Here his mentor was Reginald Garrigou-Lagrange, who even in the 1940s was known as "Reginald the Rigid." After graduation in June 1948, Wojtyła returned to Poland. After brief stints in parishes, he completed a doctoral thesis on the German phenomenologist Max Scheler at the Jagiellonian. Scheler was essentially an ethicist who posited an absolute and eternal order of values in the world that we perceive not through intellect but through an intuition of the heart, what Blaise Pascal calls *logique de Coeur* (logic of the heart), a kind of spiritual intuition. Scheler (and Wojtyła) highlights the absolute value of the person; a person is more than just an individual, but is a spiritual being that is capable of moral values that far transcend mere impulses.

But in all this talk about "personalism," the Anglo-American reader needs to be careful, because personalism as used here is an abstract notion. As a "personalist," Wojtyła is not interested in psychology, personality theory, sociology, counseling, psychiatry, or guidance. For thinkers like Wojtyła, the whole focus is on the absolute value of each individual with no broader context. This is an approach that I think is profoundly flawed because it is toxically anthropocentric. Wojtyła says, "A person cannot be put on the same level as a thing. . . . Between the psyche of an animal and the spirituality of a man there is an enormous difference, an un-crossable gulf."[2] This is profoundly wrong. "To make humanity the be all and end all of existence is to forget the other five days of creation and is an insult to God's creativity."[3]

After completing the Scheler doctorate, Wojtyła began lecturing in theological ethics at Kraków Seminary in 1953, and in 1957 he became a professor of ethics at the Catholic University of Lublin. On July 4, 1958, he was ordained auxiliary bishop of Kraków. As bishop Wojtyła attended the whole of Vatican II and generally

identified with the majority bishops. On January 13, 1964, he became archbishop of Kraków and was created cardinal in May 1967.
As archbishop he was mildly reformist, close to the people, and
popular. What is significant is his successful clerical trajectory that
took him at age forty-one to the archbishopric and three years
later to cardinal. His entire ecclesiastical career was lived out in the
unique situation of the Polish church's eventually successful struggle with an avowedly communist, atheistic state. His strong personality, physical toughness, determination, and single-mindedness
stood him in good stead in this struggle; whether that transferred
well to the papacy is more problematic.

Wojtyła's academic interest was in philosophy and interpersonal
ethics. Here it is important to emphasize that he was not really a
theologian, let alone a biblical scholar or historian. The two latter
disciplines would have rooted him more firmly in the reality and
relativity of human affairs. He was very much the European intellectual, a man of theory who looked down on the more practical
sciences as utilitarian, or "Anglo-Saxon," as supercilious continental
academics would say. Wojtyła claimed that he learned much from
the young people to whom he ministered and who were often his
companions on camping trips to the Tatra Mountains and the Ma-
surian Lakes in northeastern Poland. He talked a lot about sex both
with and to young people. His first book was *Love and Responsibility*, published in 1962. Its open discussion of genital issues, including the rhythms of female fertility, was very explicit for the time.
Nowadays, this all seems rather quaint, but in Catholic Poland in
the early sixties, it was unusual for a priest.

He worked closely on *Love and Responsibility* with Kraków psychiatrist Dr. Wanda Półtawska. A member of the Polish resistance,
she had spent four years in Ravensbrück concentration camp, where
Nazi doctors experimented medically on her and other Polish
women. She survived and returned to Poland. She met the young
Wojtyła, and they became lifelong friends. A strong woman, married with four children, she helped camp survivors with what today we would call post-traumatic stress disorder. She influenced
Wojtyła deeply and helped him develop his ideas on marriage,

sexuality, contraception, and the so-called theology of the body. As a result of her Ravensbrück experience, she believed that contraception undermined respect for life, had harmful medical effects on women, caused neurosis, and led directly to abortion. Półtawska had an idealized, romantic notion of the "mystery" of woman, revealed in motherhood. Wojtyła picked up her views particularly on womanhood and contraception. In a somewhat banal talk entitled "The Mystery of Woman Revealed in Motherhood," Wojtyła says, "The woman stands before the man as a mother, the subject of the new human life that is conceived and develops in her, and from her is born into the world."[4] Thus, women are biologically (and morally) bound by their maternal role. Wojtyła argues that sexual intercourse is truly human and moral only within the context of marriage. Intercourse in any other setting is "using" another person; it is "utilitarian," not "personalist." He maintains that natural law determines that every act of intercourse must be open to the possibility that a child might be conceived. Contraception, he says, degrades women by using them as sexual objects. In a feminist and post-Freudian world, this makes little sense. Wojtyła strongly supported *Humanae vitae*; he may even have influenced Paul VI in formulating it. He considered the encyclical infallible.

Biographer George Weigel says that "John Paul's *Theology of the Body* . . . challenges us to think of sexuality as a way to grasp the essence of the human—and through that, to discern something about the divine."[5] Wojtyła argues that at the heart of every person is a search for transcendence; everyone is, as Scheler says, a *Gottsucher* (God searcher). This requires a strong, even radical, commitment, and Wojtyła has no time for slackers, those who, like former priests, abandoned their God-given vocation. This kind of absolutism fits in well with Polish messianism. His first philosophical work, a dense and obscure tome, *Osoba i Czyn* (Person and act), appeared in 1967. It was never properly edited, and an oft-repeated joke among the Kraków clergy was that it would be required reading in purgatory. The confusion of phenomenological rhetoric with uncompromising Catholic traditionalism left people floundering as they tried to sort out what Wojtyła was actually saying. It is sometimes assumed that because a text is incomprehensible, it is profound, whereas the opposite is usually true.

However, someone who saw potential in *Osoba i Czyn* was Polish American philosopher Anna-Teresa Tymieniecka, who contacted Wojtyła in late July 1973, proposing that she edit and prepare an English version of the book. He consented, and a remarkable intellectual and personal relationship began. Over the next five years, they met for extended periods in Kraków, Rome, the United States, and Switzerland as they discussed his ideas and she worked on the manuscript. Of Polish and French extraction, Tymieniecka was born in German Pomerania (now part of Poland) in 1923. A graduate of the Jagiellonian, the Sorbonne, and Freiburg, she married Dutch-born economist Hendrick Houthakker and joined him in the United States. As well as working with him on *Osoba i Czyn*, Tymieniecka published Wojtyła's articles and papers and arranged lectures for him at Harvard and the Catholic University in Washington, DC, when he came to the United States in the summer of 1976. He also visited her holiday home in Vermont.

In February 2016, a BBC *Panorama* program made public some 350 letters of Wojtyła that clearly show that what began as an intellectual collaboration ended as a profound personal friendship that was, at least for Tymieniecka, deep love.[6] To fit the relationship within the framework of priestly celibacy, Wojtyła seemingly idealized and spiritualized their love. This is not to claim his sublimation was insincere, but it is to say that in this way he absolved himself from responsibility for the painful and difficult position in which Tymieniecka was placed. "I don't think he understands what she's coping with when she's in his presence," Dr. George H. Williams, author of the first major book on John Paul and longtime friend of Tymieniecka, says.[7] And what about the difficult position of her husband, Hendrick Houthakker, and her children? The other element here was the danger posed by the Polish secret police, the SD, who were particularly interested in Wojtyła and would have been delighted to have a "scandal" they could pin on him. That is why most of his letters to her were written when he was visiting Rome and she was in the United States.

When the English edition of *The Acting Person* was published by Tymieniecka in February 1979, the "Polish Mafia" in Rome—made up of Monsignor Stanisław Dziwisz, John Paul's secretary, and close friends Archbishops (both later cardinals) Andrzej Deskur and Stanisław Ryłko—tried to eliminate her from the picture. They were concerned that John Paul had already signed over to her the rights to the English-language edition of *The Acting Person*. They tried to deny her work in rewriting, editing, and certainly improving the book. They even mounted an unsuccessful legal challenge to her copyright. She looked to Wojtyła, now pope, to speak up for her, but he failed to deliver. In a revealing interview with Carl Bernstein and Marco Politi, she says she felt "betrayed" by John Paul. She claims that her role in *The Acting Person* was "influential" and that he thanked her for the book's "final shape." The relationship was strong enough to survive this crisis, and their intimacy continued right through until his death. Tymieniecka, however, was never befuddled by her love for Wojtyła. She said bluntly that his book *Love and Responsibility* was silly. "To have written [as he has] about love and sex is to know very little about it. I was truly astonished. . . . I thought he obviously doesn't know what he's talking about. . . . He doesn't have experiences of that sort. . . . He is sexually innocent." Asked about a sexual component in their relationship, Tymieniecka described herself as "an old-fashioned Polish lady" who was not interested in discussing sexuality, because "this is not a matter for conversation of any sort." In contrast, in his dealings with the Polish government, she says he was streetwise. "To be a cardinal under the Communists he had to be extremely shrewd. . . . He is a very clever person who knows what he is doing."[8]

IN HIS ATTITUDE to Vatican II, Wojtyła was never a die-hard reactionary, determined to resurrect preconciliar Catholicism. He was, after all, the pope who excommunicated the schismatic archbishop Marcel Lefebvre, who rejected Vatican II. Wojtyła's view of Vatican II was idiosyncratic, personal, and rooted in his Polish experience rather than in the council's actual teaching. His contribution to the council was modest, although he often acted as spokesman for the Polish bishops. Wojtyła was elected pope on October 16, 1978, and the next day said it was his "primary duty" to achieve "the implementation of the decrees and directive norms of [the council]." But the problem was his interpretation of Vatican II.

In 1972 he published a book in Polish, *U podstaw odnowy* (Foundations of renewal).[9] He emphasized what an "experience" Vatican II had been for him and the other bishops; it was as though it were an in-house, bishops-only love-in that had nothing to do with the rest of the church. None of the passion, debate, anger, and hard work appears in Wojtyła's book, and the expectations of down-to-earth Catholics are ignored. The reason was that there was little enthusiasm for Vatican II in Poland, and theologian Stanislaw Obriek speaks of Polish "nonreception" of Vatican II. "After the Council ended, given the political circumstances of Communist Poland, its documents were not openly discussed with lay Catholics and only partially implemented." Also, Cardinal Stefan Wyszynski, the then archbishop of Warsaw, had an "authoritarian temperament [that] blocked any pluralism and theological discussion." Wojtyła's "interpretation was a very conservative one and avoided . . . controversies."[10] He didn't like the term *people of God*, preferring the notion of *communio* (communion), an idea given currency by Swiss aesthete and theologian Hans Urs von Balthasar, who didn't attend Vatican II. Wojtyła felt that the council was far too sympathetic to the world and to the theology of Karl Rahner and too willing to "baptize" secular and religious movements from outside the church. Balthasar's theology, in contrast, is elitist and concerned about the loss of a specifically Catholic identity and sense of mission. This appealed to Wojtyła (and Joseph Ratzinger), neither of whom was sympathetic to Rahner's more open theology. Wojtyła was also suspicious of *ecclesia simper reformanda* (the church in constant need of reform), and he disliked the notion of a pilgrim church, an image of a people on a journey of discovery. Wojtyła was firmly convinced that the church had arrived and was already perfect.

He also favored the council's notion of religious freedom when it meant the freedom to oppose an atheistic state. But he was suspicious of the notion of religious liberty as the freedom to believe as your conscience dictated. For him, liberty, truth, and responsibility must be linked. Like the Polish bishops, he was worried about secularism and was pessimistic about consumer-oriented Western society. He objected to what he saw as the "optimism" that pervaded the council document on the church in the modern world, *Gaudium et spes*. Given the long struggle of the Polish church, first against the brutal Nazi regime and then against the communist government, a struggle in which Wojtyła played an important role, it was understandable that he saw Catholicism as a beleaguered "sign of contradiction," and *Sign of Contradiction* was in fact the title of a book that emerged from a spiritual retreat Wojtyła gave to Paul VI and the papal household (that is, those who worked most intimately with him) in March 1976. Here his assessment of the modern world was pessimistic. While human knowledge and technological know-how were increasing, human thought and philosophy were disoriented. While humankind, Wojtyła says, "has extended so very far the 'horizontal' thread of knowledge, what strikes one most forcibly is the lack of balance in relation to the 'vertical' component of that knowledge."[11] Humankind has lost its sense of the transcendent in a postmodern morass of relativity.

So Wojtyła came to the papacy with a powerful and dominant personality, an absence of self-doubt, and an articulated view of what was happening in the church, with a determination to do something about it. He had a profound sense that God had called him as pope to save the church almost from itself, and he had a messianic conception of himself as a kind of savior who, like Christ, had to endure suffering for others. The beautiful "servant songs" of the prophet Isaiah (scattered throughout Chapters 42–53) appealed to Wojtyła, as he made clear in his 1984 apostolic letter *Salvifici doloris* (Salvific suffering). In Isaiah God's faithful servant is "despised, rejected . . . a man of sorrows and acquainted with grief," as the King James Bible (and Handel's *Messiah*) beautifully puts it. Christ is identified with the suffering servant, the one who lays down his life for the salvation of all. Wojtyła had a profound sense of his own identification with the suffering Christ. For him, this seems to have gone beyond the biblical notion that all Christians are baptized into the very life structure of Christ so that, as Saint Paul says, "it is no longer I who live, but it is Christ who lives in me" (Gal. 2:20). John Paul was deeply conscious that his priestly ordination made him *alter Christus* (another Christ). In 1999 he told a group of priests that they were "ontologically configured to Christ the Priest . . . which is why we can say . . . that every priest is *alter Christus*."[12] The term *ontologically configured* means that the priest in his personal essence, in the core of his being, is identified with Christ. It implies that the ordained go beyond the baptized Christian to become a kind of "super-Christian." This notion of *alter Christus* gained traction only in seventeenth-century spirituality, and while there are theological problems with it, nevertheless, to some extent it is accepted Catholic theology.

But John Paul took the so-called ontological configuration much further. Polish philosopher Zbigniew Kaźmierczak has shown that in Wojtyła's understanding, he sees himself as *alter Christus* in the literal sense. He so appropriates Christ that he himself becomes Christ acting in the contemporary world. Thus, as pope, his subjective intentions, beliefs, plans, and priorities become Christ's. Kaźmierczak correctly describes this as "an act of religious narcissism." In "identifying with the divine he is a Christian, whereas while identifying the divine with himself, he becomes Christ himself, the second Christ, i.e. *alter Christus*." While his papal motto, *Totus tuus* (Completely yours), refers to the Virgin Mary, it can also refer to complete self-giving to Christ. Wojtyła has turned this on its head to mean *Totus meus*, that is, Christ becomes identified with Wojtyła, whose will replaces Christ's. The shift is subtle but real. In the traditional Catholic understanding, Christians freely lay themselves open to God so that Christ's Spirit guides and impregnates everything that they do. Kaźmierczak says that John Paul has appropriated Christ and God as tools to pursue his own subjective intentions. In the same sense, he identifies the church with himself. "Within this framework he presents himself as a powerful man who is able to do great, heroic things, that is actions that Christ himself would do if he still lived on earth."[13] It is not suggested that Wojtyła does this consciously, but, rooted in his inherent narcissism, the fact is that both his theology and his actions point to his radical identification of Christ with himself. In this context, many of his actions, such as his conviction that he was the one called to save the church or the one who overthrew Polish communism, begin to make sense.

Linked to this messianic conviction is his notion of suffering and celibacy. There is a very difficult text in the Letter to the Colossians where the writer says, "In my flesh I am completing what is lacking in Christ's afflictions for the sake of his body . . . the church" (1:24). Referring to this text in *Salvifici doloris*, John Paul seems to say that human suffering gives expression to the redemptive suffering of Christ, and he offers his own suffering—especially his prolonged dying—for others, linked to the redemptive suffering of Christ. Kaźmierczak says that John Paul links this to priestly celibacy. He sees chastity as central to the life of Christ, and clerical celibacy "is regarded by him as a self-sacrifice which is meant to supplement the redemptive suffering of Christ."[14] Much of this doesn't quite fit into traditional Catholic theology and spirituality. As Kaźmierczak says, his ideas on suffering seem to be found only in the writings of marginal nineteenth-century mystics and are "present in the revelations of Fatima."[15]

THE LATE AFTERNOON of October 16, 1978, saw the beginning of the most influential papacy in history. No pope, neither Pius IX, who loved crowds and adulation, nor Pius XII, who was regarded as godlike, has strode across the world stage like John Paul II. His high public profile enormously enhanced the power of the papacy. He stamped his idiosyncratic interpretation of Vatican II on the church and never hesitated to suppress dissent from it. He was simply not interested in the concerns and questions of faithful Catholics. He had no comprehension of the Anglo-American world, which he regarded as decadent. Tymieniecka's husband, Hendrick Houthakker, says, "He tended to regard Western countries and especially the United States as immoral. . . . He had no real appreciation of the virtues of democracy."[16]

He was the first pope to exploit to the full the possibilities and reach of modern media to become a world celebrity. Here the importance of the actor in him emerged into full view. Certainly, the pope's message to the crowds was rooted in *his* interpretation of the Gospel and church teaching, but there was also a cultlike element. This appeared when in April 2005 enormous crowds invaded Rome (some say 4 million) for his funeral, many with signs saying *Santo subito* (Sainthood immediately). In a perceptive piece in the *Independent*, Peter Popham spoke of the cultlike way people responded to John Paul: "It's as if faith in Jesus and God, in these secular times, is a challenge too far—while faith in that amazing old man [Wojtyła] . . . comes easy. Nobody really knew him, apart from a small, tight-knit group of intimates. . . . Yet millions felt they knew him well, so powerful was his charisma. And that intense but somewhat unreal emotion—like the fake sense of intimacy we enjoy with secular celebrities and royalty—survives his death unscathed."[17]

Popham put his finger on something here. People saw John Paul, especially on television, as an accessible figure, a man of the people who stood for a return to traditional values and justice. But this was a false sense of intimacy, because the focus was on him alone as superstar and papal monarch. Local leadership, bishops, and Catholic communities faded into insignificance. What John Paul had instinctively grasped was, according to the anonymous author of *Against Ratzinger*, that he had "to sell himself and his product according to the rules of mass marketing. . . . Wojtyla understood the concept of stardom as the consumer society's ersatz divinity." In the process, he "transformed his own body, his voice and his gestures into secular commodities."[18]

John Paul saw himself as a populist evangelist. Yes, he was trying to bring the crowds—and they were usually enormous—to Catholicism as he perceived it, and he shaped his liturgies and sermons to the local church. He embraced "enculturation" with gusto, especially in liturgy, to the absolute horror of traditionalist purists. But it was always *his* message that was communicated. He spent very little time with local conferences of bishops, from whom he might have learned something about local conditions, and the ministries and views of others paled in significance to his own. His was a one-man show. This easily transmuted into a personality cult, a form of manipulative demagoguery.

John Paul also had his own shock troops in the so-called new religious (or ecclesial) movements (NRMs), such as Opus Dei (OD), the Neocatechumenal Way, Communion and Liberation, Focolare, the Legionaries of Christ, and others. They were intimately involved in the so-called new evangelization, Pope Wojtyła's attempt to reach out to Catholics who had become "secularized" and abandoned the church. It was also a kind of attempt to bring the church to the marketplace, and the NRMs were seen as the people to make the pitch. For John Paul, the future lay with the NRMs rather than the traditional religious orders, many of which had experience reaching back centuries. Given that 13 percent of people in the United States are ex-Catholics—and these numbers are replicated right across the developed world—the NRMs certainly had a big task ahead of them. But the real question is whether these movements are the way to evangelize the contemporary world. What the NRMs actually do is to move in a sectarian direction by cutting themselves off from normal parish life, forming closed, sect-like, rigid communities that center around founding gurus like OD's Josemaría Escriva and the Neo-Catechuminate's Kiko Argüello, whose eccentric interpretations of what is Catholic are more important than the mainstream Catholic tradition. Anything that deviates from the founder is perceived as a threat, and Catholics who attempt to negotiate their belief with the surrounding culture are seen as "backsliders" and compromisers, "cafeteria Catholics" who pick and choose what they believe and what commitments they make. Sponsored by John Paul and the Vatican, the NRMs unquestioningly supported the papal power structure.

There was also an apocalyptic element in John Paul's approach to his papal role. He believed that the Virgin Mary had directly intervened in an assassination attempt on him on the feast day of Our Lady of Fatima (May 13, 1981) in the Piazza of Saint Peter's. The factual background to the assassination and the political issues surrounding it are complex, involving the KGB, the Bulgarian intelligence agencies (the DS and RUMNO), and the CIA.[19] The Turkish-born assassin, Mehmet Ali Aðca, was an experienced killer, and he was using a Browning 9mm semiautomatic pistol. He got off three shots, one of which penetrated the pope's abdomen, perforating his colon, causing an enormous loss of blood. His life was saved because the Vatican was well prepared for this kind of emergency, with a standby ambulance ready for the four-mile trip to the large, well-equipped Agostino Gemelli University Polyclinic. His wounds were extremely serious. John Paul believed that his life had been preserved so he could fulfill his destiny as pope.

What is important here is not so much the strategic and geopolitical issues as the interpretation of the event by John Paul. He believed that a miracle had occurred to save him so he could save the church. We have already seen the details of the Fatima apparitions in 1917. The Blessed Virgin entrusted three "secrets" to the children at Fatima, the third of which had remained unrevealed, causing enormous speculation among devotees of Fatima and conspiracy theorists. The content of the "secret" had been sent in a letter to Pius XII in 1952 by the only surviving Fatima visionary, Lucia, now a Carmelite nun. Subsequent popes had pretty much ignored this "secret." But after the assassination attempt, John Paul asked to see Lucia's letter, in which he read the words, "We saw a bishop dressed in white . . . killed by a group of soldiers who fired bullets and arrows at him." The child visionaries took this white-clad bishop to be the pope. We now know the text of the "secret" because Ratzinger's Holy Office published it in 2000, and Cardinal Tarcisio Bertone published a book entitled *The Last Secret of Fatima* in 2008. John Paul, who was already involved in the initial stage of his struggle with communism, had a special devotion to this feast, and he claimed Our Lady intervened to change the trajectory of the bullet and save his life, so he could free Poland and Eastern Europe and save the church. In a letter to the Italian bishops, he later mused that "it was a mother's hand that guided the bullet" past his vital organs, so that he could live to bring about the fall of communism.[20]

Whatever one thinks about the Blessed Virgin's guiding hand, John Paul was also a shrewd politician who played an influential role

in the fall of Polish communism. The Polish communist government had cautiously welcomed Wojtyła's election but anticipated
his first visit to Poland in June 1979 with considerable trepidation.
The visit went off without a hitch, with 2 million people attending
his last Mass in Kraków. Something of his messianic sense appeared
in a sermon in Gniezno, when, emphasizing his attachment to Poland, he spoke of "this pope, in whose heart is deeply engraved the
history of his own nation . . . and the history of . . . neighbouring
[Slavic] peoples." Never one for false modesty, he continued, "Is
it not Christ's will, is it not what the Holy Spirit disposes, that this
Polish pope, this Slav pope, should at this precise moment manifest
the spiritual unity of Christian Europe?" Not since the High Middle Ages had a pope claimed to "manifest" Europe's unity.

John Paul had been pope for almost two years when, in August
1980, economic dislocation and food-price hikes led to a series of
strikes across Poland, the most important of which was in the Lenin
Shipyards in Gdańsk, when an electrician named Lech Wałesa seized
the initiative. The strikes quickly assumed the status of a social revolution, or "counterrevolution," in the words of Soviet leader Leonid
Brezhnev, with workers, intelligentsia, and clergy coming together
to form defense committees. By the end of August, the Polish government had surrendered and agreed to permit trade unions to
operate freely. But Moscow was furious, and at a Warsaw Pact meeting in early December the Eastern bloc demanded a crackdown on
Solidarity and the church. John Paul, however, kept contact with
Moscow through his secretary of state, the skilled diplomat Cardinal Agostino Casaroli. Throughout 1981 Solidarity continued to
flex its muscle, with strikes and pressure on the government. With
the economy deteriorating, there was constant apprehension that
the Soviets would invade Poland. Then General Wojciech Jaruzelski
took power, and on December 13, 1981, he declared martial law.
Solidarity was banned and its leaders arrested. However, the pope
and Jaruzelski also kept the lines of communication open, allowing
John Paul to mediate. The contact between them "marked the start
of a very special and subtle relationship that at the end of the decade
would render possible the historical transition from communism to
democracy."[21] Biographer Tad Szulc says the Reagan administration

stumbled ham-fisted into this delicate arrangement, and in a meeting on June 7, 1982, with the pope, Reagan offered intelligence sharing on Poland and collaboration in supporting Solidarity. John Paul thanked him but declined; he already knew far more about Poland than Reagan and the CIA. Also, the pope made it clear to the Soviets that if they invaded Poland, he would return and stay with the people, and this may have dissuaded them.

A return papal visit for June 1983 was agreed upon and went off pretty much without a hitch, largely because the pope played his cards cautiously. In June 1987 John Paul was back in Poland. Gorbachev and *glasnost* had arrived in Moscow in March 1985, but "openness" had not yet reached Warsaw. This time John Paul made no concessions to Jaruzelski; he used the word *solidarity* (both with capital *S* and lowercase) often; praised Władysław (Jerzy) Popieluszko, a priest murdered by the SB, the Polish secret police, in 1984. He had been a strong supporter of Solidarity and highly critical of the communist government, and his murder by three SB operatives led to widespread protests across the country. The pope visited Popieluszko's grave and condemned atheism. *Glasnost* eventually arrived in Poland in 1988. Solidarity reemerged, the economy was in serious trouble with food-price hikes, and the Polish communists had no support from Moscow because the Soviets were deeply preoccupied with their own problems. Between February 1988 and April 1989, the country went through a period of strikes and negotiations that led to talks that, in turn, led to free elections, and the communists were democratically swept from power. It was the beginning of the end for the Soviet bloc, with the Berlin Wall falling in November 1989. A new, free Poland emerged. The papal use of soft power had been a very important part of the equation.

But John Paul was soon bitterly disappointed with the new Poland. He returned home for his fourth trip in June 1991. He had identified himself with an idealized nation, but what he found on his return were normal people longing for the kind of consumerism that he had denounced in the West. Intolerance with church interference in politics and in the bedroom was growing, and the Polish Mafia in Rome and conservative Polish bishops kept feeding

Pope John Paul what he wanted to hear: that all of this was inspired by ex-communists and atheistic anticlericals. So the June 1991 trip was one long, bitter denunciation of the influence of Western European secularism, the separation of church and state, abortion (which he equated with the Holocaust), adultery, "utilitarianism," and the whole "civilization of desire and pleasure." Needless to say, he received a hostile reception from a country where 2 million people were unemployed, where women, trying to feed their children, at last had some control over their fertility, and where people who had lived with endless shortages of basic goods were still struggling to make ends meet. The pope was also embittered by public criticism of the bishops and clergy for their interference in politics. His deepest disappointment was that there was no "spiritual renewal" emerging from the East. Even leading Wojtyła apologist George Weigel admits that this visit "was not well suited to the psychology of the moment."[22] John Paul's 1997, 1999, and 2002 trips to Poland were much better prepared, and the final trip in 2002 had a strong nostalgic tinge to it.

The pope had played a prophetic role, especially in his early visits to his homeland, and his conviction that Poland was to be some form of spiritual model for the rest of Europe never wavered. But in fact, the Polish church had fallen far behind mainstream Catholicism because it never really embraced Vatican II. But then neither had John Paul II.

IT IS IN his overseas trips that the messianic-celebrity John Paul is most obvious. No world leader, including Queen Elizabeth II, has traveled as much and as far as he. Excluding internal trips in Italy, he made 104 international trips, or so-called pastoral visits, during his twenty-six-year papacy, 4 per year. He visited 129 countries, some of them several times. He went to Poland nine times, France eight, the United States seven, Spain five, and Portugal, Brazil, and Switzerland four times. As a result, an entirely new phenomenon arose in the church: an omnipresent papacy. Pope John Paul also initiated the idea of World Youth Days in 1984, and the first was held in Rome in 1986. Since then there have been fourteen WYDs, the last in Kraków in 2016. These events work on the basis of vast crowds, with youth coming from all over the world. About 5 million young people attended WYD Mass in Manila in January 1995.

Contact with youth seemed to give the pope a new lease on life, but all of this travel and performance must have required extraordinary personal effort on his part. What drove it? John Paul said that these visits strengthened the faith of the local church and gathered people around himself as the symbol of unity in the universal church. He saw himself as a catechist and evangelist, bringing Christ's message to the world. Certainly, these large crowds give Catholics a sense of belonging and some pride in being Catholic. My sense is that these visits were brief respites for Catholics who live in secular societies that would prefer to see religion privatized and out of the public square. But the flip side is that when you have a dominant personality like John Paul, these trips reinforced the notion of the papal monarchy and of the identification of Catholicism with the pope. Driven by his narcissistic-messianic conviction that he alone knew what was good for Catholicism, he became the *de facto* bishop of the world, and his agenda became Catholicism's agenda. The Vatican II counterbalancing of bishops, pope, theologians, and community was lost, and the distortion of papal centralism and power became predominant again.

———

A BY-PRODUCT OF the pope's constant travel was neglect of the minutiae of church government. In one sense, John Paul marginalized the Roman Curia, and he learned more through discussion than reading reports. So access to him was important, and this was largely controlled by his secretary, Stanisław Dziwisz. The Polish Mafia and Cardinal Joseph Ratzinger were also influential, and John Paul left the curia to itself as long as it generally followed his policies. He had two secretaries of state: from Paul VI he inherited Casaroli, who retired in 1990, to be replaced by the incompetent Angelo Sodano. Other bad appointments to the curia were

Colombian Alfonso López Trujillo, a supporter of the national security state and the dictatorial juntas of the 1970s–1980s in Latin America, and Chilean Jorge Medina Estévez, a close friend of dictator Augusto Pinochet.

The John Paul papacy also appointed many weak, conformist bishops who constantly looked over their shoulders to Rome with little concern for their dioceses. The selection process for bishops explicitly excluded independently minded priests who had spoken out on contentious issues or disagreed with the official line from Rome. The pope also subverted several episcopal conferences that he considered too progressive. The first was the Dutch. With only seven dioceses, it was easy to replace more pastoral bishops with traditionalists. In the United States, the situation was more complex. Instructed by Paul VI to renew the hierarchy, Archbishop Jean Jadot, apostolic delegate from 1973 to 1980, appointed 103 bishops and 15 archbishops. Most of them were pastoral priests, such as Archbishop John Quinn in San Francisco and Cardinal William Borders in Baltimore. "Paul VI was very much aware of the fact that previous apostolic delegates had been pawns in the hands of powerful kingmaker American cardinals . . . [and that] most American bishops were . . . more big businessmen than they were pastors."[23] But the Jadot bishops were not cultural warriors, so John Paul set out to replace them. Rome had been upset by two excellent consensus documents developed by the US bishops over several years, *The Challenge of Peace* (1983), on nuclear war, and *Economic Justice for All* (1986). In response, John Paul and Benedict XVI appointed many nondescript conformists and traditionalist cultural warriors to the US hierarchy.

During his papacy John Paul directly intervened to make some utterly disastrous appointments of bishops. One was in Vienna, when the man responsible for his election as pope, Franz König, retired in 1986. Instead of following König's advice, John Paul picked an obscure, ultratraditionalist Benedictine abbot, Hans Hermann Groër, and made him archbishop of Vienna. From 1995 to 2003, accusations of sexual abuse of seminary students dogged Groër, by now a cardinal. He was defended by John Paul, who on several occasions compared his "sufferings" to those of Christ. There is no doubt of Groër's guilt, with the pope stubbornly defending the indefensible when it came to sexual abuse. Groër was eventually forced to resign.

Another example of shockingly bad judgment was the appointment of Wolfgang Haas to the diocese of Chur, Switzerland, a diocese that dates back to the fifth century and includes the city of Zurich. The canons of Chur cathedral have a traditional right to choose their bishop, but this was anathema to John Paul. He appointed Haas, a dogged, inept ultratraditionalist, as coadjutor bishop in 1988, despite widespread protests from the diocese. Haas succeeded to Chur in 1990 and held out until 1997, when John Paul arbitrarily created the new Archdiocese of Vaduz, Liechtenstein (which had been part of the Chur diocese for centuries), as a face-saver. Haas has now created toxic tensions in the Principality of Liechtenstein. These disastrous errors of judgment were the result of John Paul's stubborn determination to ultracentralize the appointment of bishops, completely ignoring collegiality.

Paul VI had set up the Synod of Bishops as a way of giving expression to episcopal collegiality. But John Paul had little time for cooperation with the world episcopate. He knew what the church needed; he didn't need bishops to tell him. He was lucky because the synod had never really gotten off the ground, and under John Paul it became nothing more than an episcopal rubber stamp. Six synods were held during his papacy. The pattern was that he set the topic; the bishops debated, always aware of what the pope wanted; and John Paul wrote up the conclusions, which often completely ignored what the bishops had actually said. Essentially, he wanted the bishops to endorse his views. John Paul was uninterested in collegiality, which was simply a hindrance to his messianic conception of the papacy.

Assisted by Ratzinger, he also attempted to rein in bishops' conferences. Reaching right back to the earliest days of the church, local bishops' synods, or gatherings, were always more important than the papacy in terms of ecclesial governance and had always been able to make decisions for local churches. The Vatican II doctrine of collegiality gave renewed expression to this theological tradition, and Paul VI encouraged the formation of national bishops' conferences. The Vatican II *Decree on the Pastoral Office of Bishops* says unequivocally, "Therefore, this sacred synod considers it to be supremely fitting that everywhere bishops belonging to the same nation or region form an association which would meet at fixed times." Back in 1965, even young Joseph Ratzinger saw real virtues in bishops' conferences. "These," he said, "seem to offer themselves today as the best means of concrete plurality in unity." He traced them back to the early church and called them "a legitimate form of the collegiate structure of the church." But after becoming CDF prefect, he changed his tune. John Allen says that "his doubts surfaced only when he arrived in Rome and started facing the assertiveness of well-managed conferences," and these "doubts" found expression in John Paul's apostolic letter *Apostolos suos* (May 21, 1998).[24] This letter said that bishops' conferences cannot teach authoritatively unless their statements are unanimous and then only when approved by Rome. Ratzinger now argued that the *madatum docendi* (the right to teach) belongs to the pope or to an individual bishop, but not to bishops' conferences.

John Paul had no tolerance for dissent of any sort in the church. The Polish experience taught him that a completely united front was needed to deal with a communist government, and he applied this ruthlessly to the church. He used direct, coercive power to deal with those who didn't share his peculiar view of Catholicism. His main supporter here was Ratzinger, whom he appointed in 1981 as prefect of the CDF. Not that John Paul invented intolerance of dissent. In a scathing assessment of Roman interference, Yves Congar in 1956 said that the curia didn't want things being said "that they don't like being said." He said that they wanted "to impose behavior on the whole of Christendom which is: to think nothing, to say nothing other than: there is a pope who thinks everything, who says everything, and the whole quality of being a Catholic consists in obeying him." Pius XII, Congar said, wanted to reduce theologians to commentators on his discourses and "to think [nothing] . . . beyond this commentary."[25] This is exactly what John Paul wanted.

Thus, a whole group of prominent Catholics, including Hans Küng, Edward Schillebeeckx, Leonardo Boff, Charles E. Curran, Lavinia Byrne, Tissa Balasuriya, Jacques Dupuis, and many others, were tackled by the CDF and tied up for years in endless knots, answering often absurd accusations from Ratzinger's CDF. (Here I acknowledge that my book *Papal Power* was investigated by the CDF between 1997 and 2001.) Many theologians and others suffered various penalties after dealing with an arcane process in which the CDF often didn't even follow its own procedures. But it wasn't just individuals who were pursued. Several "schools" of theology were also condemned. The best known is liberation theology, which is the theology that developed in Latin America in the 1970s and emerged from oppressed groups' attempts to articulate Christian faith and read the Bible from within the context of injustice and politico-economic exploitation. It is intimately related to the base Christian community movement. Liberation theologians were falsely accused of using so-called Marxist analysis that John Paul said turned the church into a political institution and minimized the salvation that came through Christ and the institutional church. What he ignored was his own explicitly political involvement in the Polish opposition to communism. Again, it was his vision that alone was normative.

Parallel to the suppression of dissent was Pope John Paul's relationship to ecumenism. In terms of the Jewish faith, his record is excellent. He was born just sixteen miles from Oświęcim, the site of the concentration-extermination camp Auschwitz-Birkenau, where 1.1 million people died between 1940 and 1945. This deeply affected him, because he grew up with many Jewish neighbors and sometimes played goalkeeper on a Jewish soccer team. Despite the anti-Semitic tendencies common among many Poles in the 1930s, often at the personal, local level people maintained good relationships with their Jewish neighbors. Polish anti-Semitism was rooted in the caricature of Jews as the principal proponents of secularism, communism, and liberalism, which was supposedly destroying Catholic culture. Theologian Ronald Modras says that by the late 1930s, "A significant if not overwhelming majority of the nation now appeared to accept the nationalists' narrowed definition of a Pole as a Slavic Roman Catholic who was the product of Polish culture. Jews were explicitly excluded."[26] After his personal experience of the Holocaust, John Paul decided that there could never be any theological or religious justification for any form of anti-Semitism. At Mass at Auschwitz-Birkenau on June 7, 1979, he said, "I come and I kneel on this Golgotha of the modern world." For him, there were no answers to this gigantic monstrosity, except spiritual ones. In light of this cosmic struggle, for the pope the Western progressive Catholic agenda paled into effete insignificance.

Other than relationships with the Jewish faith, Tad Szulc says, ecumenical relations were "one of the great disappointments of [Wojtyła's] pontificate."[27] Throughout this long papacy, little was achieved in relationship with the Eastern Orthodox churches. After the fall of the Soviet Union, relationships with the Russian Orthodox soured due to efforts by some aggressive Catholics and other evangelical Christians to penetrate Russia. There were also difficulties linked to Eastern churches in union with Rome whose property had been given to the Orthodox by the Soviets. There were several agreed-upon statements with Anglicans and Protestants, but real ecumenical work at the base level slowed to a walk. However, in May 1995 the pope issued the interesting encyclical *Ut unum sint* (That they may be one), focusing particularly on the "Petrine ministry." He said it is the duty of the bishop of Rome to work for unity, but that (quoting Vatican II) "the church of Christ subsists in the Catholic Church," while acknowledging that elements of "sanctification and truth" are to be found in the other churches. He speaks of the papacy, again quoting Vatican II, as "the perpetual and visible principle and foundation . . . and guarantor of unity." His role, he says, is not to lord it over the brethren but to act as "the first servant of unity," while admitting that the papacy "constitutes a difficulty for most other Christians." He commits the Catholic Church to finding a way of exercising the primacy that, while not renouncing what is essential, is nevertheless open to ecumenism. His ecumenical credentials were enhanced by the interfaith gatherings at Assisi in 1986, 1993, and 2002, when religious leaders from many traditions gathered with him to pray for peace, but he was strongly criticized for these gatherings by ultratraditionalists.

While there is no doubt that John Paul was sincerely committed to ecumenism and hankered after a more genuinely catholic approach, this was compromised by an exclusivist, "one true church" mentality promoted by Ratzinger's CDF, especially in the declining years of the Wojtyła papacy. It was Ratzinger, in fact, who became increasingly concerned about religious pluralism. This was why he pursued Sri Lankan theologian Father Tissa Balasuriya between 1992 and 1998 and later Father Jacques Dupuis, both of whom were strong proponents of openness to the other great religions.[28]

Early in Ratzinger's tenure at the CDF, it had been liberation theology that was condemned. Then the CDF turned its attention to other theologians from the developing world, like Balasuriya. He had worked to integrate Catholic faith with Asian culture. Inspired by Vatican II, he and other Asian theologians questioned the old missionary approach—salvation through conversion and conformity to a European-Roman model of belief, spirituality, and religious practice, as though this were the only possible way of being Catholic. Balasuriya's work upset several Sri Lankan bishops, including one particularly ambitious prelate, Bishop (later Cardinal) Malcolm Ranjith, who reported Balasuriya to the CDF. In July 1994 Balasuriya received a CDF critique of his book *Mary and Human Liberation* (1990). In March 1995 he responded, pointing out that the congregation's consulter's report "contained unproved generalizations, misunderstandings, misrepresentations, distortions and falsifications." The CDF was so confused that Balasuriya showed that "in the process of translating English into Italian and then back again they had actually injected heresy into what I had said." But this didn't stop them. They demanded a personal "profession of faith" from Balasuriya. "The whole thing seemed designed to force me into a corner, almost to give me a heart attack!" He refused and was excommunicated on January 5, 1997. It was an extraordinary overreaction to a seventy-three-year-old priest who had spent his entire life fighting for social justice, often under threat of murder; his priest friend and colleague Michael Rodrigo was murdered while saying Mass. There was an immediate outcry throughout the church, and the excommunication was eventually lifted.

The Balasuriya case made it clear that the CDF was targeting interfaith dialogue when Jacques Dupuis, a Jesuit who had spent thirty-six years teaching theology in India and fourteen years at the Gregorian University in Rome, was tackled over his book *Toward a Christian Theology of Religious Pluralism* (1997). He was accused of "ambiguities" and informed that any truth or goodness in other religions "derives ultimately from the source-mediation of Jesus Christ" and that "other religions are oriented to the church and all are called to become part of her."[29] Cardinal Franz König, retired archbishop of Vienna, came strongly to Dupuis's defense, and an "astonished and sad" Ratzinger claimed that the CDF's action "had consisted simply in sending some confidential questions to Father Dupuis and nothing more than that." This was simply untrue. Dupuis had been directly accused of violating church teaching. The whole business dragged on through 1999 and 2000. Dupuis's health declined, especially after he had signed an agreed-upon statement that was later published with an extra sentence added that he had never approved. It was a blatantly dishonest move. He was again attacked in 2004 by the CDF, this time accusing him of undermining the uniqueness of Christ. Sick at heart, he died on December 28, 2004, before anything was resolved. Not for the first time, the CDF had driven a sick man to his death.

Ratzinger's concern was the uniqueness of Christ and Christianity, and this is central to the CDF declaration *Dominus Jesus* of August 6, 2000. *DJ* is directed against those Catholics involved in the "wider ecumenism" who are trying to find common ground with non-Christian religious traditions. While *DJ* would seem to be a retreat from the Assisi ecumenical prayer days sponsored by the pope, its worst impact was on the Anglican and Protestant churches. It referred to them as "ecclesial communities" and explicitly said that "they are not churches in the proper sense." Leading Catholic ecclesiologist Francis A. Sullivan is critical of *Dominus Jesus*, saying that "there can be no doubt about the life of grace and salvation that has been communicated for centuries through preaching . . . and other Christian ministry in the Anglican and Protestant churches."[30]

Like everything else about him, John Paul's encyclicals strongly reflect his own preoccupations. His first, *Redemptor hominis* (1979), focuses on a basic Wojtyła theme: the kind of human freedom that is brought by Christ. Running right through the encyclical are issues from the pope's Polish background and his dealings with an atheistic state. He says that the most "objective and inalienable" human right is "the right to religious freedom together with the right to freedom of conscience." This leads directly into his social teaching, where, like his predecessors, he places himself within the papal social justice tradition. *Laborem exercens* (1981) strongly reflects his Polish background as he continues a kind of dialogue with Marxism. He offers a positive assessment of work, which he sees as a way of sharing in God's continuous creation. Firmly within the papal tradition, he says that "the right to private property is subordinated to the right to common use, to the fact that goods are meant for everyone." He calls for a family wage so that women can remain at home and "be able to fulfil their tasks in accordance with their own nature." This very much reflects his view of women, and he says that labor should be structured so that women don't have to abandon "what is specific to them and at the expense of the family, in which . . . mothers have an irreplaceable role." This was widely criticized as keeping women in the home and out of the workforce. *Solicitudo rei socialis* (1987) and *Centisimus annus* (1991) are also highly critical of the gap between rich and poor and "blind submission to pure consumerism." He also mounts a radical critique of free-market capitalism. *Solicitudo rei socialis* is the first encyclical to mention ecology, where he says that industrialization leads to "the pollution of the environment." In *Evangelium vitae* (1995), he confronts the hard issue of world population; by 1995 the world population was 5.7 billion people. The pope admits that "public authorities have a responsibility to intervene," but always respecting "the primary and inalienable responsibility of married couples and families." He says it is "morally unacceptable to encourage, let alone impose, the use of methods such as contraception, sterilization and abortion in order to regulate births."

The 1993 encyclical *Veritatis splendor* (*VS*) deals with fundamental moral questions. Given his preoccupation with contraception, there was much speculation as to whether John Paul would declare *Humanae vitae* infallible. He was talked out of it, most likely by

Ratzinger. In *VS* he attacks the moral relativism that he claims is characteristic of Western societies and says that the church's moral teaching is in crisis because of theological dissent. The problem, he claims, is a defective understanding of freedom of conscience that he believes means the freedom to act according to the moral law as revealed by the papal magisterium. Historian Michael Walsh points out that *VS* resembles Pius XII's *Humani generis*, where various groups of theologians were criticized with descriptions of their opinions that were "travesties" of their actual views.[31]

BIOGRAPHER GEORGE WEIGEL describes John Paul II as a "deeply pastoral man" and argues that in his "theology of the body," he found a way of addressing the challenge of the sexual revolution and of "exorcising the Manichaean [dualistic] demon and its depreciation of human sexuality from Catholic moral theology."[32] John Paul developed this "theology of the body" in a series of talks he gave to public audiences between 1979 and 1984, claiming that nowadays we have lost the genuine meaning of love. What we call "love" today is actually using another person merely for selfish pleasure. While it was good that a pope acknowledged that sexual love was actually virtuous and that Catholicism is still crippled by dualism, whether his theology is the sleeping giant that Weigel imagines is another question. Here we need to remind ourselves of the comment of Anna-Teresa Tymieniecka that regarding sexuality, John Paul "obviously doesn't know what he's talking about." While he has much to say about sexuality, the question remains as to whether what he says has any real resonance in actual human experience. Nowadays, his "theology of the body" is promoted by John Paul II Institutes in Rome and Washington, DC.

While he was happy talking about "bodily theology," he had absolutely nothing to say on the sexual abuse of children. Yet this issue has done incalculable damage to thousands of victims and their families, as well as to Catholicism worldwide. John Paul's defense of Hans Hermann Groër, even when it was clear that he was guilty, and his total lack of response to overwhelming evidence in the case of the appalling Mexican priest Marcial Maciel Degollado are incomprehensible. Maciel remained a favorite of the pope right to the end, despite his being an egregious sexual predator of numerous teenage seminarians in the Legionaries of Christ, the religious order he founded. He also fathered at least three children (and possibly six) by several women, while sometimes posing as a CIA agent. He actually abused two of his own children. But Maciel was a genius at raising money, especially from the wives and widows of multimillionaires, and for decades he was a regular around Rome, where he greased palms in exchange for influence. The Legion became cult-like, with members bound by a vow never to criticize *Nuestro Padre* (Our Father), who was honored as a living saint. He was patronized by John Paul, who appointed him to several bishops' synods, took him with him on three visits to Mexico, and in 1994 (when there was already extremely good evidence of Maciel's guilt and serious questions about his integrity) still described him as "an efficacious guide to youth." Several of his victims had tried to get through to the pope to complain about his abuse, and eventually they took out a canon-law case against him with the CDF. Then journalists Gerald Renner and Jason Berry published a series of articles on Maciel's abuse and the Legion's property and financial affairs in the *Hartford* (CT) *Courant* in 1996.

But Maciel had powerful protectors: John Paul and Secretary of State Sodano. What appealed to the pope was Maciel's so-called orthodoxy, the Legion's clerical conservatism, and its production line of clerics who fulfilled the John Paul image of the priest: handsome, youthful, traditionalist, and dressed in a cassock, with a short back and sides. For Maciel's other patron, Sodano, it was all about the money. In the end, when the evidence was overwhelming, it was Benedict XVI, not John Paul, who sent Maciel off to "a reserved life of prayer and penance" in 2006, which was lived out in an elite and luxurious gated community in Florida, paid for by the Legionaries of Christ.

Since Maciel's death in January 2008, the Legion has been through a relatively superficial Vatican investigation, supervised by papal delegate Cardinal Velasio de Paolis. Many of the best priests left the Legionaries, and there was discussion that the only proper thing to do was to close down the whole organization. Part of the problem is the extraordinarily complex financial dealings of the Legion. A book published in Mexico in late 2015, *El imperio financiero de los Legionarios de Christo* (The financial empire of the Legionaries of Christ), by journalist Raúl Olmos, says that "de Paolis left virtually intact the business structure that Maciel created. It was a change of image rather than substance."[33] The reality is that the Legionaries of Christ order still has vast property, investment, tourism, and financial holdings, and it owns an international building conglomerate. Many of Maciel's old guard, who knew all about his crimes, have survived the de Paolis "reform." They also know where the money is. Accounting for all the wealth is a massive problem, and senior members of the Legionaries who had been close to Maciel persuaded de Paolis that the order was redeemable. An extraordinary general chapter was held that ended in early 2014 with de Paolis praising them lavishly and telling them they "have been reconciled with themselves, with their history, with the world and the church" and that they have been "freed of the burden that weighed on their backs." However, they have certainly not broken their connections to Mexico's wealthy elite, and as Jason Berry says, they are still arguably "the most extreme example in the Catholic Church of religion as a form of capitalism."[34]

In a very powerful April 2014 article in the *National Catholic Reporter*, the priest who has done most about the sexual abuse issue in the United States, Thomas Doyle, says bluntly that John Paul's "sainthood is a profound insult to the countless victims of sexual assault by Catholic clergy the world over." Doyle is unequivocal that John Paul was informed right from the beginning of the crisis but that he deliberately refused to do anything about it. "The excuse that he did nothing because of his 'purity of thought' is as ridiculous as the excuse that he wanted to preserve the priesthood for which he held such high esteem," Doyle says. Writing just before John Paul's canonization, Doyle added, "The institutional church will accord its highest honor [sainthood] to the one man who, more than any other alive, could have ended the nightmare and saved countless innocent and vulnerable victims. But he did not . . . [and] would not."[35]

His failure to act is incomprehensible and has puzzled Bishop Geoffrey Robinson, retired auxiliary bishop of Sydney. Giving evidence to the Australian government–appointed Royal Commission into Institutional Responses to Child Sexual Abuse, Robinson was asked to explain John Paul's response. "What we got from him was silence," Robinson said, and the crisis "didn't fit into [John Paul's] image of church. . . . Maybe he had never met it back in Poland, I don't know, but he dealt with it badly." Robinson continued that papal leadership is still lacking, "even from Francis." The tendency, Robinson said, was to blame the media, or to minimize the issue, or to say it was "an American" or "an Anglo-Saxon problem." It was something abstract because, Robinson said, they had never met any victims. Also, "they tended to look down . . . on our Anglo-Saxon legal system. . . . [T]hey felt that their [canon] law was far superior to ours."[36]

While he may have been remiss about sexual abuse, John Paul II certainly was no slouch when it came to saint making. All told, he declared 482 people saints. Originally, individual Christians were declared saints when a popular local cult grew up around them, so it was the people who decided who were to be honored with the title "saint." But by the twelfth century, the papacy had gotten control of the process of canonization, and nowadays it is administered by a bureaucratic body, Rome's Congregation for the Causes of Saints. John Paul's 482 saints far exceeds the 300 or so officially declared saints in the past six hundred years.

If saints are held up as model Christians, then making people saints is a political process: their lives are models of the way Christians should live. Almost 75 percent of those canonized by John Paul were martyrs for Catholicism, which indicates that he considered that heroically giving one's life for the faith was the ultimate commitment. Most were killed in groups from countries as various as Mexico, Korea, Spain, and China. Among the nonmartyrs declared by this pope, most are priests or members of religious orders;

there are very few laypeople. Again, this is an indication that for John Paul, a commitment to a dedicated life was required for saint-hood. The nationalities of the nonmartyrs are also significant. The vast majority are Latin (Spanish or Italian), with some French and a significant number of Poles. There are hardly any Anglo or Ger-man names; the three that stand out are Edith Stein, the convert German Jewish Carmelite nun and philosopher; Arnold Jansen, the founder of the Divine Word Missionaries; and Katharine Drexel, the Philadelphia-born foundress of the Sisters of the Blessed Sacrament.

IN 2003 THE Vatican finally admitted what was obvious to every-one, that John Paul had Parkinson's disease. This degenerative con-dition had been diagnosed in the early 1990s. So for a decade or more, the church was governed by an increasingly sick man. We also know that popes can and have resigned and that John Paul prepared two letters of resignation, in 1989 and 1994, in which he secretly offered his resignation to the College of Cardinals if dis-ease or other causes prevented him from carrying out his ministry.[37] That is all well and good. But the trouble is that there is still no set process in canon law to deal with a pope who, for whatever reason, refuses to resign if, for instance, senility, dementia, or madness of some sort occurs.

So began the long, public process of John Paul's dying. In a death-denying and youth-obsessed world, this was a good thing, as he turned his long last illness into a kind of parable. This was most obvious when he visited the pilgrimage center of Lourdes in France in August 2004 and struggled through Mass, a very sick man among very sick people. Seven months later he was dead. Near the end he lost his voice, and his appearances became a kind of mime, the speechless communication of a dying man. He embraced physical suffering and was trying to model a Christian death, a way of iden-tifying with Jesus on the cross. These were his greatest moments, with his vulnerability on display for all to see. By Holy Week 2005 (late March), it was clear that the end was near. He died peacefully on Saturday evening, April 2, 2005. The largest funeral in human history—larger than that of Princess Diana—followed, with the population of Rome (2.6 million) almost doubling in the days leading up to the event. A million people came from Poland alone. Ten reigning kings and queens, three crown princes, and seventy-four presidents and prime ministers attended, and there was saturation television and media coverage. It was a long way from the anonymous death of Pius VI in 1799 in Valence. No pope in church history had wielded this much influence.

So was he, as some maintain, John Paul the Great, "Great" in the same sense of Leo the Great (440–461) or Gregory the Great (590–604)? Or was his papacy more problematic? Did he bequeath a church triumphant, or Catholicism in serious trouble? Hans Küng says that John Paul was not the greatest pope of the twentieth century "but the most contradictory. A pope of many great gifts and many bad decisions."[38] He was certainly a colossus who in his time participated in world events and was probably the most powerful and influential man of the second half of the twentieth century. He instinctively knew how to promote himself and create an image that transmuted into a celebrity cult. He became Catholicism incarnated for hundreds of millions of people, and in achieving this he had a master promoter behind him: the Spanish Opus Dei lay member Joaquín Navarro-Valls, who was Vatican spokesman and media supremo from 1984 to 2006. Originally a medical doctor and psychiatrist, Navarro-Valls was also a genius who was able to create a celebrity persona for John Paul that transmuted after his death into a call by the pope's followers for an immediate declaration that he was a "saint." All around Rome during and after the funeral, there were signs that read *Santo subito* (Sainthood immediately). Convinced that he had been specially called by God and that he represented Christ in the world, he certainly embodied "the fullness of supreme power."

In the 206 years since Pius VI, the papacy had come a very long way. From probably the lowest point in papal history, the popes had not only recovered their power and authority within Catholicism, but also turned the papacy into an institution that influenced not just politics and international relations but social and ethical issues as well. An example is the papal social justice tradition that offers an alternative to ruthless capitalism. What we have seen is the willingness of the popes to use soft power usually in relationship to political and international affairs and hard power in the interior life of the church. Never has the papacy been so powerful and influential, but the problem is whether what happened in the past two centuries was what Jesus, the poor man of the Gospels, the man who had nowhere to lay his head, intended.

PART IV

"THE SMELL OF THE SHEEP"

10

"REFORM OF THE REFORM"

ALL THE *VATICANISTI*, the Vatican media commentators, myself included, were completely wrong. We all said that Joseph Ratzinger would *never* be elected pope, given his record as prefect of the CDF. He would be a great elector, yes, but pope, no. We also thought that the conclave of 2005 would be a long, drawn-out affair because there was no clear candidate after the second-longest papacy in history. Again, we were wrong; it was all over in twenty-four hours.

I was there in Rome, commenting on the election for various international media organizations, when 115 cardinals entered the conclave on April 18, 2005. For the first time in centuries, they were not locked up in the uncomfortable Borgia Apartments and rooms surrounding the Sistine Chapel, but resided in the recently constructed, comfortable, but modest motel-like Domus Sanctae Marthae, just to the left of Saint Peter's. This conclave was run under rules set up by John Paul II that removed the long-established requirement for a two-thirds majority vote for election. The new rules decreed that after thirteen days of inconclusive voting, the cardinals could decide to revert to a simple majority to elect a pope. This meant that a strong minority could hold out until day thirteen and then get their man via a simple majority vote. Several names had been mentioned as possible *papabili*. Most of them were relatively ordinary characters: Dionigi Tettamanzi of Milan was seen as belonging to the traditionalist school, but as John Paul entered his last years Tettamanzi began burnishing his more "progressive" credentials for broader appeal. He too obviously wanted to be pope, always a bad move. Another often mentioned was Angelo Scola of

Venice. He was a kind of Italian Wojtyła, influenced by Balthasar and close to the NRM Communion and Liberation. Nigerian Francis Arinze, a curial cardinal who had been in Rome for years, was also mentioned, his main appeal being that he was an African, but in reality he was more Roman than the Romans. The most impressive of the more traditionalist candidates was Christoph Schönborn of Vienna, a former student of Ratzinger, but at age sixty he was considered too young. The church didn't need another long papacy like John Paul's.

There were only two "progressive" candidates, both Jesuits: Carlo Maria Martini, retired archbishop of Milan, and Jorge Bergoglio of Buenos Aires. There was also a small, far less cohesive group, centering on Cardinal Godfried Danneels of Brussels, supporting a Bergoglio candidacy. However, a particularly nasty "Stop Bergoglio" dossier began circulating among the cardinals that accused the Argentinean of complicity with the military junta (1976–1983) in the arrest and torture of two of his fellow Jesuits when he was Jesuit provincial in Argentina. The dossier was most probably leaked by conservative Argentinean bishops out "to get" Bergoglio. It is also clear that Martini was never really a candidate; he was already suffering from Parkinson's disease, although if he had been elected, he may well have been a real catalyst for change. When he died in November 2012, an interview with the Milan daily *Corriere della Sera* was published in which he said bluntly that the church "was 200 years out of date." He told the newspaper, "Our culture has aged, our churches are big and empty and the church bureaucracy rises up, our rituals and our cassocks are pompous. The Church must admit its mistakes and begin a radical change, starting from the Pope and the bishops. The paedophilia scandals oblige us to take a journey of transformation." Ratzinger always had much respect for Martini, and his comments may well have influenced the pope's 2013 resignation.[1]

In the week before the conclave, Marco Politi of the Rome daily *La Repubblica* noted that support had been coalescing around Ratzinger. Actually, support had been growing for a couple of months, with strong backing from a significant group of cardinals that had been meeting regularly for a number of years at the Rome headquarters of Opus Dei. It included two OD cardinals, Julian Herranz (curia) and Juan Cipriani Thorne (Lima, Peru); curial cardinals Camillo Ruini, Darío Castrillón Hoyos, and Alfonso López Trujillo; and Australia's George Pell. There was also strong support from Tarcisio Bertone (Genoa), Schönborn, and most of the North Americans. During the interregnum, Ratzinger, as dean of the College of Cardinals, had been eloquent at the funeral of John Paul and was impressive at the daily meetings of cardinals before the conclave, striking all "the right chords" and "reminding his confreres both of the legacy of the deceased pontiff . . . and of the challenges that it—and the church—faced."[2] His sermon on the morning of the conclave was almost a policy speech, and he entered with widespread support among a cross-section of cardinals.

The facts of the conclave seem to be that Ratzinger was well ahead from the first scrutiny, with some forty or more votes. By the third scrutiny, with approximately sixty-five votes, Ratzinger's only challenger was Bergoglio, with about forty votes. At lunch on the second day, to prevent an impasse with either the Ratzinger supporters digging in for thirteen days or an undesirable curial candidate emerging as a compromise, Bergoglio seems to have persuaded most of his votes to go over to Ratzinger, thus ensuring the German's election at the fourth scrutiny. At age seventy-eight he was clearly seen as a transitional pope.

His election received a mixed reception. While the traditionalists were ecstatic, Vatican II Catholics respectfully welcomed him, the feeling being that he should be given a chance. Margaret Hebblethwaite wrote, "People have been saying 'Cardinal Ratzinger is no more. *Viva* Pope Benedict XVI.' It is like Simon being transformed into Peter."[3] The German press were critical but quietly proud. Typical was the *Frankfurter Allgemeine Zeitung*: "Ratzinger is the Counter-Reformation personified, not with fire and sword, but with the power of his mind."[4] Hans Küng wrote, "The name Benedict XVI leaves open the possibility for a more moderate policy. Let us therefore give him a chance." This optimistic expectation was reinforced when Pope Ratzinger and Küng held a friendly meeting at Castel Gandolfo in late September 2005. However, Benedict also met Bishop Bernard Fellay of the schismatic Lefebvrist group. Clearly, he was trying to build bridges, but as time would tell, Benedict was much closer, at least liturgically, to the schismatics than to Küng, who was still an active priest and theologian in good standing. Another with respect for Ratzinger, while disagreeing with him theologically, was Uta Ranke-Heinemann. She had completed a theology doctorate with him at the University of Munich, where they were friends and worked together. She drew an interesting contrast between Ratzinger and his predecessor: "The enormous difference between John Paul II and Ratzinger is intelligence. Ratzinger is much, much more intelligent. . . . John Paul was tedious without end. . . . Ratzinger has much more of what the French call *esprit de finesse* [delicacy, sensitivity]. And John Paul had none."[5]

Catholics in Latin America, Africa, and Asia were far less enthusiastic. Viewing him as a key figure in the condemnation of liberation theology and religious pluralism, Catholics from the South saw him as deeply Eurocentric, lacking any understanding of their reality, which turned out to be an accurate assessment.

LIKE JOHN PAUL, Ratzinger's education and formation are centrally important in understanding him as pope. He grew up under the Nazis in small-town Bavaria. There was no sympathy whatsoever for National Socialism in his family. Drafted unwillingly into the Hitler Youth at age sixteen and then into the German army, after the war ended he entered the Munich-Freising archdiocesan seminary. He was unhappy with the narrow neoscholastic theology taught there, and he was increasingly influenced by Saint Augustine, from whom he imbibed a skepticism about the possibilities of human nature, the brevity of our time in this "vale of tears," and the enormous need we have for grace and the help of God. He was interested the *resourcement* movement, the recovery of knowledge of early church theology and liturgy. The other major influences on him were Jesuit Erich Przywara and secular priest Romano

Guardini, both of whom were attempting to open up theology to contemporary culture. Ratzinger's biblical and historical studies seem to have been relatively superficial. He is essentially a theologian lacking a sense of historical context, his experience was almost totally academic, and he lacked pastoral experience as a priest.

Ordained in 1951, his doctoral thesis was on Augustine, and his *Habilitationsschrift* (postdoctoral lecturing qualification) topic was Saint Bonaventure, successor of Saint Francis as head of the Franciscans and eventually a cardinal. Through Bonaventure he became aware of the Franciscan Spirituals, radicals who believed in absolute poverty and who followed the radical Joachim of Fiore, who looked forward to a "new age" and a "spiritual church" that would replace the corrupt established church. Ratzinger later saw something of this "false messianism" in liberation theology. After a stint teaching in the seminary, he began his university career in 1958 at the University of Bonn. He then went to Münster and in 1966 was appointed professor of dogmatic theology in the Catholic faculty at Tübingen University. His *vocatio* (calling) to the university was sponsored and promoted by Hans Küng.[6]

Prior to the Tübingen appointment, he had played an important role at Vatican II. In the lead-up to the council, an essay of his was published together with two essays by Karl Rahner in a book titled *The Episcopate and the Primacy*.[7] In this essay Ratzinger unequivocally sets out the Vatican I teaching on the primacy of the pope: "Only he who is in communion with the pope lives in true *communio* . . . with the true church." But he balances this view by arguing that the bishops are true successors of the apostles; they are not mere agents of the pope, and "they are as much part and parcel of the divinely appointed structure of the church as he." At Vatican II he served on a subcommittee dealing with the role and function of bishops, and he envisaged the church as a communion of local churches, thus making the Eucharist the center of the bond of unity. He also played a major role in the development of the important council document *Dei verbum*, on divine revelation. He was an important theologian at Vatican II and was associated with the reformist majority.

But after the council, something changed. He was deeply disappointed by the crassness and banality that he felt characterized the vernacular liturgy, by the exodus from religious life and priesthood, and by the radicalism of the student riots of 1967–1968. At Tübingen the theology students described the New Testament as an "exploitative text" and the Crucifixion as a form of sadomasochism. It was all late-adolescent, immature posturing, but Ratzinger saw it as an attack on Catholicism, resigned his chair in 1969, and retreated to the faculty of Catholic theology at the newly founded University of Regensburg.

The clue to Ratzinger is that he is a European intellectual. He is saved from being an "ideologue" by his genuine Bavarian Catholic piety, his profound love of music, and, as Ranke-Heinemann says, his *finesse*. He is a concert-standard pianist, and he grew up close to Salzburg, Mozart's birthplace. "Mozart thoroughly penetrated our souls," he says, "and his music still touches me very deeply, because it is so luminous and yet at the same time so deep. His music is by no means just entertainment; it contains the whole tragedy of human existence."[8] What he lacks is a historico-critical sense. He is first and foremost a dogmatist; that is, theory trumps history. He also uses, perhaps unconsciously, the argumentative method of absolutizing and thus caricaturing his opponent's viewpoint. He creates dichotomies, either-or situations, when both-and resolutions are possible.

In 1977 he was plucked by Paul VI from Regensburg and appointed archbishop of Munich-Freising. He was made a cardinal the same year. Something of a failure as archbishop, he was not well received by the local priests, who found him remote. In 1981 John Paul II appointed him prefect of the CDF, where he remained until his election as pope in 2005. He was a very busy CDF prefect, issuing statements, disciplining theologians and authors, condemning liberation theology, issuing a joint declaration with the Lutheran Church on the doctrine of justification, publishing *The Catechism of the Catholic Church*, and doctrinally reviewing all documents of other Vatican departments. In many cases, a softer approach may have achieved much more. It was hard to be sympathetic when Ratzinger and his officials complained they were "overworked."

Then, in 2001, with the sexual abuse crisis exploding and impatient with slow-moving local bishops, the CDF decreed that all credible cases of sexual abuse of minors were to be reported to the congregation for review. Bishops were warned that everything was subject to "pontifical secrecy"; this was taken as an instruction that these accusations must be kept completely secret, and bishops were not to report cases to the local police. It was not until 2010 that this was changed, and accusations were to be reported to the police. The real scandal is the hopelessly inept way the abuse crisis was dealt with and the way the reputation of the church and priesthood was put before that of the pastoral care of victims and their families. Irish psychologist Marie Keenan argues—correctly in my view—that abusive priests are not isolated monsters or deviants but are products of a human and psychological formation that fixates them at an adolescent level of sexual development. They also suffer from an inbred clericalism and a seriously inadequate moral theology, and until these issues are addressed the church will not solve the problem, no matter how many protocols are put in place.[9]

At least the centralizing of abuse cases in the CDF made Ratzinger aware of the extent of the problem. This became obvious when, replacing the dying pope, Ratzinger led the traditional Holy Week Stations of the Cross in Rome's Colosseum on Good Friday 2005. At the ninth station, when Jesus falls the third time, the CDF cardinal gave vent to his frustration. First, he seemingly denounced dissenting theologians: "What little faith is present behind so many theories, so many empty words." He then went on to utter a sentence reported across the world: "How much filth there is in the Church, and even among those who, in the priesthood, ought to belong entirely to [Christ]!" He continued: "Lord, your Church often seems like a boat about to sink, a boat taking in water on every side." But he ended on a note of hope: "You [Lord] will rise again. You stood up, you arose and you can also raise us up."[10] Perhaps he had the egregious Maciel in mind?

As Parkinson's disease took hold of John Paul II after 2000, Ratzinger's influence increased. The church became increasingly leaderless, and there was deep concern as to what would happen if the pope slipped into complete senility or unconsciousness or was kept alive artificially. Who would have the authority to switch off life support? There was nothing in canon law to cover such contingencies. The curia and the government of the church ground to a halt as Catholics awaited the death of John Paul II.

————————

RATZINGER CAME TO the papacy in 2005 with considerable knowledge of the Vatican. Many expected that he would use it to begin a reform by getting rid of dead wood and making the curia more responsive to local bishops, less bureaucratic, and, preferably, smaller. But nothing happened; under Benedict the power plays, infighting, and lack of financial accountability continued unabated, and even increased. A loyal man, in September 2006 Benedict XVI brought in the incompetent Tarcisio Bertone, his former assistant at the CDF, to be his secretary of state. This was a disastrous move, for Bertone intensified problems rather than solving them. He had no diplomatic experience whatsoever, and he brought in his own people, who marginalized the professionals in the secretariat. He also attempted to sideline the Italian bishops in their dealings with the Center-Left Italian government of Romano Prodi and then, from 2008, the right-wing government of Silvio Berlusconi, who professed "Catholic values" on issues like abortion but whose personal life was more scandalous than any Renaissance pope or prince. While Benedict defended him, Bertone continued to stir up personal animosities and added to his list of enemies. The pope also brought in Monsignor Georg Gänswein, who since 1996 had also worked with him in the CDF and from 2003 had been his live-in private secretary. Gänswein replaced Dziwisz as the one who controlled access to the pope.

From the start, it was obvious that Benedict was concerned about the post–Vatican II church. In an address to the Roman Curia in December 2005, he claimed that the reception and implementation of the council had been "somewhat difficult." He then went on to quote Saint Basil, commenting on the aftermath of the Council of Nicaea in 325: "The raucous shouting of those who through disagreement rise up against one another, the incomprehensible chatter, the confused din of uninterrupted clamouring, has now filled almost the whole of the Church, falsifying through excess or failure the right doctrine of the faith." This is an inept and unjust comparison and doesn't represent the experience of the postconciliar period, except perhaps that of a small minority who could not deal with change. He claimed that everything depended on the proper interpretation of the council, "on its proper hermeneutics, the correct key to its interpretation and application." He claimed that there were two conflicting understandings: "There is an interpretation that I would call 'a hermeneutic of discontinuity and rupture'; it has frequently availed itself of the sympathies of the mass media, and also one trend of modern theology. On the other hand, there is the 'hermeneutic of reform,' of renewal in the continuity of the one subject-Church which the Lord has given to us." Clearly, Benedict had opted for the "renewal in continuity" image of Vatican II. Actually, the vast majority of Catholics agreed with him that the council had maintained and developed the ongoing Catholic tradition. But they also knew that Vatican II introduced new ideas (for example, religious liberty and ecumenism) and revived old ones (such as the collegiality of bishops). But Benedict somehow needed to create a myth of discontinuity that he defined as going "beyond the texts [of the council] and making room for the newness in which the Council's deepest intention would be expressed, even if it were still vague. In a word: it would be necessary not to follow the texts of the Council, but its spirit. In this way, obviously, a vast margin was left open for the question on how this spirit should subsequently be defined and room was consequently made for every whim."[11]

The real problem here is the setting up of a false dichotomy, something Benedict XVI often does. It is easy to demolish a caricature, and this is exactly what his description of the "rupture" school is—a caricature. No sensible pastoral-progressive theologian or thinking Catholic says the council was a complete break with the past and a completely "new beginning," nor do they think that you can make things up as you go along by merely appealing to "the spirit of the Council." Of course, it is a case of both-and, of continuity and change. In fact, as historian Massimo Faggioli correctly points out, the only people who have created a "rupture" in the church since Vatican II are the ultratraditionalist followers of schismatic archbishop Marcel Lefebvre, with whom Benedict has fallen all over himself in trying to make peace.[12]

This "continuity-rupture" dichotomy masks a deeper division that runs right through postconciliar theology and whose roots were found long before Vatican II. This is the rift or fault line between a kind of neo-Augustinianism and neo-Thomism.[13] What it comes down to is a different anthropology and cosmology, a different understanding of our place in the world. Like Pope Benedict, most theologians of the continuity school are Augustinian in orientation; they tend to be pessimistic about contemporary culture and are critical of *Gaudium et spes*, the council document on the church in the modern world. They are also doubtful about human goodness and tend to emphasize weakness and inclination to sin. They seriously question optimistic views about the world as a source of goodness and rectitude. Their theology tends to be "from above." While never denying our spiritual aspirations, theology for them begins with God's greatness and God's revelation of self in the vulnerability of Jesus's humanity. Their view of the church tends to emphasize the communion of *saints* rather than the church of *sinners*. For them, the continuity of church history is what is important, especially the period from the sixteenth-century Council of Trent until now. The church is defined narrowly as the *communio* of committed believers. Balthasar, Henri de Lubac, Jacques Maritain, and others espoused this form of neo-Augustinianism, but it's most important disciple is Joseph Ratzinger, because he became prefect of the CDF and then pope and was able to use these bully pulpits to promote this theology.

In contrast, the so-called rupture group is neo-Thomistic; that is, its adherents follow the basic anthropology of Saint Thomas Aquinas and its modern articulation in the theology of Karl Rahner and in the evolutionary philosophy of Pierre Teilhard de Chardin. It represents the view of the large majority of contemporary post–Vatican II Western-educated Catholics. It is a theology "from below." It begins with human life and experience, with the profound longing that people discover within themselves for spiritual transcendence. It sees the church as open to the world and active in it. This doesn't mean that Catholicism passively embraces an uncritical approach; the church has a prophetic vocation to offer an outspoken critique of contemporary culture. But it remains a broad vision, all-embracing and "catholic" in the very best sense of the word. It envisages the church as a community of imperfect, sinful, but struggling believers, making up a community that constantly needs to be reformed (*ecclesia semper reformanda*).

Benedict's theological and historical background is important because he came to the papacy with articulated views on the church, and these views influenced his ecclesial governance. Part of his theology was the concept of a "remnant" church. By this he meant that the days of church and state in league are long over and that the church will increasingly be a minority of committed believers in a larger secular society. In this he left his nineteenth- and twentieth-century papal predecessors far behind. He believed that "camp-follower" Catholics would drop away, leaving only those who are prepared to engage in a struggle against social and personal evil and proclaim the presence of God. He says that the Kingdom of God will be the "little flock" of which Jesus spoke (Luke 12.32); it will resemble "a mustard seed which a man took and planted in his field" (Matt. 13:31) or the leaven or yeast in the dough (Matt. 13:33). It has been claimed that he talked about "a smaller, but purer church," but seemingly he never used this phrase. But he certainly seemed to lean in this more sectarian direction. Interestingly, Karl Rahner suggests something similar when he says that the church of the future will be a "little flock," but in contrast to Ratzinger he says this church will be "declericalised," "concerned with serving," be "open" and "non-moralizing," and be committed to "real spirituality."[14] Here both Rahner and Ratzinger reflect their Eurocentrism and the decline of the church in Europe from the late 1960s. This decline has now spread to the whole of the developed West. It may well be that Ratzinger is right and that the future lies with creative minorities, but certainly not with sectarian, hyperorthodox in-groups focused on intramural issues like the

Latin Mass. The world church, of course, especially in the global South, is not a "little flock." It is growing rapidly.

FRENCH ARCHBISHOP MARCEL Lefebvre, former archbishop of Dakar, Senegal, was one of the most extreme members of the minority at Vatican II. At heart he was a nineteenth-century French reactionary who had not accepted the Revolution, democracy, or the separation of throne and altar and had supported the pro-Nazi French Vichy regime. In his view, Vatican II was modernism rejigged. In 1970 he founded the Society of Saint Pius X (SSPX) in Écône, in French-speaking Switzerland, to train priests to celebrate the so-called Tridentine Mass, in opposition to the new vernacular Mass introduced by Vatican II. But there was more involved than liturgical eccentricities. Essentially, the SSPX is a right-wing integralist movement that harks back to the reactionary, anti-Semitic Catholicism of the Dreyfus period. This was obvious to the French bishops, to Paul VI, and to his secretary of state, Cardinal Villot. Lefebvre was soon in conflict with all of them.

In 1975 the Vatican ordered the SSPX suppressed. Ignoring the instruction, Lefebvre went ahead with priestly ordinations that year and was suspended from ministry. The conflict dragged on unresolved until 1987, when Lefebvre decided that since he was eighty-one, he needed some "orthodox" bishops—that is, bishops who agreed with him—to continue the SSPX. At first Rome vacillated, and Ratzinger at the CDF was inclined to go along with him. This was seen as weakness by the arrogant Frenchman, and on June 30, 1982, he ordained four members of the SSPX as bishops. The next day Rome announced that he and his four bishops were excommunicated *latae sententiae* (that is, automatically).

Since then there have been extraordinary efforts on the part of the Vatican to try to placate the SSPX. Where liberation theology was summarily dealt with and theologians who questioned the John Paul "line" were subjected to an "investigation" by the CDF, John Paul and Benedict went to extraordinary lengths to ameliorate the SSPX. Rome set up the Ecclesia Dei Commission to keep talking to them and run by cardinals sympathetic to the SSPX position. As late as May 2016 even Pope Francis was making overtures that were rejected with the arrogance typical of the hyperorthodox. For three decades, right-wingers in the Roman Curia have been falling all over themselves to offer concessions to SSPX. The letter *Quattuor abhinc annos* of the Congregation for Divine Worship (CDW) of October 3, 1984, told Catholics, "Respect must everywhere be shown for the feelings of all those who are attached to the Latin liturgical tradition, by a wide and generous application of the directives already issued," so that they could use the Latin liturgy according to the Tridentine rite.[15] Later, John Paul II spoke of his desire to keep the SSPX group onside by guaranteeing "respect for their rightful aspirations." No such respect for "rightful aspirations" was ever shown to anyone at the more pastoral-progressive end of the spectrum. The SSPX is not a large organization. In December 2016, it claimed to have 613 priests, 215 seminarians, and 195 sisters and to be present in thirty-seven countries.[16]

On January 21, 2009, Pope Benedict suddenly lifted the excommunication of the four bishops ordained by Lefebvre in 1988. It turned out that one of them, Richard Williamson, was virulently anti-Semitic and even denied that the Holocaust had happened, as well as having eccentric and retrograde views on the role of women. All of this information was available to anyone through a simple Google search. The reaction to the lifting of the excommunication was immediate from both Catholics and Jews. What Benedict called a "heated discussion" began, with some "openly accusing the Pope of wanting to turn back the clock to before the Council: as a result, an avalanche of protests was unleashed, whose bitterness laid bare wounds deeper than those of the present moment." These words from Benedict's letter of March 10, 2009, on the "Williamson affair" reveal that he simply didn't understand that he had made a bad mistake and needed to back down and apologize. He had been appallingly advised by the ineffectual Cardinal Darío Castrillón Hoyos, head of the Ecclesia Dei Commission, who should have known better.

POPE BENEDICT'S FIRST foray into international affairs was acciden-
tal. On his first visit back to Bavaria in 2006, he gave a lecture at
the University of Regensburg titled "*Faith, Reason and the University: Memories and Reflections.*" At first sight, this innocent topic had
nothing to do with international affairs, but the lecture was widely
criticized and caused riots in Muslim countries, including the killing of an innocent nun. In the lecture, the scholar-pope was tackling an important theological issue: the interplay of faith and reason.
Catholic theologians have been discussing this for centuries, and
maintaining balance between the two is a key element in preventing
Catholicism from degenerating into sectarian irrationality. To para-
phrase Saint Anselm of Canterbury: faith must always seek a basis in
reason and human experience. What the pope wanted to show was
that without that basis in reason, faith can degenerate into violence
and that "not to act in accordance with reason is contrary to God's
nature."[17] It is within this context that the pope in typical German
academic fashion refers to the work of Professor Theodore Khoury,
who had edited the "Dialogue Held with a Certain Persian" by Byzantine emperor Manuel II Paleologus (1391–1425). Manuel II was
writing at the tag end of the Byzantine Empire, which had lost almost all of Asia Minor to the Ottoman Turks and was reduced to
a small area around Constantinople. In the dialogue the emperor,
given the historical situation, is understandably highly critical of Islam and speaks to his Persian interlocutor with what Ratzinger calls
"a startling brusqueness . . . which we find unacceptable." Manuel
challenges the Persian to show him "what Mohammed brought that
was new." In Mohammed's teaching, he said, "you will find things
only evil and inhuman, such as his command to spread by the sword
the faith he preached. . . . God is not pleased by blood—and not
acting reasonably is contrary to God's nature."[18] This, Benedict concludes, is an argument against violent conversion. It was a mere passing reference in a much longer lecture and was certainly not central
to his argument.

Violent reactions erupted in the Islamic world from Pakistan
to Somalia and in the Islamic press and media.[19] This papal *obiter
dictum* was seen by Muslim mobs as part of a concerted Western

conspiracy against Islam, with Benedict the leader of the Christian crusaders. To most fair-minded people, this response to a passing reference in an academic lecture seemed completely over the top. Oxford University Muslim scholar Tariq Ramadan commented that this "uncontrollable outpouring of emotion ended up providing a living proof that Muslims cannot engage in reasonable debate and that verbal aggression and violence are more the rule than the exception."[20] Pope Benedict quickly apologized, but from the Vatican point of view, the real fault here lay with Bertone. This was a diplomatic *faux pas*, and a competent secretary of state would have checked the lecture and foreseen the fallout. Several commentators have subsequently said that in the long term, the pope was probably right and that Christians generally need to take a more up-front and truthful approach to dialogue with Islam.

Linked to this foray into the faith-and-reason debate is Benedict XVI's emphasis on what he calls "the dictatorship of relativism." He referred to relativism in his sermon at the Mass before the conclave that elected him:

How many winds of doctrine have we known in recent decades, how many ideological currents, how many ways of thinking? . . . Today, having a clear faith based on the Creed of the Church is often labelled as fundamentalism. Whereas relativism, that is, letting oneself be "tossed here and there, carried about by every wind of doctrine," seems the only attitude that can cope with modern times. We are building a dictatorship of relativism that does not recognize anything as definitive and whose ultimate goal consists solely of one's own ego and desires.

The only absolute these days, he says, is that there is no absolute.

By relativism he really means a kind of postmodernism that refers to the overall subjectivist direction of culture, art, literature, and criticism in the Western world. In philosophy it refers to the tendency to relativize everything and to deny the possibility of generally accepted norms of truth, beauty, goodness, or taste, what postmodernism calls "metanarratives." There are no objective standards by which reality can be measured; everything is relative to the individual, and the judgment of the ill-informed and ignorant is as important as that of the professionally informed. In this kind of context, moral and theological truth is lost in a morass of subjectivity. The tag end of the relativism that Benedict speaks about is Donald Trump's so-called post-truth, the 2016 *Oxford Dictionary*'s word of the year. It refers to circumstances, particularly in the public sphere, where reality and objective facts are less important than what you "feel" to be right. The norm of judgment is emotion, and personal belief dominates rather than reality. As Benedict said in his sermon at Mass at Glasgow, Scotland, in September 2010: "The dictatorship of relativism threatens to obscure the unchanging truth about man's nature, his destiny and his ultimate good. . . . Society today needs clear voices which propose our right to live, not in a jungle of self-destructive and arbitrary freedoms, but in a society which works for the true welfare of its citizens and offers them guidance and protection in the face of their weakness and fragility." Here Benedict has put his finger on one of the real problems we face, but we need to be careful. We should not replace relativism with absolutism, particularly in moral issues. The truth is somewhere close to the center.

As FAR AS the broader English-speaking world is concerned, the great disaster of the Benedict papacy is the so-called reform of the reform, especially in the liturgy. In some ways, the phrase *reform of the reform* has become an accurate and general descriptor for this papacy. It refers to the reining in of the reforms of Vatican II. It was coined by Sri Lankan archbishop (now cardinal of Colombo) Malcolm Ranjith, who was previously secretary of the CDW. He argues that what happened after Vatican II often veered away from the intentions of the council. Speaking specifically about the liturgy, Ranjith said that practices that Vatican II's Constitution on the Liturgy never envisaged had become commonplace in the postconciliar period. Examples he cites are Mass facing the people, Communion in the hand, concelebration, and the abandonment of Latin chant and polyphony. Ranjith argued that these "reforms" needed "re-forming," and with the election of Benedict the liturgical tradition-alists knew they had a supporter.

But Ranjith's so-called reform reaches back much further, both to a tiny reactionary rump of priests and laypeople who simply refused to accept Vatican II's liturgical changes and to the activities of the CDW. First, the reactionaries: For this minority, the renewal of worship and the introduction of vernacular languages rather than Latin became the clearest signs of the abandonment of the church's liturgical tradition (which in fact reached back only as far as the sixteenth-century Council of Trent) and what they interpreted as Vatican II's compromise with the modern world. For them, the council abandoned the sacred and mysterious elements of worship and lost the "vertical" aspect of the liturgy. They perceived the English translation as banal, untrue to the original, and insufficiently "sacred." They were constantly critical of what they saw as liturgical excesses (such as folk Masses and liturgical dancing), which were often really just attempts to involve children and young people in the liturgy and adapt worship to their intellectual development. The traditionalists' model was the Tridentine Mass, more accurately the "Mass of Pius V," because it comes from the missal this pope issued in 1570 after the closure of Trent. These people turned the liturgy into a battleground, a symbol of everything that horrified them about contemporary Catholicism. They knew that if they could persuade the Vatican to roll back the liturgical reforms, they would have won a symbolic victory over the other "excesses" of Vatican II. They have succeeded in the English-speaking world.

Second, the CDW: After the liturgy constitution was passed at the end of the second session of the council in 1963, the English-speaking bishops immediately set up a commission to carry out the work of translation, the International Commission on English in the Liturgy. Based in Washington, DC, ICEL's line of responsibility was explicitly to the English-speaking bishops' conferences, not to Rome and the CDW. Rome simply approved of their work. The *General Instruction on the Roman Missal* (1969), issued by the Post-Conciliar Commission on the Liturgy, was set up by the bishops at Vatican II to do the practical work of renewing the liturgy after the council emphasized that the translator's task was to find a "faithful but not literal" equivalent of the Latin and that "the unit of meaning [was] not the individual word, but the whole passage." This is called the "principle of equivalence."

ICEL was a genuine expression of the kind of collegiality mandated by the council, because it involved the English-speaking bishops in developing the translation that was to be used in English-speaking countries. This was not just about vernacular liturgy but also about collegiality. This was where the CDW entered the fray. From about 1970 onward, the CDW came under the control of liturgical traditionalists. The crunch came when Chilean cardinal Jorge Medina Estévez was appointed cardinal prefect in 1996 by John Paul II. Medina immediately set about systematically dismantling the whole liturgical renewal. His arrival in the mid-1990s coincided with ICEL submitting the revised and improved English translation for a *recognitio*, an approval for use throughout the English-speaking world. Also at this time, the centralizing process that had come with John Paul II was well under way, and it was intolerable to the Spanish-speaking Medina that English-speaking bishops' conferences were making decisions about the English used in the liturgy. Bishops were there to do what Rome decreed.

Medina's strategy was clear: if he could bring the English-speaking bishops to heel, the second-largest linguistic group in the Catholic world after the Spanish, he would have no trouble bringing other language groups under Roman control. So, in March 2001, the CWD issued *Liturgiam authenticam* (*LA*). This is an instruction on the principles of liturgical translation, which was meant to replace *The General Instruction on the Roman Missal*. Medina claimed that the pope had asked the CDW to prepare *Liturgiam authenticam*, but these were the declining years of John Paul and the curia was doing pretty much what it wanted. The document reflects Medina and the liturgical reactionaries' views rather than those of mainstream liturgical scholars and mainstream English-speaking Catholics who were perfectly happy with the translation. Medina was supported by Ratzinger, who had made it clear for years before he became pope that he thought that vernacular Masses were to blame for the drop in church attendance and vocations to the priesthood, while offering no empirical evidence to support this view.

Liturgiam authenticam shifts the emphasis from the congregation making prayerful sense of the English to a focus on a literal rendering of the Latin. It says that translation "is not so much a work of creative inventiveness as one of fidelity and exactness in rendering the Latin texts into a vernacular language." No care or sensitivity is shown for the praying people or their needs. It's as though the Latin text had a priority call on God's attention, and unless the English followed the Latin text literally, the prayer of the community went nowhere. *LA* is especially critical of any attempt to integrate gender-inclusive language into the translation. It also maintains that "translations must be freed from exaggerated dependence on modern modes of expression and in general from psychologizing language." No clarification is offered as to what "psychologizing language" might mean in this context. All this assumes that there is a thing called "timeless English," a moment when the language was somehow perfectly adapted to the sacred. In the process of trying to discover this wording, the new translation falls into the trap of using a kind of pseudo-mid-Victorian English, the kind that a third-rate nineteenth-century romantic novelist might have used on a particularly bad day. The language that results is not so much "sacred" as pompous and affected. This translation is the product of a new ICEL stacked with traditionalist translators. Supervising the whole process was a committee of English-speaking bishops chaired by Australian cardinal George Pell. The committee was misnamed *Vox Clara* (Clear Voice); the translation produced by ICEL under *Vox Clara*'s supervision was anything but clear. The new text, translated according to *Liturgiam authenticam*'s instructions, was approved by reluctant and craven English-speaking bishops' conferences and sent to Rome for a *recognitio* in 2008.

This "new" English text was imposed on Mass-goers in December 2011. But what was imposed was *not* the text the English-speaking bishops had approved in 2008. Some ten thousand or more changes had been made by unknown persons (the suspicion is that it was done by a small group from the *Vox Clara* committee), even after Pope Benedict had given his approval to the text. This Rome-tampered text was leaked in October 2010 and analyzed by liturgical experts. A liturgist who worked on the 2008 translation, Anthony Ruff, says that "the scope of the debacle is simply mind-boggling." Nevertheless, this defective and in places dog's breakfast of a translation has been imposed on weary, long-suffering English-speaking priests and faithful in order to satisfy a tiny ultratraditionalist rump, an arrogant Chilean cardinal with no knowledge whatsoever of English, and a text according to the principles laid down in *Liturgiam authenticam*, a document that has been described by Peter Jeffery, a very conservative liturgical historian, as "the most ignorant statement on liturgy ever issued by a modern Vatican congregation," adding that "it should be summarily withdrawn."[21] What is interesting is that the German-speaking bishops simply rejected out of hand the CDW's attempts to impose a similar translation regime on them; the English-speaking bishops gave in far too easily.

While local Catholic communities had this inadequate translation imposed on them by the CDW, Pope Ratzinger liberalized the celebration of the Tridentine Mass. In the apostolic letter *Summorum pontificium* (2007), he speaks about bringing "interior reconciliation in the heart of the Church" by making it possible for those attached to the Tridentine Mass to remain within the church. Any priest can now celebrate this form of the Mass, and priests have an obligation to celebrate this form if a group of laity requests it. No such consideration was given to the mainstream English-speaking faithful.

Even as pope, Benedict never stopped being a scholar. He was happiest when completing his three-volume book, *Jesus of Nazareth*, which he worked on and published as pope. The book received mixed reviews, especially from biblical scholars. Benedict explicitly claimed that he wrote in the context of the "historico-critical method," but it is precisely this that reviewers have questioned, arguing that the book takes a premodern, somewhat sermonizing approach to the life of Jesus. It is sensitive to Vatican II's exoneration of the Jewish people from deicide (killing God); it is Pontius Pilate who is finally blamed. The book is devotional, a kind of extended sermon that might strengthen the faith of some, while not sustaining a more intelligent readership. As a result, he wrote only three encyclicals, claiming that "after the great wealth of encyclicals bequeathed to us by John Paul II," he wanted to establish "a slower rhythm."[22]

BENEDICT IS A shy man, and part of him seemed really uncomfortable as pope. Still, he attended World Youth Days in Cologne (2005), Sydney (2008), and Madrid (2011), and he was warm with the young people and engaged with them. He also met with victims of sexual abuse in several countries, including the United States and Australia. He was committed to environmental issues and spoke passionately about care for the earth: "Preservation of the environment, promotion of sustainable development and particular attention to climate change are matters of grave concern for the entire human family," he told Orthodox patriarch Bartholomew I in a 2007 letter. Unexpectedly, he turned out to be gentler and less condemnatory in his speeches and writing than he had been as prefect of the CDF. He accented the positive aspects of faith rather than issuing a catalog of negatives and castigations.

But by early 2012, his papacy started unraveling. He wasn't interested in administration, and he "turned out to have virtually zero interest in actually running the Roman Curia."[23] It was in very bad shape when John Paul died, and between 2005 and 2012 it became increasingly dysfunctional. Benedict tended to surround himself with people he had known for a long time and trusted. That's why he appointed Bertone as secretary of state and Gänswein as his personal secretary. But the influence of both men was resented by old-guard curial bureaucrats, and they became the primary targets of growing opposition. Bertone was incompetent, but like many incompetents, he was also power hungry. Gänswein, who controlled access to the pope, was remarkably handsome, and he was popularly known as "Gorgeous George," inspiring *fashionista* Donatella Versace to design a more "clerical look" for men with "more brain and less muscle." To protect Benedict, Gänswein limited access to him. Cardinals and members of the curia were miffed, not only by the lack of access but also because of the overt sexual overtones surrounding Gänswein. Family was always important to Ratzinger, and in a way Gänswein had become the son he never had. By 2012 Benedict was eighty-five yet still in reasonable health, so the transitional pope was looking rather permanent. With the Vatican effectively leaderless, the curia did what it always did in such circumstances: it disintegrated into competing power centers engaged in ferocious infighting and character assassination.

The signs of trouble were clear. First there was the Viganò case. After a career in the papal diplomatic service, Archbishop Carlo Maria Viganò was appointed secretary-general of the Vatican City government in July 2009. The pope instructed him to clean up the Vatican government's financial administration, a thankless task. Viganò discovered a network of waste and corruption and through strong-arm tactics turned a deficit of €7.8 million into a surplus of €34 million. But this earned him the enmity of the "old-boys" network that had consistently awarded contracts to the same companies, no doubt run by family members or friends. Suddenly, in August 2011 he was moved out of his job by Bertone and appointed papal nuncio to the United States. Then in January 2012, a television program titled *Gli intoccabili* (The untouchables) was aired on the Italian La7 channel. It published several letters from Viganò to Benedict and Bertone in which he talked of financial corruption and a campaign of defamation against him and unsuccessfully begged the pope not to send him to the United States.

But Viganò was just the beginning. For months, the Vatican leaked like a sieve, much of the material focusing on the Vatican Bank and money laundering. In May 2012, the chairman of the Vatican Bank, Ettore Gotti Tedeschi, a traditionalist Catholic with links to Opus Dei, was dismissed without explanation by his board. He had tried to clean up the bank, make it accountable, and close down suspicious accounts, but he was accused of treating the Vatican job as part-time, spending most of his time in Milan, running the Spanish Santander Bank. He claimed that he had sought to conform Vatican operations to European Union standards, but that he had ended up "defamed and exposed to the defamation of churchmen without so much as a trial."[24] He had one particular "churchman" in mind—Bertone. In July 2012 the Council of Europe's MONEYVAL group, which investigated money laundering and financing of terrorism and had been brought in by Benedict XVI in 2011, gave the Holy See a cautious vote of approval, saying that they had "come a long way in a very short period of time and many of the building blocks of an . . . [effective] regime are now formally in place." However, they still had to address "further important issues" before "a fully effective regime has been instituted in practice."[25]

But Bertone himself was now the target of destabilization, possibly stirred up by his predecessor Cardinal Angelo Sodano and his allies, who saw Bertone as diplomatically untrained and power hungry. While control of Vatican finances and individuals and groups protecting their turf were important issues in the destabilization process, other people were already looking to the future, thinking about Benedict's successor. Since late 2010 the pope claimed he was not "depressed" but admitted that "things weren't going well for me."[26] As a result, cardinal insiders were jostling for pole position, with the expectation that a conclave would soon be in the cards.

The leaking intensified. The journalist leaking material was Gianluigi Nuzzi, and he claimed that his source was an insider codenamed "Maria." "Maria" revealed all sorts of interesting details: who was giving money to the pope (for example, television hosts and bank chairmen) and who was writing to Gänswein and what they wanted—mainly access to the pope. After a massive amount of material had been leaked, "Maria" turned out to be Benedict's butler Paolo Gabriele, who was confronted by Gänswein on May 23, 2012, and then arrested by Vatican gendarmes. Gabriele claimed at his trial that he had leaked the material to help the pope eliminate the corruption in the curia. He claimed that Benedict was not sufficiently informed of what was happening. "I felt like a secret agent for the Holy Spirit," he said. But it seems inconceivable that he acted alone. Much of the material he had would have been incomprehensible to him; clearly, he was a patsy for senior clerics in the curia who were involved but have never been named or charged. Sentenced to eighteen months' imprisonment—he served his time under house arrest in his Vatican apartment—Gabriele was pardoned by Benedict seven months later.

While all this scandal was swirling around Benedict, the rest of the church was struggling to deal with an issue of far greater significance for Catholicism than the squabbles of the Vatican, the sexual abuse crisis. Here was an issue that affected the whole church and the pope, and the Vatican had nothing to offer. This was the real scandal.

The Gabriele trial had hardly begun before another crisis broke, that of the "gay lobby" in the Vatican. To seasoned observers and locals, there was nothing surprising in this news. In this secret netherworld, individuals struggled with celibacy and sexuality, and acting out was tolerated as long as they kept the golden rule: never admit you're gay, especially in public. The Italian daily *La Repubblica* on February 21, 2013, said that this "gay lobby" was a secret cabal of power-broker cardinals, bishops, and monsignors. Italians love conspiracy theories, and there was a whiff of this around the gay lobby. But this was not a "lobby" in the Anglo-American sense. They weren't trying to get the church to change its teaching on gay marriage or even to stop referring to gay people as suffering from an "objective disorder." The Vatican gay "lobby" was just a group of men working for the Vatican who were homosexual, some active, some not. The really problematic aspect is the secrecy, the lack of personal accountability for one's moral behavior, the pretense, and sweeping the issue under the rug.

And then, out of the blue, the English newspaper the *Observer* reported on February 23, 2013, that the archbishop of Saint Andrews and Edinburgh, Cardinal Keith O'Brien, had been accused by three serving priests and one ex-priest of "inappropriate sexual behaviour," with homosexual affairs going back to the 1980s. By early March O'Brien admitted the accusations. It simply added fuel to the fire of an active gay lobby, not just in the Vatican but in the church as well. While the gay lobby was something of a media sensation, informed observers of the Vatican knew that a gay sub-culture had existed for centuries. They also knew that was *not* the main reason Benedict resigned. It had much more to do with the man himself.

Benedict's resignation, however, still came as a complete shock. On the morning of February 11, 2013, the pope announced that he would resign the papacy effective February 28. One of the few popes ever to resign and the first certain resignation since Celestine V in 1294, Benedict's action is one of the most important acts of any pope for centuries, because in this way he relativized the papacy and very much drained it of its "mystery." It is ironic that the man who denounced relativism actually relativized papal authority and set a precedent that frees subsequent popes from the obligation to sit it out no matter how incapacitated or sick they are.

The key to understanding Benedict's resignation is not the scandals in the Vatican but the prolonged and public dying process of John Paul II. Ratzinger was the closest public figure to John Paul when his illness became apparent to everyone during the last five years of his life. Benedict feared that something similar might happen to him. Catholicism has no process to deal with senile or incapacitated popes, and modern medicine can keep people alive artificially, whereas in the past medicine was more likely to kill rather than cure. Benedict felt that his strength was beginning to wane, and, as we saw, Cardinal Carlo Maria Martini, former arch-bishop of Milan, in a interview two weeks before he died, said that he thought the church was already two hundred years out of date. Benedict must have heard this and might have interpreted it as being directed toward him. The two men had considerable respect for each other, and Martini's words might have persuaded the pope that it was time to go.

BENEDICT IS THE first pope to write a commentary on his own papacy. He was interviewed by German journalist Peter Seewald and the result published in *Last Testament: In His Own Words* (2016). It is a curious book, matter-of-fact in approach, detached, sometimes defensive. When asked about "the Paolo Gabriele affair," he says, "I was not to blame. . . . I am not aware of any failures on my part."[27] What is clear from the book is that he lives at a level of abstraction from everyday reality, and it is because of this that his papacy has to be judged as a mere interlude in church history. His lack of interest in governance meant that power questions scarcely arose during his papacy.

Nevertheless, the Ratzinger papacy is highly significant for two reasons: First, it marked the end of the Eurocentric era. He is the last pope whose entire reality was defined by Europe. Second, he resigned. Now that is really significant.

THE "FIELD HOSPITAL"

THE CONCLAVE THAT began on March 12, 2013, had few precedents in church history; the previous pope was still alive. Also, given
that Benedict XVI had announced his resignation on February 11
(effective February 28) and there was no funeral to organize, there
were seventeen days of informal *prattiche* (discussion among the
cardinals about possible *papabili*), as well as the more formal General Congregations (meetings), where cardinals sized up one another. One thing was clear: many cardinals and others in the church
were furious with Tarcisio Bertone and the Vatican's endless scandals and incompetence. The feeling was that an outsider with administrative experience needed to be brought in to clean up the
mess. If Benedict XVI had been a failure in terms of governance,
many also disagreed with his emphasis on relativism, criticism of
secularism, and notion of a remnant church. The Roman Curia, of
course, had its defenders, and they wanted an "insider" who, in the
usual fashion, would carry out some window dressing outfitted as
"reform." But most cardinals, as well as informed Catholics generally, wanted the Vatican brought to heel, with authority devolved
collegially to bishops and local churches.

Nevertheless, just like in 2005, the *Vaticanisti* got it wrong
again. The problem is that we (I was again present in Rome for
the election) uncritically followed the Italian journalists, who, in
turn, were too close to manipulative Italian cardinals who conned
the journalists into touting their line on the election. Two cardinals
who emerged representing the insider, business-as-usual approach
were Angelo Scola of Milan and French Canadian Marc Ouellet,

prefect of the Congregation for Bishops. These were clearly the favored nominees of Pope-Emeritus Benedict, as he decided to call himself; many felt he should have been titled "bishop of Rome emeritus." Other candidates mentioned were Odilo Scherer, a Brazilian conservative and former curial official; Peter Turkson from Ghana; Christoph Schörnborn (Vienna); the fifty-five-year-old Luis Tagle (Manila); and Americans Sean O'Malley (Boston) and Timothy Dolan (New York). It was a seemingly wide-open field of candidates and would therefore probably be a long conclave. One person scarcely mentioned in the *prattiche* was Jorge Mario Bergoglio. Twelve days before the conclave, Irish bookmaker Paddy Power had Scola at three to one, Ouellet at six to one, and Bergoglio at twenty-five to one.

One hundred and fifteen cardinals entered the conclave on Tuesday, March 12, 2013. Two who were eligible didn't attend: Julius Darmaatmadja of Jakarta was very sick, and Keith O'Brien of St. Andrews–Edinburgh was caught up in his gay scandal and sensibly ruled himself out.

What started to emerge in the last days before the conclave was a feeling that the time had come to jettison the European dominance of the papacy that Pope Benedict represented. The Italians were divided—as they usually were—and the Americans, with eleven votes, were influential and held daily press briefings. Bertone, as Camerlengo, told them to stop the briefings, which they did, but Italian cardinals, including Bertone himself, continued to leak "off the record" to Italian journalists. Scola failed to impress his colleagues in the General Congregations with his rather convoluted way of speaking, probably from reading too much Balthasar. One who impressed was Bergoglio. His talk on March 7 moved beyond intramural issues and challenged the church to get out of the sacristy and into the world. Evangelization, he said, "presupposes a desire in the church to come out of herself . . . and to go to the peripheries, not only geographically, but also the existential peripheries: the mystery of sin, of pain, of injustice, of ignorance and indifference to religion." A self-engrossed church is "sick," he said, because it is caught up in "a kind of theological narcissism . . . [that] keeps Jesus Christ within herself and does not let him out." The self-referential church "gives way to that very serious evil, spiritual worldliness." There are, he said, "two images of the Church: the church that evangelizes and comes out of herself . . . and the worldly Church, living within her-self, of herself, for herself."[1] It's as simple as that.

Many cardinals were impressed. They began to look again at Bergoglio's record: runner-up to Benedict in 2005, a man who lived poorly, who used public transport, who visited the slums, and who was no fan of the curia. He spoke good Italian (his father was from Piedmont), believed in collegiality, was a critic of careerism and bureaucracy, was a non-European who supported Gospel val-ues, and was a man of genuine spirituality. Although Bergoglio was seventy-six, Benedict XVI had set an example of resignation, so age and health faded as major issues. Bergoglio went into the conclave with growing support.

What actually happened is speculation. The first scrutiny was held in the late afternoon on Tuesday. The favorite, Scola, had about 35 votes, less than expected because Italian knives were out to stop him. Bergoglio had about 20, Ouellet 15 or so, and Scherer a few. There seem also to have been some votes for Dolan. That evening Scherer asked his backers to support Bergoglio, and Cardinal Don-ald Wuerl of Washington, DC, persuaded the US cardinals to back him as well. On the first scrutiny the next morning, Scola stalled, and Ouellet and Bergoglio (who got around 50 votes) emerged as representing the conservative and more progressive camps. At lunch Scola and Ouellet asked their supporters to go over to Bergoglio. This lunch was crucial, according to *La Stampa*'s "Vatican Insider." The cardinals "talked things through," and the myth that Bergo-glio had only one lung was dispelled.[2] He would have won on the fifth scrutiny, but there was a technical irregularity. A sixth and final scrutiny was held around six o'clock, and it produced a pope, Jorge Mario Bergoglio, SJ. He was the first Jesuit ever elected to the pa-pacy, with 90 votes out of a possible 115. He chose the entirely new style Francis.

When he emerged on the balcony of Saint Peter's, he was smiling but looked slightly shell-shocked. Gone was the papal regalia of an elbow-length red-velvet mozzetta, or cape, trimmed with ermine, and the ornate, jeweled pectoral cross. He kept his old pectoral cross with its image of Christ, the Good Shepherd. It had been wet and windy in the piazza, but the 150,000-strong crowd cheered. He said, almost intimately, "*Buona sera!*" (Good evening!). He asked the crowd to pray for him, and an extraordinary silence descended, something completely unexpected with Italians, who usually never stop chattering. I know; I was there, and it was a miraculous moment. The pope then almost reluctantly donned an ornate baroque stole for the blessing *urbi et orbi* (to the city) and, as he put it, to "all people of goodwill" in the world. Once the blessing was over, he couldn't get the stole off fast enough, handing it back to the papal master of ceremonies, Monsignor Guido Marini. It was clear that baroque was not Pope Francis style.

Then he said something enormously significant: "Now let us begin this journey, bishop and people, this journey of the Church of Rome, which is the one that presides in charity over all the churches—a journey of brotherhood, love and trust among us."[3] He was a man on a journey; he had not arrived, like so many of his predecessors, at final truth and the summit of absolute power. And it was a journey together with sisters and brothers, not in isolated splendor like Pius XII. He was bishop of Rome, not "pope" or "supreme pontiff." The Church of Rome "presided in charity," he said, leading in love and companionship, not with "the absolute fullness of supreme power." He was placing himself in the church, not over and above it, and he was inviting bishops and people to join him. He was actually quoting Syrian bishop Ignatius, probably Saint Peter's successor as bishop of Antioch (ca. 35–ca. 107). And he got Ignatius right. In his *Letter to the Romans*, Ignatius doesn't talk about the *bishop* of Rome "presiding in charity," but the *Church* of Rome. It was a subtle but important distinction. It was the point people like Cardinal Guidi and others were trying to make at Vatican I.

It was clear that a new style of papacy had begun. The culture wars were over, and a more merciful, welcoming church was being recovered that was in touch with the poor, pastoral care, forgiveness, and mercy. Right from the start, people sensed that something genuinely new was on the horizon, and they were right. When Francis talks about poverty, you know he knows what he's talking about. He also seems to have changed as a person, literally, between his election and first public appearance. He has somehow fitted into the papacy like he had been doing it all his life. The rather reserved, at times severe-looking man was gone. In Buenos Aires, he was not a great speaker; now he speaks in a simple, direct way that connects with people. It is as though his whole life was a preparation for this moment. Joseph S. Nye says Francis "has a good deal of soft power, and it is not only among Catholics." Other popes have talked about poverty, but "what Francis has been able to do is put a focus on it that isn't blurred or distracted by other things."[4] This is a man who leads, not dictates.

––––––––––

ALMOST IMMEDIATELY AFTER Francis's election, accusations were made that he had cooperated with the military junta that ruled Argentina between 1976 and 1982. These charges had also been leaked before the 2005 conclave, so it was clear that someone back in Argentina didn't like him. The source of the accusations was Horatio Verbitsky, an Argentine journalist whose own connections with the military junta have been revealed more recently. Essentially, Bergoglio was accused of betraying two of his Jesuit colleagues to the junta, resulting in their imprisonment and torture. The implication was that he was sympathetic to the military government. As with John Paul II, Bergoglio's background is important in understanding him.

It is also important to remember that he is Jesuit. He entered the Society in 1958 after briefly studying chemistry. He underwent the usual Jesuit training: two years in the novitiate, three years' study of philosophy and the humanities, and four years of theology, intersected by a three-year period of teaching literature and psychology in two elite Jesuit high schools. Ordained in December 1969, he took his final solemn vows as a Jesuit in 1973, being appointed

Argentinean provincial by the general of the order, Spaniard Pedro Arrupe, in July that year. As provincial Bergoglio was the head of all Jesuits in Argentina and Uruguay. At thirty-six he was remarkably young to be provincial; usually, only more mature men are appointed. It was a difficult period in Catholicism generally and in Argentina particularly. These were the turbulent years after Vatican II that many people embraced enthusiastically, but there were also those who resisted. This was the period when liberation theology was sweeping across Latin America, and many of the young Argentinean Jesuits embraced it with a strong move away from traditional ministries like elite high schools to engagement with the poor in the slums. This was happening in religious orders one way or another right across the world. It was a time when good leadership was needed, which Bergoglio clearly lacked. His family was strongly pro-Peronist, that is, they supported military strongman Juan Perón, with his firebrand combination of socialism, fascism, militarism, and Catholicism.

Perón ruled Argentina from 1946 until a military coup in 1955. He went into exile until 1973, when he returned as president and died in 1974. Between 1973 and 1976, the country was torn apart by terrorism from both the Right and the Left, leading to another military coup in 1976. Opponents of the regime were rounded up, tortured, and murdered by the military in a "Dirty War" that led to the disappearance of some 30,000 people. In April 1982 Argentine forces occupied the British Falkland Islands, which the Argentineans claimed as the Islas Malvinas. But the junta was already on a downward spiral. The country had been wracked by the imposition of neoliberal economics, the banks collapsed in March 1980, and there was internal dissension within the military. The invasion of the Malvinas was the final straw. With the islands retaken by the British in June 1982, the junta collapsed in 1983. The Falklands War left 649 Argentines, 255 British, and 3 civilians dead.

Bergoglio was provincial, or head, of the Argentinean Jesuits from 1973 to 1979, right through the worst of the terrorist period and Dirty War. The Jesuits were divided: the more progressive priests sided with the poor and wanted to identify with the grassroots and left-leaning liberation theology. The more conservative men wanted to maintain traditional ministries, and they looked to the state to provide protection against communism and the extreme Left. Bergoglio was inclined to side with the anti–liberation theology side; there was also something rather authoritarian in his personality at this period. He later confessed that he was too inexperienced when appointed provincial, that he didn't consult and made abrupt decisions. This all came to a head over Jesuit involvement in the Buenos Aires slums. Four Jesuits who had full-time jobs as university lecturers ministered in the slums on weekends. At that time, Bergoglio was opposed to the preferential option for the poor, and he wanted them out. A long, convoluted contretemps ensued, leading to two of the four, Fathers Orlando Yorio and Francisco Jalics, being kidnapped in May 1976 by a death squad from the notorious ESMA, the School of Naval Mechanics. After being tortured, they were eventually released and exiled. Bergoglio worked hard behind the scenes to get them out, including confronting the execrable and dangerous Emilio Massera, head of the navy. Bergoglio certainly did more than most Argentinean churchmen and bishops for prisoners, who simply remained silent, like Cardinal Juan Carlos Aramburu of Buenos Aires, or who tacitly or actively supported the junta, like the three military bishops and the appalling chief police chaplain, priest Christian von Wernich, now jailed for life. Papal nuncio Pio Laghi, a friend and tennis partner of Massera, was absolutely no help to anyone.

Bergoglio's unhappy period as provincial came to an end in 1979. For the next six years, he worked as a theology lecturer, but he was a constant headache for his successor because the province was divided between those who were pro- and anti-Bergoglio. He was sent to Germany in 1986, working on his doctorate, and then in 1990 the Jesuit general in Rome instructed him to live in Cordoba, some 435 miles (700 kilometers) west-northwest of Buenos Aires, effectively silencing him completely. Here he underwent a "dark night" and emerged a very different man. But the world had also changed. Liberation theology's notion of structural sin was generally accepted, and it was vividly illustrated in neorationalist, "trickle-down" economics and the exploitation of the poor. The demise of the Soviets and communism meant that Marxist ideology was no longer a threat to the church. Bergoglio began to think and talk like a liberation theologian.

Suddenly, in June 1992 he was plucked from Cordoba and appointed auxiliary bishop of Buenos Aires. He owed this to Buenos Aires cardinal Antonio Quarracino, who had known him as provincial. He was a success as auxiliary and was appointed vicar general. In June 1997 he became coadjutor archbishop with right of succession, and on February 28, 1998, he became archbishop of Buenos Aires. He was made cardinal in early 2001.

As bishop and archbishop, he became well known for his humility and commitment to a simple life. He lived in a small apartment in the archdiocesan offices next to the cathedral, took public transportation, and was a regular visitor to the "misery villages," or slums. Argentina is a wealthy country, but historically it has been badly governed, and many slum dwellers are people structurally excluded from the economic system. As archbishop he appointed priests to live in these slum areas, and the church became deeply involved in social justice. One of his prime targets was and is the neoliberal economics that created the structures of poverty and exclusion. Postjunta democratic governments, particularly that of Carlos Menem, were committed to neoliberalism, and the country was brought to its knees with a bank crash in 2001–2002 that devastated the middle class. It was directly connected to the country defaulting on a $132 billion debt. Bergoglio's suspicion of neoliberalism deepened.

Significantly, most of the opposition to Bergoglio in Argentina came from the Right, not from the Left, in both church and state. As archbishop Bergoglio was consultative with priests, laity, and experts but made final decisions himself; he is not afraid of power. He also reached out to the broader Argentinean society and made many friends across the religious and social spectrum. He sorted out the archdiocese's convoluted financial affairs and divested the archdiocese of bank shares and involvement in any form of banking. In 2005 he was elected president of the Argentinian Bishops' Conference, and in that role he had to negotiate a number of difficult issues with left-leaning President Néstor Kirchner and his wife and successor, Cristina Fernández de Kirchner. The Kirchners were latter-day Perónists who had already done much to assist the poor. But as secularists, they sometimes clashed with Bergoglio. On the question of gay marriage in July 2010, Bergoglio tried to negotiate a compromise in the bishops' conference to support civil unions but not marriage. He was unsuccessful and handled the response to the proposed legislation badly. It passed despite the bishops' objections. Bergoglio was usually able to unite the bishops' conference, but in this case he failed. However, Cristina Kirchner was the first head of state to visit him after his election. Generally speaking, he had good relations with Argentinean politicians. Most of his problems were with Rome, which he visited as rarely as possible, or conservatives in the local bishops' conference.

He also played an important role in CELAM, the Latin American and Caribbean Bishops Conference. At the 2007 CELAM conference, at the Marian shrine in Aparecida, Brazil, he chaired the drafting committee and was closely involved with the final document. In many ways, this document sets out the program for the Bergoglio papacy. The Aparecida document begins with the experience of people on the ground, and it asks them to see what is going on in their communities, judge it in the light of the Gospels, and act to transform it. The essence of the church, it said, is missionary, going out to the peripheries as disciples of Jesus. When Catholicism stays in the sacristy, it gets sick from stuffiness. The conference renewed the commitment of previous CELAM conferences to the preferential option for the poor. "We commit ourselves to work so that our Latin American and Caribbean Church will continue to be, with even greater determination, a travelling companion of our poorest brothers and sisters, even as far as martyrdom. Today we want to ratify and energize the preferential option for the poor made in previous Conferences."

Among the issues highlighted is the return to democracy in countries after military rule, as in Chile and Argentina. Another issue the document highlights is the assault on nature, the degradation of the environment. An example is the destruction of the Brazilian rain forest. "Nature has been, and continues to be, assaulted. The land has been plundered. Water is being treated as though it were merchandise." Coming in for particular criticism is globalization, which focuses power and wealth in the hands of a few, while the poor are marginalized. "Market forces easily absolutize efficiency and productivity as values regulating all human relations. . . . In its current form, globalization is incapable of interpreting and reacting in response to objective values that transcend the market and that constitute what is most important in human life: truth, justice, love, and most especially, the dignity and rights of all, even those not included in the market."[5]

At Aparecida Bergoglio worked closely with two men who were to become close colleagues when he became pope: Cardinals Óscar Rodríguez Maradiaga of Honduras and Francisco Javier Errázuriz of Chile.

––––––––––

THUS FORMED, JORGE Bergoglio came to the papacy. He immediately struck a chord with people; he seemed like a reincarnation of John XXIII. He travels in a Ford Escort, abandoning the Mercedes-Benz S600 papal limousine, paid his own bill at the *residenza* where he stayed before the conclave, refused to live in the papal palace, and moved permanently into a small suite in the Casa Santa Martha, where he generally eats with other residents and guests. On his first Holy Thursday, he washed the feet of prisoners, including a young Bosnian Muslim woman at the Casa del Marmo young-offenders prison outside Rome. He has invited the homeless who sleep at night around the Via della Conciliazione into the Vatican for meals and has provided permanent showers and lavatories near Saint Peter's for Rome's homeless. His informality has become a hallmark of his ministry, and this has contributed to a much more positive image of the papacy.

The month after he was elected, Francis set up an advisory group of eight (later nine) cardinals from all continents to advise him, including his colleagues from Aparecida Rodríguez Maradiaga and

Errázuriz. On September 28, 2013, he formally set up this group "as a 'Council of Cardinals' with the task of assisting me in the governance of the universal Church and of studying a project for the revision of the Apostolic Constitution *Pastor bonus* on the Roman Curia." *Pastor bonus* was John Paul II's tinkering with the structure of the Roman Curia that essentially changed nothing. The reality is the curia needs either root-and-branch reform or to be abolished completely and replaced by a newly staffed and largely lay papal secretariat. He has had more success with his secretary of state, professional diplomat Pietro Parolin, who from 2009 to 2013 was nuncio in Venezuela. One of Parolin's first successes was negotiating the reconciliation between the United States and Cuba. He has also worked hard to normalize relations with China and to assist the situation of the 12 million Catholics in the People's Republic. A proponent of the papal use of soft power to achieve reconciliation, Parolin has raised the international influence of the papacy after the disasters of the Bertone period.

A contemporary example of the papacy's negotiating skill are the negotiations that brought the United States and Cuba together in December 2014 after fifty-five years of antagonism, trade bans, and isolation. Back in the late 1950s, John XXIII approved a chaplain for Castro's guerrillas, and despite his Marxism Fidel Castro never cut his ties with Catholicism.[6] John Paul II's visit to Havana in 1998 strengthened a personal connection with Castro, despite the pope's lecturing him about human rights, family values, and political prisoners. Benedict XVI visited Havana in 2012 and was more conciliatory. He criticized the US trade embargo on Cuba and called for reconciliation with Washington. By then Fidel had been replaced as president by his brother Raúl. Building on this, Pope Francis sent letters to Presidents Barack Obama and Raúl Castro in the summer of 2013, initiating a dialogue that brought the two sides together. The Vatican then helped negotiate a successful conclusion that both presidents later acknowledged.

While important, these are not the top priorities for Francis. The most significant shift that he has achieved is to reemphasize the pastoral ministry of Catholicism. Emphasis is basically important in theology, and where you place your priority is what determines your attitude. Theology is not an either-or choice. Generally, recent popes placed their emphasis on "right" doctrine, on what they saw as "Truth." Everything else was subsumed to that. Francis doesn't deny this, but his emphasis is on pastoral care, on living the Christian life, rather than believing or mouthing right doctrine. It is this that has destabilized the traditionalists. For them, right belief is everything. What Francis has done is recover the deep Catholic tradition of mercy, forgiveness, nonjudgment ("Who am I to judge?" Francis asked), reaching out, an inclusive Catholicity—put simply, the church's pastoral tradition. For decades, Catholicism has desperately needed to recover this emphasis.

Pastoral care is a core message of Francis's November 2014 apostolic exhortation *Evengelii Gaudium* (Joy of the Gospel). A long document (206 pages in English)—it needed a good editor—it is a passionate call to the church to reach out and evangelize, to "proclaim the good news." Francis wants the church to go out into the world with a sense of joy and confidence, reflecting Jesus and the Gospel. He quotes the Aparecida document: "Life grows by being given away and it weakens in isolation and comfort." He says that evangelization does not come from those "who are dejected, discouraged, impatient, or anxious, but from [those] who have first received the joy of Christ." *Evengelii Gaudium* is above all an expression of Latin American Catholicism, with its emphasis on discipleship, the preferential option for the poor, and, an issue largely neglected in the developed West, the role of popular piety. He is also ruthless on trickle-down, neorationalist economics. The free market, he says, "expresses a crude and naïve trust in the goodness of those wielding economic power and in the sacralized workings of the prevailing economic system." The use of the word *sacralized* points to the pseudoreligious nature of belief in the forces of market capitalism; he calls it an "impersonal economy lacking any truly human purpose."

His criticism of Catholicism is equally severe. He wants a church "with open doors," one that is generous with baptism (as archbishop he was furious with priests who refused baptism to children of unmarried mothers), one that cares for the poor and the sick. He turns on Catholics who are "querulous and disillusioned pessimists, 'sourpusses,'" as well as "the self-absorbed promethean neo-pelagianism of those . . . who feel superior to others because they observe certain rules or remain intransigently faithful to a particular Catholic style from the past." He talks about their "narcissistic and authoritarian elitism" that is completely contrary to the attitude needed by someone committed to evangelization. In the end, he wants "a church which is poor and for the poor," who, he says, "have much to teach us. Not only do they share in the *sensus fidei*, but in their difficulties they know the suffering of Christ. We need to let ourselves be evangelized by them."

There is also much about preaching, faith, reason and science, ecumenism, relations with Judaism, and ecological theology. It is a rich document.

———————

HIS FIRST ENCYCLICAL letter, *Laudato si' mi', Signore* (Praise be to you, my Lord) of May 24, 2015, is an extraordinary document that addresses "everyone on the planet" on "care for our common home." The title *Laudato si'* (*LS*) is not Latin but the medieval Tuscan of Saint Francis of Assisi, whom the pope calls "that attractive and compelling figure, whose name I took as my guide and inspiration when I was elected Bishop of Rome." French philosopher Edgar Morin says that Francis "takes a complex view that is global in the sense that . . . it takes into account the relationship among all the parts . . . and invites us to rethink our society." Morin says that in a time of fragmented, postmodernist thought, Francis takes a completely integrated approach.[7] The pope puts it more humbly: "Rather than a problem to be solved, the world is a joyful mystery to be contemplated with gladness and praise."

The traditional Christian notion of the human person has been that of the body-flesh/soul-spirit dualism, and the emphasis has been on the dominance of humankind over the rest of creation. This notion of the body-soul is derived from Neoplatonism, and it enters the Christian tradition via Origen and Augustine. Francis reroots the whole tradition in the creation account in Genesis: "The creation accounts in the Book of Genesis contain, in their own symbolic and narrative language, profound teachings about human existence and its historical reality. They suggest that human life is grounded in these fundamental and closely intertwined relationships: with God, with our neighbour, and with the earth itself." That is, our relationship to the earth is equally important to our relationship with God and neighbor.

This leads directly to another basic issue: Francis's repudiation of anthropocentrism—human dominance over creation. This is quite extraordinary for any theologian, let alone a pope! He says that "the Bible has no place for a tyrannical anthropocentrism unconcerned for other creatures." The word *anthropocentrism* crops up regularly in *LS*, usually in a negative context: he talks of "distorted anthropocentrism," "excessive anthropocentrism," and "misguided anthropocentrism." He reinforces negativity to anthropocentrism by saying that "nowadays, we must forcefully reject the notion that our being created in God's image and given dominion over the earth justifies absolute domination over other creatures. . . . [Rather,] this implies a relationship of mutual responsibility between human beings and nature."

This signals a profound shift because what Francis has done is undermine the whole anthropocentric paradigm and restored a genuine sense of what Catholic cosmologist Thomas Berry, following Pierre Teilhard de Chardin (who is mentioned in *LS*), has called our "biological connectedness" with the whole cosmos. By this Berry means that life is an interactive continuum, from the most primitive forms to the most highly evolved and complex. This immediately emphasizes our real place; we are not separate from and over and against the world but an intimate part of it. Francis says, "It would also be mistaken to view other living beings as mere objects subjected to arbitrary human domination. When nature is viewed solely as a source of profit and gain, this has serious consequences for society. . . . The ultimate purpose of other creatures is not to be found in us." This is a very different approach from that of John Paul II.

Flowing from this, Pope Francis has little patience for technological solutions and "fixes." Linked to this is his view of an extractive mentality that presupposes that "there is an infinite supply of the earth's goods, and this leads to the planet being squeezed dry beyond every limit," an idea that, he says, "proves so attractive to economists, financiers and experts in technology." He says that "technology tends to absorb everything into its ironclad logic" and promises "quick fixes" that favor "the interests of certain powerful groups." Conservative *New York Times* columnist Ross Douthat has critically but correctly understood that *LS* is "an attack on the whole 'technological paradigm' of our civilization, [on] all the ways (economic and cultural) that we live now."[8] That's not far off the mark, because Francis says unequivocally that we cannot continue along the trajectory on which we are now headed, for it will lead to environmental and human catastrophe.

Another group that is criticized in *Laudato si'* are those—like me—who say that world overpopulation is the key problem we face. Francis repudiates this notion. "Some can only propose a reduction in the birthrate. . . . To blame population growth instead of extreme . . . consumerism . . . is one way of refusing to face the issues." He links the issue of population control to that of reproductive health, which he sees as a Western plot to protect its own overconsumption. However, with the world population reaching 7.5 billion people in April 2017, it is clear, to me at least, that we have to do something about overpopulation.

A key to *LS* is Francis's attempt to integrate care for the environment with social justice and equity for the poor. Until now the Catholic emphasis has been almost entirely on social justice. Sure, there has been a recognition of ecological issues in the church by previous popes, but that hasn't been where the *emphasis* has been placed. Francis is trying to rebalance this by focusing equally on the environment and on equity for the poor. He sees the two as intimately interconnected. "There can be no renewal of our relationship with nature without a renewal of humanity itself. There can be no ecology without an adequate anthropology." Everything is interrelated. This is close to the essence of his message. Nevertheless, the pope says, "a misguided anthropocentrism need not necessarily yield to 'biocentrism,' for that would entail adding yet another imbalance, failing to resolve present problems and adding new ones." I'm not so sure of that. There will always be tension between human beings and the environment, especially when human beings become greedy or when there are just too many people.

LS is probably the most important and positive encyclical ever written by any pope, for it confronts the most basic issue we face as humankind: the future of the planet and our future as a species. It has already had an extraordinary impact far outside the usual range of influence of the church. The pope has influenced not just science but politics, economics, and social policy. It shows how far the papacy has come since 1799.

———

IN OCTOBER 2013 Pope Francis called a Synod of Bishops, choosing the topic "the pastoral challenges of the family in the context of evangelization." This was a shrewd choice because it involved the vast majority of Catholics, and not just a small theological coterie. The synod met in two sessions: in October 2014 and October 2015. For Francis, the synod was first and foremost an exercise in collegiality. He made it clear that bishops should not be looking over their shoulders to check how he was responding to their remarks, as they certainly did with John Paul II. He even encouraged disagreement, something unheard of previously. The three issues that emerged were Communion for divorced and remarried Catholics, polygamy, and the language used by the church surrounding homosexuality.

Taking the divorced-remarried issue first: The traditional position has been that a divorced Catholic without an annulment who has entered a second marriage cannot receive Communion because the validity of the first marriage stands. But since the 1970s, many have decided on an internal-forum or good-conscience solution to this. That is, having talked it over with a priest, a Catholic in a second marriage can make a conscientious decision to return to Communion. This is the line the Orthodox churches follow when they allow a civilly remarried divorcé to return to the reception of

Eucharist. However, this solution was condemned by John Paul in the 1981 apostolic exhortation *Familiaris consortio* that said they could receive Communion only if "they lived as brother and sister." One solution proposed in the 2014 synod meeting was streamlining the annulment process, which Pope Francis immediately supported by eliminating time-wasting appeals processes. At the 2015 session Cardinal Walter Kasper, a theologian with a decade of pastoral experience as bishop of Rottenburg-Stuttgart, proposed a modified form of the internal-forum solution by suggesting that divorced and remarried Catholics go through a penitential process, guided by a priest, eventually moving toward the reception of Communion. Francis clearly favored Kasper's solution, but many literal-minded bishops would have none of it. For them, this was a deviation from church doctrine on the indissolubility of marriage. With many marriages ending in divorce in the developed West, this issue became a test case for the synod, and it ended with no agreement reached.

Another issue was polygamy in Africa, which was also condemned by *Familiaris consortio*. But as Archbishop Charles Palmer-Buckle of Accra, Ghana, says, there are real pastoral problems embedded in polygamy that can't be solved easily. Polygamous wives can't be cast adrift "without hurting the children," let alone without hurting the wives themselves. Palmer-Buckle says that polygamous marriages often work, with "harmony between the husband and his different wives, among the different wives, and among their children." But in other instances, "there is so much hurt going on among the different women, among the different children." He asks, "How do we help all of those involved to look at Christ, and to what Christ invites them to?"[9]

Regarding homosexuality, no one at the synod was proposing that gay marriage be approved, but in the 2014 session bishops spoke positively about gay people. The church has to find a more pastoral and respectful way of speaking. If not, the church won't seem like "a home for all," as Pope Francis put it.

At the end of the synod, the bishops issued an anodyne agreed-upon statement, and Pope Francis created a new Vatican department for laity, family, and life, replacing two pontifical councils. Putting a positive spin on it, the editors of *Commonweal* said,

"Engagement rather than denunciation marked the synod's formal pronouncements, a pastoral style deeply rooted in the documents of the Second Vatican Council, and profoundly embodied in everything Pope Francis does."[10] In his speech at the end of the synod, Francis asserted that a "synodal church is a listening church . . . in which everyone has something to learn." Perhaps more important than the conclusions were the processes whereby bishops were free to speak their minds, but the problem was that most of the bishops appointed by John Paul II and Benedict XVI had little to say beyond their inadequate theology and pastoral rigidity. They found it difficult to adjust to ministerial rather than doctrinal answers.

The key thing was the pope's response to the synod. On April 8, 2016, he issued the apostolic exhortation *Amoris laetitia* (Joy of love). Unlike John Paul's postsynodal documents, *AL* genuinely reflects the synod, the bishops' conferences, and Vatican II. He acknowledges that the Christian experience is central in discerning moral truth: "I want to make it clear," he says, "that not all discussions of doctrinal, moral and pastoral issues need to be settled by the intervention of the magisterium." This is a departure from his predecessors, who constantly intervened. He continues: "Unity of teaching and practice are certainly necessary . . . but this does not preclude various ways of interpreting some aspects of that teaching or drawing certain consequences from it." He says that the church cannot "impose rules by sheer authority" and that it is "called to form consciences, not replace them"; being "defensive" actually wastes "pastoral energy," denouncing decadence without achieving anything positive.

However, the real flash point of *AL* lies in paragraphs 301–306, where Francis writes of "mitigating factors in pastoral discernment" and the need for "special discernment in certain 'irregular' situations." The word *discernment* is the key here. Francis is a Jesuit, and for Jesuit spirituality discernment is the key to decision making. Discernment presupposes that the Spirit of God is working in each of our lives and that our conscience is a key guide in ascertaining the direction in which God is calling us. In that context, Francis says that it "can no longer simply be said that all those in any 'irregular' situation are living in a state of mortal sin and are deprived of sanctifying grace." He quotes Aquinas, the *Catechism of the Catholic Church*, and the synod that speaks of "a person's properly formed conscience" to support his claim. He says that "individual conscience needs to be better incorporated into the church's praxis" and that "it is reductive simply to consider whether or not an individual's actions correspond to a general law or rule, because that is not enough to discern and ensure full fidelity to God in the concrete life of a human being," again quoting Aquinas.

It is paragraph 305 of *AL* that has caused the most controversy. He starts by saying, "For this reason, a pastor cannot feel that it is enough simply to apply moral laws to those living in 'irregular' situations, as if they were stones to throw at people's lives," and he quotes the International Theological Commission to say that the natural law is not a mere set of objective rules that governs everyone, but "a source of objective inspiration for the deeply personal process of making decisions." The key sentence reads: "It is possible that in an objective situation of sin—which may not be subjectively culpable, or fully such—a person can be living in God's grace and charity, while receiving the church's help to this end." He adds a footnote (351) to this in which he says, "In certain cases, this can include the help of the sacraments." It is this footnote that has most upset the traditionalists.

Essentially, their objection is that it directly contradicts paragraph 84 of John Paul II's *Familiaris consortio.* Traditionalists argue that Francis has created uncertainty and confusion that they claim will lead to chaos. The pope's response is simple: "There are two ways of thinking which recur throughout the Church's history: casting off and reinstating. The Church's way, from the time of the Council of Jerusalem, has always been the way of Jesus, the way of mercy and reinstatement. . . . The way of the Church is not to condemn anyone forever." Clearly, the traditionalists favor "casting off," whereas Francis speaks of "mercy and reinstatement," by which he means reconciliation and acceptance.

———————

AFTER *AL* WAS published, the resistance to Pope Francis that had
been simmering under the surface in parts of the Vatican and elsewhere became quite public. The most spectacular expression of it
came from four cardinals, all retired; two have subsequently died.
They are American Raymond Burke, former prefect of the Tribunal of the Apostolic Signatura (the Vatican equivalent of the US
Supreme Court); Carlo Caffarra, former archbishop of Bologna;
Walter Brandmüller, former president of the Pontifical Committee
for Historical Sciences; and Joachim Meisner, former archbishop of
Cologne. All are traditionalists and not new to controversy.

In September 2016 they sent a letter and a set of *dubia*, os-
tensibly a set of five questions seeking clarification, to the pope. A
month later, they published the letter in an attempt to put pressure
on Francis, who had not answered them. They claimed the faithful
were confused, and they were "compelled in conscience" to ask the
pope "to resolve the uncertainties and bring clarity." In what was
essentially a caricature, they tried to line up Francis in opposition
to John Paul, contrasting his pastoral approach with John Paul's
"absolute moral norms." They also claimed that Christ's teaching
against divorce was clear and that scripture and tradition supported
them because this is what the church has "always thought and prac-
tised." They seem to have no realization that marriage was recognized as a sacrament only in the twelfth century and that Christ's
comments in the Gospels on marriage applied to Jewish practices.

Pope Francis ignored these confected *dubia*. His aim was to devolve authority to local churches to make decisions about remarried
divorcés in light of local experience. He wanted laity, priests, bishops, and bishops' conferences to assume collegial responsibility for
their churches. Several bishops' conferences (for example, Malta,
Germany, and the Buenos Aires region) understood this and began
developing pastoral guidelines for divorced and remarried people
to receive Communion, essentially on a case-by-case basis. In fact,
this "internal-forum" solution is what has been happening for many
years in many countries, despite John Paul's strictures against it.
But the confected *dubia* gave traditionalists and anti-Francis elements in the curia permission to attack the pope. They saw this

devolution of authority as the thin edge of the wedge and were determined to resist it.

At first the prefect of the CDF, Cardinal Gerhard Ludwig Müller, seemed to support Francis when he claimed that it harmed the church to talk about the *dubia* in public and that *AL* "is very clear in its doctrine and we can read into it all of Jesus' doctrine on marriage" and the tradition of the church.[11] But by early 2017, Müller was backing away from the broadscale interpretation of *AL*. "I don't like it," he said. "It is not right that so many bishops are interpreting *Amoris Laetitia* according to their way of understanding the Pope's teaching. This does not keep to the line of Catholic doctrine." He retreated to the John Paul line: "For us marriage is the expression of participation in the unity between Christ the bridegroom and the Church his bride. . . . This is the substance of the sacrament, and no power in heaven or on earth, neither an angel, nor the pope, nor a council, nor a law of the bishops, has the faculty to change it."[12] No equivocation there! Another critic was German philosopher Robert Spaemann, who says, "The Pope must have known that he would split the church with such a step and lead toward a schism."[13] These critics make the teaching on marriage the equivalent of the doctrine on the divinity and humanity of Christ. They have no understanding of a hierarchy of truth and don't realize that while marriage is important, it is not a central doctrine of Catholicism.

Significantly, the CDF's Müller was not appointed the official interpreter of *AL*. The pope gave that job to Cardinal Christoph Schörnborn of Vienna, a former student of Joseph Ratzinger. In an interview with *La Civiltà Cattolica*, Schörnborn responded to the claim that *AL* was a minor document, a personal opinion of Pope Francis that could be ignored. Schörnborn said that "this is an act of the magisterium. . . . It is clear that the pope is exercising here his role of pastor, of master and teacher of the faith, after having benefited from the consultation of the two synods." Schörnborn says that Francis has clarified "something that had remained implicit in *Familiaris consortio*," and that is "the link between the objectivity of a situation of sin and the life of grace in relation to God and to his church, and—as a logical consequence—about the concrete imputability of sin."[14] What Schörnborn is saying is that there is a difference between an objectively immoral situation and the subjective reality of a remarried divorcé. They may well experience God's grace because they are in good conscience, and sin cannot be imputed to them. There is continuity of doctrine, but also something new. As Cardinal Newman has said, doctrine is not set in stone; it is dynamic, constantly responding to circumstances, and open to the world. Belief and theology are continuously changing, sometimes slowly, sometimes rapidly, but always related to a specific historical context. This is precisely what Pope Francis achieved in *AL*. Catholicism is a way of life before it is a doctrine or ideology. What Pope Francis is attempting to do is to shift the power and authority out of Rome to the peripheries. He is conscious that the *sensus fidei* of married people might have something theologically significant to say about married life. As ecclesiologist Richard Gaillardetz maintains, people perceive that "church leaders were more preoccupied with preserving the status quo than with faithfully discerning the impulse of the Spirit in the Church" and that "this has been exacerbated by the sexual abuse crisis."[15]

What is really happening here is a battle for the heart and soul of Catholicism. The sheer decency and openness of Francis have restored the fortunes and reputation of the papacy in the wider world after the overbearing John Paul and the maladroit Benedict. Also, part of what Francis is facing is that he is from another world from the Vatican bureaucrats, who are very Eurocentric. The opposition to him began soon after his election, and it has intensified as his inclusive agenda emerged more clearly. This brings us back to Francis's emphasis on the pastoral and ministerial rather than the dogmatic and ideological. This is what traditionalists cannot bear; psychologically, the ambiguity involved in a pastoral approach leaves them with an uncertainty that they seem to find intolerable. They are besotted with papal centralism and cannot deal with the devolution of power to local churches. Their problem is that they have to choose between popes: either John Paul or Francis. Once they opt for John Paul, they become what they have always accused progressive believers of being—"cafeteria Catholics" who pick and choose what they believe.

———————

FROM THE BEGINNING of his papacy, Benedict XVI found himself mired in financial scandals, and it was an element leading to his resignation. Francis tried to confront this soon after his election, and his first problem was the *Istituto per le Opere di Religione*, the Vatican Bank. In Buenos Aires he inherited an archdiocese caught up with the Trusso family *Banco de Crédito Provincial*, which went bust, with the church losing seven hundred thousand dollars. He then witnessed the Argentinean bank crash of 2001–2002 that devastated the middle class. As a result, he was deeply suspicious of the church being tied up with banks.

So after he became pope, he was at first inclined to close down the IOR. He was dissuaded, but ordered a root-and-branch reform. The Vatican bank has now somewhat modernized its operations and is well regulated, and its detailed annual reports are audited by the international accounting firm Deloitte. Francis also inherited a Vatican financial mess, with warnings of a possible deficit, although lack of clarity meant that nobody had an overall view of the accounts, and in fact the Vatican might have really been flush with cash. To try to tackle this situation, in 2013 Francis formed an ad hoc committee on finance and administration, COSEA, that encountered deep-seated resistance from the curia. He also brought in outside auditors to try to get around the resistance. But this backfired, and two Italian journalists, Emiliano Fittipaldi and Gianluigi Nuzzi, wrote books about the corruption that abounds inside the Vatican, with most of their information coming from leaked COSEA documents.[16]

In February 2014 Francis established a Council for the Economy that set policy, a Secretariat for the Economy to oversee implementation, and an auditor for independent verification. At first APSA, the Vatican's asset-management agency, lost many of its functions to the Secretariat for the Economy, but in early July 2016 that relationship was recalibrated, with APSA regaining its old powers over purchasing, contracts, asset management, and support services. The Secretariat for the Economy still controlled human resources and payroll and still oversees the finances of all departments of the curia, the Vatican government, and APSA. This resolved strains that had developed because the Secretariat for the Economy had at first been given very wide powers, but after tensions with APSA and the Secretariat of State, its statutes were revised. The Secretariat of State has now had its authority confirmed as the central bureaucratic body in the Vatican.

Part of the problem was the early 2014 appointment of the blunt, forceful Australian George Pell as prefect of the Secretariat for the Economy. Pell was used to getting his own way as archbishop of Melbourne and later Sydney, and he is an able, if unsubtle, manager. While he has brought some order to Vatican finances, he has upset many along the way. Much of the opposition came from the Vatican "old guard," who oppose any diminution of their power or any form of accountability. Pell is also opposed by the Secretariat of State, whose authority his secretariat challenges. This opposition was on public view when Pell commissioned a broadscale audit by PricewaterhouseCoopers that aimed at getting a complete picture of the Holy See's finances was "suspended immediately" by a letter from Archbishop Giovanni Becciu, undersecretary of state. The problem, Becciu said, was not transparency but elements of the PwC contract and the fact that Pell had signed it. However, the future of the Secretariat of the Economy was up in the air at the time of writing because Cardinal Pell has been accused by the police in Melbourne of "historical sex offences," and he returned to Australia in early July 2017 to face the first of a series of probably drawn-out court procedures. At the very same time, Pope Francis declined to renew Cardinal Müller's appointment as prefect of the CDF when his first five-year term came up for renewal. Müller has made no secret of the fact that he is furious that he was not reappointed. His deputy, Archbishop Luis Ladaria Ferrer, a Jesuit who maintains a low public profile, has replaced him.

Another serious problem Francis inherited from his predecessors is the sexual abuse crisis. Benedict XVI attempted to deal with it, even if inadequately. He reduced 171 priests "to the lay state" (that is, stopped them from practicing as priests) in 2008–2009 and almost 400 more in the years 2011–2012. By the time of his resignation, he had reduced some 800 priests to the lay state. The papacy was very slow to respond to the crisis. But from May 2001, when bishops were instructed to refer all abuse cases to the CDF, Ratzinger began to understand the extent of the problem. Another element in the slowness of the Vatican to respond was that Rome for centuries was traditionally the last court of appeal for priests who were in trouble with their bishops—and I am not referring only to sexual abuse here. The Roman legal system moved slowly, but it often supported priests in conflicts with bishops. So when abusive priests appealed to the Congregation for the Clergy or the Apostolic Signatura, the Vatican appeals court, the same scenario was applied. Bishops who had attempted to discipline some of their worst abusers found that Rome supported the priests, often on a legal technicality, and ordered the bishops to reinstate them. A few bishops had the courage to refuse to do so, but most complied with Vatican orders. It is also clear that there was a culture of denial, which was exemplified by Cardinal Darío Castrillón Hoyos, who argued in 2002 that the abuse crisis was an "American problem" and praised a French bishop who served three months in prison for not reporting a priest who had abused eleven boys over a six-year period. "I rejoice to have a colleague in the episcopate," Castrillón Hoyos wrote, "who, in the eyes of history and all the other bishops of the world, preferred prison rather than denouncing one of his sons, a priest." This Colombian cardinal, formerly prefect of the Congregation for the Clergy, was part of the Vatican "old guard" that opposed any reform of dealing with priest abusers.

Pope Francis's record on priestly abuse is mixed. In March 2014 he set up the Pontifical Commission for the Protection of Minors, whose task was to propose to the pope "the most opportune initiatives for protecting minors and vulnerable adults, in order that we may do everything possible to ensure that crimes such as those which have occurred are no longer repeated in the Church." The commission was also tasked with involving the local churches, while "uniting their efforts to those of the Congregation for the Doctrine of the Faith." Cardinal Sean O'Malley of Boston was appointed commission president, and originally it had two survivors of sexual abuse as members, Irishwoman Marie Collins and Englishman Peter Saunders. There were also ten laypeople, two religious sisters, two priests, and a priest secretary. The commission met regularly but lacked an adequate budget and has faced curial opposition. An attempt in June 2015 to set up a tribunal within the CDF to hold bishops who failed to prevent abuse or covered it up was stymied by the CDF, because Müller felt that since it was already dealing with abusive priests, it could not also take on problem bishops. Exactly a year later, Pope Francis issued a decree, *Come una madre amorevole* (Like a loving mother), that instructed "the competent Congregation in the Roman Curia," presumably the Congregation for Bishops, "to open an inquiry" into bishops who had failed to act or covered up sexual abuse, which would presumably lead to a forced resignation. So far, no bishop has faced the music.

It is hard to avoid the impression that all of this is ad hoc and not thought out. Peter Saunders stepped down from the commission in 2015, and in March 2017 Marie Collins resigned. She cited obstruction of the work of the commission by the CDF and Müller. She claimed that the CDF had refused to set up the bishop's tribunal and even refused to answer letters from abuse victims. Understandably, she was anxious to get things done, but the curia moved at its usual snail's pace, claiming that cultural change takes time and effort. And the failure to answer letters is par for the course for the CDF. They never answer any letters, even from those who are the subject of one of their theological investigations; I know from experience. In an essentially specious reply, Müller claimed that the CDF always refers letters to the local bishop, "that he might take pastoral care of the victim," saying that the CDF "will do all that is possible to give justice." Secretary of State Parolin was blunter: he said it was "shameful" that some Vatican offices resisted the pope's efforts to confront this issue.[17] At the time of writing, the papal response to sexual abuse seems to be in limbo.

IF THERE IS one fundamental weakness in Francis's papacy, it is his failure to engage meaningfully with or recognize the contribution and status of women. At times, he trivializes women, and he often sounds confused and almost childish, such as referring to women theologians appointed to the International Theological Commission as "strawberries on the cake." He has also talked about "old maids," "masculinity in a skirt," and priests being "under the authority of their housekeeper." Like John Paul, he has talked condescendingly about the so-called feminine genius, but he has done nothing structural about acknowledging women's absolute equality as baptized members of the church. "By virtue of their feminine genius," he told the International Theological Commission, "[female] theologians can detect, for the benefit of all, some unexplored aspects of the unfathomable mystery of Christ."[18] He has talked a lot about women playing leadership roles and having greater decision-making powers in the church, but he has clearly excluded the possibility of women's ordination to the priesthood or even appointment to the College of Cardinals. The latter is certainly possible, as cardinal is merely an honorary title, but it would allow women to participate in papal elections. The disparagement of gender theory and the bifurcation of gender roles have become endemic in some parts of Catholic theology, and certainly it was a leading leitmotif of John Paul's papacy. While Pope Francis sometimes mirrors this line of thinking, he knows there is a problem with the role of women; the truth is that he doesn't know how to deal with it. He has never really escaped from the ridiculous machismo that characterizes many Argentinean males. The Synod on the Family also reflected this failure when it avoided the issues of women and contraception. The only reason contraception was sidestepped was because the church would have to admit that *HV* was wrong. This is certainly what the vast majority of Catholics in developed countries think, but bishops in the developing world, particularly Africa, see this issue as linked to reproductive health, which they caricature as a Western plot to control their populations. So it suits them to avoid it, and they have increasing influence in the church.

Francis has said clearly that he doesn't support the ordination of women to the priesthood, but he has ordered an investigation into the possibility of women deacons. He set up a group of seven male and six female experts in mid-2016 under the auspices of the CDF and chaired by Archbishop Ladaria Ferrer to study the history of the issue. It's not as though the historical aspects of this issue have not been studied exhaustively before. We know there were women deacons in the early church; we know they were part of ministry in both the West and particularly the East until the eleventh century. We know that they were ordained just as male deacons were ordained. We also know what functions they carried out. Those opposed the restoration of the deaconate to women run the specious argument that they were not "ordained" in the real sense, that is, in the same way that men were "ordained." What this argument tries to do is to make sure that the sacrament of ordination of deacons, priests, and bishops is confined to men because only men provide the right "matter" (that is, a male body) for the sacramental form. Again, this is specious nonsense.

This matter-and-form approach to the sacraments, just like the substance-and-accidents approach to the Eucharist, is a medieval philosophical invention that actually drains the sacraments of their powerful symbolic value as channels of the dynamic love of God and turns them into "things." Also, the meaning of ordination for men, particularly ordination to the priesthood, has changed substantially over the centuries. The meaning of priesthood in the fourth and fifth centuries is very different from its meaning in the twenty-first century. The decision of John Paul II in *Ordinatio sacerdotalis* (1994) to "definitively" exclude the ordination of women does *not* mean that it is infallible teaching. That is demonstrated by Cardinal Ratzinger's response to a *dubium* regarding the ordination of women. He claimed that the exclusion was part of "the deposit of faith" and the "ordinary and universal magisterium," which he tries to equate with infallibility. But the fact is that if it is part of the ordinary magisterium, it is changeable and therefore not infallible. Further, there is overwhelming evidence that this teaching has *not* been received by many of the faithful. So the whole question of the ordination of women remains open. Many who oppose women's ordination to the deaconate see it as the thin edge of the wedge, and that is why they oppose it.

Two other questions on which Francis seems to be moving more decisively are the questions of ordination of married men and liturgical translation. On the ordination question, Francis has repeated on several occasions that he is open to the ordination of *viri probati* (tried and trusted men) where there is a shortage of celibate priests. This is not a theological question but one of numbers. Across the world there has been a sharp and, in some places, catastrophic decline in the number of priests and those presenting for training as priests. Francis seems to see the ordination of *viri probati* as an emergency measure in response to an "enormous problem," something his predecessors swept under the rug, hoping against hope that there would be a turnaround in numbers offering for ordination. The statistics are unequivocal: According to Georgetown University's Center for Applied Research in the Apostolate, between 1975 and 2008 the world Catholic population increased from 709.6 million to 1.166 billion, while the number of priests increased from 404,783 to only 409,166. The center's research in 2008 also shows that half of the active diocesan priests in the United States plan to retire by 2019.[19] A similar pattern is obvious in Australia. Eric Hodgens, who has studied this issue carefully, takes as an example one Australian seminary, Corpus Christi College in Melbourne. He shows that for the past thirty-five years, the college has averaged nine entries per year. Only a third of these entries stay until they are ordained. That results in three or four ordinations a year. Over that same thirty-five years, the Catholic population of Victoria and Tasmania, the states the college supplies, has increased by 75 percent. He says that the college "should be ordaining at least twelve a year if it wants to have a ratio of one priest for each 5000 Catholics" and that "because numbers have been so steady for the last 35 years you are entitled to predict it's not going to change."[20] Unless the church changes, the local priesthood will die out; it's as simple as that. Importation of foreign priests from developing countries is almost always not the answer to the shortage. Not only does this asset-strip the Third World of personnel, but it also creates difficult cultural problems that are not easily solved, especially when these priests come from tribal and patriarchal cultures that have no comprehension of the role of women in the developed West. This can often lead to disastrous situations.

So we really need these *viri probati.* In developing countries, they will come from the ranks of established and experienced married catechists who live locally and know the culture. It is not as though this is a new idea. Back in the mid-1970s Bishop Pierre Guichet of Tarawa, Kiribati, in the central Pacific, proposed to ordain his married catechists on the grounds that they were more mature, experienced, and grounded in local culture than smart youngsters who left village life behind for a seminary education.[21] The same applies in developed countries: here there are many mid- and late-career men with some theological training who could be considered for ordination after supervised training.

Second, on the question of liturgical translation, Pope Francis has ordered a review of the CDW decree *Liturgicam authenticam* (March 2001). As we have already seen, *LA* was a disaster that led to an overly literal English translation that, in the words of a *Tablet* editorial, "constitutes a barrier that separates us from God."[22] While the Japanese, French, and German bishops stood firm against this decree that was issued in the dying days of the John Paul papacy when "the Vatican curia became a law unto itself," the English bishops cravenly caved in to a Chilean cardinal, Jorge Medina Estévez, and the group of English-speaking bishops forming the misnamed *Vox Clara* committee. The result has been a translation disaster.

On January 28, 2017, Pope Francis established a committee of bishops, chaired by Englishman archbishop Arthur Roche, presently secretary of the CDW, to review *LA*. Then, on September 3, 2017, the pope issued the apostolic letter *Magnum principium*, granting much more control in the translation process to local conferences of bishops. It essentially limits the role of the CDW to the end of the process. It can't demand a whole series of amendments to the text; it can only say yes or no. While this letter will not immediately lead to the jettisoning of the literal and dreadful and illiterate English liturgical translation currently in use, it does indicate that the initiative is now back with those who support the dynamic equivalence principle in liturgical translation—that is, using a text that conveys meaning through comprehensible language rather than a stolid, literal translation of the Latin text. Following his notion of collegiality and devolution of authority, Francis wants to give bishops' conferences more say in deciding matters like liturgical translation. It makes sense that English-speaking bishops know more about English than non-English speakers in the CDW.

Also, *LA* was a disaster in its attempt to find some form of "sacral" language that is "characterised by pretentious Latinisms and pseudo-Victorianisms."[23] Many bishops and priests and the English-speaking Mass-going community have been unhappy with the translation produced by *LA*, and most feel the best thing to do is to consign it to oblivion. We already have an excellent 1990s English translation prepared by ICEL before it was emasculated, and it is this that should be reintroduced.

————————

SO WHAT ARE we to make of Pope Francis five years into his papacy? What has he done with papal power and influence? First, he has already decisively changed the pattern established by his predecessors. No longer is the emphasis on the dangers of secularism, relativism, and the false distinction between the so-called hermeneutics of continuity and rupture. Francis's emphasis is in tune with the genuine Catholic tradition focusing on God's mercy, the love of Jesus, and Catholicism's pastoral care for the vulnerabilities, sins, and failures embedded in the human condition. The church has become a "field hospital," where sinners are cared for and the wounded healed. He is also concerned with making collegiality work and strengthening the centrality and authority of the local church. The emphasis on absolute moral norms, on an uncompromising orthodoxy, has been replaced by a focus on pastoral care and forgiveness. Single-handedly, Francis has recovered Catholicism's pastoral tradition, largely forgotten by popes for centuries.

He has also brought to fruition the opening toward environmental ethics that was first perceived by John Paul II and developed by Benedict XVI. The encyclical *LS* is an extraordinarily pioneering work that is comprehensive in its scope and offers a searing, wide-ranging critique of contemporary economics, technology, and industry, such that it will now be difficult to remain a Catholic in good standing and still embrace the conclusions of neorationalist economics and trickle-down theories about the economy. Mind you, this has been obvious to anyone who followed papal social teaching since John Paul II, or even before him.

As I said earlier, at the time of writing, the Francis papacy is still a work in progress. Whether he will be able to break the stranglehold of the traditionalists on the central government of the church remains to be seen. In terms of the devolution of authority outward and downward to the local church, clearly the biggest problem is the mediocrity of the bishops appointed over the past thirty-five to forty years. Many of these men have no leadership ability and lack emotional intelligence. They are fearful and constantly look over their shoulders to Rome for permission, or they take refuge in superficial enthusiasms of the new religious movements or the charismatic renewal. They have been appointed bishops basically because they are yes men. It is going to take a long time to replace them, but the problem is that the gene pool is so shallow. The type of experienced men who would show leadership are now too old, and the few being recruited to the priesthood nowadays seem wedded to traditionalist forms and are often emotionally immature. And quite a few of them are bone lazy. So Francis has a job on his hands in terms of episcopal appointments, especially in the developed West. He also needs to recruit like-minded cardinals so that his vision will be continued by a successor who shares his decentralized model of the church. And he has not even begun to address practically the equality and role of women in leadership, ministry, and decision making.

The other important thing about Francis is his nationality. He is non-European, from the global South. His election broke the stranglehold of Europeans on the papacy. No matter how global his predecessors tried to be, they could not escape their Eurocentrism. Francis brings a completely new perspective, although as an Argentinean of Italian extraction, he is the perfect person to bridge Eurocentrism and the developing world. He grasps both cultures and brings an understanding of the extraordinary diversity of contemporary Catholicism. Catholicism is now a world church, and Francis understands that.

He has pointed the church in the right direction, and in the end all that those of us who share his vision can do is trust the Holy Spirit—and keep our fingers crossed!

12

DEATH AND RESURRECTION

CATHOLICISM IS RIFE with contradictions. Perhaps the most dis-junctive of these is the contrast between Jesus, the poor man who had "nowhere to lay his head" (Matt. 8:20) and who died like a common criminal on a cross, and the reality of the enormous power and influence of the twenty-first-century papacy. It is difficult if not impossible to see what has happened to Catholicism since the death of Pius VI in 1799 as a lineal and continuous development of the Gospel, or even of previous papal history. A basic challenge the church faces today is to reconcile the New Testament's vision of a community of loving service with the contemporary papacy. The election of Pope Francis has given hope to Catholics that he will bring the papacy down to earth and recover something of the hu-mility of Jesus. But even he, a genuinely good man, is *still* a pope.

At the root of the problem is Catholicism's attachment to power. In May 1935, when French premier Pierre Laval requested some relief for Catholics in the Soviet Union, Stalin asked, "The Pope! How many divisions has *he* got?" Stalin is long dead, but the pa-pacy is still with us. Stewart A. Stehlin is exactly right when he says, "Countries, then, if they cannot have God on their side, at least would like to have the pope there." Soft power is becoming increas-ingly important in the contemporary world, and the papacy is the oldest and most experienced proponent of soft power in history. Pope Leo I (440–461) personally confronted Attila and the Huns on the river Mincio, near Mantua, in northern Italy, in AD 452. In a contemporary account, Prosper of Aquitaine says that Attila "was so impressed by the presence of the high priest [Pope Leo] that he ordered his army to give up warfare and, after he had promised peace, he departed beyond the Danube."[1] For sure, this is a pious, idealized account, but it shows that Pope Leo was willing to try to use his spiritual influence and authority, his persuasive power.

Perhaps even more important than intervention in interstate disputes is the papal tradition of using its influence to promote the values of social justice, equity, and the rights of all people to share in society's benefits. Papal social teaching since Leo XIII has largely embraced the clear biblical teaching, especially in the Hebrew scriptures (Old Testament), that there must be an equitable distribution of wealth in society so that no one corners the market completely. Modern papal teaching supports workers' right to form trade unions in order to negotiate for fair wages, decent working conditions, and the right to strike. While supporting the legitimacy of private property, the papal tradition has always been suspicious of "unchecked capitalism." This has been a consistent theme of recent popes, including Pope Francis, who in the exhortation *Evangelii gaudium* (2013) has attacked the "opinion, which has never been confirmed by the facts, [that] expresses a crude and naive trust in the goodness of those wielding economic power and in the sacralised workings of the prevailing economic system. Meanwhile, the excluded are still waiting."

The papacy also has a long tradition of using hard power the moment it suits it, particularly in dealing with internal dissent in the church. Perhaps the most famous victim of this was Galileo, whose espousal of the Copernican understanding of the universe led to his forced abjuration before the Roman Inquisition in 1633 and to house arrest for the last nine years of his life. But one doesn't have to retreat to the seventeenth century to find papal hard power in operation. It can be seen in the activities of the Congregation for the Doctrine of the Faith, the lineal descendant of the Roman Inquisition that condemned Galileo. We have seen it in play later in the heresy hunt after the condemnation of so-called modernism when entirely orthodox Catholic scholars were pursued by a cabal of spies sponsored by the Vatican. Under John Paul II, the CDF took on a new lease of life, especially after the arrival of Joseph

Ratzinger as prefect in November 1981. He moved against a long list of Catholic theologians, moralists, and movements like liberation theology. Some of these people were treated abominably. Because of CDF secrecy, the numbers of people investigated are hard to arrive at, but, just counting those known publicly, well over one hundred theologians and others have been investigated since 1981.

Of course, there is a contradiction in even using the word *power* in the context of the papacy. The pope, like every Christian, is supposed to be a follower of Jesus, the man who said that power of any sort had no place in the community he founded. He replaced power with a call to service. He explicitly identified power with the "Gentiles," a New Testament word that specifically refers to idolaters, unbelievers, and worshipers of idols. "You know that among the Gentiles those whom they recognize as their rulers lord it over them, and their great ones are tyrants over them. But it is not to be so among you; whoever wishes to become great among you must be your servant, and whoever wishes to be first among you must be the slave of all. For the Son of Man came not to be served, but to serve and give his life as a ransom for many" (Mark 10:42–45). Sure, the popes have been calling themselves the "servants of the servants of God" since Pope Gregory I (590–604), but papal history has a very mixed record on popes serving God's servants, let alone anyone else.

The Vatican I decree *Pastor aeternus* bestows on the pope "the absolute fullness of supreme power." The text uses the Latin word *potestas,* which implies coercive, forceful, controlling power—power pure and simple—thus providing the theological underpinning for the modern papacy by giving the pope jurisdictional authority over the whole church. There is something almost demented about such a claim. The decree also defined papal infallibility, the claim that the pope is divinely protected from error when defining what the church believes. This means that the pope can't "make up" doctrine. In the end, he can only teach what the church already believes. But the definition of *primacy* is not hedged in like infallibility. It hands the church over to the pope, "lock, stock and barrel." With "the absolute fullness of supreme power," the pope can act in the church without check or hindrance, other than the law of God and the defined teaching of the church. And according to Vatican I, the pope is the final interpreter of both. This definition leads straight to the view that the pope owns the church, without any countervailing centers of authority to restore balance. In this theology, the pope equals the church and the church equals the pope. It is this unlimited, full expression of supreme power that I have explicitly addressed in this book—and rejected.

It was in this raw-power sense that popes like Innocent III (1198–1216) saw themselves as rulers of Europe, but their power was limited by their ability to project that force outward. No matter what medieval popes thought or taught, the lines of communication were only as fast as the speed at which news could travel, and by modern standards that was very slow. They also lacked the coercive ability to make that power work on the ground outside their own immediate bailiwick. There was always resistance from local bishops, church councils, priests, laypeople, and regional rulers. Up until the nineteenth century—the point at which this book began— papal claims to power ebbed and flowed. Popes were always limited theologically, legally, politically, and, above all, practically. Modern communications have given contemporary popes unimpeded ability to spread their instructions and make their presence felt.

Nowadays, several factors have coalesced to produce what I have called elsewhere an "omnipresent" papacy that is globally powerful and influential.[2] With instant communications and ubiquitous air travel, the popes can not only communicate their message but deliver it personally. No one understood this better than John Paul II. His heyday was the late twentieth century, the period before social media took over our lives. When people saw him on television, they felt he was an accessible figure who stood for a return to strong traditional values. He was no longer remote but present, a man of the people. But the focus was always on him; he was Catholicism personified. The role of the modern media in enhancing the power of the contemporary papacy has been largely neglected, but it is tremendously important. It has given the papacy the ability to project its power outward and to identify Catholicism with itself.

This leads me, as a Catholic, to ask another, specifically theological, question: Has the papacy become too powerful in the internal life of the church, so powerful, in fact, that the nature of the church has become distorted by supreme papal power as defined by Vatican I? This raises another question: Is this heresy? *Heresy* is not a word one tosses around lightly. Nevertheless, the question must be asked: Is the contemporary governance of Catholicism out of synchronicity with the Gospel, the teaching of Jesus, and the tradition of church government?

————————

THE SECOND VATICAN Council consciously tried to rebalance the unbalanced theology of Vatican I with its emphasis on the role of the bishops and the laity, the people of God. Its call for reunion with other Christians put Catholicism in contact with other forms of more representative, synodal, democratic styles of church governance. On a practical level, the council tried to rein in the bureaucratic and centralizing tendencies of the Vatican. To some extent that rebalancing worked, until 1978. But then for the long papacy of John Paul II (1978–2005) and that of Benedict XVI (2005–2013), the implementation of the reforms of Vatican II were stopped in their tracks, as a widespread attempt was made to wind back and "reform the reform." What has happened is that "the church moved away from its theological identity as a communion of eucharistic communions and became structured as a universal, corporate entity governed by a monarchical power," the papacy.[3] This rollback was partially reversed with the resignation of Benedict XVI and the election of Pope Francis. But "rolling back the rollback" is not easy, even with as charismatic a figure as Pope Francis.

In terms of the internal life of Catholicism, I will argue that the church needs a considerably humbler, less centralized papacy, with authority devolved downward to local communities. Bishops should be elected by their dioceses, and important decisions, including issues like worship, morality, and Christian living, should be decided by the very ancient notion of the *sensus fidelium* (sense of the faithful). This is difficult to define precisely because it refers to the instinctive, intuitive ability that believers have of discerning "right" teaching. Vatican II is very clear on this: "The body of the faithful as a whole . . . cannot err in matters of belief."[4] Another way of putting it is that the experience of faithful Catholics has to be a source for both church teaching and theology; as Cardinal John Henry Newman says, the faithful should be consulted in matters of belief. The notion of the "sense of the faithful" is closely related to the doctrine of reception. The acceptance or rejection of a papal or church teaching by the faithful validates or invalidates that teaching as true Catholic belief. If it is not accepted, then the magisterium (teaching authority) needs to go back to square one and ask why it was not accepted. This is precisely what needs to happen regarding the papal teaching on contraception in the encyclical *Humanae vitae*.

But where does an emphasis on the local church leave the papacy as an international geopolitical actor playing a role, as *Time* put it, "at the very center of the central conversations of our time about the issues that matter"? If papal power is limited theologically, what are the implications for popes as influential actors in ethical and geopolitical affairs? I argue that if the church were to address some of its pressing internal issues, like the role of women, the devolution of authority, the need for theological pluralism, a less centralized system, and the development of more democratic, consultative, accountable structures, then its credibility would be increased and its influence would become less dependent on the personality of the papal incumbent. It would be able to rely on the fact that Catholicism incorporates the values it proclaims. Joseph Nye argues powerfully that an institution that uses soft power to persuade others must manifest its core values within its own structure. "The resources that produce soft power," Nye says, "arise in large part from the values an organization . . . expresses in its culture, in the example it sets by its internal practices and policies, and the way it handles its relations with others."[5] So a humble, accountable papacy might well have more rather than less influence in the world at large.

Most Catholics appreciate Pope Francis and the way in which he is leading the church. But ironically, there is a sense in which he is even more dangerous to the development of local churches and a Vatican II vision than John Paul and Benedict. He is still pope, with all that that means, even though he is genuinely trying to make devolution of power to the local church a reality. Feminist theologian Mary Hunt says correctly that "all of the enthusiasm about Francis' style does not change the fact that the institutional Roman Catholic Church is a rigid hierarchy led by a pope—the warm feelings in response to Francis shore up that model of church by making the papacy itself look good." The modern papacy is still modeled on absolute monarchy, whether it is occupied by a superstar like John Paul, a culture warrior like Benedict, or a self-confessed sinner like Francis. The pope still absorbs so much of the church's oxygen, and the papacy still overshadows the local churches. "My concern," Hunt says, "is that this spate of marvellous press renders it harder, not easier, to make a case for a horizontal model of church."[6] While Francis might point in the right direction, what has to happen to give the local church a chance to breathe and prosper?

The history outlined in this book offers certain lessons. The papacy was at one of its weakest points in 1799. But it has an amazing ability to recover, and by 1870 it was theoretically claiming "the absolute fullness of supreme power" and by 2000 had achieved it in John Paul II. Never in church history had the popes been so powerful and influential as under John Paul. Medieval popes made all types of claims to unlimited authority, but they were nothing more than claims. It is often forgotten that medieval monarchies, including the papal monarchy, were never absolute. Medieval kings were hedged in by considerable limits on their power. The basic reason Thomas More protested against Henry VIII's seizure of control over the English church was not about papal authority but fundamentally because the king was acting beyond the traditional medieval limits on royal power. More was a legal traditionalist, and he saw himself as protecting the rights and privileges of England. Papal power was also seen as limited by a general council of the church that many in the early sixteenth century, including More, saw as superior to any pope.

Nowadays, papal power also knows how to use the media. The first pope to understand this was Pius IX. Early modern transportation—regular rail and shipping services—allowed people to come to Rome to see the pope personally. He made himself available in general audiences to give people a sense of personal closeness. Following him, Pius XI was smart enough to grasp the importance of radio in the 1930s, and, assisted by Marconi, he used radio as a means of getting his message out to people. Pius XII was a consummate communicator whose skills were evident in the way he projected a persona, an image of an almost godlike figure. He used print, radio, and film; television was still in its infancy in the 1950s. John XXIII was the first TV pope, and he had the perfect personality for it. He was a smiling, friendly man with a warm personality who exuded an acceptance of people, and viewers loved him as a kind of benign father figure. A shy, thoughtful man, Paul VI was never the media personality that his predecessors and successors were.

With John Paul II we entered an almost new papal reality. Not only did this man genuinely believe that he was especially chosen by God to be pope with the absolute power that accompanied that choice, but he also believed that God was calling him to save the church. Here was an iron-willed man who believed that he alone knew what was best for Catholicism and instinctively grasped how to achieve his vision. His endless world travels brought about "a shift at a deeper level of perception" because they made the pope "seem *present*. . . . He was no longer remote, like the 'quasi-divine' Pius XII, but a man of the people."[7] But the reality was that he only *seemed* present. Compounding the unreality was TV. Television loves big events, the bigger the spectacle or the crowd, the better. John Paul was a performer who knew exactly what to do with huge crowds. It never really mattered what he said. The medium was the message, and there he was at center stage. Everything was focused on him. The local church faded into insignificance. He also knew how to use gesture—adapting the liturgy to local customs, kissing the ground at airports, dancing and joining hands with young people, and responding to the spontaneity of those he met, particularly children. John Paul had a great ability to fit into a scene and dominate it. He was even able to use his suffering from Parkinson's disease and his dying as a public parable. He made absolute papal power a reality through media, especially television and big events.

This man turned the church into a one-man band and, in the process, did great harm by focusing attention on himself. Everything came back to the pope. He was Catholicism incorporated, take it or leave it. John Paul distorted traditional church government by turning it into an autocracy. The danger is that while Benedict XVI and Francis have been careful to avoid this fate, the way is still left open for another autocrat in the John Paul mold.

Lord Acton's aphorism in his 1887 letter to Anglican bishop Mandell Creighton of London discussing the Renaissance popes is right: "Power tends to corrupt and absolute power corrupts absolutely." Acton adds, "Great men are almost always bad." Absolute power has certainly corrupted the papacy and institutional church, so much so that nowadays it is a far cry from the humility of Jesus, who is the norm by which a Christian institution must judge itself. Catholicism is completely out of kilter when one aspect of church governance, the papacy, dominates and absorbs the whole. As Saint Paul says, the body of Christ is made up of head and members, and one cannot exist without the others. The simple fact is that the church needs to find a structure that is more in keeping with Jesus, the Gospel, and the New Testament. So what are we going to do? How are we going to get the papacy back into perspective?

It is not as though we don't have models on which to draw. As I pointed out earlier, on the night of his election Pope Francis said that the Roman *church*, not the Roman *pope*, presides in charity at the heart of Catholicism. Ignatius of Antioch's *Letter to the Romans* (ca. AD 110–115) says that Rome holds the presidency of love in the church, and this evolved into the notion that Rome was central to the Eucharistic concord of local churches throughout the world. Ignatius also recognizes in passing that the Roman church "instructs" others, which seems to refer to its emergence as the norm of orthodoxy. There is no doubt that from the earliest Christian times, the Roman church held a degree of preeminence as the capital of the empire and the place of the martyrdom of Saints Peter and Paul.

In fact, the early Roman church was itself a communion of communions. This was because the earliest Christian communities in the period after the New Testament followed the structure of the Jewish synagogue, because most of the early converts were Jews. First-century Rome was a very big city of about 1 million people, with a sizable Jewish population spread across fourteen or fifteen synagogues. The first Roman Christians would have been converts from these synagogues, and by about AD 100 we know there were already several Christian communities, each meeting regularly in their own place, in what today we would call a "house church." Each community had its own householder leader. These communities saw themselves not as separate but as intimately interconnected with each other, making up the whole reality of the Roman church. In smaller first-century cities, there was usually just one Christian community, so it was understandable that a single bishop appeared very early in these churches. For instance, the church in Antioch was founded very early and seems to have had a solo bishop before AD 100. In contrast, the first solo bishop in Rome was probably as late as Pius I (ca. 142–ca. 155) or even Eleutherius (ca. 174–189).

The model that emerges from all of this is the church as a communion of communions. The word *communion* is clearly linked to the Eucharist, which is the primal celebration of the community. The church was originally conceived of not as a vertical hierarchy from the pope down but as a local community in intercommunion with other local communities; the model was horizontal and circular. Hierarchical notions came much later and developed fully only after the church adopted Roman law in the Middle Ages. In the early church, we have a precedent that we can draw on as a model for today. Everything begins with the local community. Here Catholicism is most truly itself.

Gradually, the church also developed a system of synods, where local churches got together to decide local issues. The Orthodox, Anglican, and Protestant churches still retain this structure. Francis is clearly committed to making Catholicism more synodal, and he is using the World Synod of Bishops as a structure for a more collegial model of church governance. During the first millennium, synods were local, regional, and ecumenical (general). They were called by various people: local bishops, metropolitans (senior bishops of various regions), or even by laymen like Emperor Constantine, who called the Council of Nicaea in 325 when he was not even a baptized Christian. Various other councils have been called by laymen, including the Council of Constance (1414–1418) called by Emperor Sigismund. Synods as a form of decision making need to be recovered in Catholicism locally, regionally, and universally.

This means that decision-making power needs to be devolved. An example of this is liturgical translation. I have already mentioned the document *Liturgicam authenticam* (2001), which imposed a literal translation of the Latin of the liturgy. This has led to the turgid, pseudosacred "translation" being imposed on the entire English-speaking Catholic world. This fiasco proves that Rome has no role to play in issues like this, as Pope Francis has now recognized. These are decisions that should be made by English-speaking bishops and skilled laity. The sexual abuse crisis should also have been handled locally or regionally. Each country has its own legal system, and Rome's role should have been to step in to force bishops to deal with the issue proactively, but not to take the whole thing over.

Another decision that must be devolved to the local church is the selection of bishops. Pope Leo the Great (440–461), who certainly had a high notion of the papacy, says unequivocally that "he who is placed over all should be elected by all."[8] He himself had been elected by the clergy and people of Rome, so he supported the principle of episcopal election right across the church. People today in democratic societies are used to electing officials and politicians; we vote responsibly and peacefully. We would have no trouble electing our bishops; the Anglicans (Episcopalians) do it all the time, without much ado. The best system would be for an elected diocesan synod of clergy, laity, and religious to draw up a list of three names, with the bishops' conference usually approving the first name. Rome would not participate in the process unless there were disputes. I mentioned earlier that the gene pool for possible candidates for the episcopate is very shallow. Thus, the group of people from whom bishops could be elected and ordained needs to be expanded from just priests. There are precedents: the election of laymen as bishops was relatively common in the first seven centuries of the church, and the election of laypeople as bishops would be closely linked with the acceptance of married men into the priesthood. A famous example of a nonordained person being elected bishop is Ambrose of Milan. He was an administrator and lawyer, and, although already a believer, he was a nonbaptized catechumen at the time of election as bishop of Milan in AD 374. He became one of the greatest preachers of the age and was influential in the conversion of Saint Augustine.

Given that women do up to 75 percent of the church's pastoral work, their role as leaders and ordained ministers cannot be ignored. The priesthood has operated through various different models, and the meaning of ordination has changed throughout church history. The real question Catholicism faces is not so much whether women can be ordained but what ordination really means. Its present-day link with the celibate, clerical priesthood is on its last legs in the developed West, with only a tiny number of men presenting for seminary training for priesthood, many of them not really suitable for priestly ministry. The spike in the number of young men coming forward in developing countries for ordination will also decline as other opportunities beyond the church open up for ambitious, talented youngsters. It was just that the church was the first to offer a Western education and the chance for a male from a lower social order to become a "big man" as a priest or even a bishop.

The understanding of ordination today is different from that of the early church or the Middle Ages. So there's no reason that development in theological understanding cannot continue today and all ministries be opened to women. It is clear from recent historical work that the meaning of ordination has changed. For instance, the evidence is overwhelming that as late as the tenth century, women acted in roles that would now be confined to male priests. Historian Gary Macy has shown conclusively that female abbesses were ordained into their role and exercised priestly functions. Macy says that according to the understanding of the time, abbesses "were just as truly ordained as any bishop, priest or deacon."[9] The implication is that the meaning of ordination has changed. If so, it can change again. Pope Francis has opened a bigger can of worms than he might have imagined when he put the ordination of women to the deaconate on the agenda in 2017.

There is a sense in which these days, the parish is in crisis, and the great temptation for bishops is to close small parishes and absorb them into larger clusters. The fundamental reason is the shortage of priests. But many of these smaller communities are very viable because they have a committed group of people who have been loyal to their community through thick and thin. One bishop who has resisted the tendency to close parishes is Cardinal Reinhard Marx of Munich. Rather than closing local communities, he has set up a training program to develop "new models of parish leadership. Specifically, he said full-time and voluntary lay personnel would take over parishes."[10] Maintaining viable communities should be a priority, because it is so difficult to form intentional communities these days due to our highly individualistic society. The old common religious and social ties that held people together in structures like parishes have largely gone, so why throw away those that have survived? Certainly, some people still form intentional communities, groups that constellate around specific issues. The most common examples are people getting together to fight environmental issues, and already groups of Catholics are forming communities that constellate around the renewal of the church. The challenge is to form and maintain these kinds of intentional communities that are inspired by faith and formed around sacramental symbols, especially the Eucharist, that then go out into the world to be of service. This far less structured approach will need a flexible, dynamic leadership, not the type offered by clerical priests and bishops trained in the seminary system. The early church's house-church model may well provide a blueprint for many local communities of the future.

Turning to the contemporary papacy, Catholicism must deal with structural reform of this institution; it is inevitable, and the longer it is delayed, the more painful it will be. The first significant move was made by Benedict XVI when he resigned in 2013 and in a radically honest statement conceded that "after having repeatedly examined my conscience before God, I have come to the certainty that my strengths, due to an advanced age, are no longer suited to an adequate exercise of the Petrine ministry." It probably would have been better if he had retired to Germany and dropped the title "pope" altogether, but dealing with a retired pope is a whole new ball game. Benedict has opened the way for Francis and his successors to confront their mortality and resign when their strength is failing. There are probably grounds for a retiring age for popes.

There are also good reasons to extend the franchise for the election of the pope. This is an effective way of preventing sharp U-turns as one pope follows the other. So clearly, not only do bishops need to be elected by local churches, but the franchise for the election of the bishop of Rome also needs to be widened. There is no reason it is confined to the College of Cardinals. They have had the right to elect the pope only since the early thirteenth century. It was then that the clergy and people of Rome were totally excluded from the election process, but even then a precondition was that the Romans "accepted" the man elected. So essentially, for twelve hundred years popes were elected by the clergy and people. We need to recover that notion. Clearly, confining the election to cardinals is too narrow. At the very least, they need to be joined by the elected presidents of national and regional bishops' conferences. Others who could be drawn into the process are representatives of superiors general of religious orders, both men and women. It is hard to lay down a process for the participation of laity, but we need to find one whereby they can participate. And because the pope is primarily the bishop of Rome, the church of Rome must be given some say in the choice of their bishop.

It is not only the pope but also the Roman Curia that needs to be confronted. This bureaucratic incubus should be summarily swept away. Every attempt to "reform" it has failed dismally; it is irreformable and should be abolished and replaced by a smaller papal secretariat whose task would be to support the bishop of Rome in his ministry, not to micromanage the universal church. Totally new personnel, mainly laity with specialized skills, are needed to run this secretariat. Nevertheless, the Holy See should be maintained as an independent entity within the territory of the Vatican City State, with its international status and connections preserved. This is extremely important in terms of the soft-power influence of the church in the world. The Secretariat of State, with its strong diplomatic connections, is also useful. Suggestions of abolishing this form of soft power are misguided and are usually put forward by people with blinkered vision or an ax to grind. I believe that the papacy should maintain its influence for good in the world.

Finally, there is a sense that the story this book tells has come at a terrible cost to the message of Jesus. For the Christian, *Jesus probat omnia* (Jesus is the test of everything), to adapt a saying of Martin Luther. Jesus is certainly the test for the papacy and the church, and it will be true to itself only when it is true to him. That is something Catholicism constantly struggles to recover.

NOTES

Unless otherwise noted all biblical references are from the New Revised Standard Version (Division of Christian Education of the National Council of Churches of Christ in the USA, 1989).

All references to ecumenical councils are from Norman P. Tanner, ed., *Decrees of the Ecumenical Councils.*

Quotations from papal encyclicals, writings, and speeches are from the Vatican webpage or www.papalencyclicals.net.

A PERSONAL INTRODUCTION

1. For an account of my dealings with the CDF, see Paul Collins, *The Modern Inquisition.*

2. Pew Research Center, "America's Changing Religious Landscape," May 12, 2015, www.pewforum.org/2015/5/12/americas-changing -religious-landscape.

CHAPTER 1. A DEATH IN VALENCE

1. Adrien Dansette, *Religious History of Modern France*, 1:44.

2. Helen Maria Williams, *A Residence in France During the Years 1792, 1793, 1794 and 1795 and Letters Containing a Sketch of the Politics of France*, 2:25, 181.

3. E. E. Y. Hales, *Revolution and Papacy, 1769–1846*, 105.

4. John Martin Robinson, *Cardinal Consalvi, 1757–1824*, 66–73.

5. Colman J. Barry, ed., *Readings in Church History*, 13–15.

6. Fondation Napoléon, *Correspondance générale de Napoléon*, 6:450.

7. Bernardine Melchior-Bonnet, *Napoléon et le pape*, 122.

8. E. E. Y. Hales, *Napoleon and the Pope*, 157–158.

9. Robinson, *Cardinal Consalvi, 1757–1824*, 77.

10. John F. Pollard, *Money and the Rise of the Modern Papacy: Financing the Vatican, 1850–1950*, 25–26.

11. Robinson, *Cardinal Consalvi, 1757–1824*, 147.

CHAPTER 2. THE "NEW CONSCIOUSNESS" AND "NEO-ULTRAMONTANISM"

1. Kenneth Clark, *Civilization: A Personal View*, 274.

2. Hugues-Félicité de Lamennais, *Essay on Indifference in Matters of Religion*, 1:30.

3. Barry, *Readings in Church History*, 41.

4. John Henry Newman, *Letters and Diaries*, 231.

5. Roger Aubert, *Vatican I: Histoire des Conciles Ecumeniques*, 35 (author's translation).

6. Frank J. Coppa, *Cardinal Giacomo Antonelli and Papal Politics in European Affairs*, 35.

7. Roger Aubert quoted in Hubert Jedin and John J. Dolan, eds., *History of the Church*, 8:222, 223.

8. Barry, *Readings in Church History*, 70–74.

9. David I. Kertzer, *The Kidnapping of Edgardo Mortara*, 260.

10. Cuthbert Butler, *The Vatican Council, 1869–1870*, 49, 59–60.

11. Roger Aubert, *Le pontificat de Pie IX*, 302–304 (author's translation).

12. Butler, *Vatican Council*, 57–59.

13. Frederick William Faber, *Devotion to the Pope*, n.p.

14. Hubert Wolf, *The Nuns of Sant'Ambrogio: The True Story of a Convent in Scandal*.

15. Butler, *Vatican Council*, 89.

16. Aubert, *Vatican I*, 100–101.

17. Butler, *Vatican Council*, 158, 236–239.

18. Norman P. Tanner, *Decrees of the Ecumenical Councils*, 807 (emphasis added).

19. Aubert quoted in Jedin and Dolan, *History of the Church*, 8:325.

20. Paul Collins, *Papal Power: A Proposal for Change in Catholicism's Third Millennium*, 159–185.

21. Butler, *Vatican Council*, 330, 332.

22. Tanner, *Ecumenical Councils*, 814–815 (emphasis added).

23. Butler, *Vatican Council*, 345.

24. Ulrich Horst, *The Dominicans and the Pope: Papal Teaching Authority in the Medieval and Early Modern Thomist Tradition*.

25. Butler, *Vatican Council*, 352.

26. August Bernhard Hasler, *How the Pope Became Infallible: Pius IX and the Politics of Persuasion*, 89–92.

27. Luis M. Bermejo, *Infallibility on Trial: Church, Conciliarity and Communion*, 132–133; Butler, *Vatican Council*, 355.

28. Butler, *Vatican Council*, 413.

29. Tanner, *Ecumenical Councils*, 816.

30. Janus [Ignaz Döllinger], *The Pope and the Council*, 49; Brian Tierney, *The Origins of Papal Infallibility, 1150–1350: A Study on the Concepts of Infallibility, Sovereignty and Tradition in the Middle Ages*, 281.

31. Paul Collins quoted in Hans Küng and Leonard Swidler, eds., *The Church in Anguish: Has the Vatican Betrayed Vatican II?*, 52, 56.

CHAPTER 3. TACKLING A WHOLE NEW WORLD

1. Bruce Duncan, *The Church's Social Teaching: From Rerum novarum to 1931*, 52.
2. Denis Mack Smith, *Italy: A Modern History*, 98.
3. Dansette, *Religious History*, 2:33.
4. David Thomson, *Europe Since Napoleon*, 455.
5. James Hennesey, *American Catholics: A History of the Roman Catholic Community in the United States*, 197.
6. John Ireland, *The Church and Modern Society*, 369.
7. Hennesey, *American Catholics*, 199.
8. Margaret Mary Reher, "Pope Leo XIII and 'Americanism,'" 686.
9. Duncan, *Church's Social Teaching*, 34.
10. John Molony, *The Worker Question: A New Historical Perspective on Rerum novarum*, 51–60.

CHAPTER 4. "GOD AND THE REVOLVER!"

1. Paul Collins, *Upon This Rock: The Popes and Their Changing Rome*, 254.
2. Congregation for the Doctrine of the Faith, *To Promote and Safeguard the Faith*, 2.
3. Richard R. Gaillardetz, "In the Service of the People," *Tablet*, April 16, 2016.
4. Jedin and Dolan, *History of the Church*, 9:386.
5. George E. Griener, "Herman Schell and the Reform of the Catholic Church in Germany," 438, 439.
6. Alfred Loisy, *The Gospel and the Church*, 211.
7. Maurice Blondel, *Letter on Apologetics and the History of Dogma*, 221.
8. Jedin and Dolan, *History of the Church*, 9:444.
9. David Schultenover, *A View from Rome: On the Eve of the Modernist Crisis*, 111–112, 208–216.
10. Ibid., 149.
11. George Tyrrell, *The Church and the Future*, 32–34, 153–154.
12. M. D. Petre, *Autobiography and Life of George Tyrrell*, 255.
13. *Acta Sanctae Sedis* 40 (1907): 266–269 (author's translation), www.vatican.va/archive/ass-40-1907-ocr.pdf.
14. Barry, *Readings in Church History*, 112–120.
15. Gabriel Daly, *Transcendence and Immanence: A Study in Catholic Modernism and Integralism*, 232–234.
16. Ibid., 198–199.

17. All quotations from *Lamentabili* and *Pascendi* are from H. Denzinger and A. Schrönmetzer, *Enchiridion Symbolorum, definitionum et declarationum de rebus fidei et morum*, 3537–3550 (author's translation).

18. *Times*, September 30, 1907; George Tyrrell to Augustin Leger, December 24, 1907, in Petre, *Autobiography and Life of Tyrrell*, 339–340.

19. Mercier's Pastoral in George Tyrrell, *Medievalism: A Reply to Cardinal Mercier*, 9.

20. Ibid., 111–112.

21. Gabriel Daly, letter to the editor, *Tablet*, July 16, 2016.

22. Schultenover, *View from Rome*, 180–188, 242.

23. Emile Poulat, *Catholicisme, démocratie et socialisme: Le movement catholique et Mgr Benigni de la naissance du socialisme a la victoire du fascism*, 116.

24. *La Croix*, August 12, 1910.

25. Giordano Guerri, *Eretico e profeta: Ernesto Buonaiuti, un prete contro la Chiesa*, 3.

26. John Molony, *The Father of Social Democracy: Don Luigi Sturzo*, 19.

27. Jedin and Dolan, *History of the Church*, 9:452.

28. Molony, *Father of Social Democracy*, 30.

29. Pius X, *Notre charge apostolique*, August 25, 1910, www.papalencyclicals.net./piusx/10.notre.htm.

30. J. N. D. Kelly, *The Oxford Dictionary of Popes*, 314.

31. Aubert in Jedin and Dolan, *History of the Church*, 9:387–388.

32. Owen Chadwick, *History of the Popes, 1830–1914*, 357.

CHAPTER 5. "*OBBEDIRE*, OBEY"

1. John F. Pollard, *The Unknown Pope: Benedict XV (1914–1922) and the Pursuit of Peace*, 62, 64.

2. Agnes de Dreuzy, *The Holy See and the Emergence of the Modern Middle East: Benedict XV's Diplomacy in Greater Syria (1914–1922)*, 28, 29.

3. Smith, *Italy: A Modern History*, 298–299, 300–301.

4. *Text of Treaty* (London: His Majesty's Stationery Office, 1920), Article 15.

5. Ronald G. Musto, *The Catholic Peace Tradition*, 171, 172.

6. Pollard, *Unknown Pope*, 113.

7. A. Scott Berg, *Wilson*, 438.

8. *Peace Action of Benedict XV*, 9–12.

9. Woodrow Wilson, "Letter of Reply to the Pope," August 27, 1917, in Gerhard Peters and John T. Woolley, American Presidency Project, www.presidency.ucsb.edu/ws/?pid=65401.

10. Pollard, *Unknown Pope*, 130–131.

11. https://virus.stanford.edu/uda/.

12. Joseph McAuley, "Pope and President, Benedict XV and Woodrow Wilson: 'Are There Any Catholics Here?'"

13. Tim Pat Coogan, *Michael Collins: A Biography*, 202.

14. *Tablet*, May 28, 1921; Brenda Niall, *Mannix*, 173.

15. H. Eugene Bovis, *The Jerusalem Question, 1917–1968*, 6–7.

16. John Pollard, *The Fascist Experience in Italy*, 40.

17. Smith, *Italy: A Modern History*, 326, 327.

18. Pollard, *Unknown Pope*, 155.

19. Stewart A. Stehlin, *Weimar and the Vatican, 1919–1933: German-Vatican Diplomatic Relations in the Interwar Years*, 54–55.

20. Pollard, *Money and the Rise of the Modern Papacy*, 125. See also 110–115.

21. Jedin and Dolan, *History of the Church*, 9:403.

22. *Maximum illud*, www.svdcuria.org/public/mission/docs/encycl/mi-en.htm.

23. Pollard, *Unknown Pope*, 207.

24. Smith, *Italy: A Modern History*, 340.

25. *Tablet*, February 11, 1922.

26. Anthony Rhodes, *The Vatican in the Age of the Dictators, 1922–1945*, 19.

27. *Tablet*, February 11, 1922.

28. Molony, *Father of Social Democracy*, 125.

29. John Pollard, *The Papacy in the Age of Totalitarianism, 1914–1958*, 139.

30. Giuseppe Pizzardo, *The Pope and Catholic Action*.

31. George L. Mosse, *The Fascist Revolution: Toward a General Theory of Fascism*, 11.

32. Rocco in Rhodes, *Vatican in the Age of the Dictators*, 32–33.

33. David I. Kertzer, *The Pope and Mussolini: The Secret History of Pius XI and the Rise of Fascism in Europe*, 90–97.

34. *Time*, July 22, 1946.

35. www.state.gov/r/pa/ei/bgn/3819.htm.

36. Pollard, *Papacy in the Age of Totalitarianism*, 161n1.

37. Duncan, *Church's Social Teaching*, 120.

38. *New York Times*, February 13, 1931.

39. Rhodes, *Vatican in the Age of the Dictators*, 60.

40. Julio de la Cueva, "Religious Persecution, Anticlerical Tradition and Revolution: On Atrocities Against the Clergy During the Spanish Civil War," 355, 361, 369.

41. Catholic Truth Society, *The Spanish Terror*.

42. Rhodes, *Vatican in the Age of the Dictators*, 124.

43. William L. Patch, *Heinrich Brüning and the Dissolution of the Weimar Republic*, 295.

44. Hubert Wolf, *Pope and Devil: The Vatican's Archives and the Third Reich*, 172–173, 178 (quote).

45. Gerhard Besier, *The Holy See and Hitler's Germany*, 166.

46. Jim Castelli, "Unpublished Encyclical Attacked Anti-Semitism," *National Catholic Reporter*, December 15, 22, 1972, and January 19, 1973; Georges Passelecq and Bernard Suchecky, *The Hidden Encyclical of Pius XI.*

47. Wolf, *Pope and Devil*, 211, 206.

CHAPTER 6. PONTIFICATING ON EVERYTHING

1. Holy See webpage, www.vatican.va/archive/index_en.htm.

2. Robert A. Ventresca, *Soldier of Christ: The Life of Pius XII*, 4, 6.

3. Jacques Kornberg, *The Pope's Dilemma: Pius XII Faces Atrocities and Genocide in the Second World War*, 8–9.

4. www.ewtn.com/library/papaldoc/p12ch42.htm.

5. Carlo Falconi, *The Silence of Pius XII.*

6. Paul O'Shea, *A Cross Too Heavy: Eugenio Pacelli—Politics and the Jews of Europe, 1917–1943*, 328.

7. Kornberg, *Pope's Dilemma*, 119–120.

8. O'Shea, *Cross Too Heavy*, 332, 334.

9. Ernst von Weizsäcker, *Memoirs of Ernst von Weizsäcker*, 60.

10. Mark Reibling, *Church of Spies: The Pope's Secret War Against Hitler*, 248, 28.

11. Ventresca, *Soldier of Christ*, 303.

12. John Cornwell, *Hitler's Pope: The Secret History of Pius XII*, 343.

13. Paul I. Murphy with R. Rene Arlington, *La Popessa: The Controversial Biography of Sister Pascalina, the Most Powerful Woman in Vatican History*, 218–219, 244–246.

14. Paul Collins, *Judgment Day: The Struggle for Life on Earth*, 187–190.

15. Giancarlo Zizola, *Il microfono di Dio: Pio XII, padre Lombardi e i cattolici italiani.*

16. *Tablet*, October 18, 1958.

17. Ibid.

18. Peter Hebblethwaite, *John XXII: Pope of the Council*, 270.

CHAPTER 7. GOOD POPE JOHN

1. John XXIII biography, http://w2.vatican.va/content/johnxxiii/en/biography/documents.

2. Meriol Trevor, *Pope John*, 132n; Gianni Gennari, "That Modernist Heretic Friend of Pope John XXIII's," *Vatican Insider* (August 29, 2013).

3. Hebblethwaite, *John XXIII*, 124.

4. Ibid., 169, 196.

5. Trevor, *Pope John*, 228.

6. James Martin, "Blessed Angelo Roncalli"; Trevor, *Pope John*, 208.

7. Trevor, *Pope John*, 244.

8. Hebblethwaite, *John XXIII*, 290.

9. John XXIII, *Acta Apostolicae Sedis* 51 (1959): 68.

10. Ibid.; Giancarlo Zizola, *The Utopia of Pope John XXIII*, 240; Yves Congar, *My Journal of the Council*, viii, 11.

11. Congar, *My Journal*, 299.

12. Oscar Beozzo quoted in Giuseppe Alberigo and Joseph Komonchak, eds., *History of Vatican II*, 1:386.

13. Xavier Rynne, *Letters from Vatican City*, 40.

14. Ibid., 4.

15. Congar, *My Journal*, 4.

16. Arthur J. Schlesinger Jr., *A Thousand Days: John F. Kennedy in the White House*, 825.

17. Zizola, *Utopia of John XXIII*, 3–10.

18. Brian Hehir in de Dreuzy, *Vatican and the Modern Middle East*, 111.

CHAPTER 8. "THROWING OPEN THE WINDOWS"

1. *Acta Apostolicae Sedis* 54 (1962): 786–796 (author's translation).

2. Congar, *My Journal*, 14.

3. Ibid., 87.

4. Alberigo and Komonchak, *History of Vatican II*, 2:12.

5. Ibid., 1.

6. Ibid., 3:127.

7. Xavier Rynne, *The Second Session*, 188–189.

8. Xavier Rynne, *The Third Session*, 292.

9. John-Peter Pham, *Heirs of the Fisherman. Behind the Scenes of Papal Death and Succession*, 122–124.

10. Congar, *My Journal*, 305.

11. See Karl Rahner, *The Church and the Sacraments*.

12. René Laurentin quoted in P. Huizing and K. Walf, eds., *The Roman Curia and the Communion of Churches*, 96.

13. Morris West, "One Man's Voice."

14. Peter Hebblethwaite, *Paul VI: The First Modern Pope*.

15. Alberigo and Komonchak, *History of Vatican II*, 4:310.

16. Ibid., 5:373.

17. *Canberra Times*, August 5, 1968.

18. Cormac Murphy-O'Connor, *An English Spring: Memoirs*, 78.

19. Christian Duquoc quoted in Giuseppe Alberigo, ed., *The Reception of Vatican II*, 298.

CHAPTER 9. THE POLISH COLOSSUS

1. ABC Radio National, *The Religion Report*, March 17, 2004; Paul Collins, *Mixed Blessings: John Paul II and the Church of the Eighties*, 154–165.

2. John Paul II, *Love and Responsibility*, 121.

3. Collins, *Judgment Day*, 11.

4. John Paul II, "The Mystery of Woman Revealed in Motherhood," *L'Osservatore Romano*, March 17, 1980.

5. George Weigel, *Witness to Hope: The Biography of John Paul II*, 343.

6. BBC One, "The Secret Letters of John Paul II," on *Panorama*, February 15, 2016.

7. Carl Bernstein and Marco Politi, *His Holiness: John Paul II and the Hidden History of Our Time*, 135.

8. Ibid., 131–133, 135.

9. John Paul II, *Sources of Renewal: The Implementation of the Second Vatican Council*.

10. Stanislaw Obriek quoted in Sabrina Ramet and Irena Borowik, eds., *Religion, Politics and Values in Poland: Continuity and Change Since 1989*, 47.

11. John Paul II, *Sign of Contradiction*, 11.

12. John Paul II, "Take Holy Pride in Being 'Other Christs,'" *L'Osservatore Romano*, July 21, 1999.

13. Zbigniew Kaźmierczak, *Alter Christus: Krytyczna rekonstrukcja światopoglądu Jana Pawła II* (English summary).

14. Ibid.

15. Zbigniew Kaźmierczak, *Jan Paweł II w labiryncie ciała* (English summary).

16. Bernstein and Politi, *His Holiness*, 145.

17. Peter Popham, "In the Roman Sun the Cult of John Paul II Is Born," *Independent*, April 4, 2005.

18. *Against Ratzinger*, 38.

19. Nigel West, *The Third Secret: The CIA, Solidarity and the KGB's Plot to Kill the Pope*, passim and 17–57.

20. John Paul II, *Insegnamenti di Giovanni Paolo*, 17:1061.

21. Tad Szulc, *John Paul II: The Biography*, 378.

22. Weigel, *Witness to Hope*, 643–644.

23. John A. Dick, "Cleric Who Shaped US 'Pastoral Church' Dead at 99," *National Catholic Reporter*, January 21, 2009.

24. Joseph Ratzinger, "The Pastoral Implications of Collegiality," 30; John L. Allen, *Cardinal Ratzinger: The Vatican's Enforcer of the Faith*, 63.

25. Congar, *My Journal*, 543–544.

26. Ronald Modras, *The Catholic Church and Antisemitism: Poland, 1933–1939*, 34.

27. Szulc, *John Paul II*, 484.

28. Collins, *The Modern Inquisition*, 80–108.

29. http://vatican.va/roman_curia/congregations/cfaith/documents/rc_con_cfaith_doc_20020124_dupuis_en.html.

30. Francis A. Sullivan, "The Impact of *Dominus Jesus* on Ecumenism."

31. Michael Walsh, *John Paul II: A Biography*, 272.

32. Weigel, *Witness to Hope*, 334–343.

33. Jason Berry and Gerald Renner, *Vows of Silence: The Abuse of Power in the Papacy of John Paul II*, 125–221; Jason Berry, "Francis Heads to Mexico amid Legionaries of Christ Disclosures," *National Catholic Reporter*, February 8, 2016, translates and quotes Raúl Olmos, *El imperio financiero de los Legionarios de Christo*.

34. Berry, "Francis Heads to Mexico."

35. Thomas Doyle, "Records Show That John Paul II Could Have Intervened in Abuse Crisis—but Didn't," *National Catholic Reporter*, April 25, 2014.

36. Royal Commission into Institutional Responses to Child Sexual Abuse, Case Study 31, August 24, 2015, www.childabuseroyalcommission.gov.au.

37. Thomas Reese, "Can a Pope Resign?," *National Catholic Reporter*, February 11, 2013.

38. *New York Times*, April 3, 2005.

CHAPTER 10. "REFORM OF THE REFORM"

1. *Independent*, September 3, 2012.

2. Pham, *Heirs of the Fisherman*, 159.

3. *Tablet*, April 30, 2005.

4. *Guardian*, April 21, 2005.

5. Hans Küng, "The Result of the Papal Election," www.logosjournal.com/kung_special.htm; Uta Ranke-Heinemann, "A Humble Intellect," www.beliefnet.com/faiths/catholic/2005/04/a-humble-intellect.aspx?

6. For Ratzinger's intellectual development, see Paul Collins, *God's New Man: The Election of Benedict XVI and the Legacy of John Paul II*, 137–192.

7. Karl Rahner and Joseph Ratzinger, *The Episcopate and the Primacy*, 37–63.

8. Peter Seewald, *Salt of the Earth: Christianity and the Catholic Church at the End of the Millennium*, 47.

9. Marie Keenan, *Sexual Abuse and the Catholic Church: Gender, Power and Organizational Culture*, 255.

10. http://vatican.va/news_services/liturgy/2005/documents/no_lit_doc_20050325_via-crucis_en.html.

11. http://vatican.va/content/benedict-xvi/en/speeches/2005/December/documents/hf_ben_xvi_spe_200551222_roman-curia.html.

12. Massimo Faggioli, *Vatican II: The Battle for Meaning*, 24; see also 24–35.

13. Ibid., 66–90.

14. Karl Rahner, *The Shape of the Church to Come*, 45–89.

15. *Quattuor abhinc annos*, in *L'Osservatore Romano* (English edition), October 22, 1984.

16. John Paul II, apostolic letter, *Ecclesia Dei*, July 2, 1988; SSPX website, www.laportelatine.org/quisommesnous/statistiques/stat.php.

17. http://catholic-en.org.uk/home/news/2006/full-text-of-the-pope-benedict-xvi-s-regensburg-lecture.

18. Theodore Khoury, *Manuel II Paléologue: Entretiens avec un Musulman*.

19. Ana Belén Soage, "The Muslim Reaction to Pope Benedict XVI's Regensburg Address."

20. Jane Kramer, "The Pope and Islam."

21. Anthony Ruff, *Pray Tell*, October 31, 2010, www.praytellblog.com/index,php/2010/10/31/the-report-leaked; Peter Jeffery, *Translating Tradition: A Chant Historian Reads "Liturgicam authenticam,"* 100–101.

22. Benedict XVI, *Last Testament: In His Own Words*, 208.

23. John L. Allen, "Benedict XVI a Pope of Ironies," *National Catholic Reporter*, April 20, 2012.

24. Sandro Magister, "The Devil Has Retired," February 1, 2016, www.chiesa.espressonline.it.

25. Council of Europe, *Anti-money Laundering and Combating the Financing of Terrorism: The Holy See (Including the Vatican City State)*, July 4, 2012, executive summary.

26. Benedict XVI, *Last Testament*, 16–17.

27. Ibid., 23.

CHAPTER 11. THE "FIELD HOSPITAL"

1. Vatican Radio, March 27, 2013, unofficial translation.

2. *Vatican Insider*, March 13, 2014.

3. Paul Vallely, *Pope Francis: Untying the Knots*, 166.

4. *New York Times*, September 18, 2015.

5. CELAM 2007, Aparecida document, para. 84, 61, 396, celam.org/aparecida/Ingles.pdf.

6. Austen Ivereigh, "How Fidel's Faith Remained a Mystery to the End," *Crux*, November 26, 2016.

7. Edgar Morin, "L'encyclique *Laudato si'* est peut-être l'acte 1 d'un appel pour une nouvelle civilisation," *Le Croix*, June 23, 2015.

8. Ross Douthat, "Pope Francis Call to Action Goes Beyond the Environment," *New York Times*, June 20, 2015.

9. www.aleteia.org/2015/02/25/african-archbishop-lays-down -daring-challenge-for-synod-on-the-family.

10. *Commonweal*, October 27, 2015.

11. *National Catholic Reporter*, January 9, 2017.

12. *Settimo Cielo di Sandro Magister*, February 1, 2017.

13. Catholic News Agency, April 29, 2016.

14. Catholic News Service, July 7, 2016.

15. Richard R. Gaillardetz, "Growing Pains," *Tablet*, February 23, 2017.

16. Emiliano Fittipaldi, *Avarizia: Le carte che svelano ricchezza, scandali e segreti della chiesa di Francesco*; Gianluigi Nuzzi, *Merchants in the Temple: Inside Pope Francis's Secret Battle Against Corruption in the Vatican*.

17. Joshua J. McElwee, "Cardinal Müller Responds to Collins and Defends Not Answering Survivor's Letters," *Vatican Insider*, March 9, 2017.

18. *Tablet*, December 11, 2014.

19. www.futurechurch.org/future-of-priestly-ministry/optional -celibacy/priest-shortage-at-a-glance.

20. Eric Hodgens, www.catholicview.typepad.comatholic_view/priest seminarian-demographics.

21. Personal communication, mid-1970s.

22. *Tablet*, February 18, 2017.

23. Paul Collins, *And Also with You: Is the New English Version of the Mass a Betrayal of Vatican II?*, 25.

CHAPTER 12. DEATH AND RESURRECTION

1. Stehlin, *Weimar and the Vatican*, vii–viii; Prosper of Aquitaine, *Epitoma Chronicon, an 452*; J. H. Robinson, *Readings in European History*, 1, 49.

2. Paul Collins, "The Peripatetic Pope," in *Church in Anguish*, edited by Küng and Swidler, 52.

3. Richard Gaillardetz and John Heuls, "The Selection of Bishops: Exploring Canonical Alternatives," 17.

4. Constitution on the Church, 12.

5. *Time*, December 11, 2013; Joseph S. Nye, *Soft Power: The Means to Success in World Politics*, 8.

6. Mary Hunt, "The Trouble with Francis: Three Things That Worry Me," *Religion Dispatches* (January 10, 2014).

7. Collins, "The Peripatetic Pope," 54.

8. Leo I, letter 10, quoted in Jacques Paul Migne, *Patrologiae cursus completus*, 54, 634 (author's translation).

9. Gary Macy, *The Hidden History of Women's Ordination: Female Clergy and the Medieval West*, 86.

10. *La Croix*, March 27, 2017.

BIBLIOGRAPHY

Against Ratzinger. New York: Seven Stories Press, 2008.

Alberigo, Giuseppe, ed. *The Reception of Vatican II.* Washington, DC: Catholic University of America Press, 1987.

Alberigo, Giuseppe, and Joseph Komonchak, eds. *History of Vatican II.* 5 vols. English translation. Maryknoll, NY: Orbis, 1995–2006.

Allen, John L. *Cardinal Ratzinger: The Vatican's Enforcer of the Faith.* New York: Continuum, 2002.

Aubert, Roger. *Le pontificat de Pie IX.* Paris: Bloud et Gay, 1952.

———. *Vatican I: Histoire des Conciles Ecumeniques.* Vol. 12. Paris: Editions de l'Orante, 1964.

Barry, Colman J., ed. *Readings in Church History.* Vol. 3. Westminster, MD: Newman Press, 1963.

Baumgartner, Frederic J. *Behind Locked Doors: A History of Papal Elections.* New York: Palgrave Macmillan, 2003.

Benedict XVI. *Last Testament: In His Own Words.* English translation. London: Bloomsbury, 2016.

Berg, A. Scott. *Wilson.* New York: G. P. Putnam's Sons, 2014.

Bermejo, Luis M. *Infallibility on Trial: Church, Conciliarity and Communion.* Westminster, MD: Christian Classics, 1992.

Bernstein, Karl, and Marco Politi. *His Holiness: John Paul II and the Hidden History of Our Time.* New York: Doubleday, 1996.

Berry, Jason, and Gerald Renner. *Vows of Silence: The Abuse of Power in the Papacy of John Paul II.* New York: Free Press, 2004.

Bertone, Cardinal Tarcisio. *The Last Secret of Fatima.* New York: Doubleday, 2008.

Besier, Gerhard. *The Holy See and Hitler's Germany.* English translation. Basingstoke: Palgrave Macmillan, 2007.

Blondel, Maurice. *Letter on Apologetics and the History of Dogma.* English translation. London: Harvill Press, 1964.

Bovis, H. Eugene. *The Jerusalem Question, 1917–1968.* Stanford, CA: Hoover Institution Press, 1971.

Butler, Cuthbert. *The Vatican Council, 1869–1870.* 1930. Reprint, London: Collins, 1960.

Catholic Association for International Peace. *Peace Action of Benedict XV*. Washington, DC: Catholic Association for International Peace, n.d.

Catholic Truth Society. *The Spanish Terror*. London: Catholic Truth Society, 1936.

Chadwick, Owen. *History of the Popes, 1830–1914*. Oxford: Clarendon Press, 1998.

Clark, Kenneth. *Civilization: A Personal View*. London: BBC, 1969.

Collins, Paul. *And Also with You: Is the New English Version of the Mass a Betrayal of Vatican II?* Canberra: Catholics for Ministry, 2009.

———. *God's New Man: The Election of Benedict XVI and the Legacy of John Paul II*. London: Continuum, 2005.

———. *Judgment Day: The Struggle for Life on Earth*. New York: Orbis, 2011.

———. *Mixed Blessings: John Paul II and the Church of the Eighties*. Ringwood, Victoria: Penguin, 1986.

———. *The Modern Inquisition*. Woodstock, NY: Overlook Press, 2002.

———. *Papal Power: A Proposal for Change in Catholicism's Third Millennium*. London: Fount, 1997.

———. *Upon This Rock: The Popes and Their Changing Rome*. New York: Crossroad, 2000.

Congar, Yves. *My Journal of the Council*. English translation. Adelaide: ATF Theology, 2012.

Congregation for the Doctrine of the Faith. *To Promote and Safeguard the Faith*. Vatican City: Libreria Editrice Vaticana, 2015.

Coogan, Tim Pat. *Michael Collins: A Biography*. London: Hutchinson, 1990.

Coppa, Frank J. *Cardinal Giacomo Antonelli and Papal Politics in European Affairs*. Albany: State University of New York Press, 1990.

———. *The Life and Pontificate of Pope Pius XII: Between History and Controversy*. Washington, DC: Catholic University of America Press, 2013.

Cornwell, John. *Hitler's Pope: The Secret History of Pius XII*. London: Viking, 1999.

———. *A Thief in the Night: The Mysterious Death of John Paul I*. London: Penguin, 1989.

Daly, Gabriel. *Transcendence and Immanence: A Study in Catholic Modernism and Integralism*. Oxford: Clarendon Press, 1980.

Dansette, Adrien. *Religious History of Modern France*. English translation. Edinburgh: Nelson, 1961.

de Dreuzy, Agnes. *The Holy See and the Emergence of the Modern Middle East: Benedict XV's Diplomacy in Greater Syria (1914–1922)*. Washington, DC: Catholic University of America Press, 2016.

de la Cueva, Julio. "Religious Persecution, Anticlerical Tradition and Revolution: On Atrocities Against the Clergy During the Spanish Civil War." *Journal of Contemporary History* 33 (1998).

Denzinger, H., and A. Schrönmetzer. *Enchiridion Symbolorum, definitionum et declarationum de rebus fidei et morum.* Freiburg: Herder, 1911.

Duncan, Bruce. *The Church's Social Teaching: From Rerum novarum to 1931.* North Blackburn: Collins Dove, 1991.

Faber, Frederick William. *Devotion to the Pope.* London: Thomas Richardson, 1860.

Faggioli, Massimo. *Vatican II: The Battle for Meaning.* New York: Paulist Press, 2012.

Falconi, Carlo. *The Silence of Pius XII.* English translation. London: Faber, 1970.

Fittipaldi, Emiliano. *Avarizia: Le carte che svelano ricchezza, scandali e segreti della chiesa di Francesco.* Rome: Feltrinelli, 2015.

Fondation Napoléon. *Correspondance générale de Napoléon.* Paris: Fayard, 2009.

Gaillardetz, Richard, and John Heuls. "The Selection of Bishops: Exploring Canonical Alternatives." www.richardgaillardetz.files.wordpress.com/2014/04/election_of_bishops.pdf.

Griener, George E. "Herman Schell and the Reform of the Catholic Church in Germany." *Theological Studies* 54 (1993): 427–454.

Guerri, Giordano. *Eretico e profeta: Ernesto Buonaiuti, un prete contro la Chiesa.* Milan: Mondadori, 2001.

Hales, E. E. Y. *Napoleon and the Pope.* London: Eyre and Spottiswoode, 1966.

———. *Revolution and Papacy, 1769–1846.* Notre Dame, IN: University of Notre Dame Press, 1966.

Hasler, August Bernhard. *How the Pope Became Infallible: Pius IX and the Politics of Persuasion.* English translation. New York: Doubleday, 1981.

Hebblethwaite, Peter. *John XXIII: Pope of the Council.* London: Geoffrey Chapman, 1984.

———. *Paul VI: The First Modern Pope.* London: HarperCollins, 1996.

Hennesey, James. *American Catholics: A History of the Roman Catholic Community in the United States.* New York: Oxford University Press. 1981.

Horst, Ulrich. *The Dominicans and the Pope: Papal Teaching Authority in the Medieval and Early Modern Thomist Tradition.* English translation. Notre Dame, IN: University of Notre Dame Press, 2006.

Huizing, P., and K. Walf, eds. *The Roman Curia and the Communion of Churches.* New York: Seabury, 1979.

Ireland, John. *The Church and Modern Society.* New York: D. H. McBride, 1897.

Janus [Ignaz Döllinger]. *The Pope and the Council.* English translation. London: Rivington, 1870.

Jedin, Hubert, and John J. Dolan, eds. *History of the Church*. Vol. 8, *The Church in the Age of Liberalism*. London: Burns & Oates, 1981.

———. *History of the Church*. Vol. 9, *The Church in the Industrial Age*. New York: Crossroad, 1981.

Jeffery, Peter. *Translating Tradition: A Chant Historian Reads "Liturgicam authenticam."* Collegeville, MN: Liturgical Press, 2005.

John Paul II. *Insegnamenti di Giovanni Paolo*. Vol. 17. Vatican: Libreria Editrice Vaticana.

———. *Love and Responsibility*. English translation. New York: Farrar, Straus and Giroux, 1981.

———. *Sign of Contradiction*. English translation. New York: Seabury, 1979.

———. *Sources of Renewal: The Implementation of the Second Vatican Council*. English translation. San Francisco: Harper & Row, 1980.

John XXIII. *Journal of a Soul*. English translation. London: Geoffrey Chapman, 1965.

Kaźmierczak, Zbigniew. *Alter Christus: Krytyczna rekonstrukcja światopoglądu Jana Pawła II*. Kraków: Universitas, 2015.

———. *Jan Paweł II w labiryncie ciała*. Warsaw: Instytut Wydawniczy, 2014.

Keenan, Marie. *Sexual Abuse and the Catholic Church: Gender, Power and Organizational Culture*. New York: Oxford University Press, 2012.

Kelly, J. N. D. *The Oxford Dictionary of Popes*. Oxford: Oxford University Press, 1986.

Kertzer, David I. *The Kidnapping of Edgardo Mortara*. New York: Alfred A. Knopf, 1997.

———. *The Pope and Mussolini: The Secret History of Pius XI and the Rise of Fascism in Europe*. New York: Random House, 2014.

Khoury, Theodore. *Manuel II Paléologue: Entretiens avec un Musulman*. 7e Controverse, Sources Chrétiennes, 115. Paris: Éditions du Cerf, 1966.

Kornberg, Jacques. *The Pope's Dilemma: Pius XII Faces Atrocities and Genocide in the Second World War*. Toronto: University of Toronto Press, 2015.

Kramer, Jane. "The Pope and Islam." *New Yorker*, April 2, 2007.

Küng, Hans, and Leonard Swidler, eds. *The Church in Anguish: Has the Vatican Betrayed Vatican II?* San Francisco: Harper & Row, 1987.

Lamennais, Hugues-Félicité de. *Essay on Indifference in Matters of Religion*. English translation. London: John Macqueen, 1895.

Loisy, Alfred. *The Gospel and the Church*. English translation. London: Isbister, 1903.

Macy, Gary. *The Hidden History of Women's Ordination: Female Clergy and the Medieval West*. New York: Oxford University Press, 2008.

Martin, James. "Blessed Angelo Roncalli." *America* (October 11, 2010).

McAuley, Joseph. "Pope and President, Benedict XV and Woodrow Wilson: 'Are There Any Catholics Here?'" *America*, September 3, 2015.

Melchior-Bonnet, Bernardine. *Napoléon et le pape*. Paris: Amiot Dumont, 1958.

Migne, Jacques Paul. *Patrologiae cursus completus*. Series Latina, no. 54. Paris: Garnier, 1844–1855.

Modras, Ronald. *The Catholic Church and Antisemitism: Poland, 1933–1939*. Chur, Switzerland: Harwood Academic, 1994.

Molony, John. *The Father of Social Democracy: Don Luigi Sturzo*. Ballarat: Connor Court, 2016.

———. *The Worker Question: A New Historical Perspective on Rerum novarum*. Blackburn: Collins Dove, 1991.

Mosse, George L. *The Fascist Revolution: Toward a General Theory of Fascism*. New York: H. Fertig, 1999.

Murphy, Paul I., with R. Rene Arlington. *La Popessa: The Controversial Biography of Sister Pascalina, the Most Powerful Woman in Vatican History*. New York: Warner Books, 1983.

Murphy-O'Connor, Cormac. *An English Spring: Memoirs*. London: Bloomsbury, 2105.

Musto, Ronald G. *The Catholic Peace Tradition*. Maryknoll, NY: Orbis, 1986.

Newman, John Henry. *Letters and Diaries*. Vol. 25. Oxford: Clarendon Press, 1973.

Niall, Brenda. *Mannix*. Melbourne: Text, 2015.

Nuzzi, Gianluigi. *Merchants in the Temple: Inside Pope Francis's Secret Battle Against Corruption in the Vatican*. English translation. New York: Henry Holt, 2015.

Nye, Joseph S. *Soft Power: The Means to Success in World Politics*. New York: PublicAffairs, 2004.

Olmos, Raúl. *El imperio financiero de los Legionarios de Christo*. Mexico City: Grijalbo, 2015.

O'Malley, John W. *What Happened at Vatican II*. Cambridge, MA: Harvard University Press, 2008.

O'Shea, Paul. *A Cross Too Heavy: Eugenio Pacelli—Politics and the Jews of Europe, 1917–1943*. Basingstoke: Palgrave Macmillan, 2011.

Passelecq, Georges, and Bernard Suchecky. *The Hidden Encyclical of Pius XI*. English translation. New York: Harcourt Brace, 1997.

Patch, William L. *Heinrich Brüning and the Dissolution of the Weimar Republic*. Cambridge: Cambridge University Press, 1998.

Peace Action of Benedict XV. Washington, DC: Catholic Association for International Peace, n.d. (mid-1930s).

Peters, Gerhard, and John T. Woolley. "Letter of Reply to the Pope." American Presidency Project. August 27, 1917. http://www.presidency.ucsb.edu/ws/?pid=65401.

Petre, M. D. *Autobiography and Life of George Tyrrell.* Vol. 2. London: Edward Arnold, 1912.

Pham, John-Peter. *Heirs of the Fisherman: Behind the Scenes of Papal Death and Succession.* New York: Oxford University Press, 2006.

Pizzardo, Giuseppe. *The Pope and Catholic Action.* London: Catholic Truth Society, 1937.

Pollard, John F. *The Fascist Experience in Italy.* London: Routledge, 1998.

———. *Money and the Rise of the Modern Papacy: Financing the Vatican, 1850–1950.* Cambridge: Cambridge University Press, 2005.

———. *The Papacy in the Age of Totalitarianism, 1914–1958.* Oxford: Oxford University Press, 2014.

———. *The Unknown Pope: Benedict XV (1914–1922) and the Pursuit of Peace.* London: Geoffrey Chapman, 1999.

———. *The Vatican and Italian Fascism, 1929–32: A Study in Conflict.* Cambridge: Cambridge University Press, 1985.

Poulat, Emile. *Catholicisme, démocratie et socialisme: Le movement catholique et Mgr Benigni de la naissance du socialisme a la victoire du fascisme.* Tournai: Casterman, 1977.

Prosper of Aquitaine. *Epitoma Chronicon, an 452.*

Rahner, Karl. *The Church and the Sacraments.* English translation. New York: Herder, 1963.

———. *The Shape of the Church to Come.* English translation. New York: Seabury Press, 1974.

Rahner, Karl, and Joseph Ratzinger. *The Episcopate and the Primacy.* English translation. New York: Herder, 1962.

Ramet, Sabrina, and Irena Borowik, eds. *Religion, Politics and Values in Poland: Continuity and Change Since 1989.* New York: Palgrave Macmillan, 2016.

Ratzinger, Joseph. "The Pastoral Implications of Collegiality." *Concilium* 1 (1965).

Reher, Margaret Mary. "Pope Leo XIII and 'Americanism.'" *Theological Studies* 34 (1973): 679–689.

Reibling, Mark. *Church of Spies: The Pope's Secret War Against Hitler.* New York: Basic Books, 2015.

Rhodes, Anthony. *The Vatican in the Age of the Dictators, 1922–1945.* London: Hodder and Stoughton, 1973.

Robinson, J. H. *Readings in European History.* Boston: Ginn, 1905.

Robinson, John Martin. *Cardinal Consalvi, 1757–1824.* London: Bodley Head, 1987.

Romanelli, Raffaele, ed. *Dizionario biografico degli Italiani.* Vol. 53. Rome: Trecanni, 2000. www.treccani.it/enciclopedia/giovanni -genocchi.

Rynne, Xavier. *Letters from Vatican City.* London: Faber and Faber, 1963.

————. *The Second Session.* New York: Farrar, Straus, 1964.

————. *The Third Session.* New York: Farrar, Straus, 1965.

Schlesinger, Arthur J. *A Thousand Days: John F. Kennedy in the White House.* Boston: Houghton Mifflin, 1965.

Schultenover, David. *A View from Rome: On the Eve of the Modernist Crisis.* New York: Fordham University Press, 1993.

Seewald, Peter. *Salt of the Earth: Christianity and the Catholic Church at the End of the Millennium.* English translation. San Francisco: Ignatius Press, 1997.

Smith, Denis Mack. *Italy: A Modern History.* Ann Arbor: University of Michigan Press, 1969.

Soage, Ana Belén. "The Muslim Reaction to Pope Benedict XVI's Regensburg Address." *Totalitarian Movements and Political Religions* 8 (2007): 137–143.

Stehlin, Stewart A. *Weimar and the Vatican, 1919–1933: German-Vatican Diplomatic Relations in the Interwar Years.* Princeton, NJ: Princeton University Press, 1983.

Sullivan, Francis A. "The Impact of *Dominus Jesus* on Ecumenism." *America* (October 28, 2000).

Szulc, Tad. *John Paul II: The Biography.* New York: Scribner, 1995.

Tanner, Norman P. *Decrees of the Ecumenical Councils.* London: Sheed and Ward, 1990.

Thomson, David. *Europe Since Napoleon.* London: Longmans, Green, 1957.

Tierney, Brian. *The Crisis of Church and State, 1050–1300.* Englewood Cliffs, NJ: Prentice Hall, 1964.

————. *The Origins of Papal Infallibility, 1150–1350: A Study on the Concepts of Infallibility, Sovereignty and Tradition in the Middle Ages.* Leiden: E. J. Brill, 1972.

Trevor, Meriol. *Pope John.* London: Macmillan, 1967.

Tyrrell, George. *The Church and the Future.* 1903. Reprint, London: Priory Press, 1910.

————. *Medievalism: A Reply to Cardinal Mercier.* London: Longmans, Green, 1908.

Vallely, Paul. *Pope Francis: Untying the Knots.* London: Bloomsbury, 2013. Expanded edition, *Pope Francis: The Struggle for the Soul of Catholicism.* London: Bloomsbury, 2015.

Ventresca, Robert A. *Soldier of Christ: The Life of Pius XII.* Cambridge, MA: Harvard University Press, 2013.

Walsh, Michael. *John Paul II: A Biography.* London: HarperCollins, 1994.

Weigel, George. *Witness to Hope: The Biography of John Paul II.* New York: HarperCollins, 1999.

Weizsäcker, Ernst von. *Memoirs of Ernst von Weizsäcker.* English translation. London: Victor Gollancz, 1951.

West, Morris. "One Man's Voice." *Eureka Street* (Australia) 4, no. 6 (1994).

West, Nigel. *The Third Secret: The CIA, Solidarity and the KGB's Plot to Kill the Pope.* London: HarperCollins, 2000.

Williams, Helen Maria. *A Residence in France During the Years 1792, 1793, 1794 and 1795 and Letters Containing a Sketch of the Politics of France.* London: G. G. and J. Robinson, 1795–1796.

Williams, Rowan. *Why Study the Past? The Quest for the Historical Church.* Grand Rapids, MI: Wm. B. Eerdmans, 2005.

Wolf, Hubert. *The Nuns of Sant'Ambrogio: The True Story of a Convent in Scandal.* Translated by Ruth Martin. Oxford: Oxford University Press, 2015.

———. *Pope and Devil: The Vatican's Archives and the Third Reich.* Cambridge, MA: Belknap Press, 2010.

Yallop, David. *In God's Name: An Investigation into the Murder of Pope John Paul I.* New York: Bantam Books, 1984.

Zizola, Giancarlo. *Il microfono di Dio: Pio XII, padre Lombardi e i cattolici italiani.* Milan: Mondadori, 1990.

———. *The Utopia of John XXIII.* English translation. Maryknoll, NY: Orbis, 1978.

INDEX

Paul Collins is a historian and broadcaster with degrees from Harvard and the Australian National University. He has worked as a religious commentator for Australian Broadcasting Corporation, BBC, PBS, and more; as a teacher of theology and history; and as a Catholic priest. In March 2001, he resigned from active ministry due to a doctrinal dispute with the Vatican over his book *Papal Power*. He is also the author of *The Birth of the West*, published by PublicAffairs in 2013.

For more information, visit www.paulcollinscatholicwriter.com.au.

Photo courtesy of the author

PublicAffairs is a publishing house founded in 1997. It is a tribute to the standards, values, and flair of three persons who have served as mentors to countless reporters, writers, editors, and book people of all kinds, including me.

I. F. STONE, proprietor of *I. F. Stone's Weekly*, combined a commitment to the First Amendment with entrepreneurial zeal and reporting skill and became one of the great independent journalists in American history. At the age of eighty, Izzy published *The Trial of Socrates*, which was a national bestseller. He wrote the book after he taught himself ancient Greek.

BENJAMIN C. BRADLEE was for nearly thirty years the charismatic editorial leader of *The Washington Post*. It was Ben who gave the *Post* the range and courage to pursue such historic issues as Watergate. He supported his reporters with a tenacity that made them fearless and it is no accident that so many became authors of influential, best-selling books.

ROBERT L. BERNSTEIN, the chief executive of Random House for more than a quarter century, guided one of the nation's premier publishing houses. Bob was personally responsible for many books of political dissent and argument that challenged tyranny around the globe. He is also the founder and longtime chair of Human Rights Watch, one of the most respected human rights organizations in the world.

. . .

For fifty years, the banner of Public Affairs Press was carried by its owner Morris B. Schnapper, who published Gandhi, Nasser, Toynbee, Truman, and about 1,500 other authors. In 1983, Schnapper was described by *The Washington Post* as "a redoubtable gadfly." His legacy will endure in the books to come.

Peter Osnos, *Founder*